HANGAR TALK

Also by Irv Broughton

A Good Man: Fathers and Sons in Poetry and Prose

The Writer's Mind (Three Volumes)

Producers on Producing

Reindeers Don't Eat Trees: Poems

The Art of Interviewing for Television, Radio and Film

The Blessing of the Fleet: Poems

HANGAR TALK

Interviews with Fliers
1920's–1990's

BY

Irv Broughton

EWU
P·R·E·S·S

Eastern Washington University Press
Cheney, Washington 1998

Library of Congress Cataloging-in-Publication Data

Broughton, Irv,
Hangar talk : Interviews with aviators, 1920's–1990's / by Irv Broughton
p.   cm.
Includes bibliographical references.
ISBN 0-910055-40-8 (paperback)
1. Air pilots--Interviews. I. Title.
TL539.b768 1998
629.12'092--dc21
97-33339
CIP

Book and cover design by Scott Poole and Deena Lewis.

For my mother Eleanor Bavis Broughton,
flier of hopes and dreams.

CONTENTS

This we know:
we are the wind.
We will come back gently over the lake
we will lash the waves and bend the trees;
we will lie side by side on the high mountains
drinking martinis and telling the old jokes over.
Never our wings will melt or crumple with heat or hardness.
This we know.
For the man who draws the blueprints, shapes the wings, threads the
          bolts, pulls the props
is not our faith.
Ours is the wind and the wind is us
and no one shall bury us ever.

—Ann Darr
from *Flying the Zuni Mountains*

"Airplane Spoken Here"

—Sign at Williams AFB

FOREWORD

Red is the color of life.

I've always felt like a human being should do things for emotion and necessity—personal necessity, in the movies or out, and not for show, for sappy appearances. When you do that, the sincerity shows; the richness of reality takes over like a dream. That's been a kind of credo for me.

For the fliers in *Hangar Talk*, it was necessity for them to fly. They all say that one way or another. They breathe flying the way I breathe making movies. They breathe the stuff. It's that way. Call it logical or illogical. That doesn't matter. It's life and death—and both are astounding and true. One of the fliers in this book can't even go back and fly, after the real experiences he had. The old dreams are too real—pained. Too special to be anything less than the way they were when he flew earlier. Another pilot interviewed, who was downed in the Solomons during WWII, gets traded for a bag of rice. Wham. His life, he admits, was never the same. Imagine yourself. Imagine a bag of rice.

Today, in a homogenized world, we gasp for the breath of the past—for the kind of adventures that these pages hold. This book pays us back with emotion. Plenty of emotion. And heaps of contrasts. I like contrasts—always have, and what they imply. Flying impresses me as a world of contrasts: strong passion/cold analysis; technical skill/instinct; skill/caprice; constraints/freedom; beauty/ugliness; individuality/loyalty; ego/loss; and life/death.

Everything seems to contradict and contrast with everything else, and yet it all makes good sense, or if it doesn't, we take it for the inexplicable. A good storyteller will make the audience believe. When I read these interviews I think of William Wellman's *Wings*—all the great films about flying, right up to *Apollo 13*.

I served in North Africa during World War II. I was a soldier but I knew a lot of people who flew. Lots of them. I could remember them, but they are as good as here. Professionally, I've spent a good part of my life recounting stories of WWII, my own and others, on film. The stories in this book bring back the war years to me vividly. I must admit to enjoying the stories of civilian flights, as much or more. Maybe that was because we don't usually hear these, though certainly, as the voices of my generation, the WWII generation, dim and are lost, the world won't hear them anymore either. Sad to say. There's little denying that Irv Broughton did a service here in getting all this treasure down. Thirty-seven stories. Thirty-seven lives.

The breadth of experience in *Hangar Talk* is tremendous. When Clyde Ice is struggling to get his plane out of the mountains at the sight of the future Mt. Rushmore, I feel it. At the mercy of the air! When Hutchens, a Tuskegee flier, shows up in that starving Italian village and they think he's some kind of Black Christ (I won't tell the whole story), I knew it was real. It was too strange a story to be otherwise. So real I was there with him. You will be too. What the men and women in this book go through to do what they love—to fly—and what they go through when they fly, we witness in *Hangar Talk*. It's all there. I can visualize it off the page: they're taking off—every one of these pilots. They're flying everywhere in all kinds of planes. What a mix! What a skyfull! Scarves flying on some. I'll stop to read some more.

—Samuel Fuller
Acclaimed director of *Merrill's Marauders* and *The Big Red 1*

NATHANIEL LEMASTER ARMINSTEAD

The WWI Pursuit Pilot

"Judge" Arminstead was at Davidson College when the war call came. "In those days when they waved the flag, everybody jumped in," he says. Arminstead enlisted in the army because at that time—May 1917—they didn't have room in the air corps. He had been at the fort for four or five weeks when he learned he was accepted into the air corps—what they called the signal corps then. Arminstead traveled to Champaign, Illinois, for ground training and the following September transferred to Mineola, Long Island. After a couple of weeks, during which he got to see the Goddess of Liberty during guard duty, he and approximately three hundred cadets were aboard a ship heading to France. Lacking an escort ship, they traveled up the coast to Halifax, Nova Scotia, and then further north before heading down to join a convoy on the Irish coast. The trip took over a month before they landed in England. Was he apprehensive about the lack of ship protection? "I guess so," he answered, "but a bunch of wild Indians don't think much about that sort of thing." Arminstead points out that there was "a bunch of singing boys on board and they'd set a date for the world to come to an end," which couldn't have helped assuage concerns.

When I fiddle with the recorder, this keenly intelligent, bright-eyed nonagenarian from Mississippi takes a big breath and begins to describe a flying world for which very few witnesses remain.

You are a survivor. There aren't many World War I survivors around.

I've been blessed. That's the only way I can account for it.

Were the cadets treated differently on the ship?

There wasn't anybody on the ship except us. We each had our own private stateroom. It was a nice ship, with oldtime mahogany rails, and everything was fine. The food was served by the peacetime crew. Great food, great service.

How rudimentary was your training?

Have you ever heard of a Caudron plane? It was a training plane, a sort of ugly duckling, but it was a marvelous flying machine, which had no ailerons.

No ailerons?

Just bamboo. They just bent the tip of the wings, instead of having ailerons. Your controls would bend them. It was a great plane. The pilots could have wrecks with them, and pile them all over the place, and have to stop flying sometimes because so many of them had crashed. Nonetheless, you could do more things in those planes. Sometimes people got hurt, but so many accidents were without anybody really getting hurt. It had no fuselage. It had just what the French called a *nacelle*. It's a wicker seat that fits between the wings just behind the trailing edge. It provides room for two people: the instructor and the pupil. But there was no fuselage. It had these hardwood pieces running—two at the bottom, one on each side, two from the top wing—that held the tail assembly: the rudder and the elevators.

Any crazy thing happen during training?

When we landed, we went to Tours, where the flying field was. It was about three miles out of the city. The Frenchmen were our instructors, and if the weather wasn't perfect, they wouldn't fly. So it took us months to get four or five hours of actual flying time. In the meantime, we would catch what we called a "sea-going hack," a carriage, and it would plug along the road and take us into town. Automobiles were very scarce.

Of course, we would cut up a little bit in town, then come back to camp. If we did fly the next morning, we might have to be pulled out of bed. When they would wake us up like that, we were not in too good a shape, but the fresh air would revive us. Anyhow, it took us quite a while to get a few hours of experience.

Then they had what the French would call *laches*—a term for solo flight. I bet I didn't have thirty hours of flying when I was made an instructor. At that time they had more men than planes. As a matter of fact, it was that way right up to the end of the war. See, we had to get all our planes from the French—not only training planes but planes on the front. There wasn't an American plane on the front during the First World War. They had what they called a Liberty motor, which was a farce.

A farce?

It didn't work. It would catch on fire. They put it in the English de Havilland plane, an observation plane as well as a light bomber. They caught fire and that was a deadly thing in the First World War. No parachutes. Nobody had parachutes except in bombers. If your plane caught fire, then you had problems.

Were you apprehensive when you became an instructor with so few hours?

No, flying has you cocky as the devil—you could fly anything, anywhere. That's one of the things youngsters think. However, being an instructor wasn't always easy. Once in awhile some kid would not be made for flying, and he would freeze at the controls. That wasn't often, just once in awhile. But I had that happen to me one time. A great big double-jointed devil froze on the controls. I had to hit him, slap him across the face to get his attention and make him quit hanging on the stick.

What was your solo flight like?

I would say I was apprehensive, keyed up, alert. Of course, there was no problem about flying—it was just getting the plane up and down—mostly down *(laughs)*. If you could have seen the trainer I mentioned. It would flounder around up in the air. If you hit the ground, it would bounce on all the wheels but still come out of it all right. Of course, everyone had seen that happen so often, but if you had it happen to you when you had an instructor with you, that Frenchman would cuss you like the devil. He'd wave his hands and carry on. But, as I said, planes were kind of precious. Yes, I was apprehensive, keyed-up, excited, and proud to be able to get the plane up and down. I even wanted to do it again.

Any idiosyncrasies to the planes you flew?

The Newport was a very sensitive plane, and in landing, the only idiosyncrasy was the way you had to kick your rudder to keep it going straight. The reason for that was the torque of the propeller, you see. It would pull you around and you would spin around just like a top. You had to literally kick the rudder and know just how to tune your kicks to keep it going straight. The Newport really was a sensitive plane. You could hold your hand out, lean over the side, and it would turn around. But it was awfully sweet flying. It had a rotary motor. It also had a hollow crank shaft. It was a sweet flying thing with all the cylinders going. The only way you could change the speed on it was to cut out so many of the cylinders—one, three, six, or whatever. You couldn't change the speed with an ordinary throttle. Just to slow it up, slow the revolutions up, the only thing you could do was to make certain cylinders not fire. When you did this, it sounded like it was missing. It was a good idea in a way, but when you cut them back, oftentimes there was a miss—a sputter to clear all cylinders of the excess gas. Well, hell, by that time you were dead if your motor didn't catch. You were just out of luck.

To see a squadron of these things flying together, just popping and carrying on, it sounded terrible. They couldn't run right because they were with the slowest planes, and it forced the faster planes to cut out so many cylinders in order to stay in formation.

The French had what they called a *Ruliere*, which was a little plane that would scoot. Well, it wasn't a plane, either. It had one wing. Of course, all of our planes were biplanes in those days. They couldn't make a singlewing plane because they wouldn't have the strength. But this thing had one little wing, and it wasn't more than six feet off the ground. The wing itself wasn't more than two feet wide and the wing spread wasn't over fifteen or twenty feet. For training you would go down the field in that thing. Occasionally, it would get off the ground, but if it did, it would spin around and wreck. The object of using it was to practice going down the field straight. Sometimes you would think you were doing just fine and then you would hit a little bump, and it would go around and spin on you. That was to teach you to kick that rudder before you ever got up off the ground in another plane, where you could hurt yourself!

What about flying the Newport?

The Newport's wings weren't very big. A big man would make a difference in a Newport. You get a big man, say one that weighed a couple of hundred pounds, and it took a little bit to get him in the air. The plane wasn't made for carrying a load. Also, the plane had absolutely no armor. The pilots would get a little bit of steel, any kind of steel, from the shop or from the hangars, and they would put it under the seat of the plane. That's the only armament that anybody had. Everybody had an aversion to being shot in the tail, so they would just stick this little piece of metal under the seat cushion.

You never flew an American plane?

Never did. As a matter of fact, I flew an airplane before I drove a car. Cars were very scarce in those days.

Did you always want to fly as a little boy?

I never thought about it. I didn't know anything about flying until the First World War started and we found out that people were flying. I never—even in college—heard about it. Oh, we heard about Orville Wright and some things, but it was completely new in our thinking.

Did you ever get into it with a German Fokker or anything?

No. I was made an instructor and that lasted for a few months. Then they sent me to Langres, France, to a staff officer's school. When I got loose from that, I went back to Issoudun and then on up to the front. But things had gotten pretty quiet the last few months up there. We had the Germans' backs to the wall, and we were in control. We were much superior by that time. I was there, but it just happened that it was not a very hot contest at that time.

You saw some Germans up there?

Oh, yes, sure.

Would they wave to you?

Just a few months before we got to France, not the front, they were still shooting at each other with pistols. They would lean over and take a crack at each other with pistols. Of course, nobody ever got hit, or if they did, it was pure luck. Then that smart German figured out how to shoot through the propellers, synchronize the guns, you know. The Germans had a field day with our pilots until somebody got one down and figured out how they were doing it. Once in awhile, the guns would get off and clip the edge of the propeller. Then you would feel like a giant had ahold of you, you would shake so bad. Another thing: the darn ammunition belts would get out of shape. They would fold the belts back and forth. They were open cockpits, and when we maneuvered, they would get out of fold, get jammed. You had to be pretty darn agile to unjam your belt to get your guns to fire.

Did you lose any good friends in the war?

Oh, my gosh, yes. The one that comes to mind was shot, and his plane was crippled. He got back to the field and landed on fire. It was terrible to see. The ammunition was firing, because of the heat and the cloud of flame. We couldn't do anything for him. He was too far gone when he was taken out.

The only thing you could do when your plane caught fire—if you were not up too high—was what they call a wing slip. Then the flames, instead of blowing back at you, would blow across the wings. The pilot would flip it over to fly it down. Your plane would come with your wings pointed to the ground and that would mean the forward rush of the flames would go across the wings instead of back on you. If the wings didn't burn off before you got down, you had a chance. Of course, if you were over some woods, you had a chance too, but if the fire was coming back on you, you couldn't do anything about it. You had to jump out. You would still be pretty badly hurt if you hit on some trees, but you would probably get out of it.

Did you have any friends who did that?

Yes, one fellow: Earl Carruthers. His plane was on fire and he got pretty banged up, but he got out of it. I don't know how to explain it, I was just so blessed then and ever since. But some of those boys who crashed in the Newports didn't make it. If you crashed nose-down, you might get out if you weren't too high, but the darn things were so frail. If you crashed, the motor, which was right in your lap anyhow, would crush your legs. Guys would be crippled up. One of the things that bothered us the most was the idea of getting crippled up.

Tell me about the guy who came down on fire.

His name was Vincent. One of the things Vincent and I would do so often was to slip off and go into Paris. He was the best poker player I ever knew in my life. He had all the money a few days after payday—nearly all the time. He was a wealthy guy, anyhow, so I suppose if he lost, it didn't make any difference.

This was at a French camp at Tours. They had the Frenchmen there as advisors, but the Americans were in charge, and all the rules and regulations were American. At Tours, when we first got there, it was pretty crude. In fact, they weren't ready for us. Some of the barracks didn't have any windows in them, or the roofs had holes. Some of the boys got sick, but the damned head of the camp, instead of sending them to town, just let them stay there, and some of them died.

One or two of them had spinal meningitis, but the ones that died had pneumonia. We really raised cain about it. Ultimately they court-martialed one of the fellows, it got so bad. You know how you are always supposed to go through channels, but it got so bad that a delegation went into Tours to the headquarters and complained. As a result they sent somebody out, I guess undercover, and they found out this guy was responsible for the problem. I think he just didn't like fliers because we were paid the then big sum of a hundred bucks a month as cadets. The GI types like him were getting about thirty bucks a month. There weren't but a few hundred of us over there at the time.

Pursuit pilots were like fighter pilots today.

Yes, but we were pretty carefree. If we weren't on duty and didn't have anything to do, we didn't have any paperwork, no nothing. We didn't have any rules. We were the last of the people that ran free—no duties, no nothing. We just flew.

Who was the biggest hell-raiser you knew over there?

Elliot Springs of the Lafayette Escadrille. He flew for the British for awhile, then they organized the Lafayette Escadrille and he went over with them. He had a reputation as a real hell-raiser. I knew Elliot Springs pretty well. Springs was a rich man's son. Do you know the textile outfit, Springs Mills? If you were around North Carolina, you would know who they were. He was a character as a young man, and as an older man he was a smart devil. But there are some awful interesting stories about him after the war, as well as during. He was an ace.

His office was just as plush as anything could be. He had trouble with his back. Instead of wearing this little brace or corset under his clothes he would wear it outside and walk about the office, fancy as Wall Street. But what comes to my mind is the way he would handle the organized labor people. He planted this picture—he had a picture of his wife dressed up like a peasant with his son who was dressed up in rags in one of the factories there. So you had this poor woman with a child-labor boy. The labor people picked it up—they didn't know who it was—and put it in one of their labor organization's publications. Then, when they printed and carried on about it—about the way he was treating his labor—it was Elliot Springs and his wife and son. Of course, that made asses out of them.

Did you know any of the French pilots?

Rene Fonck was a big French ace. He was a very strong, healthy little cuss— a small fellow. I would see him in the bar. He and some others were great war heroes and we would just sit at their feet with our mouth open, but they were talking French.

How skilled were the World War I pilots?

They didn't have to have any brains, just skill. I'd say they were as skilled as anyone since, in my opinion, because the darn things were hard to fly, hard to land. The only controls we had were an altimeter and how fast your motor was turning. We didn't have any compass, and our gas supply was limited. You didn't stay up more than two hours because you didn't have enough gas in the little fighter planes. Nowadays you do almost everything by instruments.

Did you ever get into any fog, or incredible weather over there?

I think the most fright I had over there was at gunnery school, which was on the coast. I was monkeying around—a kid pranking around over the ocean in the sunset. I took off flying over the water. All of a sudden the fog closed in and I couldn't see land. I had to make up my mind, win, lose, or draw because I didn't have much gas to monkey around with. I had to make up my mind which way to go and stick with it.

You obviously picked right. How long did it take you to hit land?

About thirty minutes, not more than that, but it seemed like thirty hours.

Did you have any forced landings?

Yes, I had one. I was lucky because of a little field. It wasn't any real problem, even though it was a ticklish landing. Those little planes didn't have any shock absorbers, just a kind of elastic thing about as big as your thumb, that they would wrap around a kind of hook by the wheels. That was the only shock absorber you had. Your wheels were like bicycle wheels and you had to put them down tenderly because of the torque of the prop.

I was flying a Newport, which was the only thing I ever flew after training. Well, I say that, but actually I flew a Sopcamel (Sopwith Camel) just for fun, but the Newport was the only thing I flew regularly, except at the front it was SPADs. The SPADs were great planes. They had an in-line motor, with a control for your air-cooled motor temperature, which meant one more instrument. The SPAD was much sturdier than the Newport but not as much fun to fly. The SPAD, though, had one advantage over the Fokker, which was that it was sturdy, and if you could get on the Fokker's tail, you had him. It was a good plane, just not as much fun to fly. Because the SPAD was heavy, you fretted about motor temperature. There was less feel of man and plane being one.

I did have a little accident I didn't mention. Sometimes things would get a little thick on these little fields, and one time this joker came in, by golly, right on top of me and his wheels hit the top of my wings. I was already on the ground, taxiing along. I was lucky. I had only the slightest little scratch on my forehead, but it became infected, so I've got a scar still.

Were you part of the First Aerosquadron, the one that went over in 1917?

No, I went over there just as a cadet. We were not in any squadron or anything. I don't remember anyone coming over there as a squadron. We thought that those fellows training in those Curtiss planes were terrible, that anybody who was taught on those would not be able to fly the Newports. Petty jealousy between schools, of course. It was not true. When we switched over to the SPADs, we hadn't had any training on them at all. They just said, "Here it is." The SPADs were completely different. These things were not easy to fly for beginners.

When it came to danger at Issoudun, there was scarcely a day went by that we didn't have at least one funeral. We went out to what we called Field Thirteen. The funerals were every day, sometimes several of them.

I never did go to a funeral, not there. I did go to one for the friend I talked about who was burned at gunnery school.

When I say the planes were hard to fly, they are not hard to fly: they're easy to fly after you know how. But they did have things happen to them, which didn't help. You see, if you got up in a Newport and whipped it around an hour or two, you'd come back and your stick was on one side. Your rudder was this way or that way. Things had to be completely adjusted. The little wires had to be completely adjusted and lined up again.

And you didn't have a lot of support for such things, did you?

Anyone who was not good friends with the mechanic was dumb. Each mechanic took care of more than one plane. They also took care of the same plane all the time. After you had your own plane that you flew day in and day out, you had the same mechanic. Before that, on training crews, you didn't.

Did you know Eddie Rickenbacker?

We didn't like Eddie. He was a grand person. He was Pershing's chauffeur. But you see, while the balance of us were sitting around waiting to get trained and get through, he wanted to get in the air corps and Pershing let him do it. He had a green light to be trained. So he got through ten times faster than the rest of us. He was a good guy, but we were jealous of him. He got the red carpet go ahead, finished training, and was up there on the front.

Everybody felt they just had to get to the front and were mistreated if they didn't. Of course, after they got there they were just as scared as anyone else. Everybody was gung ho. We thought he got to the front to be a hero. We were just jealous.

Do you remember any practical jokes, any pilot games?

Well, we used to do foolish things. I know we would get up, particularly with those old Caudrons, and we would do some sort of maneuver with them, and then cut the motor. The other guy would have to land it. You would do it in front of the hangar—just foolhardy stuff.

What would happen if you cut the motor?

Well, you couldn't get it back on. You had to land the thing wherever you were. If you didn't have the one choice or another at the field, you had to switch it around some way to get it in.

Did you have any close calls doing that?

All of them were close calls. You didn't have but just mighty little time to make the right decision and make the landing.

Did you see any balloons?

Oh, yes, they had the captive balloons, the ones that would be on a cable. When a plane would come along, they would cable-reel them down, reel them in. There was some bad duty associated with this. You are familiar with the barrage artillery that they put over in the First World War?

Some fellow would draw the duty of flying under one end of the barrage and come out at the other and report how things were doing. The barrage would be on a timetable; it shoots so long at a certain range, and then move up a range, which changes the trajectory. Once they flew through, they would check in with headquarters at the other end just to be sure they didn't have to do it again. That was pretty ticklish flying.

What was the highest altitude you flew?

I guess maybe three miles would be as high as you'd fly, fifteen thousand feet. Those little wings would flip around up there since the air is so thin. You're struggling all the time to get up and to stay up there.

Were the guys regretful that they didn't get to pop some German out of the sky?

Oh certainly, we felt cheated and miserable because we didn't get to be heroes. Guys were fussing around because they didn't let you go.

What's the most magical experience you've had in flight?
It was always an exhilarating feeling. You see, flying was pretty new back in those days, not commonplace like it is now. You would get up in the air and you felt like you were close to the Supreme Being. I don't believe I would enjoy flying another plane like I did that Newport. We thought they were real sweet flying machines. They were better for speed, you know, when you have an open cockpit. I guess your sense of speed is as great or greater with the air flying by you than it would be in a closed cockpit. But you know planes today go so darn fast, you mush through a mile or two before you turn. The little old things I flew would turn around like a top. I don't believe I would enjoy flying any other airplane as much as I did them.

You've witnessed firsthand a lot of history. What do you think of progress?

Facetiously I always said I'm against progress. I don't think progress always brings benefits, but there is nothing to do except to progress. I don't know that it brings anything. It certainly doesn't bring anything in the way of happiness. It doesn't bring anything in the way of spiritual values that I can find. However, I really do believe that, in spite of all the problems and all the things that are wrong, that man has progressed in his character. Now that is a strange thing to say, with all the drugs and all the villainy going on, but there is more effort, more compassion, I believe, than ever.

How sad were you when you left over there, those guys in France?

It's a strange thing, but a couple of years in the army seem to leave an imprint on you for life. I kept up with many of the people for many years. As a matter of fact, until they died there were three of them: Schultz and Carruthers and Baker.

What did you do after the war?

I used to say I sat on an ash can and made a living. After the First World War, I did a lot of things. I had an automobile place, a garage and whatnot. I made a living at that and then got into the tight barrel stave business, then got into banking. I wound up in the Federal Reserve Bank in Richmond and had a pretty satisfactory career there. Then I retired. Actually before I retired, the Defense Department was looking for somebody for a year or two to go to Okinawa. The United States had 51 percent interest in the biggest bank in Okinawa. They were out of control there. The banks were a terrible mess. That was 1961. I went out there and got things straightened out. I spent time between Okinawa and Japan. Then in 1968 I went back again because we were turning Okinawa back over to Japan. Okinawa was getting off the dollar economy and into the yen economy and you could imagine there was a lot of fast footwork. The Okinawans are poor relations. We tried to make things as equitable as possible.

Did you fly after the war?

No. When I got back from the war, my parents met me at the train. We went home and, after breakfast, daddy took me into his den and asked me to promise him that I wouldn't fly anymore as long as he lived. One time this fellow, Roscoe Turner, was in Corinth, Mississippi, with a plane. He asked me to fly with him to Muscle Shoals. I called home and asked my father if it would be all right if I did. Mother went out in the yard and asked him, and he didn't answer. He just turned around and walked away. I didn't go. I never did fly as long as my father lived.

What was your father's background?

My father was in the paper manufacturing business in Richmond. He was a Civil War veteran. He went out to Tennessee. He was supposed to have consumption. This old boy says, "Kick behind the door, ain't nothin' wrong with you 'cept you need fatting up. Look behind the door and get that jug and go out on the farm with the boys." Well, that's the story. The Civil War boys were really starved. But my father lived to be 85, so I guess he didn't have consumption.

I've got a picture of father done by a pretty good artist. This fellow said, "Sit down, Will, let me sketch you." So he sketched him. Dad had a feathery beard on his face, he was just a kid. The artist said, "I'll make this sketch, but you probably won't live through the day." It was before some Civil War battle. So father stuck it in his pocket, and I have it.

What did the old warrior, your dad, say when you went off to the First War?

He thought it was the thing to do, fight for your country and all.

He just didn't want you to fly?

No, he didn't like that much. He didn't say much about it, except he let me know they were uneasy about it—that they wished I would have been satisfied to be infantry or artillery or something. You see, the flying idea was pretty cotton-picking new back in those days. I can understand how he felt about it. With me, it was sort of an ego trip, a glory job; you come back, be a big hero, you know. It's all this glamor business. It's one thing to look at it from one point of view and another thing to look at it from another. War is a pretty silly proposition nowadays. And was then. And always will be.

CLYDE ICE

50,000 Hours of Bush Piloting

L et's suppose a pilot were to log fifty thousand hours of flight time. Fifty thousand hours equals 2,083 days. Or, if one thinks of flying as an eight–hours-a-day profession (which it isn't necessarily), that number of hours would mean more than seventeen years spent flying seven days a week. If you only flew five days a week, eight hours a day, it would take twenty-four years to complete that much flight time. If you flew round the clock and nonstop throughout the calendar year, it would take 5.7 years in the ether to reach fifty thousand hours.

South Dakota pilot Clyde Ice logged over fifty thousand hours of flight time.

Ice was born a descendant of William Penn in the year 1889. A bush pilot extraordinaire, Ice attributed his longevity to good genes and "safe and sane flying." Name a type of flying and this sturdy grandfather of flight has done it—whether hunting coyotes by plane, corralling wild horses, flying passengers in the barnstorming days (he flew over five hundred passengers during one day) or operating a flying ambulance to the remote areas of the midwest.

The old days of the cherished Ox-5 engine firing away are gone, but the passion and memories of one of America's most modest and practiced masters remain with us in legend. Clyde Ice passed away in 1993.

Do you remember your solo flight?

I sure as heck do. I was just learning. I never had any training. I traded for this airplane, and the owner got a guy to fly it down. I had been selling tickets for him. He left my airplane there, and I wanted to learn to taxi it around. So I got to taxiing across this field. The first thing I knew I looked out and I was ten feet off the ground. So I thought: I'll have to land, but I might as well fly around a little. So I did. Then, I came back and shut off the power. But once I had flown solo, I could take a passenger for five dollars.

Your second flight you took a passenger for five dollars?

Yep. Well, I was selling tickets for this guy, and he went up town to get something, and he didn't come back. This other guy came who wanted a ride, so I got him all ready, and when the other guy still didn't come back, I took him for a ride.

You still didn't have a license then, did you?

This was 1919 and there wasn't any license.

Did you have some forced landings?

Oh, you can't fly for sixty years without having any forced landings. Once I was in Mexico City, and I was taking passengers in a Ford Tri-motor. An army officer came out and wondered if he could ride up front in the copilot's seat, and I said, "Sure." I was just ready to go when he stumbled over this center section, which stuck across the fuselage about even with the front seats. He stumbled over that and fell into the cabin and hit the lever that shuts the gas off. I had gotten it running and was right off of the end of the runway; I was going to take off. So when he got straightened up and got into the seat, I just opened 'em up. I didn't have a very big field. I got about fifty feet off the ground, and the engines all quit at the end of the field. I had a corrugated corn field right there in front of me. I didn't have too much speed, so I had to put it right in the corn field right now, or I would be in more trouble. I put it down there. Then we built a little bridge to get across a little irrigation ditch at the end of the field. We got a bunch of Mexicans to pull it back across the ditch, and we went on barnstorming.

Did you have a favorite plane?

Oh, that old Ford Tri-motor was about the best that I ever got in—nice and easy to fly. It was just a good airplane. You could get off in a small field, you could carry a big load, and you had three motors. A lot of people will tell you they were a dog to fly, but if they knew how to fly, they were easy. They were the easiest airplane I ever flew. The controls were awfully sensitive, and the rudders and flippers were big. But, if it got out of line just a little, you had trouble keeping it going straight.

Funny things that happened to you while flying?

I was barnstorming over Wisconsin one time—over the river—and we were putting on a little show. I got up in the air and we went up in front of a canyon a few miles from the airport. When I got in over that, I shut the motors off and went down into that canyon. I flew about eight miles up the river, out of sight. They thought I crashed up the river, and a whole lot of people started over there to the airport. But the joke was on them.

You were just doing it as a trick? How high were you when you shut off the motors?

Oh, I just saw this big canyon. The trees were high along the river, and the river was way down in the canyon, and it was big enough to fly in.

Did you do any more tricks like that?

Oh, we stuffed a coverall suit once in a while and dropped it out. Stuffed the suit with straw. People would think someone fell out.

What was your favorite stunt?

Oh, no, I didn't do too much of that. My motto was "safe and sane flying." I've seen people killed trying to do things the airplane couldn't do, or they didn't know how to do. I've been the first one to arrive at thirteen fatal accidents.

There wasn't one of them who knew he was falling from an airplane. I had two guys tear the wings off—one of them was not 300 feet from the end of my wing. Another one was about a half a mile away, and he had five people in a Ryan. He had done a 180. Well, somebody forgot to tighten the clamp on the struts. The pilot got into a loop with five people in there—four besides himself—and the bow struts pulled loose and the wing folded back into the fuselage, and he went straight down. Another guy was trying to do some kind of trick. I wasn't looking at him when he did it, but he tore the wing off. Suddenly, I looked out there again and there were pieces of covering floating in the air. I watched him onto the ground. He was only a couple of hundred feet from my Ford when he did that. That was in Broken Bow, Nebraska.

That must have been pretty hard emotionally, when you saw all these people dying.

Well, you couldn't do anything about it. I pulled one guy out of a fire. He would have burned up in it. He was knocked unconscious when I pulled him out. He got a little hot, but he made it.

So none of these incidents scared you?

Oh, heck no. They were always doing the wrong thing. It was their own fault. There wasn't one of them that was due to the fault of the airplane. They were doing things they shouldn't have done for that kind of airplane. That guy with the Ryan had one too many people in there. And they'd been drinking. I knew they had been drinking—he was that kind of guy. And they were doing things they just shouldn't have done.

When you taught flying, was there one thing you emphasized?

I told them an airplane was no plaything. They didn't want to be out buzzing their friends and doing a lot of silly things that weren't supposed to be done.

Did you get your license signed by Orville Wright?

I could have, but I was always out barnstorming when he hit our part of the country, so I missed him. I've got Number 1598, and I would have been under a hundred if I had got it the first time the inspector got there.

Did your wife mind you spending all those hours in the airplane?

Oh no, I always barnstormed in the Ford, and she came with me most of the time. I always had plenty of room. Lots of times we would drive somebody from one show to the next.

Tell me about getting the Tri-motor.

I started what we called Rapid Airlines in Rapid City, South Dakota in 1920. We were going along pretty well. In 1927, Standard Oil came out with a Ford Tri-motor—the first one I'd ever seen. Standard had done it as an advertising stunt. They'd take Chambers of Commerce and their dealers in all the bigger towns in North Dakota and South Dakota. Well, that big airplane landed mostly in pastures and fields—they didn't have airports then. In fact, they didn't hardly have any hard surfaces. I followed them along with a little airplane, carrying surplus passengers. I'd get five dollars apiece—two passengers at a time—and I'd be busy in these towns where they landed because these Standard Oil people couldn't take anybody—only the ones covered by their insurance. So when I found out how crazy people were to ride that big airplane, I told my partners about it just as soon as I got back. I said I thought we ought to have one. So the next spring I went to Detroit, and we made a deal with Ford Motor Company. We bought number 20. It took three months from the day I went into the factory, until they turned it over to me, finished and ready to go.

Did you do anything to the plane when you got it?

I took my mechanic down and we worked there, so we'd know what we were up to. I drove rivets all over that airplane. Planes were riveted together instead of being welded together like they do nowadays. The day after they turned the plane over to me, I took it to Buffalo, New York. I made arrangements with the American Legion to sponsor our passenger folly. I stayed there for ten days and sent home $13,500.

Wow, you made a lot of money.

In those days $13,500 was money. We paid the Legion 15 percent of what we took in, then paid for gas, oil, and hotel—all of our expenses. My partners—there were three of us in the deal—two brothers and me—insisted we bring the barnstorming to South Dakota. They wanted to get the benefit of the publicity; they were publicity hounds. And I barnstormed my way up here. I wanted to go to all the bigger towns down east. I could have stayed in

Buffalo another ten days and got just as much money or more. The last day I carried 510 people, and I'm pretty sure I'm the first one to carry 500 in a day. I started flying in the morning and I got done at midnight.

I've heard you've never put a scratch on a plane.

I hit a rock one time in a canyon. I was running wild horses, and my motor quit down in the canyon. I had a little narrow place to land. I only knocked off a wheel. Although, I have bent or damaged six props. That was easy to do, you know, in those days. Props were really frail at first. Twice I hit weeds taking off in a field. One time I was getting out of the airplane, going to the hangar to open the door, and my passenger turned around and hit the throttle with his elbow (we had a training plane with controls at both seats). Anyway, the plane jumped ahead ten feet and hit the door with the prop. That broke the prop. With another one, I was in a field where they had been doing a little road work. They were starting to build a runway. The wheel dropped in a mud hole and the prop hit the ground. Still another time I was hunting coyotes with a guy. We were flying, chasing coyotes, and he shot at them. He shot too soon. We had been following them and usually when you got up there in gun range, you just took the tail around a little. This gave the shooter a kind of forty-five degree angle shot, out of the way of the front end. You have to push it around—sideways. Well, he shot before I turned it, and he hit the prop.

You used to chase mustangs.

It was on the range. The mustangs damaged the range, where people were trying to raise cattle and sheep. We were hired by stockmen who wanted to get rid of them. I rounded up fifteen hundred head in a couple of years. You had to start them toward your trap and get them to go the way you wanted.

You've done a lot of rescue missions, haven't you? People who were going to have babies, etcetera.

Well, I got that baby in the blizzard one time. We were sleeping at the airport then, my son and I. The doctor called up in the middle of the night and wanted me to go northwest of here, about a hundred miles. We had a regular three-day blizzard going on. I didn't know how bad it was, but it was the day of my other son's funeral, so I didn't want to go anyway. But I told him to call these other people in the town around us. I didn't ask him why he wanted me to go. So he called back about a half hour later and said he had called all those people, but they wouldn't go—the weather was too bad.

In the meantime, I got up and saw what it was like out there and said, "They're smart—it is too bad out there!" It was white-out weather. Forty-mile-per-hour winds. You couldn't see one end of the wing to the other. So I said,

"No, I don't want to go. I'm not the one. I've got the funeral of my child, and I wanted to get back by that time. I still didn't know why he wanted me to go. I'd never turned a doctor down before in my life when it came to taking someone to the hospital. So, after my son and I talked awhile, I wondered why he wanted me to go, and I got up and called him. He said this girl had been riding a horse the evening before and the horse fell down and she was in serious trouble. She was six months pregnant. I said, "You be out there at daylight, and we'll go."

I flew the first two miles without seeing anything. I flew the airplane by what I thought was right—until I got to scrape the trees off. Do you know what I mean by white-out?

I know what you mean.

You couldn't see anything, but when you got to timber, you could practically drag your wheels in the top of the trees. You could feel it in the plane. If you were to lose that, you were sunk. You might just as well have a seat over your head; you might just as well be blindfolded, because you couldn't see anything, and you can't fly very far. I don't know how I made those first two miles, but I did. I got to timber, then I followed one bitty town to a bigger one and followed it to another town. When I crossed that town, trees all around it, I hit a telephone line at seventy-five miles-per-hour—hit my right wing over the wire. A lot of the time I couldn't see one pole to another.

I had been on this ranch, and I happened to know there was a ridge behind the barn where the snow would be blowing off. Though I still had wheels on, I knew I could land there if I reached it. I followed that telephone line to the river. Then followed the timber to the ranch. The ranch was built on the edge of the timber by the river. I landed on that ridge behind the barn. I didn't shut the motor off—the wind would have blown the plane away. They brought up a couple of big carts and pulled in front of me and we tied up to them.

The doctor took care of the baby and brought her up, and we flew right to town. Took that little thing to town. Did you ever see a three pound baby?

No, I haven't.

They're pretty little. We flew right to town and rigged up an incubator for a couple or three months. She's got a family now in Rapid City, and works in the Penney's store.

Do you ever see her?

Oh, sure. I've got birthday cards, Christmas cards, ever since.

Give me another rescue you've done. How many do you think you've done?

I've done a lot. I've gone out and picked up a lot of people that were sick, but not all of them would have died if I hadn't got there. I picked up one guy—there was about three feet of snow—who had a ruptured appendix. He had been in trouble five or six days. He had been sick to death for that long, and there was no way for them to get him out. He was way out on the range. The snow was too deep for a car or truck. The only way to get him was by plane. My plane had skis on then, and I landed in a kind of ravine—rolling country, range country on the side of a hill there. I couldn't get very close to the house on account of the slope. If I did, the skis would have slid down the hill. So I had to land up there about two blocks away. I had a buffalo robe, and I took it along and wrapped him up in it—this big buffalo hide. I carried him up there through this snow, put him in the seat, and took him to the doctor. And I have never smelled such a bad smell as his. And we got him to the hospital. The doctors said he had a fifty-fifty chance of making it after being that long with a ruptured appendix. The old doctor was a good one, and the man made it. The man lived for years.

We had that terrible winter in 1937, and I was in the eastern part of the state at the time. I had a Travel Air, a pretty good-sized airplane. It carried about seven people. I was putting skis on. I ordered them because I knew this was coming. The whole western part of South Dakota, Wyoming, and Montana were snowed in, so they couldn't move anything. In fact, the highway department broke down about half of the snowplows.

As I was getting these skis put on, the phone rang. It was the governor, and he was calling me to see if I could go out and take food to people, and pick them up and see what they needed. He knew I was the main one in this part of the country that would be able to do that. So I flew here for a couple of weeks. And I brought a lot of people in who were sick. One lady was failing badly, and she had to get to the hospital or she wouldn't have made it. I flew food and medicine out, and brought people in for about two weeks, until the snow started to go along.

It must have been exhausting trying to get your airline started.

Well, no, I didn't get tired very easily. I didn't work too hard at it. I flew a schedule. We were trying to get the line started from here to St. Paul, Minnesota. And, in those days, if you operated a schedule for six months, it would show the Post Office and CAA that you could do it. They'd then put it up for bid for airmail. Well, I flew six months from right here to St. Paul, down one day and back the next. I flew six months and only missed one half of one flight, and was never over two hours late. And I flew several trips from here to St. Paul in rain—that was in the summer. It would rain all the way, and I would never be more than two hundred feet from the ground. Now you can't do it, because they've got it covered with radio towers and power lines. I made six months of landings in the town where we intended to ask for the airmail, but I let the airplane do all the work.

Did you ever make an epitaph? What would it be?

I don't know. "Safe and sane flying." I had that painted on all my airplanes, on all my stationery. They got Joe Foss Field on the east side of the state, and they got Clyde Ice Field out here at the airport.

What was your proudest moment of flying?

The thing I'm proudest about is bringing that baby in. There is no way on earth me or anybody else could have done that if I hadn't known the country like I did. I had hunted coyotes all over that part of the country, and had been on that ranch. Otherwise, I wouldn't have dared try that with wheels if I hadn't known that big ridge was behind the barn where I could land into the wind.

You sound like a Good Samaritan—a flying Good Samaritan.

I tried to help out whenever I could. I flew quite a few people to Rochester that I didn't get paid for. I knew I wasn't going to, when I took them. But they had to go. I lived in Rochester in the '30s. I knew all the Mayos, except the grandfather who started it.

Did you ever fly the Mayos?

I never flew any of the Mayos, but I flew a lot of the doctors. They built the first airport in Rochester. And they wanted me to come up there with the Ford Tri-motor for the airport dedication. Well, there was a lot of population there, and I began to see what Rochester was going to amount to, so I said, "Why not organize an aeroambulance with the Mayo Clinic?" So that's how I came to live there. I'd be there yet if it wasn't for a disagreeable Mayo son-in-law. The one girl fell in love with him, and they wanted to do something with him, so they put him in as airport manager. He was so disagreeable and made it so disagreeable for me that I finally got disgusted and left.

Was that the first ambulance service like that?

It was the first around here. I took several trips and one of the sons, Charlie— they called him Chuck—and I got pretty well acquainted. He was a wonderful doctor. He called me one day and wanted to know if I could take a patient on a stretcher to Milwaukee. I said, "Sure."

I took a bunch of the chairs out of the plane so she could fit. She was going to be on one of these wheeled stretchers. So I got the plane all ready, and he brought a two- or three-year-old out in an ambulance. They were sending her home on a stretcher. You know what that means. They couldn't do anymore for her, so they sent her home. Well, Chuck introduced me to her when they pulled the stretcher out of the ambulance. She looked up at me and she said, "My doctor's name is Frost; my nurse's name was Snow, now my pilot's name is Ice—you'd think I had to be above the Arctic Circle." I took her home and we landed in the front yard with that Ford Tri-motor. Taxied right up to the front door.

How big was the front yard?

(*laughs*) It was big enough. Have you ever seen a picture of the Roosevelt's place up on the Hudson? Well, her home looked exactly like it.

Tell me more about people you carried around?

I was in Alabama one time and I was going to take Eleanor Roosevelt up. It was an airport dedication there. I made a lot of them in those days because I was one of the first to go barnstorming in a Ford. And, when somebody built an airport, they wanted me to come for the dedication with that big airplane. Well, they phoned me down there, and I went down. At the ceremony, Eleanor Roosevelt made a dedication speech. I stood by her side under the wing of that Ford while she made it. I was going to get to take her for a ride, but a storm came up later in the afternoon, and they didn't let her go.

What year was that?

That was about 1929.

You lost a son. Did he die in an airplane crash?

They had him flying the wrong airplane. He was flying for Western Airlines. He was going downwind, coming in to land in Rapid City in an AT-6. He had never flown anything but a DC-3 or my Waco, and he could always glide with it. When his motor quit, he didn't know that thing would not glide. He had to pull up over a power line, and he couldn't reach the runway. He was on the downwind lane, and he turned back into the wind, and he pulled up over the power line. He didn't tear the airplane up, but it knocked the landing gear off. The plane was so heavy and had such small wing surface that he went down hard. He went about one thousand feet straight in, but it came down so hard it killed him.

Tragic. Let's talk about landing with skis on.

Skis are wonderful. I helped to design the retractable skis.

What year was that?

That was in about 1950. Those are the ones you put on that saved your wheels. You could put the skis up and land on a hard surface. Put them down and land on snow. It was just like having two airplanes.

It's been a great life of flying, hasn't it?

Do you know who Borglum was? He built the Mount Rushmore monument. Well, if I had gotten rattled on that first flight, there'd be no Rushmore. You see, Borglum came up there before he ever got started, when he was trying to promote it. And he wanted to fly up there to see the place. He had climbed up it once from the back of the mountain. But he couldn't see down on the front where he was going to build the faces. So he wanted to fly up there.

I was the only one around who had anything that could take him up there. So I took him up. We made two or three trips up past the face of the rock so he could see what he had to work on. Then we started back. It was a fairly nice day, a little wind. The thing faces the northeast, and there was a little breeze from the southwest, but it wasn't bad. So we started back and he said, "Make another circle and get a little higher and a little closer." Well, I did. I just had the old Standard at that time. That was about 1921. And I made another circle, and I got a little close and a little high. The wind coming down over there pushed me down in that big valley northeast of the mountain. The trees were higher on the ridges than we were, and we just had a little ninety horsepower motor in the airplane.

When that happened, there was no such thing as pulling it up and out of there, so I had to circle in this valley. I circled there for pretty near an hour until the winds kind of went down. We were using up gas and the airplane got lighter, and we faded a little bit. Luckily, we didn't carry hundreds of tons like we do nowadays. Anyway, I flew around and around in there until it got better, then I sneaked up over that ridge of timber and went back to Rapid City.

What did Borglum say?

Well, he was this guy who was really rugged. You didn't push him around. He didn't take anything from anybody. But I know he knew aviation well enough to know we were in a problem. But he never said a word, he never complained, he never acted like he was scared or anything.

GEORGE KIRKENDALL

The Early-Day Inventor/Test Pilot

He's pioneered in everything from engineering and aviation with the Piper-Cub, to test piloting, to building the first electric incubator. He's designed the world's fastest pipe tapper, and was involved in the first night flight using lights. His license was signed by Orville Wright. He is the remarkable George Kirkendall.

Kirkendall was born in 1902. He graduated from high school and passed the teacher's exam in 1920. But his father died, so he took on the task of supporting four sisters and a brother. Through sacrifice and a lot of hard work, he was able to send his siblings to some of the best schools of his time: Madame Blakers in Indianapolis, a school for school teachers, and Riley Hospital, where his sister received nursing training.

Kirkendall scored high on a test and ended up at Kelly Field, where he took primary and advanced flight training. A classmate of his was a man named Charles Lindbergh. He studied engineering at Purdue University but went to work before graduating. A man from Detroit had a plane and needed someone to fly for him. George took the job. Winter time, he worked first in a machine shop and then for Consolidated Aircraft. He developed two early innovations: the cowl pin and the lifting stabilizer.

Kirkendall met C.G. Taylor and suggested he build a six-hundred-pound airplane. The idea seemed outrageous, but George showed him how it could be done. The result is the stuff of legend, and one of Kirkendall's most important contributions. The Cub helped simplify flying but was important for cost reasons as well. These factors helped to stimulate flight in general, and they range among Kirkendall's proudest achievements. Kirkendall later taught at Pennsylvania State University, retiring in 1967.

How did you become a test pilot?

I'm an engineer and I had been barnstorming back in the old days. Of course, when winter came along, I went for a better job and worked at a machine shop in Anderson, Indiana. I heard there was an opening in Buffalo, New York—Consolidated Aircraft was located there before they moved out to California. A friend told me, "Kirkendall, there's an engineering job up here if you come up." And I went up and talked to the engineer, and I said, "I've quit a good job in Anderson, Indiana, and have driven up here seven hundred miles, and I'm ready for a job. When do I start?" He said, "In the morning."

An old cadet friend of mine, Bill Leedy, was a test pilot for them at the time. They had found out that the Fleet airplane would go into a flat spin. You'd crash into the ground. I said, "That's not hard to handle. Just make a lifting stabilizer, so it doesn't go into a flat spin." You know how when you're in a spin, you nose down and the tail would come down and you couldn't get it back out. Overnight we made the regular stabilizer into a lifting stabilizer: an airfoil instead of just a concentric surface. By golly, it worked. You see planes today with the lifting stabilizers that keeps them from going into that flat spin.

That was looked upon as a major discovery, wasn't it?

It was a good improvement—yes, it was, definitely. And I developed what is called the cowl pin. It took the place of the cotter pin. You see them now on a variety of changeable surfaces. Even the snow plow boys use them—eight inches long. The cowl pin is a straight wire with a bent wire on the other side. They just snap in and stay put.

What year did you develop that?

1929.

Why did you develop the cowl pin?

Well, we needed it for the Fleet airplane. We were always opening and closing the cowl while it was on the ground. So we needed something we could get in and out and that would stay put, and that's the cowl pin.

Did you have experiences where you were up in the air and lost something?

No, I always took pains to make sure everything was with us. Of course, even the habit of a safety belt was part of it. Incidentally, the safety belt came about because Lieutenant Kelly was sitting on the front of the wing—before they had fuselages—and he fell off. And that's how Kelly Field got its name there in Kelly, Texas.

It sounds like you were a confident fellow to go up to Consolidated and say, "When do I start?"

I knew I had the ability. I'm a one-room schoolhouse boy, but I also put in some time at Purdue University, and that friend of mine who was up there said, "Kirkendall, you can handle it." So I went up there and I did handle it.

You flew the first night flight, didn't you?

Yes, I had night eyes; I can see like an owl. I lived in Kokomo, Indiana—this was in 1924—and they called me down to Dayton to McCook Field. It was an experimental field for the air corps. They wanted to see if we could fly at nighttime with lights. They had a DH, which was an old WWI aircraft. It was a two-place plane with machine guns in the backseat. It was a water-cooled, four hundred horsepower engine.

They had automobile spotlights out on the wing tips. There wasn't room enough to get the battery in the cockpit, so they had to set it on the lower wing. We went up to Dayton, Ohio, before dark and flew out around over Dayton until dark. I had to reach over and connect the twelve-volt battery system, so the lights would come on. It was just one of those projects where we were trying to find out what we could do with airplanes. You know that the atmosphere gets thinner as you go up and, of course, right now when you fly that high, you have to have an oxygen mask on, but they did that at that time without all the paraphernalia. They were also developing parachutes at about this time.

So you didn't actually fly the first night flight?

No, I wasn't a pilot yet. I lived in Kokomo and used to go to night school twice a week at the Indiana National Guard. So after about two years of night school they gave me an examination. It seems I was called out before the squadron one night, and the major said, "Kirkendall, you made the highest grade of the whole squadron." And for that I was sentenced to Kelly Field to take the primary and advanced courses and become a pilot. I was a flying cadet in 1926.

Any memorable things happen down there when you were a flying cadet?

Oh, Chuck Lindbergh was a classmate down there. He and this Lieutenant Maitland were up about five thousand feet practicing in WWI FE5s, a fighter plane. They put their planes in a spin, and came out at twenty-five hundred feet, occupying the same space. We had evolved the parachute—we wore them as seat packs and had the harness on all the time. When they came out in the same space they stepped out, and the planes landed together, both locked together, and they burned on the ground. This was at Kelly Field, San Antonio, Texas.

Did you ever think Charles Lindbergh was going to do the kinds of things he did?

Oh no, he was just one of us guys. We were all just cadets down there, but we ate pretty well. We were allotted a dollar a day to establish our meals, and we had a sergeant, who was later chef at the Waldorf Astoria. We ate pretty good. One time I had the cadet squadron out on the drill field and they rang the dinner bell. I just put the troops in a right half-echelon and marched them right into the mess hall.

Tell me more about this phenomenon of night vision. That's pretty rare, isn't it?

Well, it's an inherited characteristic. I have a daughter that has her own plane and flies, and my son Dave is a United Airlines pilot now. And they have night vision. They tell me it's the way the nerve in the retina of the eye is. As old as I am, soon to be eighty-eight, I don't mind driving at night at all.

What kind of physical stuff did the test pilot need?

Before we were accepted as flying cadets, we took an examination. They had a dental chair with a crank on the top of it. They spun you. You had to sit there with your eyes closed and, when they suddenly stopped, then you had to be able to put your fingers together in front of you without opening your eyes. There were only two of us out of fifty that passed.

I think we sometimes think of test pilots as daredevils. Are you a daredevil?

No, I know how far I can take the aircraft in terms of the stress and the aerodynamics situation. To a person that is trained that means quite a bit of engineering background.

What do you remember from your college days?

Well, Chuck Chevrolet—he was Louis's son—and his brother came over here in 1913. Chuck was one of my classmates and he had a Model-T Ford, and so did I, the first one with a starter on it. We took and rebuilt it. They were designed to turn over 1,250 rpm, but then we put counterweights on the crank. We had those Model-Ts pretty well educated. They were the fastest on the Purdue campus.

Did you have a favorite subject as an engineer?

I was always interested in metallurgy, the different types of metals and what you could do with them. And, as an engineer, you need to know your metals.

Talk about anybody who didn't want to fly with you.

When I was a test pilot at Pottstown, there was a little gal with one of the newspapers. Wayne Gary owned the airport; it was privately owned. Anyway, this girl came out to write a story, and she wanted the works. And the other boys all said, "We could fly you and give you a good flight, but if you want the works you better get Mr. Kirkendall." Of course, I had been military-trained and I knew about all the attitudes of stunting. I used to wear a parachute. So I took this gal up, and I had her up for twenty minutes, and I'm sure she never saw the ground or any other thing from the same angle out of the cockpit. I put her through it—she wanted the works. They had to help her out of the cockpit, and she laid down on the ground and belched her cookies.

What's the funniest thing that happened when you were barnstorming?

I went barnstorming in the fall before I went to work in the machine shop in Indiana. One time I landed on a cut hay field across from an old folk's home. They had a young fellow there that was just simple. But he was good help on the farm where they had their own produce.

They had cut the hay on the field across from there, and I was carrying passengers. You know, you would set down in the field, and people would come to see what's going on, and you'd get some riders. I did two passengers at a time, at two-fifty each. Well, that more than pays for the gas and you get a little ahead on it. Anyway, this young fellow had been such a good help— he'd been getting some hay out of the way for me—I took him up as a reward. Of course, it was an open cockpit plane. When we came back down, he said, "My goodness"—he didn't know there was so much wind— "you sure could get a good breath up there." It was real funny, sort of tragic too.

You did all right financially while barnstorming?

In 1927, when I was in Purdue, a man up in Detroit, Michigan advertised he had a four-place Standard airplane. He wanted a pilot to come up there and work for him. So I jumped out of class before I was finished with my examinations. I wasn't trying to get a degree. So I went up to Detroit and carried thousands of passengers, four at a time at two-and-one half a copy. I made enough money that spring that I was able to take the money and build my mother a home.

How big a home was it?

Oh, it's got a concrete foundation basement and a half-dozen rooms. But my sister and her husband live there now. Of course, I could have had it if I wanted to stay there, but I've been a go-getter and have been out in this world a little bit.

I guess you have. Did you dream of flight when you were a little boy?

Oh, yes, I've plowed many a field, walking, with a plow horse, and I'd see these crows fly off, up and around, why can't I?

You were known for having the largest kite in the neighborhood.

Yes. It was five feet tall, stood up as tall as I was, and probably three feet across. We used to fly it pretty high, and it sure was a novelty.

Do you remember anything that happened when you were flying your kite?

Oh, we used to have kite fights. You would put a tail on it so the bottom hung down, but not too long a tail. That way it would bob around up there. So us boys would get together and we would have kite fights. We would take one kite and it would go against another. You'd try to knock it out of the air.

Did you win a few of those?

I never had much trouble. Mine was so stable it would stay put.

You developed the Taylorcraft. Can you talk about that?

Well, first they were building the Chummy up at Bradford. It was a 1,050-pound airplane. I had my Fleet biplane with an air-cooled engine that I was trying to sell at the time; I sold engines all over the country. So I flew into Bradford, and they were talking about building this 1,050-pound plane, Taylor's twentieth airplane. And I said, "Why don't you build a six-hundred-pound airplane?" They said, "It can't be done." And I said, "Oh, yes, it can be done."

We chalked the plane out on the floor. And old dad Taylor came up with the idea to take a two-inch strip of aluminum (alloyed with nickel), and drew it into a t-section, and made aluminum ribs. I knew that was the way we had to go. I parked there a night or two. The city furnished a hangar, and the water was free out of the mountains. And gas was almost literally free as encouragement to get something going in the community. So we lay on the floor, chalked it out, and laid out the body of the first Cub. And, by golly, we kept it down and built this airplane that was under six hundred pounds. By the way, the first Cub is still owned by Bob Taylor down near Dayton. He has a barn there with some of his dad's planes. Of course, his dad later built a side-by-side, which is known as a Taylorcraft.

Tell me about some of the problems you had in developing the plane.

We needed it for primary flying. I was used to the military stuff, of course, and the general public was curious, so we had to get something down in price for them. But we came along with this six-hundred-pound airplane with plenty of wing—which was the secret. We finally found a motor besides mine that could do it. That was the Continental.

Continental had what they called an A-40. I could never get more than thirty-seven horsepower out of it. They had the thrust bearing on the back end of the crankshaft. It filled the thrust load of the propeller clear to the back end of the crankcase. Finally, after breaking several crankshafts, they decided the thrust bearing should be in the front of the engine. It's strange some of the curiosities they go through building engines. I know of an engine on the West Coast still under development. They drilled a one-inch hole through the crankshaft. With the hole in the center, they were able to heat-treat it to a high tensile. They're a successful motor, but the government's taxed the devil out of them.

When inspectors came around, were they pretty tough in the old days?

Oh yes, of course. When I was at Taylorcraft, we built fourteen thousand side-by-side Taylorcrafts. I had a friend who was a government inspector. He said that anything Kirkendall would pass, he would pass.

Tell me about Bill Piper?

Bill Piper was an oil man, and he had forty filling stations and four young boys that were coming forward. Bill Piper was a graduate of Harvard Business School—quite a businessman. First he burnt out of Bradford, then he went up to Lock Haven. There was a big, four-story concrete building there that Bill moved the company into. It was about two blocks long and a block wide. And, of course, they thought they couldn't occupy more than the first floor. But they later occupied the whole thing. They got to building these Cubs. This was from about 1930 to '34. They built ten or fifteen of them a year. The Cub had the lowest cost of operation for training people to fly. Then the war broke out. They were an excellent training plane for primary training. Same as you don't start a child with the Encyclopaedia Britannica his first day, you don't start people out flying something that is complicated. You need something that is simple and almost flies itself. Well, the Cub does that.

Is the Cub one of your proudest achievements?

Yes, it is.

Tell me what you really take responsibility for with the Cub.

Well, I showed them what the wing loading ought to be. And, of course, the four-and-one-half configuration, and the amount of material. It was a steel tube fuselage welded and covered with fabric, and it was lightweight. Well, they finally got Continental Engine to build a suitable engine for them.

What about aerobatic flying? Did you do a lot of it?

Oh yes, I'm very good at it. On Sundays, it was an entertainment for the public. People would come to the airport to see airplanes fly, and some of them would buy a ride; this was the bread and butter. I could take my Fleet up to fifteen hundred feet and hold the nose up there, then let it start sliding backwards on its tail. But then I would kick it over on its side and have the wings form an arc, and this I would take around in a sideways loop. I would always clear the ground plenty. I was able to loop the plane sideways. I think I am the only man that's ever done that—loop a plane sideways. I think you can only do it in a plane built like the Fleet. In fact, with the Fleet, you had two wings: the straight upper wing and the lower wings that came in at six degrees to the fuselage.

Can you explain how the wings affected your ability to do the trick?

I used them end over end on the wing, circulating the air end over end. With the dihedral in wings, the air did not come over the leading edge the same as in forward flight.

What did people say when they saw you do the sideways loop?

They were amazed, of course, and maybe wanted a ride.

What scared you the most while test piloting?

I've never been scared. I always knew what I was doing. I always tried things out. I had a parachute I sat on. I still have my sheepskin flying suit. That was open cockpit.

It was cold up there?

In the wintertime, yes. One time I was flying from Pottstown, and we had a show at St. Louis at Lambert Field. I had always made myself a promise that if I flew into a snowstorm and couldn't get through in ten minutes, I would turn around and get out of there. So I was coming from Pottstown to demonstrate our engine and plane at this aircraft show.

I was over western Pennsylvania, when suddenly I hit a snowstorm. I couldn't get through it in ten minutes. I did 180 degrees by the compass and got back out of it. I looked down and I could see the sun still shining where the storm hadn't hit. I put the old Fleet in a sideslip and dived down. And here was a nice farmer's field, and I landed in it. I pulled the plane over under an apple tree on one side of the field. I had canvases to put over my engine and my cockpit to keep the snow out. Then neighbors came around and wanted to know if anybody was hurt. They invited me to stay with them. He had hard and soft cider, so we had a good time. He got ready to go out and milk that night. I went out and helped him milk his cows. He was quite elated. I had to go about five miles the next day to a phone to tell my people in St. Louis that I was delayed.

Was he kind of amazed that you could milk a cow?

Oh, yes. He didn't realize that farmer boys got to fly.

What was the most difficult landing?

I instigated a landing on a Plymouth car. It happened in Kokomo, Indiana. A guy named Mike Murphy was flying out of western Ohio for the oil company.

But at the time this happened, I said to Mike, "Mike, you know these Cubs." He had a Cub, but he didn't know what the hell to do with it. I said, "You could get an attraction out here if you'd use a shorter runway for the Cub." He asked, "What do you mean?" I said, "You call up the local automobile dealer here and ask him for a Plymouth. Put some long planks on it the width of the landing gear on the Cub, then drive it down the runway—the Cub could land on it, and take off." He said, "Are you really sure?" I said, "Yes, I designed it so."

So we flew the first Cub off a "shorter" runway in Kokomo. Mike Murphy did that. I think the next time he did it was somewhere in Ohio.

You actually put planks on the Plymouth?

I put eight-inch planks on it, sixteen feet long. They were propped up off the back bumper.

Did you ever land on the Plymouth?

Oh, no, I never tried it. I did get a great deal of satisfaction from having caused it.

Was there one thing that you thought was going to set you back with the Cub?

I had a company build an engine. I've designed engines in the past, but I couldn't be in two places at once. The twenty horsepower engine that was designed originally wasn't enough. We actually ended up with almost twice that—thirty-seven horsepower. But that was probably the greatest difficulty, getting the proper horsepower.

What was the most eccentric plane you ever tested?

It was a midwing, and I remember flying that across Philadelphia, and it was almost like riding a pogo stick. The wing was fastened in the middle of the fuselage sideways. If you didn't fly that absolutely straight, you blanked off part of the wing. After I flew over Philadelphia and saw what a hazard it was, I wouldn't fly a midwing anymore.

In fact, we have one at Portage County Airport. It's a $600,000 airplane. I saw a man land it in a crosswind at the airport. He landed and thought something happened with the landing gear. All that happened was that, due to the wind blowing sideways, it blocked off the air partially on one side. That one side went down because it had more lift on the other side where the wind was more effective. He swore it was the landing gear, but I saw him land.

Any other weird planes you've flown?

Well, that's about the weirdest. We flew a two-and-one-half wing airplane. It had six Liberty engines on it—four-hundred horsepower each. This was way back in 1924 before I was a pilot. But I rode with them. The plane was made of plywood, and they were hopeful of making a bigger bomber. It was a lot of wood.

Did you baby the airplanes you tested?

I got thoroughly familiar with them and made sure they had good lubrication and good cooling and everything. And, of course, I have one of the early mechanic's licenses.

Tell me about that.

I think it was 8004—put out by the Department of Transportation. We had to prove we could do airplane engine work and do it safely. My transport license number, worldwide, is a 7781—it's a 1930 license signed by Orville Wright.

That's something. Did you ever meet him?

No, I tried to, but he was rather elusive. But Orville lived until 1948. Wilbur died of typhoid fever in 1912, I think it was. He drank branch water down in Dayton.

So Orville was kind of elusive?

I always felt that he had some kind of confinement. He never met the public. He signed licenses and things like that. I've always figured there was something he just didn't care to disclose.

Where did the idea for the Kirkendall door come from?

Oh, that was just a matter of utility, I guess, with two people getting in and out. I guess there has been more low-level picture-taking from the Cub than from any other plane.

There was a fellow in North Dakota who bought a Cub and paid for it by the coyotes he shot in the wintertime. He would take his Cub, and with the Kirkendall door down, they would fly around over the country. These coyotes would park on a wheat shock, and he would get them while they were out there sleeping in the sun. There was a bounty for them of three dollars and a half apiece, and that's how he actually paid for his plane.

Was there anything you developed on the Cub or any other early plane you worked on that people pooh-poohed, and said, "That's crazy."

The landing gear for the Cub. We tried rubber donuts, but found that the shock cord was the most reliable. In the early WWI airplanes they had wrapped shock cord around the axles. We still use it today on the Taylorcraft.

Explain.

The concept is that the shock cord is like a rope, except that it's rubber and it stretches. When you land or go up and down you need something to take the bump.

Did you have any forced landings?

Oh, yes. When I was flying out of Anderson, Indiana, I had a water-cooled Ox-5 engine, and the water pump was on the back end of the engine. I remember they had just cut the corn in Anderson, Indiana—cut it for fodder in the fall—and it was still green. I was flying this Ox-5 and the water pump went out, so the water ran out and ran down on top of the carburetor. So I had a forced landing in a corn field.

You had quite a reputation in those days, didn't you?

Yes, a very safe reputation.

Give me an unusual flight you took.

Near Pottstown we had the Pennsylvania State Prison at Perkasie, and there were about sixty-five acres that had a thirty-five foot brick wall around it. Warden Smith was head of the penitentiary. He came along one day and said, "I've got to throw the ball out; they're starting a ball game in the yard," and asked if I would fly him in to the prison. So I did. That's the shortest time I spent in prison. I had to maneuver out around those heating stacks and the power plant and all, so he could throw the ball out to the catcher.

What year was that?

I guess that was about 1931 or '32.

Did you land or did he throw it from the plane?

He threw the ball from the plane to the catcher in the prison yard. The warden used to come out to the airfield and he had a girlfriend, and she and her mother would come with him. The warden would slip me a twenty dollar bill to take her up for a special ride. So I had to please the future mother-in-law, I guess.

So your job was to impress the lady?

That's right.

Who was the wildest test pilot you knew?

Eddie Stinson was one of them. He was not satisfied unless he had his quart of booze a day. He was out of Chicago. He and I mixed it up at an air show in St. Louis. I was coming off the flight line, and he took off in any direction he wanted to, and whenever he wanted to.

I was in my Fleet and I'm still catching my breath, it was so close. He took off from his parking place on the flight line, and I came out of the line, and I was wiggling like a rabbit.

How close did you come?

Oh, I think he missed my wings by about five feet, and that's closer than I would like it to happen when I'm on the ground.

Didn't he get killed?

He was out at Soldier's Field in Chicago, where they have baseball, and doggone it if he—in one of his drunken stupors—didn't hit that flagpole and eliminate himself.

Did you think that he was a candidate for it?

Oh yes, oh yes. I had a father who was an alcoholic, although, the last ten years of his life I'm sure he didn't drink. I've taken a lot of abuse from alcohol. I don't use it.

So you knew this guy was in trouble.

Oh, sure.

What was the biggest obstacle you've seen a pilot overcome?

I've seen them in all kinds of difficulty, I guess. The thing I always feared the most in pilots was them getting drunk. I've never been drunk in my life, although I had an alcoholic father.

I taught a few fellows at Pottstown to fly. I remember two or three that I had quite a bit of difficulty with. They were older than me, and they weren't sure they were flying the airplane. They thought the other instructor had the controls. To fly in a biplane, they were in tandem with another pilot that way. So I would keep my hands up on the cowling so he could see I wasn't doing the flying and he was. It was scary. You had to swallow hard a few times.

Have you seen many crashes?

No, but I have been close to them afterwards. You know, the insurance companies wouldn't insure pilots in those days, so we had a club and everytime a pilot got killed, we contributed a buck. I contributed many bucks.

What year was that?

That was along before I got married. It was in the '30s, just after the Depression. Fred and Betty Lund were both pilots, and they both got killed stunting at a public show. I never showed off that close to the ground. I always left a little difference between myself and the ground.

Were you pretty taken back by the Lunds' deaths?

Yes, but it made me definitely decide that I was going to do my work up in the air, and not six feet under.

What was the strangest airfield you ever landed at?

I landed at the New York State Prison at Attica—just outside the prison. I flew a prison official up there. Another fellow flew over the prison at Christmas, dropped oranges out, and got a five-hundred-dollar fine, but here I flew inside the prison. I landed in the navy yard in South Carolina, which they wouldn't allow you to do today, but back in those days we were unique enough that I got away with it.

We've talked about forced landings. How about the worst landing you ever did?

One time at Pottstown I lost a wheel. I was coming in, and someone picked up the wheel along the runway and held it up and showed me it was one of my wheels. So, I had to make a one-wheel landing and, by golly, I did it without any damage to the airplane.

How did you do that?

It was just a biplane and it was not too fast a speed—that is, landing speed. It was about five to ten miles per hour. And we put the wheel on—the nut had come loose.

What's the biggest false start you ever had in developing something?

I was called in to design an engine at Kokomo, Indiana, a six-cylinder radial. These people had an order for it, and somebody told them that I was the only young man in northern Indiana that was mechanical in engines that way. But we had a drunken engineer for this Superior Spring Company that was building the engine. I wanted to use aluminum—aluminum was just coming in—to make the cylinder heads. He made the engine out of cast iron and the crankcase out of aluminum.

I had to make a test stand when I got ordered to test the engine. I had to break one fellow's hand who wouldn't turn the switch off and on. The foreman at the shop got around behind the big steel beams. He was afraid something was going to happen.

He thought it was going to break loose?

Yeah, but we had it all weighted down and had a special engine mount to run this engine. I could have made that a decent engine, but like I tell you, that drunken sot that I had to work under fouled it up. So what was the use?

What's the most important instinct one needs to be a great flier?

Self-preservation.

Did you ever do anything that you thought afterwards was a little bit foolish?

No, I don't think I ever allowed myself that privilege because, well, I love to live. I'm going to have an eighty-eighth birthday next month on May 26.

What made you a good test pilot?

I think carefulness. In other words, if you know what you are doing, you don't have to venture so much know-how. Yes, I know my mechanics. I can sharpen a drill or a tool; I have my own lathe and machine shop. I can even cast aluminum in it.

If you had to come up with an epitaph for your life, what do you think it would be?

I've been a Christian for 70 years, and I frequently say grace at church dinners; my life motto is, "I hope to leave this world a little bit better than I found it."

What do you think of the planes today?

I look at the planes today and wonder how they can fly with such little wings. They fly at such speeds they can, of course. When I see the Concorde come in: they have to drop the cabin down and still land that airplane from five stories off the ground.

So you were really born at the right time?

Oh, yes.

Do you remember your solo flight?

Yes, oh sure, that was in Texas in 1926. The instructor (Lieutenant Dudley Wadkins from Wyoming, I believe) climbed out of the plane at Lone Tree Field—as we called it—and said, "Next Landing. Touch down next opposite me." So I did. The senior instructing test pilot, Lieutenant Corkle, was going to wash me out because he thought I'd blank out in a pinch. But Lieutenant Wadkins said, "No, I've tried him in lots of tight spots over the Texas mesquites, and he never cut out or lost his purpose."

You taught college.

I taught at Penn State. The students were Korean veterans and after six weeks or so, they said, "Mr. Kirkendall"—they knew what they wanted in schooling, you know—"We just wondered if you had it, and we've been checking you out, and giving you a pretty tough time the last few weeks." I said, "Oh?" I played it innocently, like I didn't know anything about it. They found out later they were learning more than any of the other twelve Pennsylvania schools.

What's this story about the Orville Wright chairs?

Bishop Wright was the Bishop for the Brethren churches in Indiana. He had four boys and a daughter. My stepfather was a young minister and had finished five years of service before he met my mother. Bishop Wright took the two younger boys, Orville and Wilbur, with him on his calls to different Brethren churches all over Indiana. A missionary had returned from China and hadn't forgotten the little Wright boys. She had brought back a chicken feather helicopter.

A chicken feather helicopter?

Yes, you know if you take the feathers out of a wing tip of a bird—a chicken, turkey, whatever—and stick them in a cork with a spindle up and down, and roll them around, it will climb whichever direction the wing was that you took off with. Wingtip feathers are made aerodynamic. That's the reason for it.

So now Bishop Wright was calling up north, east of Kokomo, and this missionary brought them this gift. I could imagine these little twelve-year-old boys, sitting around the table, twirling this thing, and seeing it fly. By golly, if it would lift that much, it ought to lift more. I think that's the way they probably got the idea of flying.

Where'd you learn about this?

That was a story in the Kokomo Dispatch way back in the '20s. But the chairs—my stepfather lived at Hartville, Indiana near Richmond, in the 1880s. This is before the days of high school; they had academies. Chairs were a scarcity at the academies, so the students carried their chairs around with them, so they had some place to sit in class. They didn't have folding chairs like they do now. So one of these three chairs I have was used at the academy. When I went to get them recaned, on the back of it were the initials "O.W."— Orville Wright.

How many airplanes have you worked on or developed?

Oh, at least a half dozen. I never stopped to think about it before.

How many airplanes do you think you've flown?

Oh, my goodness, a couple of dozen, I guess. Of course, I never got into the modern transport flying of planes. I let my son do that. I had three sons—the oldest one, an entertainer and magician, knows nothing about flying. I bought forty hours of flying for my youngest son, but he only used up twenty-five hours of it. He lost enthusiasm when he made his first solo cross-country run. When my son David came back from the navy, there were fifteen hours left out of the forty. So David said, "Dad, would you mind if I use them?" I said, "Dave, I would be delighted if you would use that fifteen hours." Well, he took it over here at Kent State. He took it and developed on it, and the first I knew, he was flying for somebody else. He got his nine hundred hours in and got a chance to get on United Airlines, and he's been in that for twenty-five years.

As a kind of metaphor, what does flight mean to George Kirkendall?

To some people, it means fleeing from something. To me, it means rising to another altitude.

PHILIP L. CARRET

The WWI Pursuit Pilot

The year was 1915. Philip L. Caret was just a child. His father took him from their home in Lexington, Massachusetts, to Quincy to witness English pioneer pilot Graham White put on an air show. "It was considered a remarkable thing to see somebody go up in the air," Carret recalls. "But all he did was get off the ground." In 1917 Caret joined the Aviation Section of the Signal Corps.

Carret is now an internationally known figure in securities. Though he has turned over the reins of Carret and Co., his New York City company, he remains active in the business.

Carret is the author of three books on investing and is working on his fourth, *The Patient Investor.* When I mentioned that my grandfather, Chester S. Bavis, a lawyer in nearby Worcester, had written the first book on federal income tax, Carret smiled. "I wish someone would write the last book on it."

Carret's grandfather was born in 1797, the son of Napoleon's paymaster general. Carret, now ninety-nine, takes time from his busy schedule to recount an early chapter of his long, colorful, and successful life.

How did you get into flying?

I was intrigued by some friends who went into the service. They described the physical exam you had to have, and I wondered if I could pass it. So I took the exam and passed it, then went to Ground School at Massachusetts Institute of Technology for four or five weeks, then went overseas. In 1917 one hundred of us so-called "flying cadets" shipped out on the freighter bound for Liverpool. We then took a train to Winchester, where we spent three days in a rest camp. Then we traveled across the channel to France for training.

Did you have any close calls?

I cracked up three planes, but nothing extraordinary. In each case the motor on the plane quit. When the motor quits, you land as best you can. The first time I landed in a vineyard and tore up a few grapes—not much. Another time I landed in a wheatfield. The farmer came dashing out. I thought maybe he wanted to see if I had hurt myself. What he actually wanted was a receipt for the wheat I had damaged. I also landed in an apple orchard. The plane came to rest about six inches from the trunk of a large apple tree. The airfield base had to send a truck and mechanics from the airfield to take that plane apart, haul it back to the field, and put it back together.

In Cazaux I saw a couple of French pilots collide. They went spinning into the ground. I saw the wreckage: The mechanics were literally cleaning brains out of the engine.

My favorite plane was the Sopwith Camel. It was very maneuverable and great for aerobatics. I liked loops, but a loop with an underpowered plane like the Camel was quite an experience, because you'd get up to the top of the loop and just hang there. You'd have to give it an *umph* with your body to get it to come down again. I flew a Caudron for my solo flight. That plane was slow; about 65 miles per hour, and you could land at 35 miles per hour. For some time I wondered about doing aerobatics in it. I thought the tail might snap off, but it was actually pretty strong.

Remember any daredevils?

There was one pilot of ours who flew a plane between the twin spires of the cathedral in Tours. This was near the first airfield where I learned to fly. To get between the spires, the pilot had to bank the plane as if doing a sideslip. It upset the French to no end.

Did you lose any close buddies?

At flying school they had a funeral practically every day. I didn't lose any close friends, though. If someone was lost, the procedure was quite simple. The friends of the pilot that was killed would go through his effects and remove anything that might upset his family, before they shipped his stuff home.

Example?

Anything that would have suggested that he was involved in sexual encounters, say. For example, condoms, that sort of thing.

Were you anxious to get into battle?

Not too anxious. I went for a squadron assignment at the front about two months before the war ended. The captain in charge of assigning pilots said to me, "Well, there won't be much action this winter. The big push will be next spring. If you want to be a hero, that will be the time to go to the front." That sounded sensible to me. Also, I figured a little more flying experience would be good for me before I got to the front. I didn't go to the front; the captain sent me to an outfit that did ferrying. We took planes from a field about halfway between Paris and the front, and we flew them to the front. Then we went back to our airfield in a government-provided Cadillac. The government would pay us mileage for transporting us in a government-supplied car, which I always thought quite unreasonable. (*laughs*) I took the money, naturally, but I thought it was crazy.

Ever lose your bearings?

I got lost one time up near the St. Michel sector. After awhile, I located myself by looking down when I got over the trenches. I saw a plane in barbed wire that had been shot down. I'd seen this same plane before from the road, so I recognized exactly where I was. At that point I had been headed for Germany, so I turned around very fast and went back to the base near Troyes.

How elemental were some of your practice techniques?

One example: For gunnery practice we'd take a plane up and take a little paper parachute with a stone on it, throw it out, and then dive on it. We didn't shoot, we just dove on it.

Things were really rudimentary when it came to aerobatics. I remember there was a Marine major in charge of the field at Tours where I was stationed. The French didn't think we could do aerobatics with our primitive Caudron planes, but the major thought you could. He took a plane up and did various aerobatics with it. When he got down, he typed out the instructions for getting in and getting out of these aerobatic positions, and posted the sheet on the headquarters door. I was one of the first guinea pigs to memorize them and go up to try them out. I did some spins and loops. The French thought we were reckless. They thought Americans were crazy anyway.

What did your parents say when you joined?

They didn't say anything. They weren't upset, or they didn't show it. They probably were upset because I was an only child. My mother was thirty-nine when I was born; my father was fifty-two, so they were old by the time I got through college.

Were you a good pilot?

I was fair. That's why I wanted a little more flying time before I got to the front. Fortunately, I didn't get to the front. I don't think I would have done well—who knows? I'm still around.

What did you learn over there?

Nothing. I did meet some nice guys my own age. They're all dead now, but some lasted until recently.

Tell me about them.

The one I particularly remember was my friend George Goldthwaite. He was older than the rest of us. George was the most patriotic guy I ever knew. Before the war, in order to get any West Pointers to apply for flying (because they had shunned it), the government created an incentive. Upon graduation from West Point, they made a flier a first lieutenant, rather than a second lieutenant. That was the practice. When the war came along the army discovered that a bunch of college kids, like myself, all wanted to fly so badly that they didn't have to make us first lieutenants. I had just gotten under the wire and had gotten my first lieutenancy, which didn't make any difference to me really. However, my friend George didn't graduate in time to get first lieutenant. A number of the guys who didn't get that rank were upset. Some of them had political connections and sent cables back home. They managed to get the new policy reversed. My friend George, though, didn't give a damn if he went to the front as a buck private; he just wanted to serve. He went on to fly on the front as an observation pilot.

I had another friend over there named Wyman, who got halfway through training until the military gave him another eye exam, which he flunked. They booted him out and made him a nonflying officer. Later, when he got home, he discovered that he was almost blind. I used to visit him in California. He loved to play chess, and his chess pieces were four or five times the normal size. Great guy.

They're all gone, my friends from the war. In fact, of four million Americans in World War I, I read a couple of years ago that only 25,000 were left. We're probably down to 10,000 now.

The inevitable question: To what do you attribute your longevity?

I never worry. I eat and drink in moderation and, by and large, live a moderate life. My wife took very good care of me—a wonderful, perfect woman. Unfortunately, I lost her. I think she was responsible in part for my lasting so long.

How'd you get home?

I was in France for sixteen months and came home by ship from Marseilles. We landed, and I was mustered out in Long Island. We arrived home when the United States had very foolishly adopted Prohibition. The only question they asked when we checked out was, "Did you drink alcoholic beverages when you were in France?" The guy ahead of me in line answered, "When I could get them." So whoever checked us in wrote down: "moderately alcoholic." He came along to me. Of course, at that time you couldn't drink the water in most of France, so I necessarily consumed a certain amount of wine. I told him that. "Moderately alcoholic," he wrote. I thought that would go in the archives of the government, and if I ever ran for office, someone would drag that out and ruin my campaign. (*laughs*)

How would you like to be remembered?

Favorably! (*laughs*) By my children, my grandchildren, great-grandchildren, and a few friends.

From left, Capt. Boleslaw Orlinski, Dorothe Hester and Mayor Ernst Udet.

DOROTHY HESTER STENZEL

A Barnstorming Pioneer

Many people "invented" it, but one name that contributed more than her share to the acceptance and development of early flight was Dorothy Hester, now Dorothy Hester Stenzel. She was a record holder in aerobatic flying, holding early world records in loops and several other categories. She was sought after and honored in her time, offered free airplanes and large sums of money to perform her flights of daring. But despite a somewhat meteoric rise, it was not always easy getting there, as she explains forthrightly in the interview.

Dorothy Hester Stenzel was born in Milwaukie, Oregon, in 1910. Her family later built a home in Ardenwald, Oregon, where she grew up.

Dorothy Stenzel began flying in 1927 at the age of 17 and shortly thereafter began to fly in exhibitions with Tex Rankin for four years from 1928 to 1932. They performed at air shows and Rankin, the master showman, was her mentor. In the interview, Dorothy tells how she finally came to be treated as a peer by the flight pioneer, of the joys and obstacles of early flight.

At the end of the interview, I asked the long retired eighty-year-old flier if she could remember her last flight. She said, "That's what's worrying me now. Is *this* my last 'flight'? I can't breathe." Throughout the interview the courageous old flier gasped, but gamely pushed her way along, at times decrying the cigarettes she had smoked which had brought her health to this.

Amelia Earhart said you were "one girl who has made good almost from the start." Did flying come naturally to you?

Yes, very naturally.

So she knew about you?

Well, I think she was looking at my records or probably saw me fly.

Did you meet her anywhere?

Yes, at different air shows.

Do you remember the first time you were ever in an airplane?

Yes, that was my downfall. It was just about a week before my seventeenth birthday. I hadn't known there was a place that anyone could get near an airplane, and someone told me there was a place that you could go and pay for a ride—which I did. I went on a street car and got off, and I could see the airplanes flying and I started running. I was afraid they were either going to run out of gas or crack up before I could get my ride.

I liked it and I told them so. I said, "If I was a boy, I'd certainly learn to fly." And they said, "You don't have to be a boy to learn to fly. Come in the shack and we'll talk about it." So we went in, and I found out how much it was, and then I went home and I started working on it.

What did you do, save money?

Save money—I had to earn money.

How'd you do that?

There were a lot of different ways of making it and things were different then. I did it by doing parachute jumps. One hundred dollars a jump. That was before there were any regulations where you had to have a spare chute. People would say, "My God, that's dangerous!" I knew it was, but I'd tell them, "Well, if I can't learn to fly, life isn't worth living anyway." That was my thought on that one.

Remember the first time you soloed?

Yes, I do. I couldn't forget. I'd tried to get that fellow out of that cockpit for so long.

What was it like?

Well, that fellow didn't think women were here to stay, but he finally figured out it wasn't his airplane anyway. So he got out. He told me to go around once and then land. It was late in the afternoon, almost dark. So I did that. Then I saw him coming towards the airplane and I thought, "The heck with you," so I took off again. I hadn't been up when it was that dark. Fire was coming out of the exhaust stack. I didn't know it would do that. So I thought, "Dorothy, you're not as smart as you thought you were." So I came down and landed.

You were scared by the fire?

No, I was just unhappy that I had pulled a boner.

But it wasn't really a boner, was it?

Nothing is if you get away with it. I didn't want that fellow back in that front cockpit again. That was it.

You traveled with flier Tex Rankin.

They were all interesting times. We went through this more or less together, experimenting and seeing how we could perfect our flying and our aerobatics, and what an airplane would do.

What were you trying to push an airplane to do?

We were trying to prove that flying was safe. I performed everything, all the aerobatics that any man would do, ordinarily right side up, but I would do it inverted, and it was trial and error.

I know the poor old airplane cried, but we took really good care of the airplane. We had to—it was our life. We just went step by step and rebuilt the airplane. The struts, for example, were supposed to be straight, but would be bent when we'd come down. Our propellers would break! You know those kind of things happen. And, if a nineteen or twenty-year-old girl could do those things, that said something. I'm sure that's the reason Mr. Rankin taught me those things. And we learned things together. He had the flying school and sold airplanes.

What kind of teacher was Tex Rankin? Was he tough?

Oh, he really was, yes. There was no sloppy flying because it would show on his record the way I flew.

How long did it take Tex Rankin to accept you as an equal?

I tell you it took a long time. Before I could even get near one of their airplanes, I had to pay $250 for a ground course. I had to pass these tests, written and oral, before I could start my own instruction. It was a night school. His school was a large school. There were probably forty or fifty boys in the night part. After you passed your tests, you'd fly with Mr. Rankin. He did not instruct—he went out making records, handshaking, and selling airplanes. The night we graduated he came down and gave us a pep talk. He was saying, "You fellers can go to Alaska"—which was just opening up. "And you can teach flying or start an airline," do this or that. You see, mail was all there was then—there were no passengers on the airlines then. Just mail. So he told them all what they could do, and then he saw me, and looked down and said, "And the girls can work in the office." Well, you can see how that went over like a flat balloon. I can tell you I didn't care too much for that man. But I never worked in his office.

How did you manage to avoid working in the office?

Well, that isn't why I risked my life making parachute jumps, to get money to work in his office. Unh, uh, no!

So when'd you start flying with him?

He would come out to the airport about once a month, on Sunday, and go up with a boy after he had about ten hours total flying time. And he'd fly with him and give him another pep talk. But you'd have to put your name on a chalk board, and he only took about five or six.

I finally got the nerve to put my name up there, and so he had to, and

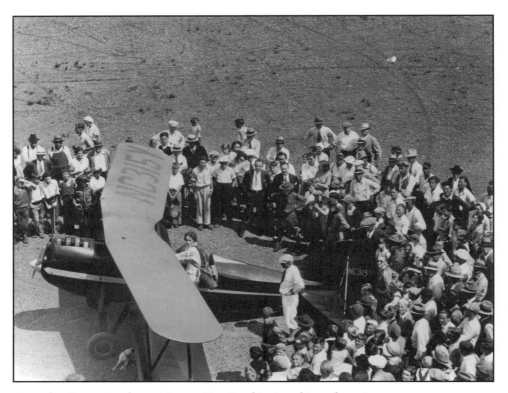

Dorothy Hester in plane; Mentor Tex Rankin in white, observing.

so he did. And I only had a fifteen-minute ticket, and he kept me up there for forty-five minutes. He said, "Hester, you fly like a boy." I liked that.

Anyway, so he started thinking about getting more students. And if he could have a female show that could fly, why any old fool could fly, see? That's how we got going.

How much money did you make when you were together doing these air shows?

Well, we'd fly to the shows with a contract, and maybe we'd fly for two or three different afternoons. About $4,200 for three days.

That was a lot of money then, wasn't it?

Yes it was, because I know we'd go into a hotel, and they'd show you about six different beds that you could sit on to see if you liked them. They'd show you four or five rooms, and you'd choose which one you wanted for the night. Then you'd get a filet mignon, a baked potato, apple pie, and everything probably for a dollar.

How much did your first plane cost?

My first plane didn't cost me anything. The Great Lakes people built me one because I had been flying their airplane, and consequently they were selling more airplanes because of me. And they felt that more people were learning to fly—that people felt it was safer and women wouldn't be as worried about their husbands learning to fly, straight and level, if a nineteen or twenty-year-old girl could do the kind of flying I was doing. It sold airplanes for them. It sold gas, it sold oil—things like that. But people were awfully nice to me.

What kind of plane did they give you?

It was a biplane. And I used that all the time.

Was that your favorite plane?

Yes. I liked it because she hung by me. She was really a tender plane—her maneuvers were quick; she would react beautifully—she was just a nice little airplane.

You make it sound like you and she were partners.

We had to be. I took care of her and she took care of me.

What was your record for loops—you held the record?

Sixty-two perfect outside loops—May 17, 1931, at Omaha Air Races, Nebraska; fifty-six inverted snap rolls—a record which still stands for both men and women. It was set May 15, 1931, at the Omaha Air Races.

Tell me how you broke the record.

Any record I broke was my own record. See, no women did the kind of flying I was doing, so I had no competition. The first outside loop record that I made I was three out of five tries in Portland June 30, 1930. They had to be perfectly round. No U's, no ovals—they marked you down on that.

Then I went through and did twenty-three at Burbank, California. I broke a record, but it was my record. I just kept building up records until I got to Omaha, Nebraska, an air show on May 17, 1931, and I did sixty-nine there, of which sixty-two were certified perfect by three observers from the National Aeronautical Association.

Did you think you were going to set the record in Omaha?

Yes. Tex told me how many to make, and that's what I did, and came down. I came real close to his record—the man's record, but he was my instructor. I couldn't break his record.

Sounds like he told you to come down so you wouldn't break his record?

That's right. And he later went up and raised his record. But that's the way the ball bounces. Anyway, that day it was pretty rough flying. I used to sleep a lot. Those Gs are hard on the body—I'm referring to pulling Gs. I could never go out at night, no, no, no. I was on a strict schedule, going to bed and getting up. Anyway, I was in the administration building, lying down afterwards, and I heard the sirens sound. But I went on and slept. They woke me up when it was my turn to fly. They always held me until the last. And so, when I came out to fly, people acted kind of funny to me. I said, "What happened?" And they wouldn't tell me. I went on and performed.

At the show there was this gold Laird airplane that belonged to Charles W. ("Speed") Holman from Minneapolis. Oh, it was a three-place open biplane, and he used to do aerobatics with it. Oh, it had more power, and it made more noise. It was beautiful. It was an expensive plane. He had flown earlier in it.

Well, what had happened, he was a big man and during his performance, he came down low, right in front of the grandstand, inverted. He pushed the stick forward to go up and when he went to pull it up, the whole seat fell off, right in front of all these people, and he was killed. So you can see what we did, hurriedly scratching around to see how our seat was put in.

Did you ever have any death-defying close calls?

I suppose so. But you always learn.

Anytime the weather was bad?

Oh, the weather's bad—I love that one! That's the only time in the world I've been frightened. And that's the truth. I was delivering this plane up to Great Falls, Montana, and it was in the fall in the smoky season. The airplane didn't have any compass on it, but that's all right. I figured I'd do pretty well with dead reckoning, but I hadn't reckoned with so much smoke that you can't see the sun. Anyway, I got myself mixed up on what speed I should be making and where I should be. And the Continental Divide, that's rough stuff up there. I actually got lost. I couldn't see anything. I didn't know where I was. That's what I mean about learning. I learned it! Little Dorothy wasn't as smart as she thought she was. It was so smoky that when I landed in Great Falls, there were ashes on the tops of the wings. Some people can't understand how there could be ashes on the top of a wing. But there was. You know how the air works around a wing. Ashes up there. So you see, I learned.

So how'd you manage to get there?

I just kept going straight. I thought something would show up sometime. I was just ahead of where I should have been in my flying.

You've said several times that "Dorothy wasn't as smart as she thought she was." Are you saying you were a little cocky or overconfident as a young woman?

No, I wasn't. But what I did I thought I did right. Well, I wouldn't have been doing the things I was doing unless I thought I could do them. And, if I thought I couldn't do them good enough, I'd find out why.

You know the Belanca people. Belanca was the airplane Lindbergh wanted to fly to Paris with. And he wrote them a letter—you've read his books. He got all dressed up and went to see them. But Belanca wanted one more man in there, and it wasn't going to be Lindbergh. Well, anyway, after the National Air Races in Cleveland, Belanca came to me and said, "Dorothy, we'd like you to fly our airplane to Paris. We'll build it to your specifications and, after you get there, we'll give you $125,000 and the airplane.

But, you see, I knew that I couldn't stay awake that long. I was good at what I was doing, these short flights, but I wasn't good on the long ones. You know they never offered that to any other woman.

What did they say when you turned them down?

They said if I changed my mind, let them know. And I said, I didn't think so. But I did appreciate it. That was quite a thing: when they wouldn't give it to Lindbergh, and they offered it to me.

Did you ever get dizzy doing loops?

No. But I was the first woman to take the G-test at Pensacola, Florida, for the navy.

Did you ever completely trash an airplane after one of your aerobatic performances?

No, I only scatched one airplane. My first time away from the Rankin School of Flying to perform and compete with men, I ground-looped. Well, I still say that that's one world's record that I hold, but it's not official—"Least Damage to Planes"

That Great Lakes airplane they built for me was one of the first that they built; it had a small tail, hard tires, and no brakes, and it was a ground-loopin' baby. If you got a side wind or something, she'd just go right into it. Anyway, Mr. Rankin and I went up to Kelso, Washington. It had two runways, and the wind was coming from the south, and people were lined up along that runway. And so Mr. Rankin said, "No, I don't want you landing into the wind there. You go down and land on the east-west one. And you're gonna ground-loop, but that's all right. I'll just tell the people that's just one more little trick that you do." Well, I did that. I went down there and naturally I felt it, and it went around. The wing hit a fence post. And, oh God, my first time showing off, and look what I did. I was bawling my eyes out and the inspector—Captain Pettis was his name—came down in his car. Oh, God, he got out and came over and put his arm around me and he said, "Honey, you just stop crying." He said, "If you knew how many airplanes I have cracked up for Uncle Sam! But I tell you what I'm going to do. I'm going to tell Mr. Rankin that if I catch you up there doing aerobatics until you've had more landings, I'm taking his license away." But that was the only time I hurt an airplane.

What did Mr. Rankin say when he heard that?

Well, I don't know what he said, but he didn't lose his license. Most people have ground-looped with that side wind.

What year was that?

1929.

Any misconceptions about early female fliers?

Yeah. I had to get a physical every six months, and there were some able men and some women who were cracking up quite a few airplanes. They would say, "Oh, I got a bug in my eye" or "This happened and that happened." And if the women couldn't come up with something new once in awhile, they'd say they were menstruating. So, when I went to get my physical, they'd tell me that I couldn't fly when I'm menstruating. I'd say, "Hummm! You haven't heard the last of this old boy, because I'm going to go straight to the president, because this is not right." I said, "I absolutely do not know— and I cannot say—whether on the days that I made my records, whether I was menstruating or not. Well, if that isn't proof enough. Maybe some people can't, but don't you say I can't. I didn't hear any more about it."

Were woman fliers treated differently in other ways, too?

I don't know. They always treated me well. I wasn't really competing with men. There was only one man that ever wasn't very nice to me. I can't tell you his name. He's still hanging on.

Did you have fierce arguments with your parents? How'd your parents take to this idea of flying?

Well, my mother died when I was nine. I had three older sisters and one younger. And we wouldn't let a lady in the house for anything. My father couldn't find a lady who'd want to be in there with us. We were very possessive.

What sort of things did you do? Ever try to break up friendships your father had?

Well, he'd bring them home, and we would just act horribly. "That finished that one."

What was the strangest comment you got from someone regarding your being a woman flier?

As I said, they'd hold me until the last at the air shows. In between acts, they would take people up for rides—the operator of the airfield would. Once in California, this fellow, his name was Hal Sweet, who had a Ford Tri-motor and would haul passengers, asked me one day, "Would you like to copilot with me?" And I said, "Oh, my God, would I like that?" So I did it and on the second day I think it was, when they came out and yelled up at me that it was my turn to fly, I came out of the front cockpit. The passengers were just leaving, and this man turned around and he saw me. He started screaming. I was nineteen at the time, and that man just kept it up all the way out to the fence, telling everyone how fortunate they were to be down. "You could have killed us."

Anyway, I used to stutter badly, and they always said I wouldn't stutter. "Ah, come on, get up here and say something," things like that. So this policeman kept coming up to me and saying, "There's this fellow out on the fence. He wants to see you." Finally, I went over there, and there's this hand sticking through the fence. He had a card or something in his hand, and he said, "Please, Miss Hester, would you sign my ticket? I was one of your passengers today. I live in Omaha and I'm sorry I hadn't realized who you were." He said, "I want to go home and show this to the people." He had flown with me, and now he was proud of the fact. I thought that was kind of nice. He did come back and apologize. But, of course, old Hal Sweet, his flying was over for the day with this feller yelling around because no one knew who I was there at that air show.

In other words, this guy found out you were this famous flier?

Yes, and he was going home to brag. But anyway, I did feel sorry for Hal.

Here's a word association game: Sideslips.

Fun. God, I wish I had some pictures of how I used to sideslip with this little airplane. Whew, whew, whew. I'd bring her on until the wing was a foot and a half from the ground, then kick her around, and she wouldn't roll at all, because I flew that airplane so much. She and I were a piece of one another, you know. Sideslips were fun.

How about spins?

That's fun too. In Cleveland at the National Air Races, they had to be very strict because everyone had a time to fly. So you flew, and boy you were out of the way so the next fellow could go. And this man—one of the earlier fliers, who was pulling four gliders in a V behind him—did his act and went out and flew over the lake, I gathered. Anyway, he left so I flew. Normally when I was through, I would roll her over and lose altitude in an inverted spin, come down into that. So that's what I did. Then I thought, "My God, what went by me?"

What had happened was this fool went out over the lake and came back and flew right over the crowd. I didn't see him, and I came down in an inverted spin right through those four gliders.

Did he see you?

The gliders saw me coming, but they couldn't do anything about it. God, I came down right through the V. Anyway, Mr. Rankin was on the loudspeaker down there and he said everyone could just imagine all this kindling coming right down on their heads.

Stalls?

Well, you've got to really stall it if you want to spin it. That's the only time I kind of fell down on Mr. Rankin. See, he would go with me—we would go together—and he would teach me these things.

So the first time I was to go up alone and do this inverted spin in front of all these people at an air show in Portland, I went up and she wouldn't stall. This was at his school. On Sundays I would perform for him—that's how I got my flying time—for nothing.

Anyway, she wouldn't stall, she wouldn't spin. So I came down and he said, "You just didn't hold it long enough. Just a minute." So he got out a wrench and lifted the cowling and tapped around. He told me that the problem was I had been doing it with him, and if the plane was heavier, it would stall easier. At that time I was just learning. I didn't have the feel of the airplane. So he told people that there was something the matter with the airplane, but that he had fixed it. And now she was going up and doing it—which I did. But that's the only time I didn't do what I was supposed to do for him.

Barrel rolls?

That's fun. All these things are fun. A smooth flier, that's what I wanted to be. You can do anything with an airplane if you do it smoothly. But just like this Holman fellow up at Omaha, I didn't see it happen. You can pull the wings off of anything by being rough. That's why you slow down in rough air, drop your gear and stuff, you know. I always did barrel rolls and everything was inverted.

Loops?

Ground loops? Loopity-loops. Well, that's the only time I'd black out. You see, when you're doing outside maneuvers, you're pulling the blood to your head, and inside, you're pushing it down. Well, I would do a vertical-eight—an outside loop where all the blood would come to my head—and when I came out of that, I'd go into an inside loop, which would push all the blood away from my head into my feet—and that's when I would black out.

What would happen?

Well, you just couldn't see. You were aware, but just couldn't see.

How long would it take you to recover?

Thirty-five degrees of a circle.

You need speed on the snap roll.

The inverted snap roll, yes. It's awfully hard on the airplane. A slow roll is practically nothing. You just roll slowly around.

When I was learning to do outside loops, I would know when I had enough speed to go around. In the open cockpits, I could tell from the windshield. When the windshield flattened out completely, I had enough speed. I could do most things beautifully, let me say, with my eyes closed.

Who were your flying heroes?

Oh, there were so many. And now most of them are gone.

Name a few.

There you go again. When I mention one, I leave someone else out.

What about Lindbergh?

Oh yes. He was really a determined gentleman, wasn't he? He was the one that really started it all off.

You named one. You better name another so you don't leave that person out.

Tex Rankin was one. Phoebe Omilie was one. She was really a good flier. She flew because she wanted to fly. She flew not for the publicity but because she enjoyed it. She was very good. She was such a nice person. She had had one airplane accident, where she'd hurt her knee and she limped.

So you looked up to her?

Oh, sure. When I was trying to climb the ladder, I told her lots of times that she's been "my star in the sky."

Do you remember what you were doing when you heard about Lindbergh landing in Paris?

Yes, I remember. I was alone. I was sixteen when he did that. But I hadn't known anything about flying at all. Most people hadn't.

Did you ever fly low to read the signs?

There weren't airports around, so you'd land in ball parks, you'd land in fields. But when you needed gas or something, you get down by the railroad, to a Standard station, spiral on down and yell, "Five or ten." See, they'd be out looking because everyone ran out to see when an airplane came. And you would have a place picked out that you were going to land, and you'd yell down to them, "Five or ten (gallons)—to the ball park." Or they'd see which direction you were going and, after you'd landed, they'd come chugging out with gas.

So you had some strange landing places?

I remember I'd go up to Hood River—they wanted me up for one of their luncheons—and I'd just go up there and land out there on the sand island, and they'd come over in a boat and get me.

I had a flying service and school on Swan Island in Portland, and I remember this fellow was a lawyer and he needed a quick trip to Byrne, Oregon. His wife was having a baby anytime so he had to get right back. There was a lawsuit up in Byrne, and he wanted to come back that night. So I took him up there.

There was this man named Hanley, a big rancher up there, and he kept a place mowed. I don't know how many sections he had up there for airplanes. Well, I thought I'd land there. But he'd died in the meantime. I got up there, and there wasn't anyplace to land.

I look around and I see this place, and it looks pretty good. It was summer and it was hot. I came in and I got right down to the place of no return, and I realized what I saw: I was landing in a wheat field, and it was deep. But it was too late, so I just finished my landing as slow as I could and everything was fine. Wheat all around us. He was in a hurry to get to town and, of course, everybody used to come out to see the airplane. The man who owned the field was there, too. He was nice even though I had ruined his wheat. He said to me, "I'll tell you what I'll do." He said, "You tell me how much of a strip you'll need and I'll mow it for you." I said, "Oh God, that's fine." But he said, "I want to tell you, there's a irrigation ditch down there."

That wouldn't work because I might have hit the ditch.

The police came and the plane was alongside a simple, gravel road. You know what people did? They just took down the fence, picked up my airplane, and set it alongside the road. And they took the lawyer into town. That left me out there, and it was hot. When it was time to go, the police came and stopped traffic up the road. That lawyer was brave; he got in. We got home a little bit after dark, and his wife had her baby just fine.

A lot of fliers lost their lives in the Cleveland Air Races.

Well, it was to be expected. I had a fellow down in New Orleans who wanted me to take him up to make a parachute jump. He was so nervous anyway, I didn't want to take him up. So he asked other people. Wiley Post was there, and he and I were sitting on the ground when someone took this fellow up and, my God, his parachute didn't open and he just missed us. Thank goodness. Poor guy, I don't know whether he packed his own chute or not.

What was Wiley Post like?

He was a real nice fellow. He liked to have a good time. He was a rascal.

Did you have a feeling of anxiety or fatalism from what happened to Wiley Post and others?

No, I didn't think it was going to happen to me but, if it did, it was going to happen—and at least I'd lived. Whoever was it who said, "If you're alive, start living."

If you could be remembered for one thing, what thing would that be?

I think, I hope it would be, that I simplified flying for a lot of people. It made it possible for them or it made them start thinking along those lines.

An early sprayer flown by Walter Ball

WALTER BALL

On Crop Spraying

Walter Ball ran a crop-spraying business for about thirty years. He has witnessed the loss of many lives in this dangerous form of flight. But the vigorous eighty-year-old says, "A lot of times I could have been killed. At the time I never thought so." Still, he has had some close calls, landing three planes that were on fire, completing forced landings, and surviving a crash that a neighboring farmer didn't bother to rush over to because he figured the worst. Ball also patented an early crop-spraying invention, the Aero-Dyne, which helped subsidize his flying business. He also developed Handi-Drain, which is commonly used to drain oil from airplanes. Those orange balls used on power lines, which have helped save countless lives, are another of Ball's inventions. He also made the parts for attaching Hoskins strobe lights to planes, door frames, and elsewhere. Ball has also served on the board of the National Aerial Applicators Association.

Walter Ball was born in Estelline, South Dakota, in 1910. His dad was a rancher. His parents got divorced, and his mother married an Iowa farmer. Ball went to country school in Orange County, Iowa, then moved to Rapid City, South Dakota.

He attended the University of Iowa on a football scholarship, but he broke his neck, ending his football career. During the Great Depression he attended South Dakota School of Mines. It was a struggle to make a living while going to school during the Depression, so he quit school and went to work for the Oldsmobile garage in Rapid City, selling Oldsmobiles, Cadillacs, GMC trucks, and Aeronca airplanes.

He flew through the thirties, and when the war broke out, he went to work training pilots for the air force. After the war Ball ran his own training service for years with a couple of instructors and a couple of trainers. "It wasn't a big deal."

Flying is very important to the Midwest, as to other rural areas. The air ambulance provides transportation in life-and-death situations. In the interview Walter Ball tells of his involvement in flying air ambulances—another fascinating form of civilian flying as told by an American original.

How did you get into crop dusting?

I never did any crop dusting. We don't do any dusting up here at all. It's a thing of the past, but they do keep calling it crop dusting. We spray, under pressure.

We had a terrible accident up here this week. One of the old operators got killed. He and his son were flying the field together—a 2,600-acre field. He thought his son had finished his part of it and was on his way back to the airport; both of them were cleaning up around the edges. When you spray a field, you spray long swaths back and forth. When you have a high line at the end of the field, you have to pull up quite a ways before you get to the high line. Some guys go under the high line, but not many of them. When you get through with the field, then you go parallel to the end to get the part that you missed. They call that "cleaning up the field." Anyway, this man's son was on one side of the high line and he was on the other, but each one thought the other one was gone, I guess. He pulled up right into his son, and his son tried to pull up to miss him. He hit the tail of his son's airplane, and his son's tail end went through the canopy and killed him. He was dead before he hit the ground. The man was only sixty years old. I sprayed until I was about seventy.

He was an old friend of yours?

He was a competitor, but we were always on friendly terms. Sprayed off of the same airport and everything. A lot of the old-timers sprayed until they killed themselves. I didn't. I quit while I was ahead.

It's a pretty dangerous business, isn't it?

Yes, I guess it is. A lot of them start and don't live the first year. If you can make it through the first year, then you can keep going. But I really never thought of it that way. I never felt it was dangerous. We had certain safety codes we made up ourselves: things we didn't do and things we did do. I think that helped us.

What was one of the codes?

When we were on the ground loading, we didn't want anybody but the pilot to touch the controls or anyplace on the airplane that the pilot would touch. When we are busy, the pilot never loads. He never would get his hands exposed to chemicals. You might get chemicals all over the controls, then smoke a cigarette and get them in your mouth. We never had anyone get sick because of chemicals.

In the early days we weren't afraid of it. We thought it was safe. I used to mix it without using gloves. I never had any ill effects. Both of my sons grew up in it. They were helping me from the time they were twelve or thirteen years old—out in the fields flagging for us. They were around it all the time. My one son still sprays a little bit now and then. His main job is flying a jet for a public utility company. My oldest son flies 747s for Northwest on the Orient run.

You're not saying that these chemicals are not dangerous at all, are you?

No, you have to understand them, you have to know something about them. You just don't go and handle them without knowing what you are doing. Yes, they're dangerous if you don't understand them.

What was the strangest thing about spraying in the old days?

Probably the strangest thing about this business is there were no books, no schools, no place you could go to find out how to spray. How do you calibrate your sprayer? How do you get a hold of a sprayer? The only thing we learned formally in those days came from colleges which had seminars. I attended them all over the U.S. That's how we learned to spray.

Do you remember any seminar that was a watershed experience for you?

One that I really remember was one of the early ones. We had a three-day seminar at the University of Minnesota. I took in all the meetings religiously. I think I learned more there than practically anywhere, but again that was in the beginning when I had an awful lot to learn. I've also been to other colleges: Arizona, California, and Mississippi. I was also selling the Sorensen sprayer, so that was a reason for going.

What was revolutionary about the sprayer you sold?

They were the first ones. You could buy a kit that would fit either a Super Cub or an Aeronca.

How primitive was it in the those days, before the Sorensen?

In the case of the first spraying we did, Sorensen made some of the equipment. He made the tanks that fit inside these small airplanes. You would take the rear seat out and fit the tank in and set it on a stand and fasten it down. Then you'd hook the rest of your plumbing up to it. That was as primitive as I can remember.

I remember the first couple of fields we sprayed, we filled the damn thing with a water bucket. We didn't have any equipment then to load them. We really didn't know how to mix it, to tell you the truth. The chemical company helped us a lot; each chemical company knew their own chemical. They would come out and hold meetings and show us how to mix it and take care of it.

What are the worst conditions you've sprayed in?

I suppose the most dangerous thing I've ever run into—the only time I felt that I almost got killed spraying—happened northwest of Huron Airport. There's an area there where there are a lot of tall cottonwood trees, maybe two or three in a group, seventy-five to eighty feet tall. The wind started up as we were spraying among the cottonwoods, and it kept getting stronger and stronger. However, it didn't really bother us flying close to the ground.

I pulled up over a cottonwood and got caught in this swirling wind. It almost rolled me over on my back over this cottonwood. I thought I was going to get killed. I did, I thought, "This is it." Finally, the controls took over, and I got out of this turbulence a little, rolled back out of it. That scared me bad. What flashed in my mind is that people would think that I spun in—they would think I made a pilot error—I stalled it and spun in.

What about forced landings?

I've had a lot of forced landings. Maybe ten or twelve. That's in my whole flying career, not my spraying career. I've had engines fail on me, especially in the early days. Some of those old engines weren't too reliable.

I had a Belanca once that had a 150-horsepower Franklin in it. For some reason or another, if you flew it in the snow, it would quit on you. We never figured out why. I had that engine quit over some tough terrain. I was only about a hundred feet above the ground. It was snowing and the visibility was bad, and that engine just quit me cold. It wasn't carburetor ice because, as long as it was snowing heavily, I ran carburetor heat on it. I know it was getting its hot air up there around the exhaust pipes and then into the carburetor. That airplane did that several times to me, and I never could figure it out.

What year did you start spraying?

I think the first year I started was the summer of 1947. Not many guys sprayed before I did.

How many hours flying?

About twenty thousand. It wasn't all spraying though—I only sprayed about five-hundred hours a year. We just sprayed in the summer here.

You invented a spray unit.

Yes, I designed a spray unit and manufactured them for awhile. It was called the Aero-Dyne. I had the copyright on that name, but the copyright ran out. Anyway, I sold them all over the world.

What was unique about yours?

Well, mine was in the shape of an airfoil, and it fitted up under the bottom of the airplane and was removable. It could carry more gallons than any other could. Because the tank itself was producing part of the lift, you could carry that additional weight. It worked good, but the factories started building regular spraying airplanes that were made for that. They stopped using these little ones, and it died out.

You did air taxiing, too.

Every ambulance trip was a story in itself. One night about one in the morning the phone rang, and it was a doctor from Gettysburg, South Dakota, northwest of here about one hundred miles. Nothing up there in the sky. Just black. The field wasn't lighted, no beacon on it. It had runway lights, but you couldn't see them til you got right on top of them. Anyway, this doctor said, "We've got to get this very sick man to Minneapolis—the University Hospital."

Once I found the airport, I picked up the patient and the nurse, which wasn't easy to do on a dark night. I had a twin-engine airplane, a Piper Apache. So they brought the patient out and put him in the airplane. I told the doctor, "I'm not sure I'm going to make it. There's bad weather between me and Minneapolis." He said, "Well, you might as well try it, because he won't live if you stay here. He will be dead by morning."

But you didn't want to go down with the ship.

Well, no. There were many times like this. Everybody in the plane is in danger. So I took him, his nurse, and his wife. I had them all in this six-passenger airplane. We started out for Minneapolis. At Redwood Falls we ran into heavy rain. Still, we kept on going. I wasn't about to go back. About fifty miles from Minneapolis, we ran out of it. Nice and clear, and the sun was just barely coming up.

The nurse was right behind me, and she was an experienced nurse of about twenty years. She said, "He's dead." I said, "Are you sure?" She said, "I've checked his heartbeat and pulse. He's dead."

I said, "Well, I'm not going to turn around." There's so much red tape to take a dead person across a border. You had to fill out forms and answer questions, weeks later. I didn't want to go back very bad. So I landed in Minneapolis. I told the nurse, "Don't tell his wife until we are on the ground." We landed in Minneapolis, and I radioed ahead to have an ambulance waiting for me. We taxied up to where the ambulance was waiting, and I looked back at this guy. Here he was smiling at me! He's supposed to be dead. I said to the nurse, "Was my landing so bad that it shook him back to life?" She said, "No, I don't think so. I don't understand it at all. I know he was dead!" And the guy is alive today!

What other rescues have you been involved in?

We had a kid dive off the diving board and hit the bottom of the pool and fracture his skull—a young guy fifteen years old. It was stormy and just before dark. They asked me if I'd take him, and I told them that the weather was impossible. Then they told me that the closest brain surgeon was about a hundred miles away. I mentioned the weather again.

The family was all sitting around, so I told the hospital that I'd call if it was at all possible to fly. I had a young experienced pilot, who had all the training for instrument flying, and I tried to get him. He wouldn't go and said, "I won't fly in this weather for anybody." Pretty soon the ambulance pulled up outside. They brought the patient out. I asked them, "Why did they bring him out here?" They said, "Well, he might as well be out here as in the hospital. If he doesn't get to the brain surgeon, he's going to die anyway."

He was in my lobby on the stretcher. I finally decided that I would take him. I didn't have radar. I had called the flight service station and said, "Will you follow me on radar until I'm out of range? I'll be flying very low. You steer me around the thunderstorms, then when I can pick up Sioux Falls, I'll have them steer me in." So we did that. It worked. I tell you, though, the lightning was so bad that when it flashed you couldn't see the instrument panel. You were almost beside the lightning. Nonetheless, I got him there, and this guy is alive today.

I suppose there were car wrecks, too.

Yes, a woman was in a car accident—she was from California—and hers was a head injury, too. Their family all got together and decided they wanted her back in California because they had more confidence in the doctors there. She lived in Burbank. So they called us to see if we could fly her to Burbank, California. We had just single-engine airplanes in those days, but we did have a Beech Bonanza. It was pretty fast. We could make it there in a short day.

I was up in North Dakota, and my boss asked me if I could be back in time to take her there—that was before I owned the business. I got home two or three hours before it was time to leave. I got a little sleep, and they brought this woman out on a stretcher with her niece and a nurse. I loaded them in the airplane, and we started for California. We went from here to Cheyenne, the first fueling stop. By the time we were there, it was really gusty, very rough around those mountains on a hot summer day. I started into the airport, past the tower; if they see anything wrong, they tell you. They didn't say anything and gave me clearance to land. But I was landing, going into the direction of the tower, so they really couldn't see my airplane. They couldn't see the nose gear—or anything.

It was a nice landing. Then I felt the nose go down, and I knew that my nose wheel wasn't down. That nose gear didn't have an indicator light; the main gear had a green light, but there was none on the nose gear. So my nose gear wasn't down, and I had no way of knowing. So when I landed, that nose went down and, I tell you, I threw pieces of propeller all over the runway. I turned it off and was able to swing the plane onto the grass. The lady, by now, was hysterical. So was the nurse. We took them into the flight engineer's place, and the old lady had to go to the bathroom. The nurse said, "I can't carry her, and we don't have any wheelchairs here and she can't walk." She said, "You carry her in there." Well, that's the first time I've ever carried a woman and put her on the toilet.

You did all kinds of things on these ambulance trips. In this case, I managed to get another ambulance plane to pick them up, and they reached Burbank the same day.

How about equipment failures?

I was coming back from Minneapolis one night with a passenger, about eleven or twelve o'clock at night, and it was cold—twenty-five below zero. We had passed Brookings, South Dakota, and everything was fine. But I looked down at my instruments after we passed Brookings, and I noticed that my oil pressure was a little lower than usual, just a little lower. I kept going, and every time I looked down at it, it was just a little lower than it had been before. I knew I was running out of oil, but at twenty-five below zero, where do you go? I told the passenger that we might have engine failure. I told him about the oil pressure, and he said, "Well, I saw that and I was going to ask you if that was normal."

We landed. As I taxied up to the hangar, the oil pressure dropped to zero. I couldn't have flown for another thirty seconds. We didn't get real scared when this was happening. It was only later that I thought, "Man, that was close." You think about things like that off and on for awhile. Of course, I've had a lot of these things happen like this. But, in this country here, you can almost always find some place to land if your engine quits.

So where is the strangest place you've landed?

I started to California. Another fellow and I were going out to an agricultural meeting. I was leery of the weather. I thought, "How can they tell me that the weather is going to be clear all the way to L.A. today?" When we landed for fuel, I went to check the weather. They said, "Oh, it's fine." I said, "Don't you think there is any danger of snow in those mountains?" He said, "Never today, maybe tomorrow."

My next gas stop was Albuquerque, and I landed there. I had talked with them about weather. I said, "Are you guys sure it isn't going to be snowing?" He said, "Absolutely not. You're just worried. It will start snowing tomorrow but not today." So I started for L.A. We got past Grant, New Mexico— that's about forty miles from Albuquerque, going west—and it started some snow flurries but not bad. I called the flight service station out in the Zuni Mountains. I called them and asked them what they thought about the weather. This wasn't the weather service, you understand, they will usually give you better weather than the weather service will. They said, "It's snowing a little bit at our station but, if you go up through Gallup Pass, you won't have any trouble; a plane just came through."

The pass is 7,400 feet high. So we started out, and I just followed the highway. It was just before Thanksgiving with a lot of traffic on the road. I got to thinking, if I get in trouble up here, I couldn't even land on that road. And it was a rough canyon. I kept on going for awhile, then I decided to go back, back to Grant. I went back for a little while, but it was getting worse so I turned around and started up the pass again. It got worse and worse and worse. We were about two hundred feet above the highway. You couldn't see anything straight ahead. Finally, I told the guy I was with, "We've got to land." He said, "Can't we climb up through it?" I told him, "We don't have the instruments, and we have an airplane that the ceiling's about ten thousand feet. Some places on the edge of the pass are eleven thousand feet." I said, "If I pull up into that, we're dead for sure. We have to land someplace."

It was very rough ground, very rocky. Just then, I went by a gravel road that went to the right and wound around by the freeway, going south. I said, "This is our only chance." So I made this low turn, cut the power, and landed on this little gravel road. I even had to go across this bridge. I rolled over it, and everything went okay.

I taxied off into an area away from the road and got out. We tied the plane down because we didn't know if it would start to blow. A highway patrolman came along and took us over to an abandoned Santa Fe railroad station, next to the highway. I had to phone in and cancel my flight plan, or I'd have everybody looking for me in that weather. I asked this guy if I could use his phone, and he said, "We don't have a phone, just a dispatcher phone here. It goes direct to Winslow. You can call the dispatcher there." I said, "I wonder if he could cancel the flight plan for me." He said, "Sure." So I stepped on this button to talk and let up on it to listen, and I told the dispatcher what I wanted him to do. He called the flight station and did close the flight plan for me.

Then we went into town, and it snowed and snowed and snowed. We stayed all night, and it snowed all night. Then a girl from the office called and asked, "Are you military men?" We said, "No, we're civilians. Why do you ask?" She said, "Well, someone called up here and asked if you were military men." Before long the phone rang again. It was colonel somebody. I don't even remember his name. He said, "Did you land an airplane on the trail about twelve miles from town?" I said, "Yeah, I had to because of the storm." He said, "You didn't fly up the canyon, did you?" I said, "Yes, it's the only way we could have gotten here." He said, "I can't hardly believe that." I said, "You don't think we carried that airplane, do you? You can see it—can't you? By the way, who are you?" He said, "Well, I'm Colonel so-and-so, and I'm commanding officer for a secret base, and you landed on the edge of the base." I said, "How the hell did I know it was there? It wasn't on the map." He said, "Well, you didn't do anything wrong." So I asked him, "Why are you so concerned? We're not going to take off tonight, that's for sure. We'll probably take off tomorrow." He said, "Well, the military has been looking for a short place to put a runway for these small planes when they come up from Albuquerque. Several experts looked the area over, and they said it couldn't be done." I said, "I had to land there; I didn't have any choice. We used to load spray off the roads, so I'm used to landing on roads." He said, "Well, when are you going to take off?" I said, "Tomorrow, when it stops snowing and warms up a little bit." He said, "Will you call me just before you take off? I want to come out and see this because I don't think you can take off from there."

So I called the guy. The passenger and all the luggage went with the highway patrolman to the airport on the other side of town—because I wouldn't have all this weight along. I took off from there without any trouble at all. So I went to the airport and picked up my luggage, passenger, and gasoline, and we got into L.A. that night. Later on there was a big story in the paper about that.

That was probably the scariest thing I had to do. I only had two choices; either land the airplane or crack it up and probably live, or go into the clouds—and if that happened, I knew we'd be gone.

When you were a little younger, were you a daredevil?

No, not really. I did hunt wild horses.

With airplanes?

Yes. I was the first guy who ever did that. Down by Senic, South Dakota. They have an area there called Fog Basin, a real rough piece of ground. These ranchers every so often would round up these horses just to get rid of them—the horses would get into their feed before the cattle would. So, when the horses got bad, they would run through these fences—especially at night. That's when the ranchers would want to thin them out.

They had this one area full of wild horses and couldn't get them out of there. You couldn't get saddle horses down there to get them out. I told them I can round them up for you right where you want them. They asked, "You think you can?" I said, "Of course, I can. You build a corral up a ways. I'll bring the horses up there. You have your cowboys up there to round them up." They said, "Well, we'll do it." So the next Sunday I went down in a Piper

Cub and took a guy with me. He was a guy who didn't weigh too much. He took a shotgun with rock salt in it. I said, "If the horses slow down on us, we may need it."

If you fly down behind a bunch of wild horses at an angle, they will run away from you. You can put them almost anyplace you want them. You can do the same thing with cattle. So I brought the horses up, about fifty or sixty of them. The cowboys gathered, and then I got them up close to the corral, and they took it from there. The Omaha *World Herald* a couple of weeks later said on the front page, "The Last of the Wild Horses." I couldn't convince the writer that this wasn't the last of the wild horses. There still are wild horses out there!

What year was that?

1938.

You were definitely the first?

As far as I know. Now Clyde Ice did it, but that was afterward. He was over in Utah. At the time I thought I was the first one and the *Herald* said I was the first.

You were telling me about the Devil's Tower—that's quite a story.

Devil's Tower is a straight-up-and-down tower of rock. It's flat on top—about fourteen hundred feet on the sides—and slopes slightly on the sides, but it's pretty much up and down.

George Hopkins was really a daredevil. He decided that he wanted to parachute on that, to be the first man to be on top of Devil's Tower. Some mountain climber had tried it and couldn't make it. It couldn't be climbed.

The first time I met George was when I worked for an automobile dealer. I was a sales manager in Rapid City. He came in the office and said, "I understand you have a parachute that is outdated." I think that when it was five years old, it had to be drop tested before it could be licensed again. Then it had to be licensed by a licensed parachuter. Then your parachute was legal once again for four or five years.

So he came in and asked, "Can I use your parachute?" I said, "It's time for it to be drop tested again." You had to send it to Denver, and it cost about fifty or sixty dollars then. That was a fortune in those days. I couldn't afford it. He said, "I'll drop test it for you if you'll let me use it." I said, "Okay, sure, how are you going to drop-test it?" He said, "I'll jump it." So he took it out and jumped it at about three thousand feet. At about two thousand feet he pulled the ripcord, and it opened. He signed it off and then he used it.

Later, he brought up Devil's Tower. He said, "I want you to fly me up there and drop me off." I said, "I don't want to lose my license. The FAA will never approve it. If you hit the side of it, or hit the tower, you're going to get killed."

How much platform was there on the Tower?

Only about two or three acres. Any map in Wyoming will show it. I said, "I know a guy in town who is a darn good pilot, but doesn't have a license. They can't take his license from him. However, if you were to take my airplane when I wasn't looking— like in the early morning; that would be the time to do it—that might protect me." He landed on Devil's Tower and couldn't get off. He hurt his leg badly. At night it got cold so they dropped him blankets and food. They dropped several ropes, but they would miss the tower, or get tangled up. He was going to take the ropes and climb down them.

He was up there for about a week. Anyway, I never did get my parachute again. They finally did hire some mountain climbers to come in and try to climb it. One group tried and gave up. Then they got some guy from Denver, and they were able to climb up and get him down.

Did you ever get credit for the plane?

Oh, yeah!

Do you remember your solo flight?

Yes, it wasn't anything exciting. I knew I could do it. After I was flying, I'd give my parents rides, I used to go down to the ranch; my dad was a rancher. I'd pick them up and take them with me on trips. Dad loved it. They decided it was safe.

Do you remember what your Dad said at first?

Well, my Dad was outspoken. He said, "You're just a six-foot damn fool. You'll kill yourself, sure as hell." My mother didn't say too much. Of course, in those early days, someone was always getting killed. When you were learning to fly, those flight instructors were terrible. When I learned to fly, they didn't even tell you the right way to use the controls. They told me that if you're in a steep turn, you just pull back harder on the stick. If you're close to the ground, you're going to lose altitude to beat the devil—so it's not very smart.

Did you have any close calls in those early days?

None at all in the early days. I only had one accident in twenty thousand hours of flying, and it wasn't bad. I was flying the next day. I had a spray plane. The telephone company was putting up a new line, and they got as far as the farmer's fence, and I guess they knocked off for the day. Then they ran the wire across the top of these fence posts—a temporary line. If you could fly even to or above the post, you knew you were going to fly clear, but these wires were on top of the posts, and one of them was in a group of bushes, so I couldn't see them. They were new steel wires, and I caught them in my landing gear when I came in. I was probably doing ninety miles per hour, and I stopped within seventy-five feet. Three steel wires caught me and yanked the landing gear right off the airplane. The airplane went right on its nose into the ground. When I came to, I was sitting in the airplane, and I can remember thinking, "You better get out of here in case this thing starts to burn." The gas tank in that airplane was right up in front. I went to get out, but the impact had driven my feet right through the floor. It was just plywood for floorboards. I cut my legs all up on the pieces of wood, trying to get my feet out of there. I had hit the instrument panel and had a big bruise on my forehead. I had all the safety equipment on, but my shoulder harness was broken. It was new, and it broke right in two. Nowadays, I would sue the harness company and the telephone company. I got out of the airplane and found my helmet. It was twenty-five feet in front of the airplane. The helmet came off when I hit the instrument panel and went right through the windshield and into the wheat field. So I went over and got it. I started back to the road, and this farmer drove up. He'd been cutting hay in the field next to it. He said, "Were you in that airplane?" I said, "Yeah." He said, "God, I didn't even hurry over here because I thought you'd be dead anyway." He took me to town. All I had was a burn on my forehead. I was fine and up spraying the next day. That's the only accident I ever had.

Some big differences between now and the early days?

The early days, when you went solo, you were then a pilot. Now, when you do, you have to train for months afterwards. There were a hell of a lot of things we didn't know. When I used to get a problem I didn't understand, I'd call Clyde Ice long distance, only thirty-five miles away.

There were two other instructors in the business, but you couldn't make a living at it. One guy in town who had an instructor's license, learned to fly in 1911. He was one of the first original Curtiss team. I used to take some instructing from him. I used to get guys like this, and I'd ask questions. I know that those questions I asked probably saved my life. I remember one thing. If you ever get lost over the country—especially over the Midwest, anyplace there are farmers—and you don't know directions, the sun is behind the clouds, there's a trick. You fly down over a farmyard, and you look for the chicken coup, and the chicken coup is always facing south. They want the chickens to get all the sunshine they can during the wintertime. And from there you can find your directions. I used that a lot of times. Today, they have so many electronics. My son flies a jet out of here, and he doesn't have to do anything! In the old days, we flew.

Ever have any fires in planes you flew or were in?

Well, I was on fire three times, in military airplanes. But I was scared to jump. I weighed about 185 pounds. You've always got to have a twenty-eight-foot parachute, but the military didn't have that type—they only had the twenty-four-foot chute at the time. So I knew that if I jumped with the smaller chute, I'd break my legs. I saved a couple of expensive airplanes for the government that way.

What kind of planes?

BT-13s. They look just like those Japanese bombers.

What did they say when you brought those planes in?

They thought I was a damn fool for doing it, if they could get a pilot who wasn't thinking.

Another time a guy and I took an old Stearman biplane—open cockpit—up, and were flying it around. We were about done testing it. The pilot was sitting in the backseat: he had been flying it then. So he yelled at me and said, "I'm going to do some rolls. Do you have your belt tight?" I reached down and pulled it, and the damn thing came out of the socket. If he had rolled us on the back, I would have fallen out. I showed him the end of the belt and said, "Let's go back."

What has flight meant to you?

It's been my whole life. I've loved airplanes since I was a little kid. The first airplane I saw was a Curtiss Pusher, when I was about eight or nine, I guess. It was flying over my hometown, and I thought to myself, "That's the life—that's what I want to do."

Charlie McAllister's second glider, The Yakima Clipper. *From The Museum of Flight (Boeing).*

CHARLES McALLISTER

The Master of Spins

Charles D. McAllister, 1945

C harles McAllister has run his own company, McAllister Aviation, out of Yakima, Washington, for sixty-four years. "There aren't many companies that have been around that long, are there?" he says with a smile.

McAllister trained to be a woodworker, and for many years he teamed up with his brother, Alastair, a welder and machinist. "Between the two of us, we could build anything." We were always getting along with inspectors because of this."

Alastair bought a Curtiss Standard in 1926. With its C-6 engine—160 horsepower in line—they flew the hills of Oregon and Washington, barnstorming.

By his own count, he's completed fifteen thousand spins in his life, and has taught over fifteen hundred students. He's held the Northwest record for endurance gliding; but for an act of fate, which he described in the interview, he might have had the national record.

McAllister has had ten forced landings, but never has he crashed a plane. Since his first flight "license," which was signed by Orville Wright, he has seen it all from this rural southwestern Washington community.

At eighty-seven, this slim, wiry man is still involved in flight, coming in daily to work and, incidentally, to inspire.

You did barnstorming in the early days.

Oh, yes. We had a lot of things happen. We had to land in small fields, and sometimes we'd just barely get up over the fence. You had to use good judgment or you'd have a wreck. (laughs)

How long did you do that?

I did that for about twenty years, until a few years ago. I traveled to Sunnyside, Washington, for thirteen years in a row. Never missed a year. They had a celebration there.

What sort of things did you do?

I took up passengers in the old Ox-5 airplane. Sometimes we'd go out and do stunts for the crowd, but mostly it was to haul passengers.

What sort of stunts?

I used to do loops and rolls and spins. I've done a lot of spins, I've done about fifteen thousand.

Fifteen thousand?

Yes. I've trained about fifteen hundred students in my lifetime—and I used to give each one of them about forty-five minutes to an hour, and I'd start out and do a couple of spins. Then I'd climb, and I'd do a couple of more, and I'd usually do about twelve spins with each student, so figuring I had about fifteen hundred students, that would be about fifteen thousand total.

There was competition among barnstormers, wasn't there?

Yes, there was a man named Frank Kammer—he was a Swede, a very compatible man to get along with. I was in Morrow, Oregon, hauling passengers with the Waco and doing very well, and he came down. I'd hauled them for three days. The third day at noon here comes someone in a big sound truck, and he started announcing. He said, "Here comes Captain Frank Kammer in a giant Tri-motor." He had a Tri-motor Stinson, and he came in and landed. When that happened, all my passengers disappeared. I'd made six hundred to seven hundred dollars already—so I didn't feel so bad. Also, I didn't have any landing lights, so I couldn't land in the dark. He had landing lights. I remember I was down at the hotel, getting ready to go to bed, and he was still flying.

What makes you a good teacher?

That's hard to say. I think that I have an agreeable disposition that enables me to get along with people. And I am very cautious and always allow margin. A lot of people don't allow margin. That's like when you're going to cross the railroad tracks and try to beat the train by about five feet. Also, I always feel that you need to plan ahead.

Did you get that attitude from your parents?

Yes, I did, I'm sure. My father was very cautious. I taught some of my mother's people to fly and they had excellent coordination, and I inherited that from them. My father never even drove a car so I don't know how he was on coordination, but I think he was pretty good. He'd been a blacksmith and later on a sheepman, but he never got hurt all his life. He lived to ninety-two.

How about an example of cautiousness?

We'd be out barnstorming—we were in a little town, Elgin, Oregon, many years ago—and we'd have to use a small alfalfa field for takeoff. So I tested the field alone first, then I'd put in one passenger and try her. And then I'd put in two. I'd have some competition people flying. They'd be using the same field. As the day warms up, the air gets thinner and your performance goes down. They've got a name for that now. They've got a formula for it now, but I used my own judgment to figure things out. For example, when I could just barely get over the fence with two passengers, I started hauling one. When I could just barely get over with one passenger, I quit. I would wait until it cooled off in the evening. But the competitors kept flying, and pretty soon they hit the fence and wrecked. *(laughs)* They were out of business. So when it cooled off, I tried to solo alone, and I got off with flying over the fence. Then I tried one passenger and got off and pretty soon tried another. I was back in business again. That's what you call being cautious.

It sounds like your competition was a scam. Did you run into a lot of that back then?

A lot of inexperienced people would take chances. I never took any chances. I took *some* chances by getting over those fences—to make money—but I used judgment, judgment in recognizing when the plane's performance was going down.

Was it tough making a living in those days?

It was. It wasn't hard work, but you didn't make much money. None of us did. We got about three dollars per passenger for fifteen minutes.

Any mistakes you made barnstorming?

I made one mistake years later. I was over in the town of Wenatchee and had been hauling passengers all day. A couple of young National Guard boys helped me. I got all through, and they wouldn't take any money for helping me. So naturally, I wanted to give them a ride. Just then a big thunderstorm was forming almost overhead. This was a pasture about three miles long—up on a plateau. My better judgment—whatever you call that—told me not to go, but I was so confident. I'd been flying in wind of all kinds so I took off anyway.

I had this old Ox-5 Waco, which had no brakes, just tail-skid. If it had wheel brakes, it might have been a little different. I took off and just as I got going, the thunderstorm broke over Badger Mountain and came right down on top of me. It had some downdrafts to it, and I'd get about four feet high but couldn't get any higher. I'd settle down and I'd get about four feet high again.

This field was long, but there was a snow fence made out of lath and posts down near the end of it. I got to worrying about that snow fence. If I hit it, it would, of course, break my propeller. We were going about one hundred plus miles per hour; the wind behind was about 60 miles per hour, a tail wind. I knew if I'd had more power, I'd have been all right. I was wondering what was going to happen if I got to that fence and just couldn't get over. So I kept watching and pretty soon, I saw it coming up. I was moving fast. I saw that I was coming down and was going to be on the ground when I got to the fence. So, instead of waiting until I settled down, I shoved it down ahead of time and I bounced again and went over the fence—I made it. *(laughs)* That's the closest call I ever had.

Are the people you taught in touch with you?

A lot of them. I just got a call yesterday. Guys come over the airport and call me. It was a friend who is a Canadian Airlines pilot. He called to say hello— he was going down to L.A.: forty-five thousand feet. He called in on what they call the Unicom.

Andy Hawkins called me up and asked if I wanted a gas boy. I said, "Sure." He said, "I'm sittin' on the ground here—on strike." He was a captain on Eastern Airlines.

I have a lot of students still flying airlines. One student retired several years ago after thirty-five years. He never had an accident of any kind. Then I probably have eight or ten of them still flying airlines. A lot of them are retired. Some of them are dead.

Do you remember your first solo flight?

I sure do. Everybody remembers their first solo flight. I don't remember everybody's solo flight that I trained, but my, I remember my own. A fellow by the name of Tex Rankin, an oldtime stunt pilot, trained my brother Alistair and me. On my first solo flight I knew I could land it every time, and so I went up and it was really a pleasure. I knew I could do it. When I trained students through the years, everyone I soloed I didn't worry about at all. I knew they could do it, absolutely, before I ever turned them loose. I'd give them all kinds of maneuvers that are not in the book. I would make them do what they call short-field takeoffs—I call them stall takeoffs, which they really are. I'd make them take off with the controls clear back and then correct and make them shove ahead on the controls, make them try it every way like that.

Any crazy things happen when you were around Tex Rankin?

Well, he had quite a sense of humor. I remember he told a story one time. He was out flying and had a forced landing. In somebody's wheatfield. He had to pay the farmer for some wheat—where he damaged the wheat. He managed to get the trouble fixed with his carburetor, whatever it was, and was trying to take off, but wasn't getting up very well. This wheat was pulling on the control stick, pulling up. Anyway, the stick pulled out of the socket and he cut the throttle and landed again. He didn't wreck it. But he had to go back and try it again. And he had to pay the farmer for some more wheat. *(laughs)* I thought that was pretty good.

Any other Tex Rankin stories you recall?

He told a story about a fellow, William Brubaker, who used to have a large camera that cost one thousand dollars. That was a lot of money then, sixty years ago. Tex took Brubaker up. One time he had this Jenny—that's all he had—and they were taking pictures over the mountains. They hit some bad air, some downdraft that was coming down. Tex wanted to throw the camera out; it was pretty heavy. But Brubaker wouldn't let him. Lucky, because they managed to make it back. I talked to Brubaker himself, and he said the story was true.

You were back at the beginning of the airport here, weren't you?

My brother, Al, wasn't interested, but I thought it would be nice to be the first one to land on it. So I got up at five o'clock and came over. And, by golly, Elrey Jeppesen was there sitting on the field with his old Alexander Eagle Rock, laying out on the wings. He said, "What are you going to do, sleep all day?" *(laughs)*

Ever train any World War II aces?

I trained students during the war. One fellow I trained flying a P-38 plane shot down a German plane with a 20 mm cannon—and he shot only one shot. That was an early, early German fighter plane.

That's a good percentage. Did you ever build any airplanes?

When I was a kid, I was going to build a Wright biplane. I was fifteen then. So I built it out of lumber. I had go-cart wheels on it. Then I tore it up. Later, I tried to build a glider, a ten-foot wing, which I decided to tear up. Then I found a book, "How to Build a 20-Foot Biplane Glider" by A.P. Morgan. So I built a twenty-foot one. I used to go out and put ropes on it, and we flew it like a kite. It got about ten feet high. I'd put some kids in it. But I never did get in it. I used to run and jump with it, and I'd get about two feet off the ground and lift up my feet. There were a lot of hills in that little town of Wasco, Oregon, where we lived. I knew I'd get killed—it didn't have any controls—so I chopped it up.

Did you know any fliers in Montana?

My father used to take sheep to the Montana State Fair in Helena, and they had a Curtiss Pusher up there. Tom Moroney was flying it. I admired that. I thought, "Oh, boy, that was great." But that was my first shot at flying. Moroney let me sit in it. It had a wood block for a brake and the block would rub against the tire.

So you were interested in flight practically all your life?

I was always interested in flight. I used to fly kites. I was an expert at building kites and everything. Then Tex Rankin came to our town—he was in Portland— and we met him. He said he could teach my brother and me to fly. And we didn't think we'd be any good at it. But by golly, my brother was a machinist. I was still going to school. I didn't have much money at the time, so he put up some money and bought an old Standard. Someone had wrecked it before my brother bought it; that's why he bought it, to fix it up. So we went down to Portland in 1926, and Tex taught us to fly. We found out we did real well at it. I could walk a high-wire at that time. I'm not sure that helped me in learning to fly, but I had good coordination. It was different than I thought it was going to be. Tex taught us very well, and the things he taught us always held water.

So you actually walk a high wire?

Not too high. Twenty feet. When I was young, I taught myself.

Did you want to be in the circus or something?

No, I did it just to prove I could do it. We stretched a wire between two trees. Years later in Yakima, I walked across a hop yard fence about eighteen feet high. I walked from one post to another, just to prove I could do it.

Didn't you build a large glider?

I went to California during the war, Twenty-Nine Palms, and flew and towed gliders for the army. And I built this glider years later, which is in the Boeing Museum right now. It was a very good glider with a fifty-foot wingspan. I designed it and built it, and my brother did all the welding on the controls for me. The rest of it was built out of plywood. I tried for an official world record. I had a barograph from Washington, DC and everything. A barograph is a tape on smoked paper to record the flight. It was an endurance record I was going after. We were supposed to be there at 7 AM, but at that time, a big storm came up they said was sixty miles per hour. But the examiner didn't show up at first. He was supposed to charge thirty dollars a day, but he cut it down to ten dollars; he knew I didn't have much money. Nice man, Herb Munter. He's dead now. He didn't show up until 2 PM so I lost about seven hours. I just about had a conniption. I got a stomachache. *(laughs)* I kept eating the jelly cake my mother put in the lunch box. Finally, the examiner showed up. He couldn't say much, but it turned out as they were leaving Seattle he got in a car accident. His brother got killed, so he had to take care of things. He said he wouldn't have come at all, but he knew how much it meant to me, so he came.

Did you lose a lot of fliers you knew?

One young fellow got killed in the war. Tex Rankin, my teacher, got killed in Klamath Falls, Oregon. He hit a wire. He was taking off on a hot day and he hit a wire with one pontoon on his plane, which I never did like, and hung way down. Hooked a wire.

You've had forced landings, haven't you?

Oh yes. I've had ten low-altitude complete forced landings—the engine failed and I had to land. I made them all.

The scariest one?

I don't think I've ever had a scariest one. You don't have much time to get scared. I learned early the first thing you should do when the engine quits is to look for a field—immediately. Pick a field and then you can fuss with the engine. These fellows who were killed recently on a hunting trip didn't do that. They fussed with the engine first and couldn't get it going so they ended up hitting some wires across the road.

Describe one of your forced landings.

Oh, I had one right here. I was taking off in the old Standard and a water connection in the water-cooled engine came loose. I didn't have any windshield but had goggles on, and it blew water all over my face and I had to duck. I was only about 400 feet high and I held my hand over my eyes so I could look and see, and I managed to land.

What happened was the water jacket had broken and lost water, and the engine wouldn't run. But I made it down. My brother then fixed the engine and put more water in it. It had Prestone in it because it was kind of cold. I had to take down a fence to take off and get back to the airport.

Another forced landing?

I was coming over from Wasco to Yakima and was flying this old Standard that never had any cowling over the engine, so you couldn't fly it in the rain. Of course, if you got in the rain, it would quit. I started across Satus Pass and this little rain started. I knew right away what that would mean. So I turned immediately and got back over wheat country, and it began to pour down. I was right handy over a six hundred-acre wheat field—nice and flat—when the engine quit, but I landed, no problem. That wasn't scary at all. People came out, and we pushed the plane over and tied it down behind the barn. The next morning the sun was shining so I started up and flew back to Yakima. I had used good judgment by not trying to go over the mountains.

Is it true that your first license was signed by Orville Wright?

The first license I ever had was. When I was going to try for the glider record, I knew you had to have a Federal Aeronautic International license, a worldwide deal. Elrey Jeppesen had one, and he was only nineteen years old. He told me how to get it. I had to fly a hundred feet high around three pylons fifteen miles around, and the committee watched me. Nobody rode with me. Then they sent it back to the National Aeronautic Association in Washington, DC, and Orville Wright signed it. That was in 1927. Then the Air Congress Act came out which said that Wright's licenses were no good. So I had to take a government test for an Air Transport license. I've had that all my life.

What does flying mean to you?

As I remember back when I was a little kid four years old I used to watch yellow swallowtail butterflies fly around, and I used to think that was pretty neat. I remember that. So later, we lived in the country in Montana, and we had pigeons in the barn. I used to get in the top of the barn. It's a wonder I didn't fall down. I used to handle them. I'd throw them out, and they'd start flying. I was intrigued by that. Later, neighbors showed us how to build kites. Flying is really, really exhilarating. I think most people think about flying more or less like that.

What number of planes have you flown?

One hundred thirty-five or one hundred forty.

What was the worst of those you ever flew?

One time I flew a plane—I don't know who made it—that had a Ford Model-A engine in it, and it was the poorest I ever flew in. It didn't have any power. You had to glide terribly steep, have the nose way down.

Which was your favorite?

I liked the Jenny Standard, but I think the Waco-10 was about the best one. Waco used to have a slogan that said, "Ask any pilot." They were easy to handle, had smooth controls, and they had pretty good torque. They were lighter, too. They weighed twelve hundred pounds whereas some other airplanes weighed fourteen hundred pounds with the same engines. So you see, you were short two hundred pounds when you started.

Any planes you flew that you thought unusual—or maybe even goofy?

The one they called the Aerocoupe. It was pretty good, though. It was a little two-place plane, and it didn't have any rudder on it and had a lot of dihedral. In other words, the wings sloped upward like a pigeon puts its wings up. Anyway, you could control it without a rudder, believe it or not. It had a little built-in rudder on the fins. You had an angle, so you had rudder on right and on left all the time. You would make turns by tipping over your wings and centering them, then pulling back on the controls.

Did that affect the turns you could make?

You could really make only two kinds of turns: steep ones and shallow ones. You couldn't make intermediate turns too well.

Any plane that fooled you in some way?

The only thing that fooled me was the glider that I built—the sailplane that's in the museum. I flew it once, and it got licensed by official inspection from the government. We towed it with a big Franklin car right at the airport in town. It got about three or four feet high and, oh man, it flew wonderful. It balanced just perfect. I was happy with it, but I had never made a turn with it. The next flight I made out of town was at at Lookout Point and about eight hundred feet high. I took it up there and was going to shoot it off there, but the wind wasn't any good. There were about one hundred people up there who'd come to watch us, so I decided to please the people. Four to twenty people could launch it with a shock cord. So the crowd launched me and everything was fine, and I went over the Nachez River and was going to turn and come back by the hill to see if I could get any lift there to soar. However, poor aileron control—it had excellent rudder and elevator control—was a problem. With a fifty-foot wing spread, when you start to turn, the outside wing starts to turn faster than the inside wing. It wouldn't stop turning. I was going to roll clear over when I got up vertically. I think if I hadn't had a lot of flying experience I would have been a goner. I was up vertical, so I centered the controls and kicked left rudder and the nose came right down, and I was level. After that I learned how to sneak up on it and not use too much control with the ailerons. But that's the only plane that ever fooled me.

You seem like a cat with nine lives.

(*laughs*) Well, I've had some experiences. One time I took up some people and got up about two thousand feet about the edge of town. I was going to pull the controls back and slow down, but a carburetor maybe wasn't adjusted just right and the engine stopped. The propeller was clear dead. I knew what to do: I could come back to the airport. I had plenty of altitude to land and I could have somebody come out and start it for me there. But I decided instead to dive it about eight hundred feet. I was at two thousand feet. You can dive about eight hundred feet and start it. I've done it many, many times. Some airplanes nowadays with high compression won't do that. Anyway, I decided to dive it, but I used the wrong language. I should have said, "I'm gonna start the engine," but I said, "I'm gonna dive." And the passengers both looked back and they had the most terrible look on their faces I ever saw. Then I got it started, and they said they thought I said, "We're gonna die." *(laughs)*

When you were barnstorming, were there any funny reactions to your flying?

Well, one time I was trying to sell rides. There was an air show here in the old days. A fellow wanted to go up, but his wife was scared. She didn't want to. At last we talked her into going up. She asked if she held up her hand would I come back, and I said, "Sure." We were about twenty feet high when she and her husband started struggling and, by gosh, she was trying to hold her hand up. Finally, she got loose and held it up. I couldn't land then because I needed to turn and come back, so I turned around and let her out. Then I took him up by himself.

Did you ever hit any big birds?

I hit a pheasant right here at this field. I was about fifteen feet high at the time. It took the propeller tip off. My mother cooked the pheasant. Anyway, we never did find the tip of the wooden propeller—it flew a long ways. I brought out a hacksaw and a measuring stick and pencil and cut the broken end off. Then I cut the other end off. We taxied back with a short propeller. That's the only big bird I've ever hit. I've hit a lot of little ones. You'd find them in the cowling, you know, sparrows and stuff.

I've chased eagles. This oldtimer, Frank Kammer who barnstormed, he showed me some pictures where he was chasing an eagle over Wenatchee, Washington. The eagle started doing wingovers and he did too. The eagle got confused and flew into the old Jenny he was flying and broke a two-by-six-foot wood strut. He thought he was a goner, but the wing didn't collapse, the other struts held. He landed and paid some kids five dollars and lunch, and they went out and stayed all day and brought the eagle back—a seven-foot eagle that weighed twelve pounds. I've learned never to get behind birds. You always want to get to the side.

Do you have any flying heroes?

Tex Rankin, my old instructor, was a hero. Of course, Lindberg was a great man. My friend, Jeppesen, I always admired him. I might also say the Wright Brothers. I honored them very much all my life, although I never met them.

What was your finest hour while flying?

I think my glider attempt at the world record. Also, I had something happen in a glider. I was flying up at Badger Gap up here. I was flying in about thirty-mile-per-hour wind, and it was pretty rough. It was about sundown and I was going to land. I saw this red-tailed hawk stretched out below that I thought was dead. I was up about fifteen hundred feet, about as high as I could get. But when you see a hawk dead on the ground, it is always crumpled, folded up, never with wings stretched out. I came down to look. He wasn't on the ground at all. He was about twenty-five feet high and sitting still in the wind. I moved right over, and he just moved right out and never flapped his wings. When I took his place, I was standing still. It was still kind of rough and then the sun went down behind the mountains. By golly, some boys came running over, and I was up there standing still! The wings on the plane were sort of flopping, like you carry a flexible pipe. I tried to stop the vibration and I finally got it stopped and I was sitting there perfectly still. I couldn't hear: the wind was blowing in my ear. The boys continued to lay down below and take sight of me. They all swore that for almost fifteen minutes, I never moved one-sixteenth of an inch. That's hard to believe, but it actually happened. You couldn't believe that you were flying in an updraft over a hill and sitting still just like the hawk. I was like a plumb bob up there. That happened two times six months apart, in 1933 or 1934.

Any really dangerous flying you've seen?

Morris McMechan was an old-timer, an Irishman who was afraid of nothing. He was going to do some stunts out here, he and Russell Schlosstein. Morris was flying a Waco, and they were flying formation looping and I tried to talk them out of it. So I watched them. They looped a long ways apart once, and they got close together. They looped and came together. One went one way; the other headed down and went into a spin and disappeared, and we thought, "That was Morris." The other fellow went down and landed. He said that what happened is they did this loop but were too close together. He said he felt a bump and the Waco's rudder was sticking up through his bi-plane's lower wing. *(laughs)* When they pulled apart, it just pulled the rudder and the fin clear apart. We thought Morris McMechan was killed, but he wasn't. Morris said he came out of a spin and didn't even nose over. When my brother and I went up to examine the plane we found that the controls were frozen. You couldn't move it at all, not even the ailerons. He was back out training students that afternoon. I figured the Lord was with him.

Other close calls?

One time I got iced up badly. They had a big flood in Yakima and the bridges were out between Christmas and New Year's. We were hauling food and passengers around. Morris McMechan was flying too. We went over to Terrace

Heights—the other side of the Yakima River. Coming back, in a period of ten minutes, we picked up two inches of ice on the wing and just barely made it. If I hadn't had a thousand-foot altitude, I couldn't have made it. Morris McMechan behind me, he didn't make it. By golly, he was okay though. He landed in a pasture, and it never hurt him at all.

You've flown a long time—any thoughts?

It's just like a feller who likes to go fishing or swimming or go out into the mountains—the beautiful mountains. It's an expression that's most exhilarating, and that's especially true of gliding. If you like to get away from it all, you go up and fly around in the clouds. It's like a dream.

I read a story about a fellow and it was true. When he was a boy he'd go fishing in the mountains by the lake and he dreamed about being an airline pilot. So he grew up, and he got to be an airline pilot. For years and years, flying over that lake, he dreamed about being down there fishing.

You must have been a little sad on your last flight.

I was. Someone made a video of it, and it was on CNN. Somebody in the army said they were down in Honduras, and they saw it on cable.

You still intend to fly?

I can fly now if I can fly with somebody. I can't pass the eye test now. My eyes are twenty-forty: they've got to be twenty-twenty. But I get one of the boys to go out with me. I take off and land. When you've flown that long, you don't forget.

If someone wrote your epitaph, what do you think it would say?

Hard to say—hard to say what it would be. "I followed the straight and narrow," I guess.

Forced landing by Ray Goss (caused by a broken oil line). The plane is a 1934 Cabin Waco-Cont 220 H.P.

RAY GOSS

Float Flying

Ray Goss began by washing airplanes at the airport, which led to his first ride in a Jenny. After he graduated from Appleton High School in Wisconsin, he got a job in a body shop north of Milwaukee. He worked there until 1939, until the shop owner got sick. Ray bought him out. In 1942, Goss enlisted as an ensign in the navy and taught three years as a naval cadet instructor at the Milwaukee Airport, then worked at Curtiss Wright Airport, in Milwaukee, Wisconsin. After a stint as a bush and float pilot, he returned to crop spraying, which he did until he was fifty-seven years old. He left that job only because the owner closed the business up. After that he moved to Hartford, Wisconsin, where he worked building airplanes for ten years. He retired at sixty-eight years young, and returned to West Bend, Wisconsin. Currently he and his friend Bill Buettner restore wrecked airplanes. Ray laughs a lot and seems surprisingly mentally and physically adept for a man of eighty-three, especially one who has seen plenty of stressful flight situations and has escaped death many times.

How old were you when you first flew?

I've flown ever since I was sixteen. When I was in high school, I used to fool around the airport. I got to watching airplanes and going up with the fellows who were flying. Then I got to flying in 1931. I had about four-and-one-half hours of flying, and the instructor said, "You've made some good landings, so I'll let you solo." So in the next takeoff, in a Waco 9, the engine quit, so we landed in a pasture filled with cows. Luckily we didn't hit any cows. We stopped just in time. The plane had a broken gas line. We got the plane fixed up and back to the airport. I made my solo. That was October 1931.

What did the instructor say when you ended up in a cow pasture?

He was cussing the OX-5 engine. But I never had more than one forced landing because of a broken gas line.

How many forced landings have you had over the years?

I guess about sixteen. The one that gave me the biggest scare was when I was working in Milwaukee right after the war. In the wintertime, I was to get one of the dusters and take the plane down south and do some experimental work. I was to put lampblack on the snow to see if it would melt it. The boss says, "Okay, go ahead, hop the airplane around the field to see if it's okay." Then I took off into the wind and was going to buzz the hangar. I turned downwind and pulled up over the hangar. I got up about three hundred feet and I ran out of gas. Across the street they were subdividing a bunch of lots to build houses. There happened to be a field big enough, and I got it into that without any damage to the airplane. But I'll never forget that one.

Another time I was working down in Tennessee with an experimental airplane, a duster, the Taylorcraft. I'd been flying over the mountains into the valleys. This one particular day I had a field real close to my strip. I never got very high, maybe fifty feet, flying through the field. I was getting ready to let down in the field, and the plane caught fire. The field was a pea field. I let the plane go, and I managed to get out of it. What happened was the exhaust system heated the carburetor, and there must have been a spark in there. The exhaust pipe had broken, and the exhaust went into the carburetor.

Once I went into Wisconsin and I bought a Fairchild-24. I was coming home with it. I had brought a friend along to copilot. We'd just cleared a bunch of bad territory—swamps and the like—so I said, "Go ahead, fly it." He took over and flew about five minutes. He looked at me and said, "This thing sure flies good." He no more said that and the engine quit. So I set it down in a farmer's field. We took the carburetor off and looked. I can't explain it, but a piece of grass got in the mixer control. This was a funny airplane. You had a left and right tank. You could fly off of either tank, but if you flew off of both tanks the engine would quit. They had quite a few fatal accidents because of that. Anyway, my friend and I flew through a little town and landed at a field where we had supper. At about ten o'clock we took off. I was living in Appleton, about twenty miles from Oshkosh. So I landed at the airport. They said, "Hey, Ray, you never gave me a ride in your airplane." So we took off. We got to about a thousand feet, and we were going to fly over the town, when the engine quit. We were still close to the airport, so I got back in all right. It seemed while I was parked at the supper club, the gas siphoned from one tank over into the other tank, so I had just enough gas to get to the airport and run out of gas.

Let's talk about bush flying.

I was a bush pilot for five years up there on the Canadian border. I was going out to pick up four people late in the evening. I got a couple of miles from the resort where they were, and the engine starts cutting out. I had enough power to taxi to the resort. This time I had a broken push rod. I managed to find a bolt and wedged it into the push rod. Then I fired it up. It seemed to run all right. I had four people in back. One couple was on their honeymoon. I told them that I wasn't sure if we were going to get back to the base or not, that we'd have another airplane up here in the morning. They said they'd take a chance. On the way back, I climbed to three thousand feet. I could see the lights of the town, and I thought, "By gosh, I'm going to make it. I no more thought that than she quit again, so I had to land in the woods. I had some pretty scared people with me, I'll tell you that.

It wasn't exactly a honeymoon.

No, they were used to the big city. I thought the bride was going to go into hysterics. She was just terrified. I told them there was nothing to worry about, just to take the cushions off the airplane seats and make themselves comfortable.

What was the hardest thing about bush piloting?

You flew most all kinds of weather. That was the main thing. You'd treat the airplane just like you would a truck. You'd load it down, so it wouldn't fly anymore, then you'd take something off and try it again. As to what we carried, you name it. We carried lumber, boats. It was a tough job, but I used to like it.

What was the strangest thing you carried?

I carried a lot of dead people, I'll tell you that. You see, we serviced quite a few resorts on the border. We'd try to fly over these places because you never knew when somebody was sick or needed help. The standard system the resort owners followed was to put a white flag up on the pole if they wanted you to stop. So I stopped at this one resort. It was the first trip in the morning. The operator came down. He was all excited and said they had a shooting last night. He had a resort with a main lodge and a bunch of cabins. On that particular night, he says everybody was in the main lodge at the little barroom. There were six or seven fellows from Chicago. Supposedly there was a gun rack on the wall, which had a 30.06. He kept it loaded because there were a lot of bears around the place. So the story was some kid got up on the chair there and fired the gun off, and it hit this guy from Chicago in the neck and took his head off. So this guy says, "Go get the deputy coroner and deputy sheriff and bring them back." So I bring them back to the lodge. We're looking everything over and, sure enough, the guy's head was off and lay about three or four feet from his body. They took the gun and dusted it for fingerprints. The deputy says, "Accidental shooting. I can't find any fingerprints on the gun." I thought, "Gee, somebody handled the gun. There had to be fingerprints." I didn't say anything. So as I'm loading the body in the airplane, a lot of people came down and said, "We don't want to stay here anymore after this happened. You take the body back to town, then come back and pick us up." So I came back. I was flying a Norseman, a ten-passenger plane, and when I got back a second time, there were still some more people on the

Wolf hunting in the border waters. One of 55 wolves that Ray and company got that year.

dock. By the time noon had come around, I'd emptied the resort out. There was nobody there. So by then the sheriff and coroner had come from a neighboring town about fifty miles away. They said, "Where are the witnesses?" There weren't any because everybody was gone. I sort of wondered about that. All the while I was hauling people out, nobody said a word about it. I often wondered what actually did happen.

Another time I had to go there, there were two fellows fishing below the falls in a canoe, and they tipped over and both of them drowned. The river there let out into a big lake. I had to haul the coroner out there, and we put the net across the river so the bodies wouldn't go out to the big part of the lake. After a day or so, the bodies came out of the river. The weather was hot, so we put them in a special rubber bag, then tied them to the float to fly them back again. Another time I hauled a logger out. A tree had fallen on him, and there wasn't much left of him. Another time I had to go out and haul in a woman. She'd been fishing with some kids during the day. A kid cast with one of those triple hooks, and it hooked her right eye, so I had to haul her back. She, of course, lost her eye after that.

Were you a squeamish guy?

Well, I wasn't after all the stuff I saw. I learned to take it as it comes.

What was the worst country you had to fly over?

Well, any of the northern country. We used to take canoe parties up there. At that time you had to be pretty careful. There weren't too many roads. Also, there was a lot of iron in that territory. As a result, you had to know the territory, because your compass wasn't always going to be reliable because of all the iron ore deposits in that area. You had to know where you were going. If you got lost, it was just too bad. I never was lost in my life.

To what do you attribute that?

I knew the country. I come from the country I was flying over. If you once got to know the country, got to know the lakes, you didn't need a compass or anything. Oh, yes, we'd fly up where we'd barely see the tops of the trees, and I never got lost.

Describe the most inspiring place up there.

I liked it best in the fall, when the leaves were turning. Then it was really beautiful, with all the color. There were lakes like you couldn't believe. If the weather got bad, we'd set down until the weather cleared a bit and away we'd go. We'd fly nearly every day. The only time I didn't like to fly was in the late fall, when the weather was getting cold and the lakes were freezing up. The weather was windy and cold, and the airplane would pick up a lot of ice. Lots of times we'd pick up so much because of the rough water. On the lake we'd take a spray from the floats, and ice would build up on the prop and plane. We'd take a plastic hammer and knock the ice off the prop. In the smaller airplanes, if the lake froze up overnight, we'd go in and land on it the next day. I never lost a float plane, though.

We'd use the Supercruiser, which was a seaplane with two back seats. We used to use those mostly as winter ships, because the big airplanes were too much of a hassle. In the deep snow we'd use the plane to haul deer hunters. We'd have two hunters in the airplane, plus the pilot, and tie the deer up on the wing struts on each side, and haul them out. That is big country up there. And there were a few hunters who would get lost. We'd have to look for them by air.

Would you find them?

We always found them. One fellow came up there one time, and the weather was real lousy. He was flying with friends to one of the lakes on the border. The lakes were frozen over, but some of them were open yet. The weather was mild, but it was real foggy that day. Of course, we knew the country so that didn't bother us, but this fellow took all his friends back. Then he went back in a plane to pick up the deer at this lake. It was getting towards evening, and the weather was getting worse. He loaded the deer up, and he got lost and headed into Canada. Of course, when he didn't show up the next day, his friends got worried. We started looking for him. After about three days, we got all the planes in Fargo River City, and finally one of the guys saw some smoke about ten or fifteen miles on the Canadian side. We flew over and landed on the ice. This guy had gotten himself lost and landed on this lake at night. By luck, it was frozen over. He slept in the airplane, and the next morning he got up and was going to turn the plane around, when the airplane broke through the ice. There he was. The guy was lucky we found him. We just happened to see the smoke.

One time we couldn't find a fellow. They sent ground parties out looking for him. They found where he'd been hunting. A lot of people panic when they get in the country. When the guy realized he was lost, the first thing he did was throw his gun away. And he started running, and he started taking his clothes off. Why he did, I don't know, but the search party was going down a logging trail, and this guy came running out of the woods and he was nearly naked. He was stark raving mad. They had to put him in a straitjacket. He was so terrified.

With sixteen forced landings, do you ever feel as if you've got nine lives?

Well, I'll tell you. I've gotten to the point where I wouldn't trust any engine anymore. In fact, we bought one of these Supercruisers, brand new, in 1946, the first year I was up here. It was to be our winter airplane. I was coming back one night, carrying somebody out. We were bucking an awful head wind, and the temperature was about thirty below zero. We were flying low to get out of the wind and had just cleared the edge of a lake when the engine quit just like that. On a brand-new airplane. I was wearing a light wool jacket because we had a good heater in the plane. The snow was about four or five feet deep. I was about five miles from town, but I realized I couldn't walk into town without snowshoes. I monkeyed around with the airplane, trying to get it running, but I couldn't get up enough power. So, I opened up the cowling—the control stick was in the baggage compartment—and I took it out and banged on the carburetor, and it fired up. We flew up and away. We had a nice shop, so we took it in and went over the plane, but we couldn't find a thing wrong with it. We used it all winter, and it never gave us a bit of trouble. The following winter some friends of mine came up who wanted to go wolf hunting. We used it a lot for wolf hunting. In the winter we had more free time, so we used to do a lot of wolf hunting. We'd land on the lake and chase the wolves with the airplane. One year we got fifty-five timber wolves. The boss got one that weighed 150 pounds. Anyway, I took these two guys out in the same airplane. We went over to the Canadian side. It was a beautiful day, sun shining, twenty-four below zero, but just a beautiful day. We were at about a thousand feet, looking for wolf tracks out on the lake. Suddenly, that thing quit just the way it did the first time. I landed on the ice, opened up the cowling but couldn't find a thing wrong. I banged on the carburetor with the spare control stick. It fired up. We flew home, and I took off the carburetor and could find nothing wrong. That occurred almost a year to the day when it quit the first time. So you wonder why I don't trust the engine. That was a brand-new one.

What was next?

When I came back up north, I went into crop dusting. I crop-dusted for about sixteen years. I went to work for this fellow. "I've got good equipment," he says. "Never have any trouble." His airplanes were so nice, no question about it. So another fellow and I went to Green Bay. We were spraying a pea field. The first load we took out, I was a couple of miles from the pea field, when my oil pump goes out. I tried to keep the airplane going and get back to the strip, but without the oil pump, it wouldn't keep going. I set it down in a pea field and went back to work.

Crop dusting is pretty hazardous work, isn't it?

Yes, you have to be pretty careful. The thing is some days I flew as many as fourteen hours a day. After eight hours, you're not really fit to fly. You're overtired. It's hard on the system, but the work was there, and I had to do it because some days you couldn't fly and had to make up for it.

Did you lose anyone you knew crop-spraying?

You had to take new fliers up in a trainer. You would show them how to do it. You'd give them a duster or sprayer and give them a field and tell them to demonstrate spraying for you. Then you'd let them solo and watch them, without a load in it. Then we'd give them a load and see how they did. Everybody didn't like it, because it took a different type of flying. If they weren't prepared, I wouldn't let them go. It was tough flying. You had no instruments, no air speed, nothing, strictly flying the airplane. I had one fellow crash.

Well, the thing is I didn't want him to go by himself yet. I was supposed to go up to North Dakota to take on some experimental work, but I told the boss, "Don't let this guy go up. He isn't ready yet." The boss says, "Ah, he'll be all right." So I left that night and went up to North Dakota. The next day I got a call, and it turned out the first trip the boss sent him on, he killed himself. I was so sad about it, because I got to know the guy pretty well. It was actually the boss's fault, because he shouldn't have sent him out.

Right after WWII, we were working in Nebraska on a big potato field. That's where I started crop dusting before I went up north. There was an old crop duster named Bob Shrock, who had started me off in it. We were working the potato field and putting kerosene on it. These were great big, rolling fields. We were using a flag man. Anyway, there was this one field man who was flying for Shrock who'd just bought a new Chevrolet sedan. He was just as proud of that! The boss just happened to be there that night, and the field man was bragging about his new car the night the boss went back to Milwaukee. The plane would make so many passes, then the guy would move his new car down to the next field, and we'd fly it. As I said, the field was rolling, so the crop duster comes over one of these hills next to the road, and here this guy's got his car parked there. He hits the car, knocks the landing gear off the airplane, and takes the top right off the car. Bob flew the airplane back to the airport and landed it on its belly, then came back to work. That night Bob called the boss back in Milwaukee and says, "Remember the nice car that field man just bought, that nice four-door sedan?" He said, "Well, it's a touring car now!"

What's the most difficult terrain you've crop-dusted?

I don't know. You took it as it came. If you had a rough spot to do, you'd go in with a lighter load. If you had a good area, nice and flat, you'd go in with a larger load. I remember we used to fly off the old airport at Rochester, Minnesota. Right next to the airport there was a three-acre patch of peas, surrounded by electric wires. The whole town would turn out to watch because they were sure we were going to go into the wires. We always pulled up.

Have you ever been frightened?

Usually you're frightened after it has happened. You don't get a chance otherwise. I suppose when I went through a bunch of electric wires in Minnesota. As I went through them, I cut them all off at the top, which created fires like you wouldn't believe. Luckily, I didn't hit the wing, or anything.

What is your proudest moment?

I guess what I'm most proud of is that I've got over sixteen thousand hours and never killed or hurt anybody and never had a real serious accident. I busted up a couple of planes but no serious accident.

You restore planes.

I've restored two, actually, with a friend of mine. We've gotten some awards, including four at the EAA at Oshkosh. One I restored was a PA-12 Supercruiser and the other was a Taylorcraft. Right now I'm working on a Tri-pacer that had tricycle gear on it. I've taken the nose gear off and am making a conventional airplane out of it. I've got it stripped down to the last nut and bolt.

How many hours can you work a day?

Oh, I can work as long as I want to. I haven't been working lately, because I hurt my back, working around the house. That's laid me up for awhile, but I feel good now. I'm going to get right back to work on that triplane.

What are you going to do in your second hundred years?

I've got so much work planned now I'll have to wait that long. I told Bob, my partner, "I don't think I'm going to live long enough to finish this." And he said, "Well, work as long as you can."

Bob Gehring of Hartford, Wisconsin owns both the Taylorcraft and the Supercruiser I restored. He also owns the Tripacer Cub and the J3 Cub I am working on now. If I finish these two, he still wants me to build a Bushmaster on floats. So you see why I have to live that next hundred years. I still hold my pilot's license and fly whenever I can.

Larson Airport, the first airport in Wisconsin, where Ray Goss learned to fly. (From left to right) an Ox 5 Waco 9, a WWI Thomas Morse Scout fighter plane, and an Ox 5 standard WWI training plane.

Gib Blackmore

G.B. "GIB" BLACKMORE

Pioneering on the Dixie Clipper

Gib" Blackmore made aviation history when he and his fellow pilots flew the first paid passenger flight, transatlantic, on the Dixie Clipper in 1939. Blackmore was born in "a wide place in the road called Bloomfield, Indiana," in 1903. He attended Purdue University, where he graduated with a degree in Science.

He went into the Navy and took Navy Flight Training at Pensacola, graduated there as a naval ensign, then spent one year with the fleet. From there he went on the airlines and stayed with the airlines 30 years until he retired in 1963.

"How many different airplanes have you flown in your life?" I asked him.

"Fifty," he said, "I'm only guessing."

Pictures of the Boeing 314, in which he made the historic flight, decorate the wall of his den.

Did you like the Boeing 314?

It was a helluva airplane. That's why I have pictures all over my wall.

What was your role on the flight?

I was first officer, checking out. Rod Sullivan was the skipper, so I was second in command.

That was a check-out flight for you?

I'd checked out as skipper in Bermuda and all through Latin America, but I'd never made a transatlantic flight.

What was Sullivan like?

He was just a two-fisted pilot — and a pretty good one, too. He later flipped one over on the Tagus River and that ended his career with Pan Am.

What happened on the flight?

I think he tried to land too short, got out of flying speed, and it flipped over on him.

How many flying hours did you have when you retired?

Thirty thousand.

That's a good number.

Well, it was great while it lasted.

Someone told me when you flew in Mexico they offered you a job as captain — which was unusual.

I went down there as a captain. I was leaving American Airlines and I was going to get a better job or else. I got a job as skipper. They had had a series of accidents and they were trying hard to eradicate that.

What kind of accidents?

Oh, I don't know. It was a mishmash. They'd run out of gas or some damn thing.

What planes did you fly for the Navy?

I flew the Consolidated NY 1's, 2's,3's — the flying boats, the TD-1's, the Douglas twin-engine flying boats. That was the beginning of my career because it was heavy equipment and the airlines were looking for pilots who had heavy equipment time.

A favorite plane?

I liked them all, but each one got a little better. The best one I got to fly was the 707, and it was my last one.

What did you think when you first saw the 707?

Oh, I thought it was a great airplane and the more I got to know it the better I liked it. I could go up to save fuel—or come down and burn it up—very flexible. It was a helluva aircraft.

Remember your first flight on the 707? Was it exciting?

I went to Honolulu and back. No problem.

What year?

1959, I think.

Was that exciting?

Oh, sure it was, because very few of us were checked out on a 707.

Were you a tough captain?

I don't think so. Everybody seemed to tolerate me. (*laughs*)

Anything you were a stickler about?

Well, I wanted to be on time for departure — I wanted to be ready to go. That was the main thing. I don't think I ever had any run-ins about it, though.

Did you lose any pilot friends?

Oh, a number of them. I had an instructor — he was flying for Hearst, I think, from Denver to El Paso, and he got wound up in a storm and got killed.

What did you think when that happened?

I don't know—apparently he stuck his neck out. The rudders are running— you can turn around, but he didn't. He was over-anxious I think—I don't know.

Did things like that bother you emotionally?

I have learned to live with it. I was always very sorry to learn about losing one.

Ever have an engine go out on you?

Oh, yeah. I had one burn off going into Fiji during the war, but nobody got their feet wet. We got off. I thought the damn thing would blow up, but it didn't. We got everybody off, and an hour and a half later we got back on board.

What happened?

They had no firewall on the DB-2Y3 and the generator caught on fire. We landed on the water and got everybody off. And later the fire went out after the engine fell off in the water. And we got back on board and that was it.

Talk about your historic flight.

Well, it was an uneventful trip. We took off from Baltimore and went to Port Washington, New York—about an hour-and-a-half flight—then we took on passengers and went to the Azores. We refueled there and went to Lisbon, Portugal; overnighted there. We would fly two hours on and two hours off. The next day we went to Marseille, France.

It was the first paying passenger flight—they'd had many proving flights, but this was the first where they had paying passengers on board. It was a kind of gala trip.

A gala trip?

Yes, they were the bigger people. Mrs. Tripp was on board—the Whitneys. Oh, hell, I don't know—about 35 passengers.

The Clipper Ships were based down in Dinner Key when you first flew them. Do you remember what it was like when you first got there?

When I first got there, it was in the middle of a hurricane. They were getting people out of the Keys. It was kind of hurdy-gurdy, but I didn't have to do any of that. I just checked in. A few days later, I got my feet on the ground and we got going.

That was quite an introduction to the place.

Yes, it was (*laughs*).

Was it pretty primitive down there?

After that storm you could drive up Biscayne Boulevard and find boats on the other side of the street. It was quite a deal.

Did you think maybe, "I don't think I want to do this."?

(*Laughs*) No, I'd made up my mind I'd roll with the blows. No problem. I always wanted to be a pilot.

Did you ever fly close to the water out of Miami?

One-hundred, fifty feet—depending on the weather. But most times you'd get up higher than that. You'd sometimes fly low to avoid a headwind or sometimes if the weather was better down there than it was up high.

Do you remember your solo flight?

We had to take three checks with two instructors and one with the skipper. You made three landings, one with each of them, and they tried to put you in a corner where you couldn't take off again. So, eventually you'd have to say, "Well, I'll turn around and taxi back." It was a very good check flight. Finally, the skipper, J.D. Price, a Naval Academy man, got out and said, "You're on your own—this is it."

Do you remember your instructors in Pensacola?

Oh, they were wonderful people. I had an enlisted pilot first and then I had a First Lieutenant who later went with TWA.

What did they teach you?

You had to make your usual amount of turns, loops and aerobatics.

What did you like best to do?

I liked the aerobatics very much—I liked to fly on my back—loop, whatever you wanted to do.

Ever any problems?

I flew too low on my back one time. Also, I froze up an engine and made a dead-stick landing at Corry Field. The prop stopped, that's all. I should have turned over and got some oil for the engine so it wouldn't freeze up, but I was too stupid to know then.

That day I thought that I was through flying, but they had an airplane there and the instructors said, "Go ahead and take it." I had a little time I could use, so I went up and did a little too much upside down flying. (*laughs*)

But you landed okay.

Yes. (*laughs*) But I was mad as hell because I'd been so stupid. But that was my problem, not theirs.

Ever have any bad landings?

Not real bad. Some were a little rough — bad fields. In Mexico, on the north coast, I had a few.

What was the big lesson that flying taught you?

Know your job and do it right. Don't fuss around with it because there's a right way and a wrong way—and if you're wrong, you're all wrong.

André Tomalino up top, October 1946

ANDRÉ TOMALINO

Flying Banners

Though fliers flew banners in the twenties and thirties, André Tomalino is nonetheless a pioneer in the field. Not only did Tomalino make advances in the techniques, as he explains in the interview, but he has had the longest running continuous aerial advertising business. He's been doing it for fifty years straight.

Tomalino was born in 1920 in Upper Darby, Pennsylvania. Several years after graduating from Upper Darby High School, he joined the Army Air Corps in 1943. By the time he completed his training, all the places for pilots were taken, so he ended up teaching glider pilots. The flying of gliders could be hazardous to one's health and at one point, he was involved in a glider accident. He was riding as a passenger when the pilot held too long and it spun in. Fortunately, they hit on one wing (the gliders he flew had a wingspan of 84 feet and 6 inches) and that absorbed a lot of the shock. He spent several weeks in the hospital and then returned to instructing.

After the United States dropped the bomb on Hiroshima and Nagasaki, they didn't need glider pilots and they were instructed they could go home. Tomalino himself was out of the military by the end of September, 1945. He immediately started a business flying banners in Florida, later moving to New Jersey, where he operates Paramount Flying Service with his daughter, Barbara, who is now the owner. One of André's proudest awards comes from the FAA, commending him on his safety record and for contributions such as aerial pickup booms and under-wing night lights. He also was the first to use the autogyro to tow.

You trained pilots on gliders in World War II.

Yes, the CG4A glider. I instructed in it toward the end of the war. Our basic goal was to teach people to glide them and also return them from behind enemy lines. Actually, the gliders were the forerunners of the helicopter, in the sense that that's how they moved troops behind the lines before the helicopter came along. During World War II they had a lot of trouble going into France, Holland, and over the Rhine. They were a high-casualty group, and what was more remarkable, it was a volunteer organization. But it really was a good organization, and they did an awful lot of good. They moved a lot of guns, howitzers, and jeeps behind enemy lines.

You had to have a minimum of 250 hours' flying to get into the glider group. We had one fellow who showed up for training who had 250 hours flying, but it was in blimps. He didn't mention that on the application. When he got in, we all chipped in to teach him to fly, but he finally got washed out.

Did a lot of people wash out?

Yes, they did. And we also lost quite a few in training. I remember one day we lost two different planes on idle turns right in front of me. We used PT-19s for basic training for gliders. We would fly them up as airplanes, then cut the engine. Anyway, they were doing hurdle flying. For that, you had to bring the plane to a minimum speed, that is, the speed right at the point where the plane would start to shake. You'd have to hold at that point and not let it go beyond to the point where it would stall. So each of these two pilots was up at 300 feet, turning on final when the plane stalled. You're not going to recover in that situation. The two died within an hour of each other.

They called the session after the second crash. I know one thing: the next day we lost a lot of potential glider pilots. They'd come down, but they somehow couldn't make the hurdles. It became obvious they'd seen enough the day before.

What was the most difficult thing about teaching people gliders?

We used regular airplanes, and once the student cut the engine off, they had a one-time shot at making a good landing. A lot of the boys didn't get accustomed to the idea that once the actual glider was loaded and coming in, it was to be coming in at a very good speed. They had to learn to slow them down when landing. For example, as soon as you hit the ground, you put the aircraft over on its nose to help slow it—along with using its brakes. Gliders always used short-field landings. The biggest problem was in keeping the glider approach slow when in a combat situation. Often in such a case, the flier would try to put it on the ground as quickly as he could by putting the nose down and getting speed. When that happened, they couldn't land at the field designated. They'd go right through that field onto the next and through that and into the next and into the woods.

Ever have any returnees with amazing stories?

Quite a few. I can remember a fellow named Concannon. He got shot up coming in on a glider, which went into a ravine in the woods in France. They shot at him through the glider all night long, but he was so far down in the ravine that none of the shots hit him, but the rest of the crew was killed. He was the only one left alive in the glider. A lot of them you never heard from, because they never came back. I had another returnee who had a successful glider landing, and his whole crew got out and secured the area. They were all dressed up with their pinks and greens (dress uniform) under their fatigues.

114

They went sailing through France with the underground. Meanwhile, though, they had him mistaken for dead and had services for him and everything. He showed up two months later in England.

When did you get started in banner flying?

I'll tell you what got me started. I was in Miami, and I saw this banner that read, "Heineken's Back."

Heineken's, the beer?

Well, I didn't know it was a beer. I thought it was some serviceman flying a banner up the beach to let everyone know he was home. (*laughs*) I said, "Boy, that's a great way to advertise," so that led to the business. Concannon (the fellow mentioned earlier) and I and several others started businesses. That was at the end of 1945.

What was it like?

It was kind of bad. Things were tight. It got so tight that you almost had to dogfight with one another over business. It finally wound up with everybody carrying guns in the airplane, so if anybody got close to you, you'd shoot at them. We'd sleep next to the airplane. Over time, you had tires cut and valve-grinding compound put in the engine of the plane when you weren't around. That was a tough way to make a living in that time. There were no jobs so it was cutthroat.

Ever catch anyone?

No, we didn't actually catch anyone, but we did catch a couple of planes in the air, so we got a group of us together and went to the airfield, armed, and told them the next time it happened we were coming over to burn their airplanes. We had a constant thing going on at the FAA. Every week we'd be over there at their offices, trying to get things ironed out. We'd walk out of there shaking hands 'til the next week when they'd start flying, and the problems would arise again.

Another example, someone would see a banner fly down the beach that was contracted for, and they'd walk right into the establishment and offer to do it for half the money. That kept on happening until it got so bad that we came up to Pennsylvania, where I was born and raised, and continued the business.

Any critical misspellings? I recall Stan Freberg did a thing with a skywriter that kept spelling Nucoa the wrong way.

Yes, we've had some critical misspellings. Leave the "R" out of shirt. That was many years ago. I think that was done by the ground crew on purpose, to see what kind of laugh they could get.

What was the greatest satisfaction you've had in the business?

One of the greatest satisfactions I got probably was when a Canadian from Montreal was trying to reach his brother. Their father had just died, and the other brother didn't know. The one brother was on vacation in New Jersey, so his brother called the state police for help and then he called us. He asked us to fly on the beach, because he knew his brother would be on the beach at three o'clock. So we flew a banner, so he could contact his brother as quickly as possible. And it worked. The lost brother immediately called his brother in Montreal, got the news, and made it home in time for the funeral. That was satisfying. Later, they wrote us a nice letter and called us with thanks.

We've done a lot of unusual things. We've towed for lost children and lost pets. One time we found a lost pet. A guy had spent $1,000 to find his lost cat. (He must have liked that cat very much.) Anyway, we flew a banner for the cat, and somebody found it.

I think my greatest satisfaction in fifty years of business was when we got an award from the FAA.

How did people look at the aerial advertising business in the early days?

In the early days it was a kind of a circus-type phenomenon. Totally unusual. One of our early customers was Ballantine beer. But when TV came in strong, aerial advertising began to lose out—skywriters, balloons, and banners, at least for awhile. But it's gotten back now to where it's a totally accepted medium. It's bigger and better than ever and going on an international scale now.

What were the technical problems you had to solve at first?

We had to modify the airplane to a great degree. See, we're flying at a very slow airspeed with a high RPM, high boost, so it's almost as if you're climbing out, constantly. As a result, you have to change the rigging of your airplane. On takeoff, of course, you use your right rudder. You have to modify that so you don't have to hold right rudder all the time. Also, you have to modify the plane so it cools at high RPM, high boost, and slow airspeed. We'd lighten the planes, too.

You did some pioneering work in the pickup of banners.

It all started with the method used in picking up the airmail. They would snatch up the mail bags and drop them at different post offices. They used a hook to catch it as you flew low. That method became the method of picking up gliders during the war. I got the idea for using it to pick up the banners.

The old method involved tying the banner on the back and taking off with it on there. That created problems. When you took off like that you were forced to take a steep takeoff and sometimes couldn't get the altitude needed.

André Tomalino in Pitcairn Autogyro, over North Wildwood, N.J July 1952.

Of course, you also needed more runway and a larger horsepower plane.

What was the most unusual aircraft you ever towed with?

I towed Noxzema with the Pitcairn Autogyro. I had one of those. It was a rotary-wing aircraft, which still had an engine up front. The engine was what got the wing going. The thing was difficult. You had no control of the rotors on all the early models. These rotors we had just went round and round. When you would slow it down, you'd just lose control because your control was aircraft control: rudder, elevator, and aileron. First, when it slowed down, you'd lose your ailerons, then your elevator, then your rudder. You'd be at its mercy if you went too slowly. Another thing was you'd never land with the wind to your right, because that's where the blades were coming up. You'd never land with forward speed because the gear would hang down and your brakes would lock up, and it would immediately throw the aircraft over. Another thing you never did with the Autogyro was to land on a concrete surface, because your wheels would spin out. Back in 1951 this employee of ours had trouble. He had dropped his banner and come in for a landing. Unfortunately, he did all of the things I mentioned not to do. He turned the aircraft inside out like an infuriated palm tree. We repaired it enough (Mr. Pitcairn was nice enough to give us some old blades.), and we gave it to Pioneer Village in Minden, Nebraska.

Did you know any old-timers?

I knew Bill James from Wildwood, Cape May, and Atlantic City. He had a prewar Stearman and a WACO. That was back when you could fly anytime. He used to fly right off the beach. He'd take passengers up, and when the passengers lessened in numbers, he'd grab a banner and go up.

Did anybody ever paraphrase baseballer Sachel Paige's words "Don't look back, the banner may be gaining on you"?

(laughs) We used to fly celebrities when they came to Wildwood. I couldn't get Louis Armstrong in an airplane. He told me, "I'll go with you. Just let me keep one foot on the ground."

(Left to right) Captain Snyder, First Lieutenant Tully, Lieutenant Jamison, Cadet Boller, and Cadet Cameron Robertson at Brooks Field

CAMERON T. ROBERTSON

Flying Airmail

"I 've always been a captain—I didn't know there was any such thing as a copilot when I started to fly. In fact, I've never had that experience where I was anything but the captain," says Cameron T. Robertson, Texas native and pioneer flier.

In 1968 Cameron T. Robertson prepared to retire from Pan American on his birthday at sixty years old. He was in Tokyo, coming to San Francisco, and his birthday was three days away. Scheduling told him to get to Bangkok. He would then have to deadhead home. Robertson, a genial man, wasn't about to take to that. He said no. So, after fifty-one years of flight, at his own insistence, he went home on his regularly scheduled flight—in time for a well-deserved birthday and retirement party all rolled into one.

Cameron T. Robertson is a graduate of the United States Army Air Corps primary and advanced flying schools in San Antonio. He flew in the air corps until the fall of 1928, then started flying airmail route #1 from New York to Albany to Montreal. In his interview he relates some of his by-the-seat-of-the-pants adventures, including one outrageous crash. In Febuary, 1929, he got a job with the National Transport Airlines. After that he flew with United Airlines until 1942. During the war he went on active duty and was director of operations at Harmon Field, Newfoundland. He later went to American Export Airlines, which eventually became American Overseas Airlines and then Pan American.

Robertson's thirty-seven thousand hours of flying, of which eight thousand consisted of long jet flying time, span several pivotal eras in the development of American aviation. He seems somewhat excited to reminisce—as excited as I am to hear—and the interview begins.

You flew contract airmail. How did that work?

In the early beginnings, back about 1918, the government started airmail service. And the government ran the whole thing. In 1924 the government contracted that service out by route: CAM-1 meant Contract Airmail #1; FAM-1 meant Foreign Airmail #1. The individual companies would operate the mail under contract to the government.

What was the worst route you had to fly?

In those days there were low mountain routes over the Allegheny Mountains between New York and Cleveland. That was even worse than high mountain routes because of the weather.

Describe the roughest flight you ever had over there?

That would be hard to say. I had one one night between Chicago and Cleveland, where the engine drowned out in the rain, and I almost had to jump. The engine was popping; I was losing altitude. Just before I got down too low, I flew out of the rain. Then the engine dried out some, and the plane picked up on a couple of cylinders, and I went on into Toledo. I got out of that plane, went in to the office, and put my parachute on the floor. I laid my head on the parachute and said, "I'm going to sleep. Call me when there isn't a drop of rain in the United States!"

What was the most challenging thing about flying contract airmail?

The hardest thing was getting from point A to point B. That was fairly early, you know, and the airplane hadn't developed all that much in terms of instruments and aids to navigation. We didn't have any of those things. That made it a little tough. And the airplanes didn't perform. They didn't go very high or very fast or very reliably

How were the flying procedures radically different in the early days?

There weren't any procedures. Each person had his own procedures in flying. Each pilot would fly how he wanted. Some would fly high; some would fly low; some would try to fly on instruments; some wouldn't. But everybody flew relatively low because the airplanes wouldn't go high to start with. A lot of people would fly low, I mean very low. I mean right down on the fence posts, assuming the weather was bad. But the way you flew just depended on the individual. Just go and get there the best way you can.

Who's the most colorful character you've known in your years of flying?

One of them would be Walter J. Adams, one of the early airmail pilots. He didn't fly government airmail, but he flew contract airmail, almost from the beginning. One time old Walt told me he was standing around Maywood Airport in Chicago when an airplane came in and landed, a DH mail plane of Robertson Aircraft, St. Louis. He watched a big, tall, lanky guy get out of it, and Walt started talking to him. It turned out to be Charles A. Lindbergh, who was nobody at that time. He was just another airmail pilot. What he was doing was going to work for Robertson Aircraft, and he was doing a familiarization by landing in the different airfields from St. Louis to Chicago.

When Lindbergh got ready to leave to go back to St. Louis, he asked Walt if he'd crank the old Liberty engine in the DH plane. So, Walt said, "Sure." When Lindbergh said, "Contact," Walt grabbed the propeller and ran through with it, and the plane started. (You used to grab the propeller with one hand and run through with the propeller.) Anyway, Slim Lindbergh waved goodbye to Walt, then he flew off. Then Walt looked down at his hand, and he had the leading edge of Slim's wooden propeller in his hand. It had pulled part of the leading edge right off. Walt said, "Next time you see Lindbergh, ask him if his engine ran a little rough that day."

What route did you start flying first?

I started flying Foreign Airmail #1, Canadian Colonial Airlines, New York to Montreal. While I was there, I had my application in with National Air Transport. I wanted to get on at National Air Transport because I wanted to fly the transcontinental routes. I was just waiting to get on there. Strangely enough, when you waited, you were actually waiting for some guy to get killed, because that's the only way you could get to be one of their pilots

Did you feel a little squeamish about that?

Not really. It was just a fact of life. But, sooner or later some guy accommodated me over near Cleveland. That's how I got my job with National Air Transport, a predecessor of American Airlines.

How long did that take?

Six or seven months.

Do you know what happened to the guy you replaced?

He spun out in a snowstorm at night up there by Vermillion, Ohio, at a little emergency field on a lake. He had gotten into this snow storm and lost contact; he had become disoriented and just plain spun in and hit the ground

What's the worst weather you've flown in?

That's hard to say. Thunderstorms are always bad. But you might say I got into some worse weather one night when I was coming down from Montreal to Hadley Field in New Brunswick, New Jersey. That was the eastern terminus of all the airmail in the United States. I was flying from there to Albany to Montreal. Anyway, one afternoon I was coming down south and getting into the New York area, and there was a dense fog all around. I was flying low, very low. Finally, it got to the point where I got right down into the middle of Newark, almost. As I did, I looked for a two-track railroad that I knew would lead me toward Hadley Field, but I never did find it. The fog was getting so bad that I couldn't see to fly. At last, in desparation, I did a left-hand turn and noticed a light spot on my right that I hoped would be an open field. I did a 270 degree turn to the left—or what I thought was a 270 degree turn—and pulled the throttle back, cut the switch, and waited for the plane to hit the ground. I lit on to a little open spot all right. I had almost stopped when the wheels went into a ditch. As this happened, the airplane went slowly up, up, up, until it sat on its nose for a minute. Then "boom," the plane went over on its back. There I was with eight hundred pounds of mail scattered around my neck. I had a flying suit on, a helmet and goggles, a six-shooter, and all this mail down around my neck

I finally crawled out and went up onto the road. I saw some guys testing out a new bus. I stuck my head in the door and asked them if they could help me get to the telephone. I said I was carrying airmail. They looked at me as if I was from another world. They said they didn't know anything about that, and announced they were busy, besides.

Incidentally, when I had gotten out of the airplane and walked down, I noticed a big concrete company building about one hundred yards away, which I would have hit had I flown another one hundred yards. I made a phone call, and the fire department got out there. Each one of the firemen had a bottle of that "Jersey lightnin'," which was grapejack that those guys made over there. When each one of them found out I had had a harrowing experience, they thought that I ought to have a nip from him. The firemen had these pike poles they used to punch holes with. They proceeded to put a rope around the tail of the airplane, and had had a truck with a hoist on the end, so they could wind up. They pulled on the airplane, trying to get it up on the wheels. After they'd get it up there a ways, they'd stick a pike pole up there to help hold it while they got another bite on it. Unfortunately, they forgot that my airplane was linen-covered, so my plane ended up all full of holes. The other damage I had was a cracked crankcase.

Finally, they had the plane up on its wheels. Now that airplane had folding wings on it—it was a monoplane—so they folded the wings, put the tail up on the truck and towed it through the Holland Tunnel, through the East River Tunnel, out through Long Island and up to the factory. The factory put a new engine in it and patched up those holes. I got it back two days later and flew it back to Montreal.

Did you have any communication problems in Canada?

On my first trip into Montreal, I didn't have a map of Canada, north of the border, except for a road map. It wasn't very good. To complicate matters, the further north I got, the worse the weather got. Before long I became lost. I was going north, up the river, looking for San Hubert Airport in Montreal. I didn't know where it was. I was lost.

I saw a farmer down in a field. I was flying right down low, on the ground. The ceiling was right on the ground. So I went past this guy plowing in the field. I took a letter from my girlfriend out of my pocket—she later became my wife—and I wrote on the letter, "Point the way to Montreal." I took and slid open the side window and went on a vertical bank right around this guy, and threw it at his feet. I came around again and he was reading it. He finally threw up his hands, as if he didn't comprehend. That made me realize that he was no doubt a French-Canadian.

I kept north up this river, and I came across a two-track railroad. I figured if there's a two-track railroad in this country, it's got to go to Montreal, but which way? So I thought, "Well, I've got a fifty-fifty chance." So I chose to turn left. In ten minutes, I crossed the southern boundary of San Hubert Airport, and there I was.

I bet that felt good to be there.

Yes. It turned out my good friend, Paul Raider, was waiting for me in Montreal. When I didn't get there, he went looking for me in his plane. He even got lost down there somewhere. So when I couldn't find him, I waited for him. I knew he'd get back there sooner or later. He did arrive a couple of hours later. When he did, he and I went down to the Mount Royal Hotel and cracked open a bottle of champagne and discussed the whole matter.

Did you know any of the earliest airmail fliers?

Jack Knight, for one. He flew the first airmail from Cheyenne to Omaha. I used to know him. I flew at the same time as he did. He was a wonderful guy. In those days, the cars would come out to the field and turn on their headlights and try to make some light for you.

Did you ever have any forced landings?

I had one. The thing I was flying was a Curtiss Carrier Pigeon Number 2, with a Curtiss-Conquerer B-1570 engine in it. I left Cleveland and was westbound, flying low to catch an east wind—a tailwind—when the crankshaft broke. I landed in a field out there, just an ordinary farmer's field, over a large ditch; this was where the engine quit. I ground-looped around and went over to the left and stopped but didn't scratch a feather.

What did this farmer say to you?

Oh, he was surprised to see me. They had to take the wings off the airplane and put it on a truck and take it down to an emergency field in Vicory, Ohio. They put it back together, and I flew it out. I didn't have any trouble with the plane after that.

You did some test pilot work?

I wasn't a professional test pilot. I was a pilot for American Export Airlines, a seaplane pilot between New York and Ireland. It turned out the Martin Company needed somebody to test the Martin Mars.

That was a huge plane, wasn't it?

Was it ever huge! It had a two hundred-foot wingspan and held twelve thousand gallons of gas, which was quite a bit in those days. Not so much now, considering a 747 carries about 325,000 pounds of fuel. The engines in jets burn pounds, they don't burn gallons

What happened on the first flight?

One of the contractual requirements was a twenty-eight-hour nonstop flight, and I flew it thirty-three hours nonstop. But because it was wartime, the navy wouldn't permit us to go anywhere on a straight line. So I picked out a route between Chesapeake Bay, which was the Martin plant, and LaGuardia, and on to Nantucket, then to LaGuardia, and Chesapeake Bay, etc., and that's all we did from sunrise one morning to sunset the next afternoon.

How did you stay awake?

Wreck of th T.C. 10 at Brooks Field

I was the captain on the flight, and I had three or four pilots with me. I would take a nap if I wanted to. I don't remember sleeping much, though. I was young in those days

What was it like to handle that plane?

There was nothing unusual because it was so damn big, and it did things slowly. It was like any other airplane. It landed on the water; it was a seaplane, you know. It was first designed as a patrol bomber, but they gave that up and turned it into a transport type. But they only got about five of them built.

What did people say when they saw this huge plane?

I showed up at the Martin plant and this thing was sitting on the ramp, on beaching gear. The top of the tail section was about five stories high. I hope to tell you, I wondered if that damn thing would ever come off the water. I spent about three days familiarizing myself with the controls and the systems of the airplane. Nobody down there could check me out. There was only one other guy in the country who could, and he wasn't available. After the three days, they towed it down into the Chesapeake and cut it loose. I went around in circles each way about three times. Then I taxied downwind, then upwind, then downwind and got the feel of it that way. Then I turned into the wind and said, "Standby for takeoff." Then I murmured, "Lord, if you ever helped anybody, help me this time." The takeoff was beautiful. We flew right over the Martin plant, and the whole personnel group of the Martin Company was out in the yard. I could see and hear them down there, screaming and shouting and waving.

We flew around for two or three hours and then landed. But while I was up there, the whole time I'm thinking, "Now this is great, but I've got to get the thing back on the water. How do I do that?" There was lots of room in the Chesapeake Bay, naturally, so I just backed off, and picked out an area to land. I started a slow descent, reduced the air speed as low as I could, and came in at a very low rate of descent. Finally, I felt the keel going click-click-click on the water, and eased those throttles on. The next thing I knew I had set that thing down as if it was a big tomcat on a Persian rug.

That was the long-distance record you accomplished with the Martin Mars, wasn't it?

You bet it was. I don't know how many international records we put in the books, but the navy wouldn't allow much publicity because it was wartime. Another reason was that I was a civilian pilot auditioning their airplane, though the plane was under the Martin Company's control until they delivered it to the navy. But the navy wouldn't allow much publicity, so the flight didn't get the publicity it deserved.

I mean, nobody even does that today, thirty-three hours nonstop. Incidentally, a 747's wingspan is slightly less than that, and the endurance on the 747 is about fifteen hours or so.

What about your parents' reactions to your flying?

My dad was 100 percent supportive, and he helped me all the way. My mother, of course, was a little bit frightened, but she went along with it, too. When I graduated from Kelly Field, from the advanced course school on February 4, 1928, my parents were there. When I got home, my Dad bought me a new 1928 Model-A Ford. A blue one with wire wheels. Don't you think I wasn't something with those wings and boots and blue Model-A Ford. You couldn't beat that for that age!

The girls must have liked that.

I had a girl. That's the only girl I ever had. I married her. She died in '78 of cancer.

What went into forming American Export Airlines?

American Export Airlines was owned by American Export Steamship Lines. They were looking for people to help them form a new airline across the ocean, and they had the idea of flying their passengers one way, then putting them on their steamships the other. They hired Charles Blair, who was a character in himself. He got killed in the Virgin Islands about five or six years ago. He had his own airline and lost an engine on one of those little two-engine Grummans. There was a strong wind blowing, and he hooked a wing in the water.

Pan Am didn't want any kind of competition around the world, so they did everything in the world they could to oppose American Export. American Export got the certificate to fly the Atlantic, but Pan Am opposed it and cut off any funds that American Export was supposed to get from the government. Actually, American Export started out as a secret arm of the navy, but that was not generally known. For all intents they were a civilian airline. When the war was over, they actually were a civilian airline.

Any unusual flights that stand out in your mind?

I met and flew General "Beetle" Smith, the chief of staff for General Eisenhower during World War II. He planned the invasion. He was in the United States at the time to have a conference with General Marshall and the President, then he was going back to London.

We planned to take General Smith as far as Ireland—that's as far as we could go. He was in civilian clothes, of course. He would go from there to England on a civilian airline. We started to take off, but the flight pattern showed that the winds were too adverse. We could stay in the air for over twenty hours, but even at that, we didn't have enough range with that wind to get to Ireland. So we decided to go to Bermuda to change the angle of the course, relative to the wind. This was wartime, and it was a tense situation. It was important that General Smith get back to England.

When we got to Bermuda, I remember Smith got his second star: he was a brigadeer general when we left New York. Anyway, the conditions in Bermuda looked bad, and they figured they'd stay for two or three days. So the next day, early in the morning, I told the general that these conditions would probably last. I had been haunting the weather office and looking at the charts, and specifically looking at Gibraltar, where a big high was centered at that time. I observed the winds were better on that track. I told him if he would like to go to some place in the Mediterranean where they had a seaplane harbor, they should give me the clearance. I just needed the clearance. He said, "Sure, you can take me to Gibraltar." He turned to Dan Gilmore, his chief of staff and said, "Dan, send the necessary signals to General Marshall." So Dan did. Then I called my company in New York. Of course, you had to be careful of how you spoke on the phone in those days; they didn't have security. I had planned this thing, so I sent them the message in code, and they called me right away on the phone and said, "Oh, no, we can't do that." I said, "Okay, fine, but you will be hearing from this in another hour, so stand by the phone."

I told Beetle Smith what my company had said, and he told Dan to call Washington. They talked to General Marshall, and within an hour, I got another call from New York. They said, "Hey, Robby." I said, "Yeah." They said, "Do you know that thing we were talking about awhile ago?" I said, "Yes." They said, "What do you think of it?" I said, "What do you think about it?" I said, "You realize I planned it, don't you?" They said, "Yeah. All right. Good luck." So that was the end of it. We started out the next morning. I told him we could get away at first light, and that it would take eighteen hours forty-five minutes. At the same time there was a Pan Am seaplane in Bermuda, which was holding because of the weather. They were heading for Lisbon, and had Eisenhower's brother Milton on board. Beetle got him off there and had him go with us.

We left the next morning, but we kept getting behind in the flight plan. The winds were not as favorable as predicted. After about seven or eight hours, we were getting further and further behind in the flight plan. I had had experience with those wind forecasts, and I figured that if they were inaccurate on this end, it would be inaccurate at the other end. Furthermore, on the other end, they indicated headwinds. Anyway, we ran out of these headwinds and into these tailwinds and went into Gibraltar exactly on the flight plan, the next morning at 0800. We landed in the bay, and they opened the boom for us in the control boat and let us in behind the breakwater there. The governor of Gibraltar met the general, along with an RAF (Royal Air Force) captain and a few other people. Smith had this B-17 from London, so he had it made then. We said "goodbye," and away Beetle went on the B-17.

Smith and I became pretty good friends and we corresponded, but the next time I had contact with Beetle was in Moscow in 1947. When I landed there in Moscow, I was the first NC (noncommissioned) licensed commercial United States airplane to land in Russia. At that time, I talked to General Smith on the phone. He was busy. He had a representative there—a captain who gave me a message that read, "You can imagine how busy I am. Otherwise, I would be there to meet you. But the captain will lead you to a telephone and will get me on the phone so I can talk with you."

By the way, they made us put two Russian soldiers on in Berlin for our trip to Moscow. One was a navigator; one was communications. The problem was the navigator didn't know how to use our navigation equipment, and communications didn't know how to use our communications equipment. So we filled out the forms for them. With their help, we'd have been up behind those what we'd call "Urine" mountains. (*laughs*)

When we left Moscow, I took off and kept flying east toward the city because I wanted to see it. But this Russian officer kept crossing his arms and beating them together. I thought he was going to break his arms, so I finally turned away from the city.

How many hours do you have in the air?

About thirty-seven thousand.

Do you remember any crazy or irregular things that happened on any flight?

I remember once coming out of Cleveland one night in the old airmail days. I was flying a Liberty engine, Douglas biplane. A good friend of mine had taken off for Chicago about fifteen minutes ahead of me. But he had to land in Toledo and take off some mail and put some on. As I got over Toledo, I saw the floodlight come on, and I thought my friend was preparing to take off. I watched his navigation lights as we went west over the river there, west of Toledo. I snuck up alongside of him and turned off my navigation lights. I continued sneaking until I put my left wing right inside of his right wing and right out to his cockpit. Underneath our lower wings, we had a great big landing light. So I slipped over there close to his plane and put that landing light practically in his cockpit, and flipped it on. Well, you can imagine what you'd think. This is all happening at two o'clock in the morning. (*laughs*) All he had wanted to do was to get a little nap. He had one of his shoes hanging on the oil cooler handle, when he was suddenly awakened by the sun rising in his face. We got a big charge out of that, but it actually scared him.

What other humorous incidents do you remember?

I remember one thing that struck me as being pretty humorous. One night Sid Nelson and Hy Little and I—all of us airmail pilots—were having a snack in Cleveland, sitting around about midnight. Sidney and I had just gotten in, and Hy was just going out. We were sitting there having a cup of coffee and Hy said, "Oh, Sid, by the way, didn't I see you over the wrong side of the course the other night over there near town?" You're used to hearing, "Everybody stay to the right side of the course or you're going to run into somebody coming the other way." And Sidney said, in his usual subdued manner, "Yeah, Hy, that was me." He said, "I always fly on the left-hand side of the course. I figure it's closer."

Who was your flying hero?

I suppose it was Charles A. Lindbergh. I was in Brooks Field and had been there several months when he flew his famous flight to Paris. A lieutenant came in to land and told us that Lindbergh was reported off the coast of Europe. He said, "You guys can have the rest of the day off." We thought that was great, except that it was four o'clock in the afternoon then, and we were about to go home anyway. A few days later we had to march down Houston Street in San Antonio to celebrate Lindbergh's trip. Years later, when I met Lindbergh, I said, "Boy, we sure were happy to get that day off, but we took a dim view of having to march down Houston Street with those GI shotguns on our shoulders." Lindbergh got a chuckle out of that. Occasionally, over the years, I would see Lindbergh around the world and have breakfast with him in some far-off place.

Any unusual things that happened at Brooks Field?

Well, one unusual thing that happened was Lindbergh threw his dog off the side of the lighter-than-air hangar in a parachute one time—just to check the parachute. Of course, he was a student there a couple of years ahead of me.

What are you most proud of?

I guess that I'm still alive. That indicates a little bit of competence, but it also indicates a hell of a lot of luck. I've never had but two forced landings in my life. That one I told you about at Newark in a Fairchild cabin monoplane. The other one I told you about was in that Carrier Pigeon II. And, in eight thousand jet hours I never had a jet engine quit (that would be thirty-two thousand engine hours). That says something , don't you think?

I had an engine I noticed was losing oil one night when I was halfway between Honolulu and San Francisco. I could see the oil quantity going down. I simply shut the engine down and went in on three engines. No sweat. The people got there and found that somebody had left a plug loose. They washed the airplane down, got all the oil off of it, put in a new plug, and filled it full of oil. Then I went to Tokyo and everywhere else around the world. That's the only problem I ever had with a turbine engine.

Did you run into problems with passengers?

I remember once I was flying from Kansas City to Moline to Chicago in a Ford Tri-motor. I had $2,500 invested in a Tri-motor. Anyway, in 1934 I went down to the terminal; they had a terminal in Kansas City, believe it or not, in those days. So I met a guy there at the terminal who was going to be my passenger. Obviously, he had been drinking. They were holding a convention in Chicago, and he was going to it. So I met him and talked with him for awhile. I said, "We're going to leave here pretty soon. It would be a good idea if you got in your seat and took a little nap. We'll be in Moline before too long—in about four and a half hours." No stewardesses or stewards in those days.

We left Kansas City and I look back in the little peephole in the door. There was a good-looking doll sitting in front of him, and she was trying to sleep. Well, he reaches up and tweeks her on the back of the neck, and continues doing stuff like that. After awhile, I went back there and I said, "Look, this young lady doesn't like this." I moved her across the aisle, but he moved behind her—and this kept on. I said, "Let's forget that and not do this anymore and everything will be fine." I got back up front, and here he's doing it again. About the third time I went back, I said, "Look, if you don't sit down and behave yourself, I'm going to land in Kirksville, Missouri, at the emergency field, and I'm going to put you off there. How to get to Chicago from there is your business, but I could care less." So he didn't say anything to me and I went back up front. I learned later that he said to one of the passengers, "Aww, Kirksville, Missouri, we passed that a half hour ago," which we hadn't. Then he reaches up and starts this little act again. This time I don't do anything except call the emergency field. We had a radio on the airplane in those days. I also called Kansas City and told my company I was landing in Kirksville, Missouri—the place we had passed thirty minutes ago. I told them we'd be there in thirty minutes. So we landed, and I confronted the guy and said, "This is where you get off." You talk about a surprised individual!

We went into the beacon house. All they had there was a beacon house, which was maybe four or six feet square, a little beacon shack right on the field. They had a telephone in there, so I had my copilot make out some sort of little slip that would refund his money. Oh, he was irate, but we were even "irater." (*laughs*) So he got on the telephone, and he called his lawyer in Chicago at five o'clock in the morning. He woke the man from out of a deep sleep. Apparently the lawyer asked his client what the charges were. At that point the man turned to me and said, "What's the charges?" I said, "The charges are drunkenness." He screamed into the phone, "Drunkenness?" You could tell his attorney said no to him. Then we took off and went to Moline. When we got to Chicago, I called W.A. Patterson, the brand-new president of United Airlines, and I told him about what had happened. He said don't worry about it. The drunk had told me that when we reached Chicago he was going to tie us up for ten thousand dollars. That was a lot of money in those days. So I told Patterson this, and he said, "Don't worry about it. If he does, we'll fix his wagon." But we never heard anything from the guy.

Tell me about the emergency fields.

Every thirty miles was an emergency field. The beacons were ten miles apart. It wasn't much but you didn't need much for those kinds of airplanes. The fields would generally be L-shaped and they would have a green

Crack-up at Brooks Field. Cameron Robertson's car, Cameron Robertson's student.

rotating flashing course light on. Green was the emergency field, and red was the light between the emergency fields. So, if you saw a green flashing light ahead, that was an emergency field.

What's the most beautiful flight you've ever taken?

I'll tell you one that was beautiful. I left New York one day—I wasn't one to continually blab over the loudspeaker. I figure the captain is supposed to be damn sure the airplane is right side up and going where it's supposed to, rather than being a commentator. But this morning we were going over

Nantucket. We were at an altitude of thirty-five thousand feet and I picked up the phone. I was just overcome by the view. I said, "Ladies and gentlemen, we can see further today than at any time I've ever flown across here. It's absolutely beautiful, and you can see for hundreds of miles. As a matter of fact, if you look out the left-hand side of the aircraft now, you will be able to see the crook of Cape Cod." This was during John Kennedy's presidency. So we went on, and sometime later I walked back and some passenger said, "Captain, just a minute, please. You said, a minute ago if we look out the left side, we could see the 'crook of Cape Cod.' I thought the son of a bitch was in Washington." (*laughs*)

As a kid were you ever ecstatic about flight? When did you first learn about flying?

My dad was in the picture show business at Fayetteville, Arkansas, and when I got big enough—about ten years old—I took tickets at the theater. I also looked at the newsreels. The newsreels were forever showing little airplanes of one sort or another. So that kind of began to play on me.

I remember the first flight I ever had. I saw an airplane flying from the town square. And I jumped in my dad's Dodge Roadster. I was about ten or eleven and, believe it or not, I followed this guy. I saw which way he was going, which was way out north of town. He landed out there, and I caught up and told him I would trade him some advertising on my dad's picture screen for one flight. He said, "That's a deal."

My dad used to take pen and ink and make an advertisement on a clear piece of glass and show it through the projector onto the screen. So I traded him a week of that while he was in town, for a flight. That was my first flight.

I took my dad with me on the flight and on the first bank he took, which was to the left—my dad was the left and on the low side— I thought Dad was going to climb out the top of it!

Later, I was digging ditches for ten dollars a week, and I borrowed five dollars from my girlfriend—my wife-to-be—and took my second flight.

DAN BRENNAN

The Bombardier And The Eighth air force

I started out as a pilot, but I washed out on a thirty-two-hour check," Dan Brennan says forthrightly. That, however, didn't end Brennan's career as a flier. He had hunted a lot with a shotgun in his youth; and when someone told him he'd make an excellent air-gunner, he signed on.

Brennan began his training in Alberta, Canada, where they were training pilots in Tiger Moths. The wind there blew so hard they found they couldn't go anyplace, so the authorities changed locations. "Some real estate agent had talked them into putting a field there," Brennan quips.

Dan Brennan is a natural storyteller. He is animated, lively, and one can almost feel the wheels turning in his active mind. In fact, Brennan has written and published more than a handful of novels, including *Never Say Young Again*.

He has the distinction of having flown with both the Royal air force and the American Eighth Air Force. He transferred to the Eighth air force in 1943.

Did you ever think you had nine lives?

I didn't then, but since then, sometimes I'd walk along the street and begin to think, "Gee, I was lucky. I was really lucky." But it was happening to everybody. I saw guys get killed who had just bags of missions.

Guy Gibson was probably one of the great bomber pilots of WWII. He headed the Mohne Raid, where they skipped bombs across the dam into Germany. After all those missions he had, he went to what we would call a piece of cake—to an engine works outside Paris. This was an easy target. We didn't bomb the city itself, so there wasn't a lot of flak there. Two hundred and fifty aircraft went in, and he never returned. They never found him or anything. That happened despite all the experience he had. Usually, you'd get knocked off in your first ten missions—through lack of experience.

You were telling me earlier about a young fellow who disappeared for several months and it turned out he'd been shot down.

In front of a Halifax he looked like a twelve-year-old with a big mustache, up there so high. He got shot down over Cologne and three months later he walked in to the mess hall. He said that he was coming down on the outskirts of Cologne and he could see the lights and everything—the city lit up by the searchlights over there. But his boot fell off—we had these leather flying boots—and he set off and the next day in the woods he heard troops. So, he said, he covered himself with leaves and he lay there. He said the Germans walked right past him. He waited until dark and he started walking. He took out the compass that was made from two buttons that were in his battle jacket. As he held them in the palm of his hand one button would swing around and point north with a little white dot. He walked; he lived off of cabbage in the fields most of the time, and drank the water off the grass and the weeds and stuff.

He was accosted by all these little Nazi kids with knives, he said—they were ten or twelve years old and they all had knives. They all came up to him and asked for money. He had German marks so he took them out and just dropped them in a canister and they just went away and left him.

Then he met some people and they rigged him out on a bicycle and a coat and they got him into Belgium to go to a factory. From there they put him in the French underground. They got him down through France and he went over the Pyrenees. He came back three months later. Any guy gone that long, we presumed he was dead. Nobody had seen him go down. But there was a British expression. "What have you heard from Bill?" "Oh, Bill's gone for a Burton." In the First World War they used to say, "He went west." The British said, "He went for a Burton"—which is a beer.

That really meant he was gone?

He was gone—he was shot down.

Quite a euphemism.

Yes, it was very common, used by everybody.

Did you ever have any trouble writing about any of your war experiences?

Never. I wrote and published six novels. I think I used up everything about everything I experienced. I wrote one novel, *Never Say Young Again,* in the afternoons after morning meteorological briefing for the night "op." I wrote some of the novel in London on leave. I was without a typewriter. I wrote some when I went to see my wife. I remember where I finished it—a hotel room in a service club in London. But before that I had two chapters typed— they were really short stories—and I went to an agent. She said, "These are fine, but I can't sell these." So I went to see Constance Cummings in a play. She was a very beautiful actress in *The Petrified Forest* at some theatre in London.

Afterwards, I went across the street to a pub. This guy came in in a leather jacket. I said, "Aren't you the guy who played the role of the old football player in *The Petrified Forest?*"

He said, "Yeah." He was a Canadian who later became very famous in film. We were talking. "What are you doing?" I said. He said, "Well, some of us are going down to Soho to dinner." I met a guy there, an actor named Terrence De Marney—a wavy-haired, good-looking guy. I was telling him about the stories. He said, "You know, a couple of years ago, I sold a man's script. The man was on a life raft in the Atlantic for a month. Let me see these stories." So he read them and said, "Could you write a novel?" I said, "Oh, sure." So I went back and I opened the story in Minneapolis, then to Canada, and then I got into combat. Then came the end—120,000 words. So he introduced me to Stanley Unwin of Allen and Unwin. He was the venerable reigning little king of publishers—not big, but well known in the business. They gave me about $3,000 and that was a fortune then.

I had to cut 20,000 words out. The novel had to open in England and that made it easier cutting. So I just went through and sliced it up like you do news stories and pasted the pieces together.

Much later, after the war, did you run into any old fliers?

Fifteen years ago a car stopped at my house in Minneapolis and a guy got out with a big Syracuse University hero jacket on, with a big football letter. He had pure white hair. He walked up and he said, "Dan, you remember me— I'm Mal." I said, "Mal, I gotta say, I don't know you." He said, "Mulaney." I said, "Oh, my God, Mulaney, you been dead since '42."

Well, it turned out Mulaney was shot down—I'll tell you the story. After he got out of a German prison, he stayed in the air force and he was in Laos and he was all over, and he did his time and got out. Then he went to Syracuse and managed the football team. That's how he got the jacket. He told me that they were over the Meuse River and he was in the tail—he was on a Wellington then—from our squadron, the Wellington squadron. They got hit and there was a fire up ahead.

He opened this little turret around and looked up through the fuselage and there was fire up by the wings. So this gunner got his chute, swiveled the doors open, swiveled the turret around, rolled over backwards and out he went. We had plastic escape kits that contained beautiful colored silk handkerchiefs that were really maps, and some food tablets, and also some German and French money. He landed in a corn field and took off all his identification tabs—just had blue trousers and blue shirt. He was lying there. They had told us to contact old people or cripples that couldn't harm us—or children that were ten or twelve years old. These were your best contacts.

So he heard a little motor bike coming along, going "dut-dut-dut-dut-dut." But it wasn't. It was a long row of geese being driven by a guy, and the geese were making that noise. So he went into town and he thought he'd go to the priest's house, but he said he'd been warned about priests. He decided he'd go anyway. He knocked on the door and the priest came out on the balcony. He called him and said, "I'm an American." The priest said, "Go to this bean field," and he gave him directions. He got there and he lay under the beans and guys were collecting beans, but they didn't come near him or anything—they left him there.

Then a woman came by and he never saw her, but she just talked to him. She told him, "Don't get up. Don't get up. I'll bring you further instructions." Well, he thought something was wrong—he didn't know what was wrong. So he got out of there. Down the street he stopped a twelve-year-old boy and asked if he would help him. The kid took him home. The next day they gave him a Belgian soldier's coat that they had, from someone discharged. Then they got on bikes and they went out to a wood and they were supposed to be picking mushrooms. They took him into a big house. He was sitting there when another man came in, who started to question him.

What was the number on a leave pass for the RAF? He said, "Well, it was a 1065." What was the thing that you towed that you shot at in practice? What was the name for that? "I couldn't think of it. They called it a windsock," Mal recalled. "No, that's not a windsock," I said. Mal said, "I still can't think of the name." "It was a drogue," I told him. They were screwed up!

Next, a girl came in the room and she had killed some German and they were trying to smuggle her out. And they took them to a castle. The guy took them in and fed them pretty well.

And then the guy in the castle said, "How come you never bomb the German radar tower that's over there about two miles?" Mal said, "I don't know why they don't bomb it. But tell me exactly where am I and tell me where it is, and if I get back, I'll bring it up." Next day the sheriff came. And he got in the car with the sheriff, who had a pistol right between them. He drove Mal all the way through where the Germans were and he took him to a place where he got into a cart and was covered with beets and vegetables. He was then driven into a city and then he was taken to a place where there were about ten or twelve other fliers. But he said he thought the Germans had a line on them, because the next day the Germans scooped them all up. He spent the rest of the war in Stalag Luft III. He always carried a two-inch piece of barbed wire in his wallet. He said, "Whenever life looked bad after the war, I looked at that, and I thought of the prison camp, and I knew it couldn't get any worse than that."

You had to be one of the more experienced fliers over there.

I warned these green Eighth air force crews, after I transferred, that German nightfighters sometimes worked in pairs. One at nine o'clock would have a green light; one at six o'clock would have a red light. The guy at nine o'clock would flash his green and then they would do a simultaneous attack. You had to turn into the attack. So I had told them and told them about this. One night I was kind of dreaming along myself in the ball turret, scanning, revolving it back and forth from eight o'clock over to four. I finally went around to nine and, Jesus, there was a green light. It blinked three times and, all of a sudden, cannon fire—great big tracers of cannon fire went right under my ass. I yelled, "Dive left. Dive left." Just as we dived, the Jerry attacked. And I heard the pilot yelling, "Oh, he hit the prop." I thought, "Well, shit, as long as they don't hit the engine." And in the meantime one of the waist gunners upstairs put his chute on, went to the door to bail out, and got shot right in the ass. (laughs)

He survived that, didn't he?

Oh, yes, he did.

But his vanity must not have.

He got kidded terrible. "You can't turn your ass to the enemy."

Did you get in some situations that were tough?

Yes, well, we were sometimes conned by searchlights right over the target. When that happens, you're in deep trouble with my job. In the RAF we'd take turns—I'd either be in the tail or mid-upper turret. When I was in the mid-upper, the attacks would come from underneath where you didn't have any protection. They'd silhouette you against the sky. My job then, when you're coming off a target, was to get out of the mid-upper turret, go down on the floor and crawl to the fishbowl. At the bottom of the fuselage on the floor, was a gigantic glass globe, like half of a huge fishbowl. I put my head in there and peered all around to see if there were any fighters coming up.

Well, one night they had us. The pilot was climbing and diving and turning and I was reacting just exactly as you see the astronauts. I would do a perfect handstand with no hands. Then, of course, he'd come down, and the centrifugal force would bring me right down on the ground then. And I'd go up again and do another handstand, and go down again. Well, as I'd do this, my head would come out of the fishbowl. On the third one, I went up and came down, back in the fishbowl, and there was a hole in it as big as my head. A piece of flak had come right through there, but my head was out of it. Another lucky break.

One night I got hit in the arm, shooting on a nightfighter. I wasn't aware of it at all. I got back to the briefing and I thought I'd pulled a muscle in my left forearm. "Geez, I wonder what the hell's wrong there?" Took off my jacket and I had a little machine-gun bullet, a 7.9, just sticking halfway in.

Tell me more about your training.

My training involved firing a machine gun on the ground. Then we got into Battles, a single-engine aircraft. Looked like a Spitfire, but only two feet behind the pilot was a scarf-ring-mounted WWI machine gun. It was a Lewis gun with a pan on it. The ring was a tube that went around the cockpit. The gun slid around on the tube. You moved it around by hand. It had a cut-off at nine and three o'clock, so you wouldn't shoot your wings. I think I had seven hours of training when they said, "You just graduated."

I won a major dance contest in New York before I went to Canada. I danced in college—I learned from a guy I used to box with. He was a tap dancer. A woman came to me after I won the dance contest that night. I was wearing an RAF uniform and dancing to "The White Cliffs of Dover"—which is like bringing on your mother and dog and waving the American flag. Later this woman phones me and has me over to tea. "When you get to London, look up these Dutch girls," she says. I looked them up. They had a very nice party. There was a squadron-leader, fighter pilot, a New Zealander, and I said to him, "I'm going to be a tailgunner in a week or two. What advice can you give me?" He said, "Just get a lot of armour plating." That I thought was funny. And then I said,"How'd you get to be a squadron leader so fast?" He was quite young. He said, "Well, there was noboby left to promote." A week later I went on Defiant nightfighters—with an electrically-operated turret right behind the pilot. Single-engine aircraft. Like the Hurricane, which the Germans thought was so fast and attacked from the rear and got clobbered. But the next day, they shot the whole squadron to hell.

They thought it was a Hurricane?

Well, the lines of the aircraft looked very much like the Hurricane fighter. And, if you saw it from a certain way and you didn't see the hump behind the pilot, then they'd come in and attack from the rear. Here was this thing you were firing, with four .303 machine guns, electrically-powered turret that could swing from three to nine and shoot the hell out of them. It had only two guns forward. Two days later, the Germans attacked head-on and just decimated the squadron.

I was pretty lucky up until the war went on. Then I went down to the Whitneys' squadron. Then I went up north to Yorkshire and flew a tour of 30 missions up there. The Whitney resembles nothing as much as a giant crow. It had wings that were gulled! We went on the first bomber raid to Cologne, I think, or was it Bremen?—in those things—Whitneys—and then they were grounded.

I went up to Yorkshire again, and there I got shot in the left shoulder, but it didn't really hurt very much. I knew I was hit, but there was just one machine-gun bullet and it didn't hurt until quite awhile later. And then it burned. Then I finished a tour there on the Halifax four-engine planes. I had a great pilot, "Crasher" Dawes. In those days, the British never carried a second pilot in bombers. So I would get out of the turret on landings and sit in as second pilot. We'd be making the approach through the funnel out on the runway. And the ground man would flash us a red or green light, telling us whether we were too high or too low. I think that Dawes was so often exhausted that he couldn't determine red from green. And he would start to let down and I'd say, "For Christ's sake, go around again. Go around again—that's red."

"We'll wind up in the next county before we land."

"That's green."

"No red, red." We argued to beat hell.

Then one night the other gunner got up in the turret and we were twenty miles south of our field, due to heavy fog. We were in 14,000 feet of milk, that was all. I couldn't see the rudders that were just outside the turret. I called him, I said, "Hey, there's a lot of hills out there in this section." Well, he forgot to reset his altimeter for the barometric pressure for what the ground level was, the sea level. All of a sudden we come out of the clouds. Just bang—there is land. I heard him yelling, "We're gonna prang! We're gonna prang!" And I grabbed the stick from him there and I looked out and saw the trees behind me. He cut the tops off of about three trees. "Bang, bang, bounce, bang, bang." And I was going up and down like someone in a cartoon. Then the right undercart broke and we spun around in circles.

Harry McDaniels said afterwards that I was out of the turret and into the RAF Mess, having a beer, before the machine stopped moving. I had jumped out about eight feet from the ground, thinking the thing would catch fire.

You actually jumped out while the thing was in the air?

No, it was on the ground and it was kind of squirming around. I was about six or eight feet up. The tail was that far off the ground then. I just ran like hell out of there.

What people will do in strange situations. We were moving once when we were on Whitney bombers. We had to put our bicycles and all our gear in certain positions so the aircraft could balance, and have a certain point of gravity. I was watching one bomber take off and suddenly I noticed a great big black piece hanging down behind them, and realized that about a quarter of the wing had come off. It came fluttering down like a big leaf and struck a pole. The next thing we heard, "Boom!" and up came the smoke because the plane went down and crashed. We got on our bicycles and went and there were people running across the field. The plane was smoking; there was a guy up on the wing and jumping down. And then, a guy who had come running out of the side door turned around and ran back into the aircraft. I thought he'd lost his mind. Guess what he came back out with? Not his gear or kit, which was by the door, but the brand-new pair of goggles and helmet he had left in the rear turret. I suppose he wondered if they were to charge him for them. He got out all right.

One time we came in crabbing in a crosswind and we were off the runway. Way down at the end of the runway was a little brick house, smaller than a small garage. A guy was leaning in the doorway, smoking a pipe. You know the little car in the circus when one dwarf would get out, then about ten would get out? Well, this guy's leaning in the door and we were headed right toward him. He runs inside and out come eleven workmen, all about seventy years old, running to beat hell, to get out of the way—across the runway. Anyway, we get the thing back on the runway and we're headed right for them again. These old guys are looking over their shoulders. They hadn't moved like that for years. *(laughs)*

We weren't supposed to fly over Switzerland because it was neutral. Well, our navigator would get lost, our G-box would pack up and he'd guess with the navigator about where we were and he'd fly over Switzerland. The Swiss would fire. We'd see the guns fire from the ground. They were telling the civilians they were doing their job.

They were faking it?

Yeah, they were faking it. No flash in the sky. It was perfect because it would cut time. We'd go to the right of Mont Blanc.

One night coming home, the pilot asked me to look down and see if we were over the ocean. I looked down and there was a natural cloud below us, which—at night—looks like ocean, white waves, mackerel cloud. I said, "Oh, yeah, we're right over the ocean." Well, in about ten seconds, a master searchlight beam hit us right away and they conned us. Then they just started to pump the crap at us. I got down behind the armor plating and peered out just to see if any fighters were going to come in. They would come into their own flak sometimes. Our pilot was turning, trying to throw them off, and the flak was coming around, just one steady burst tracking us. They had to be really good to do that because most of the flak was block barrage.

Can you explain the tracking and shooting?

Well, tracking meant that somebody was on radar, predicting where you were and where you were going to be. The guns would be automatically tracking you and then fire—as if they were shooting at ducks—leading you. The box barrage over the heavy target—you'd go diving in there and you'd see flak burst, white balls, with an orange flash in the middle. Sometimes they would get so thick that it was like clouds. Then, when approaching a cloud, you think, how could anyone go through that? Well, the sky's a hell of a big place. After the Pathfinders drop a mark on the target, wave after wave of British aircraft would come in. At that time, after the markers were down, and we were bombing, then they would start a box barrage. That meant they would fill a square in the sky, maybe 18,000–14,000 feet high and so many miles wide. They'd just fire right into that because we were coming over an aiming point. Some of the planes might run into it.

People ran into it?

I've seen a lot of guys run into it. That night we were being tracked—that's different from box barrage. We were being tracked. Our pilot was throwing that kite all over the sky. He would dive and climb, pull up to the right and dive down to the right and climb and pull up. He said—I cracked up when he said—"Sorry, chaps, but I've done the best I could." And I thought, "Jesus Christ, you better do better."

He crashed it?

No, he didn't. The searchlight could only reach so far. We managed to get out toward the end of it and then we escaped into darkness.

What happened to Crasher Dawes?

Crasher got red-lined, as they called it. That's a kind of disciplinary statement against him. When he flew into the trees, his log book showed he hadn't changed the barometric pressure on his altimeter, so we were landing under the ground, not on top of it. Then one night we went off to Stettin and this is where I think Crasher redeemed himself.

We started over the North Sea. I saw ice blowing off the wings, just chunks of it. Oh, shit. They put some kind of a big goose grease on the leading edge of it to stop it. But then the outer engine quit. We started to fall. We put out a mayday. We were going down. With the ice on there and everything, we were going down, down, down. We pulled out at 6,000 feet. Crasher climbed back up again and went on and attacked the target on the other side of Denmark, in Northern Germany. Of the twelve aircraft that went, all the great hotshots of the squadron aborted because of ice. I guess Crasher really stuck it to the Wing Commander and the rest of them. I'd say, "Oh, where the hell were you guys over Stettin? I was there." North of Stettin, between Stettin and Berlin, they had a big fake city with a little sprinkle of lights here and there—thinking that you'd drop your bombs on them. But nobody ever suckered on that.

Where were most of your attacks?

We used to call France a piece of cake, because the flak wasn't as heavy there. We fought most of the war in Germany. I would say 80% were in Germany.

B-17's Over Germany

Were there any specific targets?

I was in the first attacks on the Krupps works at Essen, which we used to call "Happy Valley." All these cities are next to each other and there are thousands of flak guns coming in all over. I used to get diarrhea when we were told we were going into Dortmund or Cologne—the heart of their manufacturing. Everything was there. It was very pertinent.

In 1985, the retired head of the RAF—he'd been group captain in '42—came to our reunion in England. It was a very big thing. His name was Gus Walker and he had a hook for a hand. Trying to pull people out of an airplane crash, he lost his hand. Gus was a little man. In 1942 he drove up in front of our briefing room in a beautiful Bentley with silver-colored exhaust tubes on it. He and Sir Arthur Harris, head of Bomber Command, came in, and it kind of reminded me of high school football locker room talks. You know, "Get out there for West High." Only this time you were gonna die. They came in and were supposed to prep us—we had a marvelous record. We were the most heavily decorated bomber squadron in the RAF. We were Number Ten, "Shiny Ten" they called it. Gus came in and Sir Arthur Harris. It was like the king came in. He prepped us up. Gus said, "I hope I'll remind you of this thirty years later." He said, "All you chaps, you've done a lot of ops." They used the word "ops" for missions. "You've done a lot of ops, I know, but I want you to know, I've been in this sort of thing very early. I shot a good arrow at Crécy." That was the big battle [1346] where the British long-bowmen beat the French with those longbows.

So, thirty-five years later in York, we're all standing around at the old aerodome, where the runway is now a drag strip, and the officer's mess is now a pigsty—which we thought very appropriate. I was telling Gus about what he said, briefing us for Essen, and he said, "Oh, really, did I say that?"

"Yes, you did. And you broke up the room—if you don't remember." (laughs)

What about the pep rally ?

They had you go into this room, like the old locker room, and the coach—wing commander—got up. The map of Europe is covered. Then he uncovers it. You see a red ribbon that shows where you're going. The target from England. The red ribbon shows the way in and the way out. He gets up and tells us the reason for going there. Then he tells what the defenses are like. The weatherman comes in and he gives the weather. Then, the intelligence officer comes in and he gives us the picture of the target. I used this in a novel later. He would say, "The German nightfighter's color of the day is red-blue." That meant if you got conned by searchlights, you fired off a pistol flare of red-blue, and it's possible they'd stop shooting at you.

Explain that.

Do you know what a Very pistol is? You'll see it in infantry movies. It's a pistol with a diameter of about two or three inches across. It fires up a colored light with a tail—something like the Fourth of July. Then, the German nightfighters—if a searchlight picked them up—would fire off the colors of the day. It might be green-green; red-red. That way the gunners on the ground would know that they were friendly and wouldn't shoot them down. The British had these German colors of the day, because they had somebody in Germany who was sending these things over by "wireless." Then one day we didn't get them anymore, so I figured they'd caught him.

How did you take the two pilots dying on you?

The first guy flew over, made another turn down when he started to let down. I wasn't flying that day. I was watching. As he turned, the propeller fell off the port, outer engine, just fell right off. He slid right into the ground and blew up. That kind of shook me. And then I had this British squadron leader. Let me tell you, he went for a Burton!

Years later, in *The New Yorker*, a British scientist wrote how the Halifax bomber had what is called a rudder stall in takeoff. I noticed that. He said it was a hard kite to handle just as it gets airborne. They didn't cure it for years and, of course, they had accidents because of that. I don't know what caused it. They changed the rudder shape. Anyway, we were only up about 50 feet and bang, down we came. It broke in half. I was in the tail and I was kind of dazed at first. Then I got up and I just ran out where it broke right in half— there was a door there. I got the hell away from it. Then the front end caught fire and the pilot and bombardier were caught trapped in there, and died. I felt terrible. I went into the city of York, went to a dance and got pretty drunk. I went to a small Episcopal church, called St. Olaf's. I was sitting there in church and I was going to miss the bus. This man Ken Harry Radcliffe—I dedicated my first novel to him—was wondering what was wrong with me. I said, "Well, I saw a couple of guys killed today, and I just feel really low." He said, "Come on and stay at my flat." That led to a friendship. I got a new crew, and we would go, on nights off there, to a big dance hall, and to the pub, and instead of having to catch the bus home, we'd stay at Harry's. He'd feed us and in the morning we'd call a taxi and away we'd go back to the aerodrome, eleven miles. I did that for one-and-one-half years. And when we finished our tour, he resigned from the church, became a padre in the RAF, and stayed in for four years. He was really a sweet guy.

Twenty years ago in Minneapolis, a couple came to my house. They said they were from Brainerd, Minnesota, and did I know a Harry Radcliffe?

I said, "My God, yes."

"Well, we were in England, in a little parish church in Yorkshire, and we said we were from Minnesota. He said, 'If you ever find Dan Brennan, be sure to say hello to him from Harry.'"

I relocated Harry and corresponded with him up until he died several years ago. He called me one day and he asked for "Dawn." I said, "There's no Dawn here!" He said, "Dawn Brennan."

Well, it was old Harry. I said, "Where are you?"

Well, he was in Yorkshire. He said, "I went and bought some whiskey the other day and felt in the mood to call you."

Were there any weird souvenirs—or anything representing good luck?

There were guys who had a talisman, a lucky piece. This one guy would play "Autumn Leaves." It had such a mournful tune. He played that before we'd go out on a mission. To me, it sounded like a dirge. I'd get out of there. Then, I had a rabbit's foot and I had a girl's stocking. I used to think they were good. But whenever I carried them, we were in more trouble than when I didn't!

A girl's stocking?

Yeah. I threw it away, finally. I figured I was going to be killed.

You actually wore it?

Around my neck.

Keep you warm?

She was bad luck, really. One night over Kiel, it was a terrible night. We got hit right over the target by flak. It blew the bomb doors off the wings—the incendiary-bomb doors that hung down from the wing. The big bombs are in the belly. When the bomb doors fell down, we stalled. Down we started to go. I got out of the upper-turret into the bomb bay. We had bundles of leaflets down there, and my job was to open a little window and kick these bundles out. Scatter Germany with them.

I was on the floor when we got the order to bail out. Because of centrifugal force, I couldn't move an inch. I was pressed down like I had twenty tons on me. We were just falling. Through the window I could see all this damn flak bursting around us, and McDaniels—whom I stay in touch with today—I could hear McDaniels saying, "God damn, son-of-a-bitch, God damn, son-of-a-bitch." Like a litany. And we're going down. The pilot—Crasher—told me later, he got his feet up but he couldn't trim it out. He got his feet up on the instrument panel and got the stick back. Saved us. Those wings must've been flapping. . . .

The next day at noon in York—we were standby that night, no flying—I went in to see Harry and tell him we were going to be in that night.

He turned to me and said, "Dan, were you in trouble about midnight last night?"

"Harry, I've never been in so much trouble in my life."

"I woke up, just suddenly, bolt upright in bed and I knew you were in trouble. I got down and prayed and prayed and prayed."

"Well, Harry, it may have worked, because we got out of it." I thought it was a coincidence. . . . Oh, you never know.

Any other great coincidences?

Well, they sent the incoming B-17 crews to us. The B-17's had just been there for about three days. There was a big old auditorium with huge windows on the right. They were bored. This Englishman had capped teeth in front and a long moose face and talked like Terry Thomas. I said to him—"Charles Izzard, you gotta get a monocle and give these guys a show." So he bought a monocle. And this moose face. I said, "We gotta give them some stories. They're gonna fall asleep."

So Charles introduced me as a veteran of four hundred and fifty missions. And I introduced him as a veteran of five hundred. Of course, these guys sat there goggle-eyed. Then Charles would start his first story. He looked out the window at his right and said, "By jove, actually, as a matter of fact, it was on a day just like this I shot down my fourth."

I thought, "What in the hell is coming now?"

He said that he was in a slow trainer craft, landed at about forty knots, had glass all around it. He said, "I was sitting there during the dire days of England. When the enemy attacked us, we put the flaps down, and we slowed up so much that he went past us. When he passed us, I let him have it with a pistol flare." The green crews loved it.

The British Pathfinder crew wore a special little wing, an albatross above their regular wing. One of these later buttonholed me and said, "Brennan, you and some Englishman are the two biggest bullshitters that ever lived in the kingdom."

"What are you talking about?"

"I was about to score with an American nurse and I was telling her about what I'd done." He'd done about eighty missions, which is a helluva lot of missions. "And she said, 'That's not many, is it? We listened to a lecture when we got over here. Some American did four hundred and fifty missions. His name was Dan Brennan.'"

I said, "Aw, Buzz, we would have given you eight hundred missions, if we would have had you at the show."

What was considered an average number of missions?

When Americans first came over, they did not expect to send any people on bombers home—they didn't expect them to survive. So they set the number at twenty-five. Then they had guys that survived and went home. Then they raised it to thirty. When I was in the British, it was thirty to start with. Later thirty-five.

After you're down long enough, you begin to feel invulnerable. But when you're close to finishing a tour again you begin to feel, "Jesus, I'm never going to get through." Then you get slap-happy again and believe you're invulnerable.

I had a tragic letter here two months ago from a Canadian who had been at the reunion at York. He wrote me that at their recent reunion a British woman turned up, obsessed with finding someone who knew about her brother's death. His letter asked, "Were you on the raid on Kiel, Jan. '42?" That was one when we all had a bad time." He wrote, "I looked in your first novel—there was a dedication among the names to someone named Mazonbacher from Cleveland, Ohio." The only other American. And I figured he was on the crew with the woman's brother. This was their last mission, number thirty. But they blew up just below us; they got hit right directly that night. Of course, they never found anything of them. I wrote her a letter.

This Mazonbacher. Here's a story. That night they died, it was so dark, I've never seen it so dark and rainy. Just terrible weather. We went out to the kites and got in them. Then they fired a signal for us to come in. So we sat in the recreation room with everybody in full flying gear. That gets very, very depressing. You know, waiting around. This Mazonbacher walks around everybody and says," Hey, what are you looking so sad for? You're gonna be dead in a couple of hours." Of course, Mazonbacher never came back that night.

Unnamed flier in ball-turret.

He actually said that?

Oh, yeah, he went all around the room saying, "Smile, buddy, quit looking so . . . " He was one mission away from completing his tour and maybe never having to fly again in combat.

Did you get shifted around a lot?

In the Eighth air force I got all these Americans on these training crews and I did some daylight missions with them. Suddenly, I got orders to report to another squadron. I got there and the colonel said to me, "You've been sent down here because we're going to bomb nights." In training in Texas, when your lights are on, you can go fifty to one hundred miles before a wind change. Here, in England, you fly ten minutes east or west and you're over the ocean. You change wind in a dog's leg, in the air, and it's fifteen to twenty miles a leg.

So I said, "We'll try it with the tailgunner."

"Have you ever been a ball turret gunner?"

"No, I've never seen a ball turret." So he took me out and showed me.

The ball is in the belly on a B-17. It's round and looks like something you'd go in the ocean with, only smaller. I used to call it the "iron womb" because you lie on your back in a fetal position, and in front of you, between you and your feet, is the gun porthole. Superimposed on the gun is an electrified circle to estimate how much lead to give. The two guns come right out of there, with two handles right above your head. There's a button to press to fire. You press the handles and the turret will go straight down; and you can go side to side, from 3 o'clock to 9 o'clock.

Of course, this would be a great thing at night. These goddam Jerries are shy when you're underneath. The Brits never had a bomber with a turret underneath, so I said, "Ok, let me go with the crews to see what they do, what they need."

I was appalled. They'd say, "Tail gunner to pilot." Pilot was up there, "Yes, go ahead." They had this *dialogue!* When I got back, I went to the colonel and I said, "You've got to change all the dialogue or everyone's gonna die. If you ever get into an attack—which could happen fast, coming out of the dark—the gunner has got to be in charge." (The British gunners yelled, "Dive port or dive starboard"—to dive and turn right away.) "You've just got time to say 'Dive right, dive left,' so that you give them a maximum deflection shot. When you turn and dive, your deflection increases. Besides, you have no damps on the exhausts." The planes going through the sky at night would be four red dots, the perfect thing for a nightfighter. A Jerry just had to come up and fire between those four red dots from the exhausts.

"I won't go unless you put damps on them because otherwise they're gonna kill us."

He agreed and asked me to write a statement about what to do under attack. I wrote, "You'll find at night that Venus is a green star. If it's flashing, it's not Venus. The German nightfighters will often attack in pairs. The guy with the green light showing will always be at 9 o'clock—level with you. The guy with the red light will be on your tail. You're going along straight and narrow and the guy with the green light will flash the green, and the guy with the red will flash red. They attack simultaneously. The one guy doesn't have to lead much—he's got a point-blank shot at you. . . ."

I went with one crew after another and, boy, were these green crews. I was very worried. They called out "flak" right away. I told them when the flak comes up, "If you don't hear it, it's not going to hurt you. If you hear it, it's going to sound like a kettle drum in a symphony orchestra. Sometimes it'll rain on top, and it'll sound like hail on a tin roof. That isn't going to hurt you. It's when you hear it and it goes "Voom, voom—like that." Then they're close. Then call out where the flak is, but don't worry the pilot all the time by saying, "Flak 9 o'clock." That would make a pilot nervous. He doesn't know how close it is and can't see it."

I went with the guys off and on. One plane at a time. I told the colonel, "This is suicide. The only way the RAF can get into Germany is with mass attacks to overwhelm their radar and searchlights."

We had stuff that looks like that silver Christmas tree dressing—tinsel — that we'd dump out and that would cloud the radar screens on the ground. I didn't admit I was worried, but I was. So off we went to Kiel. Everything was tracking us. We were a lone plane and they were tracking us all the way. But nothing happened. We bombed Kiel and got the hell out of there. Coming home, it was so dark underneath that I couldn't perceive anything. No white clouds.

All of a sudden "Pow, pow, pow"—I was hit. I was hit with a 20 mm cannon shell in the right thigh, then I was hit in the right shoulder. I yelled, "Call out the fighters." Then I looked in the darkness—it was so fucking dark I couldn't stand it. Then I saw his guns—kind of blue blobs. So I started firing right into his guns. I heard one of the guys screaming they were hit. "Oh Jesus," they were yelling. I just kept firing. Then he wound up underneath us, hanging on his nose, just like a great big fish. I bet he was twenty five yards away from us. But his nose was over, so I just fired and one of his engines caught fire right there. He just fell away. I hope he died in the ocean.

We started to go down in the North Sea. I knew we were going down, and my chute was in the radio room. You couldn't wear one in the ball turret—there wasn't room. So I reached up. They had these ejector ratchets that I pushed back to push open the top of this trap door. I pushed up. There were two bodies lying on the turret: the waist gunners. I crawled out. I knew something was wrong with my leg—I couldn't stand on it. It hurt like I was hit with a hammer there in the thigh.

I crawled into the radio room, and we leveled out, and the radio operator was sending, "Mayday, mayday." He pointed to his boot; it was full of blood. I took his boot off and rolled over against the wall and got a great big bandage and put it on. He had a piece of metal sticking out of his ankle, like an arrow.

They came in and said we were going to have to ditch in the ocean. I thought, "How the hell am I gonna get up that wire ladder out of this plane?" They brought in the waist gunners. They put one in the doorway next to me, and I held an oxygen mask on his face. He was pretty old—maybe thirty-two. He was lying there in half darkness, moaning to beat hell.

The tail gunner had gotten hit. He'd had his flak vest on around his feet and ankles. (We never wore flak vests.) The waist gunner was ripped all to hell, but the tail gunner saved his legs. He had some minor wounds.

We were slowly going down, with one engine on fire. We descended slowly toward England. The guy in the doorway died. We just crossed the coast and got to a Mosquito field, a Polish squadron. The round side of the ball turret was down, sticking out, and it was supposed to be up. Going along the runway with that thing that way, we were kicking up sparks. But we landed.

They hauled out the dead guy and then the wounded. My turn came. I knew something was wrong. Then, my foot caught on the way out and that's the last I remember. The pain hit me and I passed out and woke up in an ambulance. I thought, "My God, I'm out of it." On my thigh was a big hole; they put bandages with Vaseline on it and bound it up.

I got well. Then one day they started throwing everybody out of the hospital. They said, "Well, you're ready to go back to the squadron." I stopped off at a Red Cross club. I asked a woman, "What the hell's going on? Where is everybody?"

"Don't you know what happened this morning? They just invaded Europe."

I got back to the squadron; they had been out three times that day. The colonel asked, "How are you feeling?" I said, "I got some wet bandages on, but it's all right." He says, "You're to go up this afternoon." So off we went. But the weather was so bad we never saw any enemy aircraft, for which I was grateful.

I flew in about six more missions. I didn't quite do twenty-five. After that, I got a job giving lectures to the in-coming gunners and staff. I must say one thing, though. You know the British and Americans were very different in demeanor. The Americans were kind of informal. The British were more military. But, on the British squadron, there was less chicken shit than on the American squadron.

How did the British treat you?

They really bent over backwards. On the buses, the clippies—those were the girls on the buses in London that clipped your ticket—would say when we got on, "You guys go sit down." That was before there were any Yanks. I was appalled at the Americans—the way they complained. They were the biggest bunch of crybabies about food. My gums bled consistently on and off for two-and-one-half years in the RAF because I had no fruit juice. I used to tell them, "You know, the Germans would surrender if you guys would drop Brussels sprouts on them—and 'sweet dessert,' a terrible cake with a sauce on it. Plus your cigarettes. The Germans would surrender."

How did the Americans treat you? Did they think it unusual that you were flying in the RAF?

They'd say, "How come you're in there?" I'd say, "I made too many model airplanes." When I was transferred over to the American air force, I was sent to what I called a "concentration camp." Here were about thirty of us who had been in the Battle of Britain—fighter pilots, Americans—and now they were teaching us close-order American drill. How to salute. The articles of war. Then, if you can imagine, they had officers doing guard duty at night, wearing gas masks. This was in 1943. Marching around, I used to take my rifle, throw it in the bathroom window, crawl in and go to sleep. Then they told me, "You could be shot for that."

The ultimate came one night when they said, "There's a possible riot between black troops and white troops down in the village below." We were going to have to go down there and help the police. We'd lived this long and we were going to get shot in some bar fight. We got in this truck with this new guy from America, who had seen too many movies. The truck stopped in the dark by the road. We could hear the pop, pop, pop of gunfire. Our leader said, "All right men, this is it." We got hysterical with laughter. "All right men, this is it. Out. I'm gonna walk down to the village. You guys spread out across the field and advance." We spread out in the field, got away in the dark, and sat down in a circle. He came back looking for us. We wouldn't answer him or anything. Finally, somebody signalled him. We said we'd been down there and the firing seemed to have stopped so we came back.

Then, when the Americans went out at night, you had to sign up and get a pass. The British said, "If you're old enough to die, you're old enough to go out at night." Their attitude was that if you weren't there in the morning for meteorological briefing, tough shit. You were in trouble. No passes required.

My wife was a captain in the Royal Artillery. All the women were conscripted over there. She went up through the ranks and became a radar detector officer on a big anti-aircraft pattern. They fired at German aircraft and at buzz-bombs, that sort of thing. Anyway, she came up to see me. They wouldn't let even majors or colonels or anybody leave this transferee enclosure. Who's going to run away in England?

Helen came up in full military gear and went in to the colonel. She said later, "Dan, I don't think that he's ever had a good salute in his life." She gave him this Coldstream Guard version of a salute, where she stomped her heel—the British salute. His eyes popped open. No one on that place ever got a pass to get out, but I got a seventy-two-hour pass. All these majors were asking, "How did you get out?"

"Well, my uncle's in Congress and on the Armed Forces Committee. He's over visiting," I lied.

Any practical jokes you recall?

I'm glad you reminded me. I was training air gunners for the Eighth Air Force in Norfolk. I was teaching ground-to-air firing, how to lead and all that. The colonel had a full-blown Texas sergeant. Also, he had a major with him, a gunnery officer, who was quite a kidder.

I received a call one day from the colonel. He said, "You know Lieutenant Benson?" He was the entertainment officer who got the concerts up. He came to the town dances, wearing wings, but he had never been off the ground. He was kiting these British girls around.

"Well, he's been lying about missions. You can imitate an Englishman, can't you, on the phone?"

"Sure."

"Well, you haven't been married too long, how would you like to have a weekend pass?"

"What would you want me to do, kill him?"

"No, I want you to go to your room and phone him and tell him that you're from the British squadron over here and that they had a spare tail gunner spot tonight on a Lancaster."

Just two days before, a Lancaster had come back on fire and had gone right over us. A couple of days before that an airman had been washed up dead. So I got Benson on the phone and I said, "Hello, this is Squadron Leader Fowlenough. We heard that you would like to go with us. Tonight is really a piece of cake—we're going well into Germany and we need a tail gunner. We'd show you how to operate it, and we'd love to have you."

Benson coughed furiously. "I've got a cold."

"Is it bad or what?"

"It's been bothering me a lot lately."

"Why don't you go to medical and get it cleared up? It's a short mission, only about four hours." Benson coughed, blew his nose, everything.

I went back over to the colonel who was sitting on the floor—he'd been on the phone listening, holding his belly. The major's sitting in a chair, bent over. He says, "You're gonna get your pass, pal, but wait a minute. If he goes to the M.O., I've already tipped the M.O. off. So we'll wait a few minutes." Then he called Benson.

"What's this crap? I just got a call from the British squadron over there about you wanting to go on a bombing mission with them tonight, and I said it was okay. But, dammit, don 't you know we've got our own air force if you want to go on a mission? What the hell's the matter with you? You been hanging around limeys too much—drinking too much tea?"

This was in the morning. Then I guess the word went around the station. The M.O. okayed him. When he came back all the officers told me the guy was the color of death. Everybody's congratulating him: "Takes a lot of guts to go over there at night. But good luck." They even brought a jeep around with a driver for him. Some guys waved a farewell to him and he went out to the gate where the driver had been tipped off to drive him all the way over, then drive him back. The ironic part was that the next Saturday night in King's Lynn, at the dance hall, there he was with his wings on, and a ribbon, dancing to beat hell. He was a real flier—with the girls.

Was that the only practical joke you were involved in?

Just before D-Day, there was a demarcation line in Southern England. Those who were stationed below that could not cross and go to the north, but you could cross and go to the south. We were going to bomb Kaiserslautern. One of the engines started to fail on the way out, then started to pick up again. The pilot and the co-pilot started arguing about whether to go back or not. This was really bad to do in front of the crew. Finally, I couldn't take it anymore.

"Hey look, you guys! "Make up your mind. If we go in there, there's a full moon tonight, and if the engine packs up when we're in there and we're on three engines, the nightfighters are going to get us." (Probably they could. I didn't say necessarily they would.) Make up your mind. There's nothing to be ashamed of if you have a problem with the engine." They went "mumble, mumble" and decided to abort.

Five minutes after turning back, one engine quit right there. We came down right off the cliffs of Dover, on a grass Spitfire strip. We were there about two days. When I got back, all my shoes and equipment and everything were gone. Dead man's kit, they figured. I got all my clothes back eventually.

Tell me about the "dead man's kit."

The next morning, if you had not returned, they put all your clothes and shoes and everything together, then they usually sent the stuff home. But in a lot of cases, the guys raided the package and you got stripped bare. We came back three days later and raised some hell around there.

Most memorable lesson?

When I was being discharged from the American air force , I came home on the first boat after Germany surrendered. I was on one of the first train-loads that came in from the eastern coast to Ft. Snelling in Minneapolis. You went through a line. They'd check your teeth. You'd see all kinds of doctors before they discharged you. I was brought in and they said, "Would you like to get discharged?" I thought I was going to get sixty days, thirty days leave, and go up on B-29's to Japan, and bomb there. This was May or June of 1945. The guy said, "No, you've got more points than anybody we've ever seen in here. You have 185 discharge points." I said I was in the RAF too, and they gave me points for all of that. He repeated, "Would you like to be discharged?" I said, "How soon?" He said, "How about tomorrow?"

I had had enough. I had an English wife coming over in a month or so. When I went to the doctors, I came to a psychiatrist.

"Have you been depressed?"

"Just the last five years, Doc."

He laughed. I was kind of numb. I couldn't feel very much. I went back to work on the newspapers.

Before I went to war, blood used to bother me when I cut a finger. But now, when I went to cover a worker who had fallen off a bridge, it was different. This time I went with the photographer from the paper—this is the summer after I went home. We went to the dead man's house and I said, "Your husband fell off the bridge and he's dead. Do you have a picture of him?" She starts screaming around like Woody Woodpecker. I took her by the arm and led her over to the drawer and said, "Is that a picture of him? Do you mind if I take it?" She was just raving. I got outside and the photographer's mad too.

"What the hell's the matter with you? Jesus, how can you say it like that?"

"So the guy died, big deal." I had become immune to those feelings.

How long did it take to get your sensitive side back?

About two or three years. At first, when I came home and my wife wasn't there, talk about paranoia. I'd wake up at night. I'd go to the window and look out and I was positive—I know it was just a goofy feeling—that there was somebody behind that tree. We had these big elms. I used to have dreams. Often, even to this day, I wake up at night, seeing the most vivid, emotional incidents in my life. They don't keep me awake, but they come.

It's forty-five or more years later.

Yeah, and they're just as clear as can be. But they don't bother me.

Any recurring dream you have?

The one where I got hit in the leg with cannon fire. That night when we were going down in flames with one engine out. Guys were dead and screaming all over. That often comes back. I'm in the ball turret, turning around, and I look out and see the engines on fire. But that doesn't bother me like it did. It used to bother me when I'd think of some friends dead, but it doesn't anymore. It's so far away and yet so real.

Charles Irving

CHARLES IRVING

The Radioman

It is a brisk winter day, and a strong wind powers the snow up off the ground. Getting no answer at the front door, I wander around back of Charles Irving's modest Spokane home. I spot him and we shake hands, and he then points with pride to his woodpile, which this vigorous World War II radioman had chopped and assembled himself. The son of a lumber manufacturer, Charles worked twelve hours a day at the sawmill. He found the military a breeze after those laborious years.

Irving joined the Army National Guard in 1940. He watched a number of friends join, and though he was only two and one-half credits from graduating high school, he decided to follow them.

He has a few regrets. "My life has been interesting, and very lucky!" His voice softens. "There were so many guys I knew that are gone. Their lives just came suddenly to an end." Out of the 132 men Irving went over with, only 11 or 12 returned.

Charles Irving was born in Ethel, Mississippi, in 1920. His family later moved to Alabama. He went to radio school in the army infantry, then into the National Guard. One day in Jacksonville, he and a friend decided to go down and check out the air corps. He was accepted for the air corps and managed to gain a discharge from the National Guard. After training that included building a radio set from the ground up, his flying career began.

How long did it take to absorb what happened to you in the war?

Gee, I don't know. You would go on a mission and sometimes be gone a long time, depending on where you went. You were hyped up and didn't realize the danger. You'd get back on the ground and wake up the next day and realize just what you went through. I didn't realize fully what I'd gone through until I got back to the States.

What unit were you in?

I was in the 385th Bomb Group. We were stationed at Great Ashfield, a little town in northeastern England about eighty miles north of London.

What was your toughest mission?

They were all tough. I think the longest one I went on was when I went through Bordeaux, France. We flew right down over the coast of France, right down through France. That was quite a long ways, really. We came back out into the ocean and went back to England. Coming back, the Germans moved in on us and tracked us. They followed us all the way back to England. We flew right on the ocean, right down low in order to keep away from them. That way they couldn't fly down underneath us. In other words, when they came in they would dive-bomb us and shoot. In doing so they would throttle their props back, but when they did that they had to slow up, and when they got through, they had to turn up. Then they were really vulnerable. Anyway, that mission was a long one. It took, I think, eleven hours.

Another long mission involved going to the heavy water plant in Norway, north of Trondheim. You see, the Germans were experimenting with hydrogen-heavy water. They got the water right at this dam in Norway. I met someone from up there in Spokane not too long ago. She was from Norway and she told me, "God, you missed it by a mile. You didn't hit the target at all." I said, "What?" The lady said, "I was on that hill in Norway, and we were pointing right at it for you guys and you still missed it by a mile."

She actually said that to you?

Yes, she did. Oh, God, she really chewed me out. I was on that airplane, and she saw it all. She said, "You missed it by a mile!"

How'd that conversation begin?

This lady came over to the U.S. on a visit, I guess. I was working over off of Division Street and I got to talking to this lady. Because she was Norwegian, I told her I was on that mission over Trondheim.

We went on a mission to around Marionsberg, near Poland, and bombed the Focke-Wulf plant, which was brand new. We flew in at about eight thousand feet and just demolished it. According to our intelligence, Herman Goering was supposed to be there to dedicate the field that day, and that was one purpose for bombing it—to get him. But he didn't make it. We supposedly got two shifts of employees, coming and going. It just literally destroyed the plant. RAF Mosquitos flew over it about an hour or two later, and they took pictures of it. By the time we got back to England, they had those pictures developed, and the next day I saw the pictures.

That was quite a deal. Lucky. They didn't expect us to fly that far. I was on the lead crew so we flew over the factory first. I always managed to get on the lead crew.

Did you ever fly any big missions over the industrial sites like Schweinfurt?

I went to Schweinfurt to a ball-bearing factory. That was a shuttle run. But we had an engine go out east of Paris on that trip, and we had to fall out of formation and return to England. So I didn't get to go. When we fell out of formation, we came down low and flew right over the countryside. We were just luckier than hell that we didn't get picked off. We were safer going back than going on ahead. The fact was we lost a lot of bombers that day. We lost dozens and dozens of planes on that Schweinfurt raid.

What was your training like?

I went up to Scottfield, Illinois, and to St. Louis, and then was accepted to radio school. You either went to the aircraft mechanic school or to radio school or to gunnery school in Las Vegas.

I wasn't a very good student in school. I didn't care. All I wanted to do was play ball. The school we attended was the equivalent, they said at the time, of two years of college. There were twenty-eight weeks of it. The first thing you learned was how to type, which I didn't know. You had to type because you had to write your code with a typewriter. Then you got to learn Morse code. I had never heard of Morse code in my life. Then you learned the Z-signals, which were antiquated the moment you learned them. Then they started on Q-signals. Then you learned theory—what makes a radio work, transmitter, receiver, the whole smear. It was a good learning experience. I really enjoyed the air corps, wartime or not. I grasped the information pretty well. Surprisingly, I could figure out why. We had college graduates that were pulling their hair out and jumped off of water tanks because they couldn't take Morse code. They just couldn't figure it out.

What was so hard about Morse code?

It came so repetitiously: *de, de, di, di, da, da, da.* I guess it would just blow somebody's mind. It didn't bother me, though. I seemed to thrive on it.

It's a case of memory more than anything else. It's like learning the alphabet. The hardest part was—when you got out and found that they didn't use that code: they didn't use Z-signals. You had a book to help because you couldn't remember them all. But to look up something you almost had to have a memory of what the signal was. You'd try to remember the ones that were used more frequently. I graduated with thirty-five words per minute, but a lot of guys just couldn't get it, although we had some guys doing one hundred wpm. These guys could be standing there talking to you just like you and I are talking and, after they finished the conversation, they would go over and write down what had come over the line. I remember one guy who was that good, who had been a radio operator on a ship in the Great Lakes before he went with the Air Corps.

Did you ever feel any pressure when you were taking an important message? Did you ever make a mistake that was critical?

No, I never made a mistake in my life.

Right!

No, not really. But pressure didn't seem to bother me too much. I was carefree and a happy-go-lucky, don't-give-a-damn, eat-the-meat, throw-the-bread-away type guy. It didn't affect me like it did some people. If you knew what your equipment was capable of doing and made it work, then you were all right, especially if you followed procedure. The only thing is, the weather affects how strong your message is when it gets there. For example, when we flew overseas, I flew out of Presque Isle, Maine, to Goose Bay, Labrador, to Reykjavík, Iceland. The weather was so bad that you couldn't even see the wing tips; you couldn't see the sun and you couldn't see the ocean. You had nothing but constant static on any radio—you just couldn't hear signal one. How we ever got over there, I'll never know. The navigator just did a superb job, but there were four or five crews who didn't make it. They just got lost at sea.

Were you trying to send messages all the time?

Oh, yes, I was trying to navigate with the radio compass or digital transmission. I would send messages out, and they would hopefully send your position back—QDMs, they're called. "QDM" means "What's my position?" But nobody could hear. The constant radio compasses were spinning around like this (*gesturing*) all the time: we were in a big magnetic field. But our navigator got us there.

Were you frightened at that point?

Oh, you bet. I knew that we had only so much gasoline and a certain amount of time in the air before we had to land *some*where. We got lost one time coming back from Norway. We had a green navigator who didn't know where he was going and didn't know how to get there. I got a little nervous.

The English were way ahead of us in communication. All up and down the coast of England, they had distress receiving stations. We changed frequency every time we went out because if the Germans learned a frequency, they jammed the signal. We had a facility chart that showed a map of the coast of England, and it showed the frequency that you could broadcast on. This was not done verbally; you did it with C.W. "C.W." is "continuous wavelength" like de, de, dat, dat, etc. When you got into a problem, or if you figured you didn't know where you were going, you would send a QDM and hold your CWD key down for thirty seconds and they would hone in on your signal. A compass would tell them what your position was in relation to where they were. They would relay this information right away, and the master station would send you your position back, longitude and latitude, then you would repeat this two or three times. As you did, you would mark it down. Then the next time you would mark it down, then the next time. Your position was changing because you were flying. Finally, you would just pencil in between the lines, and you could tell where you were heading.

Anyhow, we got lost, and I sent out some QDMs. It was dark, and we thought we were heading back to England but came to find out we were not far from the coast of Germany. We were going in the other direction, straight into Germany! I called the pilot and informed him. He said, "Do it again." I did, and he finally talked to the navigator. The navigator said, "Well, to tell you the truth, I don't really know where I am. I got messed up on my paperwork here." So the pilot did a 180 and we landed in Scotland out of gas. We didn't have enough gas to get back to our own field, so we had to take the first place we could land. We refueled and flew on to Great Ashfield. But that was interesting, I thought. The name of the plane, by the way, was *The Fickle Finger.*

The Fickle Finger?

Yes, it had a big arm up—straight up. You see, we thought we'd had the fickle finger when they busted up our crew. We figured, "Hell, we've had it now." So that's what we named our airplane. It wasn't just a finger, it was an arm! Incidentally, that plane lasted seven missions and we had to ditch it. It had over a thousand holes in it.

The Fickle Finger

What happened to the crew?

Only one guy got hit and that was the bombardier. He got a little flak. A shell came in one time and took my transmitter out right behind me. That shell flew right up through the plane and went through it but didn't explode. The transmitter had a hole in it (*gestures, indicating a 6" diameter circle*).

That's enough to make you wet your pants.

It scared the dickens out of me. I had a gun in the radio room of the B-17. It was on a swivel. When you weren't using the gun, you slid it right up over the bomb bay, which was right between you and the pilot and the copilot and engineer. The engineer ran the top turret gun, but mine was a single gun on a swivel. I could only shoot straight up and back and out to the side a little ways.

Did you use your gun very much?

Oh, yes, I shot up boxes and boxes of shells. You really didn't know if you were hitting anything or not. You would just fill the air with lead. You would come back from a mission and the gunners are talking of knocking down these planes. "Did you see that guy? I was giving him short bursts." They would come back and claim five fighters. I'd say, "Hell, how do you know? Everybody was shooting at those planes."

Sometimes the enemy would fly right through your formation. I used to look out the window and see a guy with no hat and a scarf on. He looked like the Red Baron. The Germans would get up in front of you, then they would come around and fly right through your formation. They would throttle back and shoot 20 mm. cannons, synchronized through the props. They would throttle back and fly right through, wiggling their tail and putting lead out everywhere they could. Those guys were trained real well. They knew what they were doing.

I've seen the German flak shoot down their own aircraft. I think we were over Wilhelmshaven. I must have seen six or eight German aircraft that went down by their own fire. I couldn't believe it.

That many?

Oh, yes. Jeez, I'm up there throwing tin foil all over the sky to confuse their radar. That was my job in the lead plane.

It was always my job to send the message back that we bombed the place—or we didn't. I was aware that they were pretty accurate on the lead plane. So as I was throwing out bales of tinfoil, I could look back and see the Germans directing the fire into the tinfoil. It worked because the planes behind us weren't getting the intensive flak we were. There again, the Germans had JU-88s and other aircraft up there flying alongside of us. They might be too far away to shoot at, but they were flying and radioing the information down to the ground. The planes would correct it for the guns below: "You're shooting way too low. Shoot up near us."

What was the worst flak you were in?

We went on one raid and we had thirty-one straight minutes of anti-aircraft fire. We went down to the Ruhr Valley. We bombed that area a lot. It was Gelsenkirchen—an industrial town. This time we had a navigator who got us exactly where we shouldn't have been: right straight in the middle of the Ruhr Valley. Below us were over one thousand heavy guns that they knew of, plus many, many, lighter guns.

What did you think when you found yourself in the middle of that?

 You couldn't do anything about it. You know, you don't hear it when you are flying up there like that. If you would hear it, you would hear "vroom"— something like that and a long roar. Up there you would hear this "woof," "woof," something like that, and then it's gone. You'd see it burst—you'd see the puff of smoke.

We used to fly in tight formation where the fighters couldn't come through us. They would have to go up above or come below us. It was the German's idea to get you divided, then they would pick you off. But, when you were on a bombing run and you got into a lot of anti-aircraft fire and you had a lot of German fighters after you, sometimes they would break our formation. I've seen a lot of B-17s get shot down right out of the sky. They would peel right off and they were gone into the North Sea. They wouldn't survive just three or four minutes—that's maximum. The water was so cold.

Did you lose any close friends over there?

We had ten men to an airplane: a pilot, copilot, engineers, bombardier, navigator, radio operator, two waist gunners, a ball-turret gunner, and a tail gunner. Sometimes we'd have big-wigs along. So we might have eleven or twelve people on board. I understand 132 of our original flight crew died over there. Eleven of us finished it alive.

Do you remember anyone you lost that you really thought a lot of?

Yes, I lost a friend of mine by the name of Hubbard. He was from Kentucky. He went down. In England, we didn't have many boots, and it rained a lot there. He said, "If I go down today, Charlie, you can have my boots." He never came back. That touches you pretty good. He carried a carbine with him. He said, "They will never take me, never." They wouldn't have. I know they wouldn't have because he was a real strong person. He was the kind of guy who wouldn't back down an inch. He was quite a guy.

You got his shoes?

I didn't really want them, though, even though I didn't have a pair. It rained a lot, and we needed galoshes.

How many missions did you complete?

I did thirty-two, but on seven of them we didn't drop the bombs. We couldn't see where to drop them, so we brought them back.

So that didn't count as a mission?

It didn't unless you hauled off and dropped them in the ocean someplace. A lot of the guys got chewed out about that and had to quit doing that. I think on one or two missions we did drop them randomly.

That must have been frustrating to go out and risk your life, and then you don't get to drop.

We didn't even think about it. Frankly, we didn't know whether we were going to finish up or not. We thought, "What the hell, the way the army does things!" You do twenty-five and then you go to the South Pacific, and they have a hundred over there.

Did you get extra nervous toward the end of your hitch?

When you get close to leaving, you know good and well that your chances are dwindling. I finished with a friend of mine from Ronan, Montana, by the name of Don Hughes. Old Don was quite a character. He was a radio operator also. He said, "We are going to finish this and probably go home and get killed on a bicycle." I said, "You're kidding." He said, "Naw, you can never tell." Sure enough, he got home and he got killed in a car wreck right in the city.

What was the strangest message you ever got?

I think the darndest message I ever got was when we were flying to around Denver somewhere. We transmitted a message to Fort George Wright, which was headquarters then for Geiger Field in Spokane. That was before Fairchild existed. The message we transmitted came in R-1, S-1, which was the best signal we could send. The message I got back was "Upon your return, go directly to Fort George Wright."

To Fort George Wright?

Yes, for a commendation or something, I forget exactly how it was worded. So I took the message to the pilot, and he read it and couldn't believe it. But he did what the message said. He returned to Fort George Wright, and we landed on the parade field with a B-17. We got chewed out from one end to the other. Then we had to fly that damn thing off that parade field. We almost didn't make it out of there. There wasn't even a runway.

That's now a college campus, Mukagowa University. The parade field there's probably little more than a city block. I can't believe you got out of there.

They took all the crew off the plane, except it couldn't leave the ground without a radio operator, a navigator, a pilot and copilot. That was a skeleton crew. Also, they took everything off the airplane they could. We managed to get off and went right down over the Spokane River, just picking up a little bit of speed at a time. I think that's probably the only B-17 that landed at Fort Wright!

FREDDIE HUTCHENS

Tuskegee "Savior"

Freddie Hutchens was born in Blakely, Georgia on September 16, 1920, back in the days before everybody got a birth certificate. His family later moved to Donalsonville, Georgia. Hutchens graduated with honors from Douglas High School in Thomasville, Georgia.

Freddie's father, Charles, had served in the American Expeditionary Force on active duty in World War I.

At the insistence of his mother, Hutchens attended Tuskegee Institute. (Hutchens' mother died when he was a sophomore.) He completed his program in 1942. Despite having to work his way through college, he was active in campus activities. Hutchens served as the advertising manager for the Campus Digest and became a member of Omega Psi Phi. At Tuskegee he studied agriculture and took a course from George Washington Carver, something for which he was very proud. The year he graduated, the Army commissioned the first five black flying officers.

He went on to overseas duty with the Tuskegee Fliers, and to many incredible adventures, including the one he describes in the interview where he is treated as a "savior" after having been shot down over Italy.

When he returned to the states in 1945, he went back to Tuskegee where he immediately became an instructor. He instructed there until they closed the field in 1946, after which he went up to Lackland AFB, and then to ROTC School in Texas for a training course. After that, he ended up back at Tuskegee when the first Air ROTC was established there.

Freddie became an early member of an organization known as Mach-Busters, when he qualified for jets shortly after the Korean War. In his last active duty Freddie was assigned as Executive Officer under Col. Marvin Glascow of the 444th Fighter Squadron in Charleston, S.C. The squadron earned the distinguished award given by Hughes. After the war he worked at General Electric and Lockheed.

Hutchens passed away in the summer of 1991, just before his 71st birthday. He is buried at Arlington National Cemetery and survived by two sons, Eric and Fred, Jr.

When did you see your first airplane?

I was about nine or ten. I was born in southwest Georgia on a farm. I was always fascinated by airplanes. As time went on, we moved from living directly on the farm to a little farm town named Donaldsonville. I built the first model airplane in that little town.

How did you do that?

Before I got to flying airplanes, I used to look for pieces of two-by-four and scrap wood. I'd whittle those down and make fuselages out of them. I'd use coat hangers for the struts and snuff cans to make my windshields. All went well until I tried to fly them, and I realized that they were a little bit too heavy to fly! So I started off building a couple of different flying models and, after two or three failures, I built a Fokker DH.

Were you quite disappointed when you found a couple of those planes wouldn't fly?

Yes, I was.

How much did they weigh?

Oh, I don't know. I don't think I had one that weighed a pound. I was fooling around with rubber bands and I finally learned that people put out special rubber bands to wind them up. I remember I built one that had a wingspan of about three feet. It was a one-blade prop with a counterbalance on the other end of it. I got that one to fly fifteen or twenty minutes.

What did you do to get it up in the wind?

Oh, that one had enough rubber in it. You could wind that doggone thing up a lot. The rubber band was about three or four times the wingspan and, if you wound it up real tight, that propellor would run a long time.

What did people think about your apparent obsession with flight?

A lot of people used to talk to my granddaddy. They didn't want him to allow me to fool around with airplanes. They thought it was a waste of time and that I was overly ambitious. The idea of fooling with an airplane was—foolish!

What did your granddaddy say?

He was all supportive. When I was about twelve or thirteen, some man came to town with one of those barnstorming planes—it was a Stinson Reliant, a high-wing model. He was charging people a dollar and one-half to ride. So my granddaddy scrounged up two dollars and fifty cents. He didn't charge me full fare. That two dollars and fifty cents, I think, was one of the best investments granddaddy ever made.

Do you remember when you actually said, "I am going to be a flier"?

Yeah, yeah. I remember once somewhere around thirteen or fourteen, I was being responsible for people gathering peanuts. That was one of the crops that grew on the farm almost every year. It was my job when the peanuts got ripe to take a mule with a certain type of plow, run underneath the peanuts, and sack them. Well, once, I got so carried away when what looked like every airplane in the whole Army Air Corps flew over, that I forgot about all my responsibilities. I just sat there and watched them. It took them about an hour and a half to all fly over. I was still oohing and aahing when my granddaddy came up. He got plenty irritated with me because he was paying the people out there by the day to pick up and gather peanuts, and I wasn't doing my job. He gave me a pretty good shellacking about that. I told him that I was going to fly one day. Later on, granddaddy came to see me get my wings. I went out to a local airport, rented a Piper, and took him up for a ride.

What was the toughest transition to Tuskegee?

I graduated from high school in 1938. I had applied at several colleges and was given a full scholarship to Johnson C. Smith, Marshall College, and Morehouse in Atlanta. I was accepted at Tuskegee. Tuskegee had a reputation for students who came out with pretty good jobs, so I went there. I knew I was going to have to work my way through, and it was nip and tuck every quarter.

In 1939, they started the Civilian Pilot Training Program. If you could get enough time in, you could end up with a private pilot's license. I couldn't qualify for that because I didn't have forty dollars. Still, every chance I would get I would talk to the people who were in the program. It wasn't long before Tuskegee was accepting people for military training.

Bill Davis, Jr. came to Tuskegee from Fort Benning. They didn't know what to do with him at Fort Benning. His daddy had given him a canary yellow Buick, and that wife of his would go round the base at Columbus with that top skinned back—and it just irritated the hell out of them there. So they figured out a place to farm him up to, and that was the ROTC at Tuskegee.

I was in the ROTC program, but I graduated before I could get my commission. I would have to go to school another two or three months—another quarter—and I didn't want to do that. I asked Davis if he would write a letter and request a waiver on three months' training because I already had a degree. He said, "Why don't you come and join the air force?" I said, "Look, I never applied, Lieutenant." He said, "You might just make it. I'd like to have you in my outfit." So I applied and eventually I was accepted and made it through.

Do you remember your last day of work?

I was working at the military base. They were building it in those days. It was built by a bunch of brothers, the McKissick Brothers. When I stopped working there, I was making $125 a week.

Did you almost think you couldn't afford to leave?

Yeah, that was a lot of change! But no, there wasn't much of that thinking, because I was bit by the bug. All of my life, ever since I can remember, I was fascinated by airplanes.

How did you feel when you were fighting the Germans? It must have given you a little extra adrenalin to think you were fighting this idea of a superior race.

Oh, it did. It did. We had very little knowledge of what Hitler's ideas were. Most blacks at the time were not in tune with that type of news.

You were one of the first Tuskegee fliers to fly a P-51.

Yes. We had gotten word that we were going to get some airplanes. Finally, the operations officer walked by the tent one afternoon. He looked at me and said, "Hutchens, can you fly a P-51?" I said, "You bet your boots I can. Why? It's got a wing on it, doesn't it?" (I was just mouthing off.) I think the planes had arrived just a little quicker than the operations officer had expected. He said, "Okay, get your parachute on and grab nine more of your friends and meet me down there at Base Operations in thirty minutes. Bring your 'chutes."

"For what?"

"You are going to pick up some airplanes."

"P-51s?"

"Yes."

"Is there a handbook on the airplane?"

"Yeah, there is one here."

"Where is it?"

"Oh, the Colonel has it."

We had to go down to one of the white bases where they were flying them—the 325th Fighter Group. They had them all lined up on the taxi-way. They had numbers in a hat, so each one of us went into a hat and drew a number. One of the first lieutenants down there climbed into the cockpit to give us a cockpit checkout. You know how confined it is around a cockpit. You can't get more than a few people close to it at once.

Finally, we got everything squared away. The lieutenant said, "Okay, are you ready to go?" I looked at the number that I had drawn. It was the first plane in the lineup. Nobody could get past me until I took that airplane up or moved it off the taxi strip. So that's how I got to fly the first flight.

What did you learn that day?

I learned a lot that day. I guess one thing that I learned was that the fuselage tank in the plane wasn't of original design. It was put in there after the plane was designed, to provide for extra fuel. Until you burned the fuel down into that fuselage tank, the airplane was kind of off a little bit. I looked at the fuel gauge in the fuselage. It was way below the problem point. When I got out there, I proceeded to put on a show.

What did you do?

Oh, I buzzed the shit out of that air base. The one fellow thought I was going to hit him. He had an eighteen-wheel tractor trailer with eighteen P-51 engines on it. He saw me coming, and he thought I was going to hit him. So, he jumped off the tractor trailer, and the damn thing jackknifed. He put eighteen airplane engines all over the ground.

Needless to say, we put on a show for the white boys. I initiated it, and we really beat this airfield up. When I got back over, I took a look at the Old Man's tent. I was sitting there at a reasonable altitude and I thought, "Shit, I may as well buzz him too." I backed off and gave him a pretty good pass, and that tent leaned, and I said, "Why don't I put it all the way down?" So I backed off. I got up to about ten thousand feet, about fifteen or twenty miles away. I got on a full head of steam and was coming down. As I did, it looked to me like I was looking up at the top of his tent. When I saw the Old Man, I hit the war-emergency boost and boy, did that plane jump. Then I could see it in my mirror. I pulled up and went down and then I started rolling right off the top of it.

When I came back, I did an awful lot of rolls. It turned out everybody had stopped working. The cooks had stopped cooking and everything had come to a standstill. When I finally came down and landed, all the mechanics and crew chiefs and everybody was all over the airplane. They were all asking me, "How did you like it, lieutenant?" I said, "It's the greatest thing since girls." I pointed to it and said, "I'll name this one. This one belongs to me."

What did you call it?

"Little Freddie." See, when I left, I had this little wife who was pregnant. I said it was going to be a son. So I named the plane, "Little Freddie."

You didn't get into too much trouble, did you? Or did you?

Yeah, when I was coming up from the white line area, B.O. Davis' jet wasn't far from mine. I saw him standing there. Somebody had put his tent back up. He looked at me and said, "Hutchens."

I said, "Yessir." And he beckoned me over.

He looked at me like I was a damn blithering idiot. He finally returned my salute and said, "At ease."

"I bet that was you up there putting on that show."

"Sir," I said, "you know this is one poker hand that I can't call." I used to play poker with the Old Man.

"It was you."

"Yessir."

"Well, I think it's poor judgement." He was really mad. About that time his telephone rings and the commanding general of the Fifteenth Fighter Command was chewing his butt out, going and coming. He rapped him at attention from "Yes" to "No" to "Yes" and said, "Yessir, I wasn't involved. Yessir. No sir."

I said, "Oh, shit." I was beginning to feel like my butt was going to get it now. So he finished talking and he said, "Do you know who that was?"

"No sir."

"That was General Struthers, the Commander of the Fifteenth Fighter Command. The general thinks that it was a pretty poor display of common sense, too."

"Oh?"

"Yes."

"Well, I'm sorry sir."

Then he paused and said, "The General told me he wanted you all to be just as hot as you all want to be. But please you tell your people to get three or four hours in the damned airplane first (laughs)."

What about that tractor that jackknifed?

That was what started it. The commander of the outfit called the Fifteenth Fighter Command and told them what the hell was going on. The driver of the truck thought he was going to get killed and, hell, I wasn't going to hit him.

Was it a white guy driving the truck?

Oh, yeah, this was a white outfit.

You started out to say a little while ago that you showed those white people you could do it. Obviously, you felt a need to prove yourself, because people didn't believe you could do it.

Yeah, one of the things that stood up above them was that we had a whole lot more flying time than the white fliers did. See, they would come in and have anywhere between four and ten hours in the operational-type airplane. They'd sent the white pilots overseas as replacement pilots. But, at the time when we were sent overseas—I've got to say that I was an original—we had up to two hundred hours in combat-type aircraft.

Stories about flying P-47s?

The prizefighter Joe Louis had a farm up in Michigan not so far from the airfield and since we flew seven days a week, we could go up there and bug the people who were up there riding horses—watch them fall off their horses. Also, we would fly underneath the bridge that connected Michigan and Canada—the Fort Huron Bridge. I think I hold the record for that. I took six airplanes under there at one time.

Six airplanes under the Port Huron?

Yes, at center span. We had a formation of six. That was foolish on my part because we didn't have that much room. I backed them up—way back up—and I told the pilots to pack it in real tight. They packed it in real tight. I don't think we had room to breathe. I figured we had enough clearance to get through there, and we did. Word got around, and when it did, word came back that we would do no more things like that again.

Was Freddie Hutchens a little bit of a hell-raiser when he was younger?

A lot of people called me kind of loosey goosey, but I wasn't. I was really a very intense person who didn't show it. I would develop some wisecracks to sort of take some of the apparent intensity off.

Why do you think you didn't want to show it?

Well, I don't know. I would just guess, I suppose, that it was because this experience was all new to us. We were the first of our kind—we didn't see any others before us—so we had no rules for comparison. At that point all my instructors were white; the instructors at Tuskegee were white, too.

Did you have any trouble with white instructors?

I didn't. I didn't feel any indication of trouble. Most of the instructors were southerners. But we had a few good laughs sometimes.

Like what?

Oh, I had one instructor in Basic. His name was Gabriel C. Hawkins. Of course, Gabe was a very good instructor. But one day we went out there to AT-6s, and he did something that was cardinally wrong. He didn't open the fuel tanks and stick his fingers down into the tank—the wing tanks. If you couldn't feel fuel in there, you'd take the tops off, and put fuel in there until you felt fuel. Anyway, he didn't have much fuel in there, and he took off. As soon as he did, he got to about a hundred or two hundred feet in the air, and the damn thing quit on him.

He tried to turn it back into the main airfield, which was wrong. The book says, "Go straight ahead." Anyway, he lived, but he got his face cut up so badly it wasn't even funny. It so happened they needed some special kind of blood for him, and there was one man on that base with that special kind of blood. That someone looked Senegalese. Do you know what a Senegalese looks like? They all start around six-foot-six. And they've got no fat on them —call it muscle.

Well, this chap had the kind of blood that Hawkins needed, but Hawkins said, "Ah, hell, just let me die." His wife said, "Don't put that damn blood in him." The hospital commander was also a Southerner, but a very humane person. Well, he rode the fellow from Senegal over there, and they knocked out Hawkins, then rolled this black person up beside him and said, "Put in a little fuel."

Hawkins was then sewed up by a young black doctor who had graduated from Howard. The goose he gave Hawkins was so small that today you couldn't tell whether it was a scar or a little burn. And this man put two hundred and fifty stitches in him.

Anyway, Hawkins lived. But he didn't want any children after that. He didn't want any black babies.

Did he tell you that?

Yeah, he will tell you that now.

Is he still alive?

I don't know if he is now. Well, he finished off his tour up at Memphis State. I have been to Memphis State several times to see him. Every time I come up there I give him a call, and he comes out to the airport to visit with me. He made full colonel.

In 1951, when I was over in Korea, I came back to Japan. I needed some uniforms, so I went to the military base to buy me some uniforms. This damn burly sergeant up there says, "You can't take any uniforms."

I said, "Sir, to you, goddam it! Why can't I buy any uniforms?"

"Because Major Hawkins said you couldn't buy any uniforms."

"Where does it say that?"

Hawkins had put out a memo that no uniforms were to be sold to people over in Korea because there was a shortage. I thought that was one hell of a note.

"Is this Major Hawkins anywhere around here?"

"Yeah, why?"

"Get him on the phone. I want to talk to him."

I knew who it was. I read the sign that said "Gabriel C. Hawkins." I didn't think they'd have but one Gabriel C. Hawkins in the whole air force.

He was at lunch when I called him up and told him I wanted to buy some uniforms, that they wouldn't sell me any. I told him who I was.

"What in the hell are you doing over here?"

"I'm over in Korea."

"Wait, don't move a thing. I will be right down there." He stopped what he was doing and came right down to the office. He told the sergent, "Let him buy some uniforms."

The sergeant looked straight at him and said, "Are you going to violate your own directive?"

Hawkins said, "To hell with it."

After we got the uniforms, we went to his house. He was living on the base. So I went by the house, and his wife fixed up a place for me. We got to talking and laughing about the blood episode. It turned out that Gabriel and his wife had had three kids. The kids were falling apart when they learned about their parents' stupidity. At the time Gabe and his wife were damned serious—they weren't going to have children, but as it turned out they went to a party, I guess, and forgot that damn rhythm method, and she got pregnant.

So somehow they ended up with some kids. All of them were blond-headed and blue-eyed, just like the parents. We laughed and laughed about that. He laughed, too. He said he just didn't know.

We all laugh about it. Every time I'd see Gabe he would laugh about it because he made three big mistakes that day: One, he did something he'd told us not to do: Don't ever take off until you check the fuel in your tank and you can feel it in there, and two, if the engine quits shortly on take-off, don't try to come back to the field, try to go straight ahead, and the third one, he didn't want any of that "doggone nigger blood" in him. But he has no qualms about telling anybody the whole episode. He was saying, "You can understand. Hell, we didn't know any different. We were doing what we were taught."

What was the most surprise you saw from somebody who saw you black fliers flying?

In 1945, I think, they had some P-51s down at Moody Air Force Base and they wanted to take them to a base in New Mexico. We took off and went down to Valdosta, Georgia. We had special buses pick us up. I think there were twenty-five of us back there, and our job was to fly the airplanes. They had looked to Tuskegee because we were P-51 pilots, so it was logical for us to take the planes to New Mexico.

But the base commander found out who we were and he was just wringing his hands. So when they finally found out that all of us were people of ethnic descent—or whatever you call it—and they said, "Don't let them go down and pick them airplanes up."

It turned out they couldn't stop us from picking them up. The guy said, "They're out there on the highway."

The commander said, "Call the state patrol. They can stop them."

The guy said, "No, I wouldn't do that."

So they decided to let us go, and they alerted the people at Moody that there were twenty-five of us coming down to pick up those airplanes for flight. So Moody was waiting for us. We got there a little after dark. We wanted to get up early the next morning and get a good start.

The trip had three legs to it. For the first leg we were going to stop in Shreveport, Louisiana. We had a little trouble getting the airplanes—smilin', nit-pickin' stuff. The planes hadn't been flown in a good length of time, so it was maintenance stuff here and there. They finally got us off the ground, and we got into tight formation.

We went by the Tuskegee Army Airfield, and asked permission to pass in review. They said, "You're cleared to pass once from the northeast to the southwest." We came down that runway right down in front of the buildings and were packed there like sardines. We could fly some formations! We put on a good show and came back in line and buzzed a couple of times. Then I took off, pulled out of formation and did my little slow roll off the deck. I had done maybe a six-point hexagon. You would go until you got maybe six different angles within the 360 degree angles.

So, when people came out of formation, everybody was out in the streets. We had gone back up into formation and passed up over there in formation. We waved our wings and went out through the annex. We went on into Louisiana. We did what those boys do in NASA, when they taxi in formation. When one canopy comes up, all of them come up. Well, we had been used to doing this, so I taxied up in front. This fellow, who was sitting up there giving me these signals on how to park the damn thing, watched. The airplanes came down, landing one right after the other—you could hardly tell where one wing ended and another began, we were that close together. I just reached up there and shut the airplane down. The man that was parking me jumped up on the wing and, as he jumped up, I unbuttoned my oxygen mask. I could have sworn he had seen a ghost. He fainted and fell right on that goddamn wing!

By that time we were all getting out of the planes. Everybody looked to see us. They had troopers out there, and the base commander met us. He said, "We don't know if you are going to stay here tonight."

"We can't continue on. It will be dark by the time we get to the next station we planned to go to." We were going to Fort Worth the next day, and were going to stop there. Finally, they put us—not in the BOQ [Officer's Quarters]—but down on the other end of the field where they had all the other black troops. They had a nice little hut, and the beds were clean. They couldn't feed us in the Officer's Club, so they brought us a truck and sent us downtown. (They were clearly not as hospitable as they were in Valdosta.) So they sent us downtown to a nice little restaurant some black person had. We had some beautiful steaks and, of course, the base picked up the tab.

A couple of the fellows decided to look around downtown Shreveport. They didn't do a thing wrong, but a cop picked them up down there and put them in jail. "Niggers impersonating an officer." The cops called us out at the base, and the base commander said, "Yes, we got some here."

He asked for their names, and the guy gave him the names. He said, "I'll send someone down to pick them up."

So the base commander called me down at the bivouac area, where we were bunking and said, "I think they've got a couple of your troops down there. The local police picked them up for impersonating an officer."

I had to chuckle about it, because I had told the sons-of-bitches to stay put. So the Provost Marshall went down and picked them up and brought them back. One of the fellows was explaining. I said, "You don't have no explanation for this. I told you from the damn beginning that we are here to ferry airplanes, not to socialize."

The next morning we got up and were getting ready to meet. The base commander came out and said, "You can't take off in this kind of weather."

"What do you mean, General?"

"This weather is below minimum. This is below the instrument flight rules."

"Yeah, I understand that," I said, "But we are leaving here."

"Well, I will have to write you up."

"Fine, but I've got my rebuttal."

We had to leave because they couldn't give us the accommodations suitable to commissioned officers in the air force. That's why we decided to go to the next state.

So we went and lined up and got on the airplanes and went over to Fort Worth. I don't know if you know, but in Texas and Oklahoma and Kansas, they've got no trees, no rock, no nothing to stop the Arctic wind. When it's bad, they call it a "Great Northern." Well, while we were there in Fort Worth, we had one, so we were stuck there. The people were nice, though.

You never got in any trouble for taking off against orders.

Oh, no.

What was the most important thing you learned in the military?

Respect your own abilities and make sure you know your own limitations and, above all, be honest with yourself. We have had people who got into trouble because of just that one thing. You know, when I was telling you about how I had buzzed the base command and the tent fell down? What I didn't tell you was that I had gone upstairs, and I was ready to run that airplane out. I knew what it would do. I didn't try it on the deck the first time. I had plenty of altitude if there was a mistake.

I didn't feel I was in any jeopardy. Everytime I'd pull a roll on the deck I would always —before I'd start my roll—pull the nose of the airplane up. So, when I started my roll the nose of the airplane was going up by two degrees—or about fifteen or twenty degrees, maybe. That gives you some margin of error if you have to fall out.

What was your favorite air tactic? Was it the hexagon?

No, one of the things I used to like to teach when I came back after combat was the cube-and-eight. With cube-and-eights you start off and take an intersection. When you get up and start looking at the ground from up there, you can almost see yourself pulling off squares. What you want to do with a cube-and-eight is pull up and go just like you are going to go into a loop. And you go through the loop and, as you come through, while you are inverted, you roll on your way down and go into a second loop, coming back up. Then, when you roll it out again, that's a cube and eight. That means you actually become inverted in the airplane.

Let's talk about going to war.

We left Selfridge Air Force Base. That was, I think, Christmas Eve in 1944. We came out on a special troop train and went to Newport News, Virginia. That was where we bivouacked until we could get overseas.

How did you feel that night?

For awhile there was a lot of mystery to it. I remember that, the first night we got into the *Patrick Henry*. Some of the people came up to Bill Davis and wanted him to come out and shake hands and bring some of his boys. But they said, "What are they doing?"

"They want to sit anywhere. They want to sit in the movie theater."

"But they aren't sitting where they are supposed to be sitting."

Davis looked straight up and said, "I guess you'll just have to leave them because my troops are going overseas, and we have received our arms. I don't think it would be wise for anybody to get into any argument here while they are sitting in the theater."

Later on, in January, we finally got overseas. I think we had two ships per squadron. We would have these submarine drills, and they would come out and blow the whistle. We would, of course, come running on deck and put our Mae Wests and crash helmets on, go through the walkway and get into lifeboats.

We found out that the boat we were on had a thousand pounds of mercury fulminate fuses on board. They've got a problem with flash point. That's where you only need a little friction before the things will explode. But, once we knew what we were riding on, we realized there was no point in trying to get off that thing in an emergency because, if we got hit by torpedos, shit, we would never know what hit us.

What was the worst practical joke you witnessed?

It wasn't really a practical joke, nor was it on me. But I remember this time we were outside of Nome, Alaska. This was after the integration of the air force. We had about three-and-a-half to four hours of nighttime per day. Of course, we dug out slit trenches. We would go out and use them for discharge of body wastes. One fellow had to go early in the morning. The wind was blowing something awful, and the temperatures were about minus sixty degrees. I don't know what the chill factor was, but it was cold. We were in layers of clothing. So this fellow started breaking down his one pair of pants over one pair of pants. When the wind told him he was down to his bare bottom, he squatted over that slit trench and, all of a sudden, you could hear him cussing. He didn't get the last pair of pants down. He had to live in that damn stuff. It wasn't funny to him, but it was funny to us.

In Alaska the sun was bright as hell off the melted snow and ice and could create problems. Once when we had completed bivouac, which was seven to ten days, we would have to do our survival work. After that, we all came back and we were all sunburned. Of course, the whites experienced all that reflection and glare out there as well, and they burned too. But my skin was actually peeling. Just like a damn snake getting a new hide. Anyway, the first time somebody noticed it, he said, "Hey, look here at Freddie. He's been burned too." He was dead serious. He didn't think Negroes could get sunburn.

What was your first sortie like? Were you apprehensive?

I wasn't so apprehensive. I figured it had been a long time since I had been in an airplane. We got a few hours' refresher. I don't know what the first mission was about. But we were later patrolling up by Naples Harbor. Then we moved farther up and were flying out of Naples.

What was the first dogfight you got into?

We were flying long-range escort for B-47s. We spotted a few planes. I was flying B.O. Davis' wing at the time. We spotted these planes up there at about nine o'clock high. They were coming around us. "Bandits at eleven o'clock high." Pretty soon we said, "Bandits at twelve o'clock high." They first started off calling them bogeys until they were identified. They were in formation just like we were, and they were trying to catch us from the top. They'd always be over our head. We never could get above them. That day we were ready to go.

B.O. Davis hollered, "You with me, men?"

Everybody said, "We got you covered. Go ahead and lead."

"How about you Freddie?"

"Colonel, I am right on your wing."

"Let's go get them."

"Charge, men."

And we did.

We were dispatched from Italy down to Athens, Greece, and we didn't know what was going on down there in the first place. Later it became known to us what the purpose was. The British were going to parachute into Greece and then drive the Germans back north. They were using us to go down there and soften up the anti-aircraft. So we went down there several times. Every time we went down there, we lost airplanes. I don't think I was on the last flight that went down, but I got hit with ground fire. They were shooting up, and it just exploded at about the same time I was there. I got hit with 20 mm ground fire. The airplane was hit everywhere it could be hit.

I realized that I wasn't going to make it home. I started making tracks as far away as I could from that airport. The wingman saw me and he followed me. I nursed that airplane until it just wouldn't go anymore. About then, I slammed into a mountain near Athens. It was north of the city. The wingman saw the Germans making tracks over there to where I was. The wingman thought I was dead, but he gave me the benefit of the doubt.

Then some sympathizers got there. They just put me on one donkey and loaded up another donkey with my parachute and other paraphernalia. They started making tracks up into the hills. It was known the Germans weren't going to come back up to the hills. But that wingman kept the Germans off me.

Who was your wingman?

A young man named Roger Romine. He got killed later on. But he stayed there until he couldn't stay any longer.

He just shot at them?

Yes, every damn time those Germans would start out, and it looked like they were headed my way, he just turned those six fifty-caliber guns in their direction, and kept me from being captured.

What do you remember about that trip up the mountain?

After about an hour of it, I started hurting like hell. I took a look at my mouth and my teeth were raggedy. I was spitting up blood. I had also been hit in one of my legs. It was a nick in one of the bones, but I broke my jawbone and my ankle. I just took my fingers and put my teeth back in place. You see, when I hit the ground I hit the gunsight of the airplane. I was doing about 256 miles per hour. That's a pretty sudden stop! Well, I guess you don't stop suddenly, you bounce somewhere. The airplane bounced and made me accelerate through the air. The plane broke into pieces and the cockpit rolled over about three times and stood upright.

What did you think?

I realized that Saint Peter wasn't there with his harps and everything to anoint me and let me come on in. So I looked around and thought, "Well, hell, it wasn't quite my time."

I reached in back of the canopy—what was left of it—and pushed it open and got out. I ran about twenty-five yards and fell flat on my damn face. Then the underground picked me up. They realized that this man, Romine, was keeping the damn Germans off of them, so they came in.

When I realized that I was safe with them—that they were friends and weren't going to kill me—I felt a lot better. They moved me near a little village, and put me in a haystack until it got dark. I looked up at my watch: it was about nine o'clock when they got me out of the haystack and put me in a little canoe with two men in it. Those sons-of-guns rowed from nine o'clock in the evening until three or four the next morning. We made land somewhere and, by now, I was really beginning to hurt.

Then we came into a little village and all the people were in the village. They were just about as ecstatic as can be. They all wanted to see me. The Germans were up to this little village just a couple of days ago. They had taken all the food that these people had. But then that night they had about a three-hundred-pound swordfish come taxiing in up there, and he couldn't get back out there into deep water. They didn't have any food and then, all of a sudden, by coincidence they did. I didn't have a damn thing to do with it. This goddam three-hundred-pound swordfish just came in. He was thrown up against the sand and couldn't get back out with the tide. There was certainly plenty of swordfish for everybody there in the village. The people brought in staples: cornmeal, beans, and flour from other villages, and we ate. We stayed at that place for one day.

A lot of people went up there, and they spoke that I was the Messiah. It was the luck, of course, but they thought that because this being came about the time the fish came there was a connection. The next morning, about first light, a little kid walked up to me. He spoke perfect English. He was born and reared in Detroit. He and his family had come back up for a vacation and had gotten caught over there during the war.

You could tell he was an American. He had American written all over him. He was a redhead from Baltimore, Maryland, and he had green eyes. He was about six foot three, and weighed about two hundred and a half. When he walked up to me, all he said was, "All I need is your name, rank, and serial number." I gave it to him. He was going to send back that I was safe. But I don't think they got the word back.

John Swenson

JOHN SWENSON

Missing In Action

If you wonder about the experience of someone who evaded capture by the Nazis by dint of courage and guile and the beneficence of the Resistance, John Swenson can detail it for you. As this imposing man, six feet, three inches tall, tells his story of being declared missing in action (MIA) for five and one-half months, he brightens while remembering something he had not thought of for a long time. As he talks, his cat "that follows me like a dog" follows his movements.

John Swenson and his twin brother were born in Somerville, Massachusetts, at home. His brother died when they were two weeks old. When the war broke out, John volunteered for the army air corps, and was pegged for radio operator and mechanic school in Sioux Falls. Thereafter he volunteered for tail gunnery school, which took him to Kingman, Arizona, and then on to Moses Lake to begin combat flight training. He was deployed to Europe as part of the 100th Bomb Group.

After the war, John remained in the Air Force Reserves. He was recalled to active duty in 1948, to help with the return of the World War II dead. He was again recalled from 1950 to 1952, when war broke out in Korea, and again in 1962 for a year during the Cuban Crisis. In 1982, after forty years of active and reserve duty, he retired as a lieutenant colonel.

On the exterior, Swenson seems a kind of no-nonsense guy but in actuality a man with a big magnanimous heart. Today, he suffers weakness from lung cancer after years of smoking, but he is more than willing to give the interview a try.

What did you do on your first mission?

We bombed Kiel, Germany. A lot of flak, but we didn't see any fighters. We were bombing docks, harbor facilities, with two hundred planes on the mission. That was all you could get in those days.

When I flew my first mission, the flak started coming up, you couldn't believe it. The sky around us was black from the puffs of these '88s. The plane was getting hit by these little pieces of steel. When we got back, we counted more than a dozen little holes, pin-pricks in the plane.

Describe your last mission.

On our last mission aircraft, *Heaven Can Wait*, we went to Ludwigshaven, Germany. When we were over the target, we hit a lot of flak, though no fighters. We passed over Luxembourg and came over the Ardennes. Suddenly, three Focke-Wulfs came out of the sun at eleven o'clock high at 1:40 PM. Spitfires were supposed to pick us up at 1:50 PM. Our plane was flying tail-end Charlie in the low element of three elements. The Germans hit us with cannon and machine gunfire. They hit number four engine, set something on fire in the bomb bay. The fire was a roaring inferno. Then we heard over the intercom the pilot saying, "We are hit. Bail out."

After Germany's surrender, I visited the pilot, Frank Smith, who told me the plane's controls were shot out. He couldn't fly it on automatic pilot because it kept falling off on its right wing. We bailed out and came down through two layers of cloud cover. After the second layer, we could see the surrounding land. I saw the forest, rolling hills, white steeples, and a church in every village. As I was coming down, I saw a B-17 coming at us in a slow spiral. All I could think of was that it seemed like I was being followed down by two German fighters. It looked like it was coming at me. Then I saw the plane was falling off to the right. Now it was coming back the other way. All this before we hit the second cloud cover.

After that, I didn't see the B-17 anymore. I came down in the forest—the Ardennes. I didn't hit any trees but rather came down in a small clearing. I unbuckled my chute. I expected the whole German army to be waiting for me. Fortunately, the second cloud cover hid me from view, so it was only a couple of minutes before I hit the ground.

As I was unbuckling my chute, what should I see off in the distance but another chute coming down at an angle, as if on a glide path. It was a white chute, so I figured it was one of ours—not knowing what color chutes the Germans had. I ran in the direction of the chute, but I didn't see anyone. Then I came into a clearing. Who's standing there, but my navigator, Saul Herkovitch. We called him "Herky." "Where are we? I asked. He says, "I don't know." "Are we in Germany or France?" I asked him if he'd been able to make a determination on the charts.

About a hundred feet from us was a farmer. He was ploughing up a field with the help of an ox and a mule. We ran over to him and all he said was *"nix Bosch."* What he was saying was "no Germans." At the time I didn't know what he was saying, so I said to Herky, "Let's get the hell out of here before someone comes and spots us. Let's get to the treeline."

As we started to run away, we heard a voice in the distance say, "Wait for me." It was John Runsel. He had heard me stomping through the woods and thought it was Germans, so he had hidden under a bunch of weeds and leaves. He joined us, and then we heard a couple of voices yelling at us. We turned around, and it was a couple of Frenchmen, so we stopped and waited for them.

We had determined by now that we were in France. Herky was Jewish and his people were from Poland, so he tried Yiddish on the ploughmen, then he tried Polish, then he tried Latin. Nothing. So that's when we moved out. Those fellows continued to yell at us, and we determined they were French. They said, "Come with us." We decided to follow them, since we didn't have any other place to go. They took us deeper into the woods, to a shack. They said that they'd bring someone back who spoke English. Instead, they brought a little school kid, but he couldn't speak English, only a couple of words. Then they brought in a school teacher, but neither did she know anything. Before they left, they made us understand they'd be back the next morning. We settled in until 3:00 AM, when the two Frenchmen arrived and took us to their village.

Were you pretty frightened?

No, none of us were frightened. At this point there was no threat. If you were frightened, you wouldn't have been able to fly these missions. After twelve missions or so, they'd send air crews off to R and R someplace.

Unlike in America where the farmer had his house in the middle of his farmland, in this area they lived in a village. And their farmland extended in a circle beyond the village. I don't remember how many people or how many homes there were in this little village, which was called Vieux Les Morannes. It wasn't on the intelligence maps, it was so small.

On the second day we were stopped there, two gendarmes came. Of course, we didn't know what the hell they were talking about. They wanted to see us and talk to us. They couldn't make any sense of what we were saying either.

That day, who shows up in the village but Clyde Manion, the bombardier. He came down near a little railroad depot. He was hidden in a back room out of sight, then dressed up in a conductor's uniform and brought to the village. So now, there were four of us.

The Frenchmen with whom we were staying said we would be leaving the next morning to meet a priest, and then we were going to get on bicycles and travel to the priest's rectory in a distant village. We started walking cross-country through the ploughed fields. We traveled a few miles and finally made it to where the priest was waiting. He said, "We can't take you in the daylight, but we'll be back tonight with bicycles." In this area there was a red brick pumping station along the lake. We stayed there for the day. When it was dark we left, and we went back to the place where we'd seen the priest. He had four men, with a bike for each of us, and one for each Frenchman. They said, "Ride to where there's a man waiting on the road." This is at about ten at night. There's nothing on this road—no lights, no Germans, not anything. We just kept on bicycling. We start going through these small villages. And finally, after about a half-hour, there is this fellow standing in the road, pointing off to the right about a hundred yards into the village. We got off our bikes and went into a house, next to the rectory. We stayed overnight there, and the next morning moved to the rectory, and Bill Wertz and Alvin Little were there.

You guys came down all over the place yet found each other.

Yes. By bailing out at twenty-one thousand feet, we were probably spread out over a twenty-mile area. When Bill Wertz bailed out, he came down in a field. When he came down, he came down in a field and saw a steeple in the distance. He started walking towards the steeple. He was walking out in the open, and he didn't know where the hell he was. So he was walking through this village, and as he passed this store front, a hand reached out and pulled him in. That was his first meeting with the French!

After our plane had gone out of control, the German fighters also hit the last plane in the third element. Only two people got out of that: the navigator and the bombardier. That ship went down with all the other men. The following day, we met the navigator and the bombardier at the rectory. My outfit lost two ships that day. So there we were, Little, Wertz, Manion, Herky, and the two from the other ship. They told us we had to move out that afternoon, that we couldn't stay there any longer. A van showed up, and they put us in a van.

So we got in the van and we started going across country. We didn't know where in the hell we were going. We went through checkpoints and weren't stopped. We could not see out of this closed van. Now we came to this town of Vrizy. Billy Wertz, Clyde Manion, the bombardier, and I went to the home of Georges Logart. He lived there with his wife and four children. Alvin Little went to a house up the street. The rest went to another village, about five miles away. We stayed there for three weeks. During that time the chief of the local French Resistance came down and talked to us. We gave him information, including our names and organization. Also, a man and a woman came down from Paris to see us. They were also involved in collecting information and radioing it back to England. They talked perfect English and dressed the part of the French aristocracy. They took down our names and serial numbers because they needed these to know whether we were who we claimed to be. They said, "We'll get back to you."

The fourth week we moved to the next town a couple of miles away, the town of Attigny. We stayed there for a week, and all of us joined up in one house. From there we got on a train and headed for Paris. We were all dressed up in all kinds of clothing, including some military dyed black.

Were any of you in physically bad shape?

No. Alvin Little had a sprained ankle, which he thought was broken. Poor son of a bitch went on I don't know how long thinking it was broken. It wasn't in a cast, but he had a crutch. When we got on the train, everybody's smiling at us. The bloody French spotted us right away—knew we weren't French and offered their seats to us. We were on the train for a couple of hours, it seemed. We traveled with this Frenchman who had come down a week earlier to confirm with England that we were who we said we were. He had one assistant. When we got to a station in Paris, we all got off. Alvin's there with his crutch, limping along. There was a Red Cross woman, who perhaps thought we might be injured French troops. Suddenly, this Frenchman came running over to her and he said something, and she backed off. Nevertheless, we went into this station and sat down at a table to wait for the train.

In Paris we picked up another person, a Canadian. He'd been downed in France for more than a year. The British authorities, through the Resistance, had said that if he didn't get his ass back, they were going to court-martial him. That's the only reason he was going back. He had gone to movies and restaurants with the French, and he was having a grand time over there. I'm sure he didn't want to fly anymore. He was a hot tomato. He was probably about twenty-two, tall and handsome, a pilot officer.

Anyway, the plan involved some of us going into the country—the four officers were going to stay in Paris. We had a few beers and looked at magazines. A few tables over were German troops eating their sausage. A big fat German MP walked around looking at everyone. You know we stood out like a sore thumb. Talk about strange uniforms. We still had our GI shirts on, though they were dyed black. We're sitting around in our black shirts like a bunch of mafia. They didn't even spot us! Still, the worst feeling went through me, waiting there. After about two and a half hours, our train arrived. We went twenty miles west to the town of Esbly. That's where I met Charline Charble.

When we got off the train, Al Little couldn't walk very well, even with his bloody crutch. You should understand that Al was a short little fellow, but he was heavy. I said, "Al, I'll carry you." So I put him over my shoulders. What a mistake! The son of a bitch weighed a half a ton. We climbed a hill. We finally get to Charline's, and I'm in a state of exhaustion. We stayed there a week, but we left Al Little behind, thinking he had a broken ankle. So I said, "Come on, I'll carry you over the mountain." I could hardly get over the mountains myself, when the time came. So we go back to Paris and they make up phony ID travel cards. When we began flying, we carried half a dozen photos of ourselves to put on identity cards, just in case. When they made the IDs, they properly stamped the travel papers, but what they lacked was fingerprinting ink. The ink they used wasn't black; it was blue, so what you had was blue, blurred fingerprints. It would never pass inspection if an idiot looked at it.

That evening we were going to get on a train and go down to southern France. Now we had a group of Frenchmen with us who were going to leave the country. They were wanted by German authorities. They were our escorts. I was smoking in those days, but I hadn't had a cigarette. So as I was standing there waiting to change trains, I took one cigarette out I had rolled, but I had no matches. As I stood there about twenty feet from my guide, a French soldier walked by me. He stopped in front of me and began to light his cigarette, so I stick my face close to his and said "Monsieur," and he passes me a light then goes on his way. Next, a German officer comes along and sees a German soldier whose uniform is in disarray, including the fact that the epaulets on his shoulders were cut off. The soldier's uniform was in disrepair, and the officer really read him up and down. Finally, after the kid had had his dressing-down and had gone on his way, I had my smoke. My poor guide was going out of his mind, waiting for the train which would take us to the city of Tarbes.

Unlike our trains where you have the seats in a row, here you had these long seats facing each other on each side of the compartments. So my guide and I get on the train and sit down, and who should come in but two Vichy cops in their mustard-colored uniforms, carrying carbines. They took their seats kitty-corner from where we were. There was a family with a bunch of children. The kids were doing all kinds of things that kids do. They were laughing and having a good time. I didn't know what the devil they were saying, but I laughed too. What a position to be in! I'm telling you, to make things worse, we have these two idiots over there with their carbines. Nevertheless, after a time, the family with kids and the Vichy cops go their way at different stops.

We finally get to our station and somebody comes running up and says something to my escort, and we get back on the train. My guide says that the Germans knew we were coming. I think that was a bunch of crap, but nevertheless we get back on and go on to the next station. We got off, walked to a house where this young fellow lived with his mother, and there we stayed a couple of weeks. By this time we were into the second week in February. They took us on a visit to the head of the French Underground in Tarbes—a Mr. Lamousse. He and his family had us to his home for a nice Sunday lamb dinner.

I kept asking these Underground people when we were leaving for Spain, when we were moving out. They kept saying *demain, demain*—"tomorrow, tomorrow." Always tomorrow. Finally, about the first week in March, one of these good-sized charcoal-burning trucks pulls up, and we hop in the back. You know, they didn't have any gas, so they devised a method of burning charcoal. The only people who had gasoline were the Germans. We drove about an hour to a town named Bagnères. There we went into a hotel, called "The American Hotel," believe it or not. They put us in the attic for a couple of hours, a precaution if the Vichy police came by. I guess the Vichy police were bad, all bad. Although we were evading, they didn't take food up to us in our rooms; we'd just go to the dining room. Around the middle of March, the French Resistance said, "We'll leave tonight." Well, let's face it, no one was prepared to leave; no one had proper clothes or proper shoes. These idiots didn't have presence of mind to make sure we had the right gear to climb a damn snow-covered mountain.

The mountains are full of snow at this time of year because the snow hasn't melted off. So off we go in another charcoal-burning truck. We leave that night and start driving into the foothills of the Pyrenees Mountains, through the snow. All of a sudden, we stop. Now it's cold as a son of a bitch out there. It's well below freezing, and we're not really dressed for the weather. Suddenly, we stop. We have a flat tire. We leave the truck and have to move one hundred yards off the road, so we won't be seen. But nobody but us would be out on a night like this. You're not going to find any German patrols out. What are they going to patrol? This is the foothills, rolling country going up into the mountains. It takes about an hour before they have the tire changed. So we go on a bit further, about another mile, and the truck gets bogged down in the deep snow. The Frenchman tells us we have to walk from there. Now this is great. Where we get off the truck, the snow on the ground is maybe a foot deep. Now we've got to plod our way through this. We don't have the right winter gear. I had on a pair of French military boots with hobnails that were a couple of sizes too small. I wore a size 13 in those days. Because they couldn't find anything to fit me, I was stuck with a smaller size. So off we went. We had roasted veal with us, some bread, and canned military supplies. Some of us had submachine guns, and I had a pistol—as if we were going to fight the goddamn Germans. How ridiculous can you get! We'd get slaughtered.

We walk all night behind our Spanish guide, Tio, a tough little fellow about five feet four. We get to the bottom of a small valley. The sun is out now and it's a beautiful day, as we walk in the cold, deep snow. We're sweating like hell. Then as we go up a rise, we find the snow's waist deep. We had small suitcases with clothes in them. We use the suitcases to tamp down the snow. We come to a small running stream. To cross it we stand on boulders covered with coatings of ice. Be careful or you'd slip off into the water. It takes us over two hours to climb the hundred yards to the top of the rise. When we heard aircraft flying over, we'd stop and freeze. We saw one, but the rest you couldn't see.

The air is so clear and sharp in the High Pyrenees. Connie Stumphig, my waist gunner, yells out that he can't go on any further. Going through high snow like that you have to lift your knees up high. As a result, the fluid in your knees would dry up and you couldn't walk. I say, "I'll stay with you, Connie. You guys go ahead, and we'll follow your path." As a result, they tramp down the snow, and it's easier to walk then. Connie says, "What are we going to do, Swede?" They called me Swede. I answer, "I'm going to get in front of you. You're going to put your hands on my shoulders, and we're going to do it by the numbers. Left, right. Left, right. We're going to take short steps." We did, and we walk and we walk. We did it slowly so there isn't any pain. Now, we came over a small rise, and here's a Frenchman lying in the snow. He's actually a Greek, who speaks English. God knows what he was into for the Germans to be after him, possibly black market. Anyway, he's lying there, his lips cracked from the sun, and he says, "I can't go on any longer." "You can't stay here," I say. "You'll die in this cold. Furthermore, the Germans might spot you, and they'll know someone's gone by, and they'll get us." He then says, "I can't go any further." I take out my pistol and say, "If you don't, I'm going shoot you and bury you in the snow." He says, "Shoot me." Of course, I couldn't have, but I'm thinking maybe I can con him. I said, "To where we're going is just over this rise, just a couple hundred yards away. There's this cabin where we're going to stay overnight. It won't take you more than ten minutes to get there." You know, at that, the son of a gun jumps to his feet and off he goes. I don't believe this guy! After awhile, we come to the cabin, a kind of quarry-type operation, where a couple of workers had stayed the winter. I take off my shoes and my toes are covered with a coating of ice, turning black.

Did a lot of the men have frostbite?

All of the men had a touch of frostbite, some worse than others. Anyway, at the quarry they fed us soup and bread, and then we slept. When I got up in the morning, I tried to get the boots on my swollen feet. The other guys had shoes that fit; I was the only one with shoes too small. We had escape kits, which consist of money, maps, needle and thread, compass, matches, and rubber water bottles. I cut the toes off my shoes and put water bottles over my toes and wrapped my feet with burlap. A couple of hours after we left, my feet were killing me, and I couldn't go on. Neither could a couple of Frenchmen and Connie. The guide said he'd be back after he got the guys to where they were going in Spain. In a couple of hours, he came back with the rest of them still with him. It turned out he couldn't get through because of avalanches and German patrols. The navigator Herky's feet were so bad that he couldn't walk at all. They just left him there in a small mountain village. Before he died in 1991, he told me that the Germans came by the small hospital in the village. They were going to take him into custody until they saw the condition of his feet, so they said he could stay a little longer. They later took him into custody when his toes had healed and put him in jail. In June, when the invasion started, the Germans got out of the village and left Herky on his own.

We returned to that mining camp, where they had that quarry. There was an iron bucket on a cable that went down into the village below. The guide went down in this iron bucket to make preparations for us to be fed.

John Swenson's B-17 crew. Swenson is standing, extreme right.

But we couldn't use the iron bucket. The guide returned, and we had to walk down. In pain and agony, we hiked back to the village of Sainte Marie, in the foothills of the Pyrenees. There we went into the house of the chief of the Resistance for that area. He took us into the house, gave us hot food and wine, took us up before a roaring fire to thaw out. After a couple of days, he said we'd have to leave and go into the foothills. Throughout the foothills you'd see little shacks, which shepherds used. We stayed in one of those. After about a week, they brought a doctor to see us. Poor son of a gun, he wasn't young. When he looked at our feet, he immediately realized there wasn't anything he could do except to give us Vaseline and bandages to wrap our toes. During this time, the Resistance brought up the carcasses of a couple of sheep, which we prepared with potatoes. Finally, one day someone came up and said, "All right, you guys, we'll be moving out." A gunner from Philadelphia had feet so bad he couldn't leave. Neither could I, without shoes, but everyone else departed. During the second trip Connie's toes were so badly frozen that one of his toes broke off.

Finally one day someone else came out. We were sitting outside. Our toes were so bad we couldn't leave. But they brought in a fighter pilot—a kid of nineteen whose P-51 engine got hit by flak. The plane had a liquid-cooled engine, and he lost all his coolant, so he bailed out. (When we got back to the States, he gave me an autographed picture of himself with his P-51.)

So the rest of the group left the two of us behind. At this point we had only a bunch of potatoes to eat. We lived on potatoes. After awhile, we said "To hell with this noise. Let's reconnoitre and find out what the lay of the land is around here." You couldn't keep warm covered with straw. We spent some miserable nights trying to keep warm and sleep at the same time. So we started down the foothills toward the area where the house was that we had stayed in on our return.

We were seen by a Frenchman, living in a house nearby. He was looking at us, then he went into his house. He came out with a bucket and he pointed to the bucket and left. He apparently knew who we were. Every noontime for two days, he'd put out the food for us—bread, cheese, and soup. Finally, after a couple of days, I said, "Let's get back to the house where we were. We just can't stay out here in the hay." So we went back to the house, but when we got got there, we found it was a burned-out, gutted house. What had happened was that during the two days we spent there with the fires roaring in the hearth, we created so much heat that it ignited the beams underneath the hearth. After we left, the fire gutted the house and interior.

I said, "What the hell. At least there's sheets and covers. At least we can be warm at night." In late afternoon the insurance adjustor came by to look over the damage. He spoke French. We didn't know what to say. All we could say was that we were American, had been left behind, and we were hungry. He said, "I'll be back this evening with food." However, before he came back, the son of the head of the Resistance came by. He said, "I was going up in the hills to look for you guys." He says, "Jump in the truck. We're going back to Bagnères," which we did. So they took us back to the American Hotel. We stayed there one night, and then they moved us to a private home in the city. After a week they moved us to another town, and we stayed on the second floor of another house. We spent a couple more weeks there, and by now it was springtime, the latter part of April.

They were going to move us out of the country to Spain, over the Pyrenees by a different route because of the problem with my feet. They had a pair of custom-made boots made for me, which I still have.

That must have felt like Christmas.

Oh yes, it did. They said the boots cost 7600 francs to make. Now we're ready to leave. We climb in a truck with all of us sitting in the front seat with the driver. We go down a winding road and through the city of Lourdes and enter a lumberyard. They filled the truck with lumber but left a space for the two of us to crawl in. At this time we picked up a Frenchman, an architect, who was running from the Germans. He crawled under there with us. They drove toward the mountains. Finally, at some place along the road, we got off the truck and began walking. Incidentally, a new guide was in the truck. At this time there was no snow around. We started hiking and hiked all night. Around six in the morning, we came to this small, one-story house with a barn. We slept there for twenty-four hours.

We left and got up higher, toward the snowline, and it snowed. In one area we walked along the edge of a canyon, so high up that there were clouds below us, moving through the middle of the canyon. There was a little rain, and bold colors showed up on the face of the rock that were absolutely gorgeous. Finally, we reached the point where the guide stopped and pointed off in the distance. There we saw the mountains that sloped down to green fields—we realized we were in Spain. The guide said, "This is as far as I go. You're on your own." The guide didn't tell us his name, and we didn't ask. It was a policy not to ask people their name. It they volunteered, so be it. Otherwise, no name.

We found a path and started walking down the mountain. At the bottom we came to a turn in the path, and there sitting on the ground, eating a noonday meal, were a couple of Spanish border patrolmen. They called us over and told us to sit down. They fed and took us in to visit with the chief politician of the area, who wanted to know who we were. For a translator they had a stout little woman in her sixties, who as a young girl had gone and lived in New York for years, then retired to her homeland. Finally, after a day or two, the border patrol took us to Barbastro. There we were turned over to the authorities and put into a political prison. We were locked in a goodsized cell, where the lights were to stay on all night. They said, "If you go near the window, the guards have orders to shoot." During the day we could go out of our cells to walk around the prison yard. The prisoners found out we were American, and through the trusty would sneak us cigarettes.

One day while we were there, the commandant sent a guard and said that he wanted to see me. I said, "What would this guy want to see me about?" He wanted me to help him with his English. I went, and he started reading from his book. He poured me a glass of wine, and as he read, I'd correct him. That lasted for about an hour. At the end of it, he thanked me and I went back to my cell. By the fourth day, a representative of the British Embassy got us released and took us to a hotel in town.

The hotel was run by a family. A daughter, Josephina, and the mother ran the kitchen and dining room upstairs; the brother and wife ran the café downstairs. They were very kind people. People around there would promenade around the town—up and back. We used to join them. One night we heard this voice say, "Good night," in English. We turned around and here's this Spanish lieutenant, who explained that in the thirties his mother and father had come to the U.S. Later his father had returned to Spain to fight for Franco, when the civil war broke out.

Two of the officers of the Spanish air force came up one day and took us to the town of Alhama, where they kept the Allied airmen. Eventually, sixteen to eighteen of us left and went by train to Madrid, and from there to Gilbraltar. There, we were well greeted. They had two bottles of Coca-Cola. How generous they were! They gave one to me and one to Gene because we'd been MIA the longest.

Did anybody try to get the Coke from you?

No, they shouldn't have even given us the Coke, unless they had one for each of us. A short time later, we boarded C-47s at night and flew from Gibraltar back to England. When I got back I went to a British debriefing. They sent someone from my bomb group (the 100th) to identify me. In reality, I had never seen him before in my life, and he had never seen me before in his life, but that was okay.

The "Memphis Belle"

BOB HANSON

Flying "The Memphis Belle"

One of the most celebrated planes in World War II has to be The *Memphis Belle*, which made twenty-five flights over the fierce, flak-filled skies of Europe. Unlike thousands of his colleagues, Bob Hanson, radio man on the *Belle*, lived to tell about it.

Raised in Garfield, a farming region in eastern Washington, Bob Hanson grew up in a world of graneries and warehouses. Since farming didn't qualify him for exemption, Hanson was drafted in 1941. But before he got drafted, he went to a recruiting office in nearby Spokane. There the draft officer told him that, if he was drafted, he should reenlist for a three-year period. He got drafted, went to Fort Lewis, and reenlisted. When he reenlisted, he got a nine-dollar-per-month raise from the standard twenty-one dollars per month. "Guys with twenty-one dollars were really strapped," the affable, chatty Hanson says. "But I was living the life of Riley."

Later, at Jefferson Barracks, a sergeant requested that all men with previous military experience step out of formation. "You guys won't have to go through basic training," the sergeant said.

So Hanson went in and sat on the "fart sack, which was what they called our bunk in those days." Then one day the charmed life seemed destined to end. A parade caused Hanson and others to have to march. Afterwards, when he came in, the sergeant informed him that he had looked bad in the drills and would be court-martialed.

Hanson tried to explain, saying that he had simply followed orders. "When the sergeant said, 'anyone with experience step out,' I stepped out," he said.

"You didn't have any previous experience," the sergeant said.

At that point Hanson presented his discharge from when he got drafted and spent three days in the service.

The military, it turned out, couldn't court-martial him, but the powers-that-be decided instead to punish him with K.P., peeling potatoes. But luck came back. Two days later he shipped out, never to do the fourteen days of company punishment. Neither did Hanson have to take basic training.

Luck and faith prevailed when the *Memphis Belle* completed its twenty-fifth flight and Bob Hanson and the crew returned safely home.

Who were you in the film The Memphis Belle?

I was the radio operator. Eric Stoltz played my part. Some of us guys from *The Memphis Belle* went over for about ten days and pooped around with them while they made the film. We had lots of fun. I was a technical expert, a technical man, and my job was to take all these eight young men between the ages of eighteen and twenty-four down to an English pub and teach them to drink warm English beer. People ask, "Bob, why did they pick you?" I say, "Well, because that's what I excelled at when I was over here." That was my big job with the motion picture!

What did you think of the movie's rendition of events?

The movie was not what we would call authentic, but in another sense, everything that happened in the movie did happen someplace, sometime in World War II, in England. Basically, nothing was made up. It just didn't happen to one crew.

Were there situations where you were really scared?

We were scared in every situation. That's true because you just knew what the law of averages was. It was bad. You could see airplanes circling, going down, and the German fighter planes going after them. Then you'd see people parachuting. And you just kept saying, "The good Lord's gotta be with me."

The B-24s were our escort, and if the enemy saw them anywhere near our formation they always went over to hit them, because they were a lot easier to shoot down than a B-17. We were always glad to see B-24s, but they didn't last very long.

As a radio man, I was there for emergency only, to take messages. If they changed the target or we couldn't find a target, then we got our instructions that way. Also, I think *The Memphis Belle* led the Eighth Air Force only once or twice, which required the radio. Really, the radio man did very little in combat, except being a gunner.

Were you a pretty good gunner?

Oh, hell no, I was always afraid I was going to shoot the tail off, because my gun went right over the top of the tail. There was a guard that was supposed to stop you if you were shooting around behind, but I was always afraid I was going to knock that guard over when I got too excited, and just shoot the tail right off of it. But I never did that, luckily.

You seem like a pretty excitable guy.

Damn right. Anytime anybody starts shooting at you, you start saying, "Gee whiz," and holding your pants kind of close and your legs tight together, because you didn't want to start spreading you know what all over the ground. It scared the holy Jesus out of you, I'm not kidding you.

BOB HANSON

Did you shoot down some planes?

I shot *at* lots of them. I think they credited our plane with shooting down six or eight, but I don't know that I did. I don't think anybody else can say with certainty what they did because you're part of a group that's all firing at the same time.

What was radio school like?

It wasn't too hard. I can't explain it but I had a knack for taking code. Most people in the service did not know how to type, so as they were sending code they were having to learn code and how to type at the same time. It

Bob Hanson and his lucky rabbit foot given him by an R.A.F. flier.

was quite boring for me to sit there. I would take a book with me, and I would read the book while everybody else was taking the code. One day, all at once, I heard all the machines getting quieter and quieter, and I all at once realized they were sending the words, "Bob, quit reading that book."

Where'd the name The Memphis Belle *come from?*

Bob Morgan, our pilot, met this girl from Memphis and she made a great impression on him. That's where the name came from. There were ten of us on the plane, and each one of us had a vote. Problem was when we counted the votes, people had chosen ten different names. So Bob went over next to his tailgunner, Johnny Quinlan who came from New York, and he says, "Johnny, would you ever like to have a three-day pass?" Johnny says, "Oh, sure, I'd just love to have one." Morgan says, "Well, if you voted for the name "Memphis Belle,"you'd be very happy with your three-day pass." So the next vote, there were eight different names and two for *The Memphis Belle.* I deliberated between "The Walla Walla Flash" or "The Evergreen Girl," for my wife.

Actually, though Bob didn't know the girl from Memphis very well, we did stop and see her a few times. We had to put a hundred hours on the plane before we could fly it overseas, so what we did was fly to all of our crew members' hometowns, as well as the girl from Memphis. We'd fly to the closest airport, and stay overnight, so the crew member could see his parents before going overseas.

I remember when we were going to leave from Bangor, Maine, to go overseas. We got up there, but we still had to put on a few more hours, so we flew around up there. We happened to be coming down one of those rivers in New Hampshire someplace, and there was a boat down there pulling some logs, a tugboat. So the navigator says, "Why don't you give him a buzz job? Let's see what he'll do." So we went down and made a little pass over the tugboat. The bombardier says, "Hey, chief, if you can't fly this airplane better than that, then I'll come up and make that goddamned thing squeal." He did it and this time we went really low, and here's this guy down there with a gun of some sort, firing up at us. When we got back to base, somehow or another a rock had mysteriously hit our airplane as we were taxiing out. That's how we got our first hole. That's what we told them anyway. I'm not sure that that guy put a hole in the airplane, but we always said it was a rock that did it.

What was the Belle's flight like over to England?

It was just a lot of water. We stopped in Iceland. I still have some friends in Iceland that I met when the airplane stopped there on the way over. In fact, I talk to them all the time. We also stopped in Scotland and gassed up there. Later, anytime we had problems with our engines and had to replace one— we had eight engines in *The Memphis Belle* that either burned up or were shot out—we went back to the same area in Scotland because we had to put five hours on the engine before we could go back into combat. The trip was two hours up and two hours back. We got to know several people well in Scotland, particularly those in taverns.

What was it like in taverns?

I think I was the luckiest guy. We were stationed close to Cambridge, and there were nearly a hundred colleges there, separate ones. During this time nearly all of the men in England between sixteen and forty-five were shipped to Africa. There were darned few young men around that country from then on. The bartender in one of these taverns had a second job inspecting all of the newsprint for the London newspapers which was stored around in barns throughout the country. This was to protect it from being bombed. I got to go around with him. I saw more of England accidentally than ninety percent of the people did on purpose. And I did see a lot of Cambridge. Also, those young girls in Cambridge did need our help in carrying groceries home, or doing whatever else they could find for us to do. Oh, I had several friends, but I'd rather not discuss it because my wife might not be as happy as I am about it.

You were married at the time?

Yes, we were married when I was in Walla Walla. We were in the first airplane that landed at the new air base they built there. We'd come up from Tampa, Florida. I was in Spokane this last summer and I ran into Louis Zingo. We were arguing about who was on the first plane to land there in Walla Walla. He said he was and I said no, that I was. So we got a copy of our orders out, and we were on the same airplane (*laughs*).

When we first landed in Walla Walla, here comes this pickup. In fact, it followed us right in. So we landed and there were MPs all over the pickup. This driver is yelling, "Hey, what in the hell are you doing? I've been driving around this place for three years. My son comes in on this airplane and you want to arrest me." It was my father. He'd been in charge of paving the runway. The other thing about this is that because my father was arrested then, every time my brother, who was a fighter pilot for thirty years, came to the base, they checked him out extra carefully.

Is there anything from your years on The Memphis Belle that gives you goose-bumps?

Yes, mainly it's the cameraderie I enjoyed most, being together. We told stories and played a lot of cards. It wasn't everybody on the plane, of course, because the officers and the enlisted men lived separately. I have a picture of us the day they dropped the bomb on Hiroshima, and there we are. We're still playing poker.

What got you through?

Well, the good Lord did all that. He did all that. All I did was go out there. He controlled all the effects. We just happened to be together at the right time, and that's the way it was. We didn't fly any better or any worse than anybody else. All the fliers were so similar. It had to be the good Lord.

Was there anybody on your crew who was exceptionally fatalistic? They show that in the movie.

No, not that I remember. We were all in the same boat. We were going to save the country.

Early on, I wasn't interested in airplanes, coming as I did from the Palouse area of Washington. There really weren't any airplanes down there, but I had an uncle who had been in World War I. He told me these stories about how bad it had been on the front lines. I decided I was not going to be out in a muddy ditch somewhere, nor was I going to be out in the sea.

Did you ever wonder if you made the wrong decision, sitting up in the air taking flak?

No, because I remembered too vividly what my uncle had told me about the trenches. Also, because I was a bit of a history buff, I had read a lot of books in my younger days and knew the life of a ground soldier wasn't the kind of life I wanted. I was going to fly in an airplane and live a good clean life. I was going to live it as long as I could and when the good Lord said it was my time to go, I was going. Made no difference when or where.

The Memphis Belle, 1943. Bob Hanson is second from left.

Remember your worst flight?

The first flight was clearly the worst because you didn't know what to expect. Nobody could tell us because nobody had gone out ahead of us. We were one of the first missions against Germany in the war. We'd joke about going over there and making a forced landing and sitting out the rest of the war. That didn't happen, but we thought about it. We actually did have one forced landing. Just as soon as we went over the coast of England, we had to land. We had two motors shot out. Another one was sputtering, if I remember correctly. When we hit the brakes, we went off the runway and went into the soft English turf. It took about a week before we got back to our own base.

But we saw lots of planes go down. The worst thing was airplanes of people we knew. Planes going down, heading into a tailspin, from right out of our formation or squadron. We'd yell, "Get the hell out of there." Then we'd count the number of parachutes. We never heard them on the radio, going down, as in the movie..

Who was your best friend on The Memphis Belle?

Probably Harold Lock. He was the waist gunner and assistant engineer. He later became engineer. He was from Green Bay, Wisconsin. A nice young gentleman. Quite religious. At the time Harold had a roommate who was not quite that religious. Sometimes the guy would bring a lady friend back to the base and into his room. We were at a permanent air force base, living in cottages usually for families, so there were two or three bedrooms. When the roommate brought back a friend, poor Harold could hear some noises that weren't exactly what he wanted to hear, so he used to get up and go over to the church and spend the rest of the night there.

As fliers, you were celebrities of sorts.

When William Wyler made his film about *The Memphis Belle*, we came back to Hollywood and partied at his house, a lovely place. Danny Kaye, Doris Day, and some others entertained for the party. There was a famous model there, and I do remember the bombardier, who was a lady's man, chasing her around and trying to catch her. She kept saying, "You'll never catch me," and he said, "Lady, if I do I'm going to tell you some nice stories." I have a picture of everybody who was there, including Colonel Jimmy Doolittle and his wife.

Remember your last flight?

There was nothing in particular unique about it. We bombed in France. It was really what we called a "milk run," but we were scared to death. When we started, we went out over the water, one-hundred feet above the water, so they didn't track us with radar. Then we pulled up and bombed them at eight thousand to ten thousand feet. We were told that we'd be too high for the low flak and too low for the high flak. Somebody figured we'd fly right in between, but we didn't do very well. We were hit, but we made it back.

I remember the twenty-fourth flight we took over there—the raid on Lorient in France. We had the plane's tail shot off, and as a result, the captain took the plane into a steep dive. We dropped about two to three thousand feet, and it almost tossed me out of the ship. I did wonder if I should bail out of the plane. Finally, he pulled up and when he did, I fell on my back, and a frequency meter and ammo box landed atop me. Obviously, in that kind of situation the pilot doesn't have time to alert you, and I wouldn't have heard him anyway.

Biggest misconception about The Memphis Belle, *or your war experience?*

It is my opinion that *The Memphis Belle* crew were no different, ability-wise, than any other crew in England at that time. We all had the same training, same type of plane, etc. So it is my belief that it was our good fortune to survive the hardships and not be among the large percentage that were shot down in combat.

We were among the first to complete twenty-five missions, and it was our good luck to be chosen to come back to the States and inform the people of the absolute facts of the air war against Germany.

ROBERT WHITCOMB

Bird's-eye View of Cologne Cathedral

Robert Whitcomb grew up in Cincinnati, Ohio, and though he wasn't someone whose natural instincts propelled him into a flight career, he ended up there at the beginning of World War II. After sending him to Jefferson Barracks, Missouri, for basic training, the military planned to direct him to radio school. Instead he was sent to Boeing Field in Seattle to study to be a control tower operator. During that period he became interested in flying, though he still had not flown. Then one day he had the opportunity to ride in the nose of a B-17 from Walla Walla, Washington, where he was then stationed, to Mountain Home, Idaho. The experience invigorated him and helped slice away any misgivings he might have had.

At Madras, Oregon, he received word he could join the cadets for flying training. From there he went to Fresno, California, for another bout of training, then to Oklahoma City University for schooling for cadets, where he studied physics and mathematics while living at the county fairgrounds. Though he loved flying, he decided that he was too nervous to be a pilot and opted instead for navigation training. As it would turn out, he would have plenty of adventures that would tax the nerves of almost anyone—as a navigator over Germany, and later as a POW.

He was a member of the 305th Bomb Group, 365th Squadron. He remembers in 1980 returning for a reunion to Chelveston, England, where he had been stationed. All the temporary buildings were gone. Everything had disappeared except one large hangar. What were his feelings there? "Everything seemed so long ago," he says with a tinge of nostalgia in his voice.

After the war, Whitcomb graduated from the College of Music at Cincinnati and Eastman School of Music in Rochester, New York, with a doctorate. His compositions have been performed at such places as Town Hall in New York City, the Kennedy Center for the Performing Arts in Washington, DC, the Landmark Center in St. Paul, and at many universities. He is now retired from his position at Southwest State University in Marshall, Minnesota, where he was Professor of Piano, Theory, and Composition.

Talk about your experience joining the military.

December 7, 1941, the day the Japanese bombed Pearl Harbor, was my twentieth birthday. So I realized I was prime material to be drafted. The following August I was drafted at Fort Thomas, Kentucky. I lived in Cincinnati, and Fort Thomas, an old Civil War fort, was located right across the river. My father had a cousin, a veteran of World War I, who was a major in the army stationed at Fort Thomas. He and his wife had an old house on the grounds there, so they invited my parents to come visit while I tested there. I had no interest in anything military. I was interested in art and music. Later on, my vocation would be music. When I visited with Major Whitcomb, he said, "What branch of service are you interested in?" I said, "I don't know." I really wasn't interested in any of them. He said, "How about the army air corps?" I said, "That sounds as good as any."

I do remember my first afternoon overseas. There were several fighter planes buzzing the place and coming really low, and one just didn't make it. It was so low that its wings hit the wires overhead and whipped it right over, and it burst into flames, and killed the pilot. That was quite an introduction to England and the combat arena.

How many missions did you fly?

Twenty. The tenth mission was a traumatic one, because we went way into Germany near Leipzig. Coming back, we went through a corridor where we received a lot of flak. It was between Muenster and Osnabrueck. They really had it targeted because it was a frequent flight path out of Germany. I was in the lead squad plane. On this flight there were two navigators and all kinds of extra people. I looked over and saw the other navigator had been hit. I could see he had blood on his face. Several of us began taking care of him. Then he noticed, "Hey, you've been hit." I'd been hit in the shoulder and hadn't even felt it. I was lucky the wound didn't get in deep enough to penetrate a lot of bone and muscle. But we both went to the hospital for recuperation, then took leave in Southport, near Liverpool, at a big hotel. The wound did leave quite a bad scar, which I still have.

Another time, many planes in the group were disabled and our particular plane lost a couple of engines. We were forced to land in Rouen, in northern France. Though this was traumatic, it was exciting to come down in France and to see the ancient cathedral sitting up on the high hill right in the middle of the city. They took us by bus to Brussels, and we flew back to England.

Do you remember losing any good friends?

There were almost always several planes that didn't return after each mission. I remember thinking this was a real tragedy, but it would never happen to me. I didn't go over to Europe until August 7, 1944, and then on January 10, 1945, I was shot down. We thought that mission was going to be easy—if you could call any that. It was a mission to bomb an airfield outside Cologne, so we wouldn't be penetrating into Germany too far. I remember it was a beautiful, cold sunny morning. For some reason we flew over the target without dropping bombs. You see, the way we bombed was for the lead bombardier to drop his bombs, then everyone else would just toggle theirs out. But this time the lead bombardier didn't drop his bombs! So we flew over and started to go over the target again. By this time the anti-aircraft had taken aim, so the planes in our group started going down right and left.

Why was that?

I didn't know at the time, but I found out later that they had borrowed a bombsight from a neighboring airfield for the bomber. I don't remember whether it was a bombsight or the whole plane. Anyway, the switches on this new equipment turned on a different way. I think the bombardier tried to drop the bombs, but the switches didn't work. So the mission was a real disaster.

Those of us still left started to go around a second time. By this time, there weren't many planes left to shoot at—they'd shot down a lot of us. So, on that run, our plane was disabled. They shot us down. Suddenly, we were in a spin. We were flying at the time at about 26,000 feet in a B-17. We were racing toward the ground. Of course, I was in the nose. The Plexiglas had blown out and the wind was streaming in. I had not attached my chute to the harness, because it was bulky in front and interfered while working at the desk or performing navigation duties. I had just laid the chute in the corner. Clearly, that was very foolish, but that's what I'd done. When we started down, I had frantically looked around, and fortunately there was my chute. I snapped it on. Though we never heard any order from the pilot to jump, it was obvious we were going down, down. The bombardier stood at the escape hatch right behind the navigator's position. He seemed petrified. I think he didn't know if he wanted to jump. Finally, I just jumped out. I had never had any training in parachuting, but they had told us that you should make a free fall so you're close to the ground before your chute opens, so as to minimize being observed by the enemy. So I held off a long time (I thought), then opened the chute. There I was dangling many thousands of feet above earth.

How many guys got out of the plane?

I saw two other parachutes and that's all. Then I saw the plane hit the ground and burst into flame. I don't know why the others didn't get out. When I looked down, I could see the Cologne cathedral. We were supposed to bomb this airfield out in the country, so I was falling in farm country. Despite the sunshine, there was snow on the ground. Then I saw several German soldiers on horseback waiting for me. When I came down, I was the only one. (I found out later there was only one other survivor, the pilot, Art Leuthesser.)

When I landed, two German soldiers picked me up and took me to a farmhouse nearby. They kept me there a couple of days. I think they were waiting to gather up other prisoners. Finally, they corralled two others. The soldiers were not mean or unpleasant. They sat me down at the kitchen table. I tried to calm down. They gave me some ersatz coffee, made of oats or rye, and some sour black bread.

A few days later, we all went to the road and started to hitchhike. German transportation was in terrible shape at this time. A big truck came by and picked us up and took us down the road to Bonn. We got out of the truck and started walking through the town—the two guards and the three prisoners. We walked up the hill and finally got to the place used for interrogation. The soldiers realized they didn't want me. Since I was an officer, I was to go to Frankfurt. The guards and I walked back down the hill, through town, and across the Rhine River to a railroad station in another town. We waited a long time, and finally the train came. The train was very crowded. We got off just north of Frankfurt am Main. At that point we met some other American fliers who'd been brought in from other places, and we all went down to interrogation. Probably, I spent a week there. That was one of the low points. We were in solitary confinement in little dark cells—a bed, but no mattress, just straw. They'd bring food but shove it under the door. It was eerie in there, especially when you'd hear air raid sirens at night.

Occasionally, the guard would call your name and they'd take you down for interrogation. I remember going to be interviewed by a very suave German officer. He astounded me in that he knew so much about me. He knew where I was from in the United States and where I did all my training. He knew where I was stationed, what squadron I was in, and who the leader and different officers were in the squadron. I supposed the Germans got all this news from the newspapers. Anyway, I remember he offered me a cigarette to warm me up a little—to entice me to talk more. Of course, I didn't have much information. I was only a second lieutenant and not in the chain of command, so what he learned from me was not much. Since I didn't smoke, a cigarette didn't lure me. So then he decided on another tactic. He sat there and pulled out an apple and started to slowly peel it. He offered me a piece. I was hungry, so I took a slice of apple.

Later, after release from interrogation, all of us who'd been interrogated were put in a big room. After a day or so, we were put in boxcars to be sent up to Barth on the Baltic, where there was a prison camp for American airmen. We wended our way slowly through Germany. I remember stopping at Halle one night. Halle was a place we'd bombed many times. Several Red Cross women met us. The Red Cross gave us some thick soup that tasted great. We finally got to Berlin. This was just about the time the Russians were pushing hard, so the Germans stopped the train in the Berlin marshalling yards. We knew their marshalling yards to be a prime target, because we'd bombed them many times. At that point, I think the Germans didn't know quite what to do. I think they felt too harassed to take us to our destination. So we just sat there for three or four days and nights in the boxcar. I was certain we'd be bombed by our own planes. From what we could see of Berlin, it was a mess. Finally, they took us twenty-five miles south of Berlin. That's where we ended up in prison camp at Luckenwalde—a large camp of about fifteen thousand prisoners. They had it divided by barbed wire. We were in a section with the Polish prisoners and all the English-speaking people—English, South Africans, New Zealanders, Canadians, Australians, and Americans. There were a lot of Russian prisoners, whom the Germans made do all the dirty work. Also, I found out there were people (the Poles), who'd been there for six years. Though luckily I would only be there for four months.

They would bring big tubs of soup, which was frequently what I called "grass soup." You could hardly stand to eat it. Other times they'd bring pea soup, and each pea would have a bug in it. Still, it got so you didn't pay much attention to that. Occasionally, they'd give us little potatoes. We'd cook them in the little coke-burning stoves and save them until the right time to savor them in the evening. I'd always been really thin and hadn't had much of an appetite. This was the time when I learned to really have an appetite. I've been a pretty good eater ever since.

Did you have frostbite from your travels?

No, I didn't, though it was in January. I remember this one German officer who supervised roll call. He wore a long blue-and-white leather coat. Of course, we were pretty tattered. As always when I got in the plane to fly a mission, I put on my electric-heated suit. I had taken my shoes off and put on heated, felt slippers. It was not till long after I got to the prison camp in Luckenwalde that I finally got shoes. I do remember thinking of the sharp contrast between us and the natty German officer.

Could you see anything going on outside the prison?

I remember the first night after I got to Luckenwalde, the British staged a gigantic raid on Berlin. We all rushed outside to watch. It was spectacular. The planes dropped bombs and flares. As I said, Berlin was just twenty-five miles away, so we got a pretty good view of things. We cheered. We felt certain we were going to win the war, but still felt pretty downtrodden in prison.

The conditions in the prison suffered. These were old buildings, with fleas and all kinds of vermin. I remember being concerned by the place we had to go to the toilet. It looked like a cesspool of disease; however, a doctor among the prisoners told us there wasn't anything much to worry about.

Finally, we began to hear fighting very close to us, all around us. Some of the guards did smuggle in newspapers, so we had some idea sometimes of what was going on outside. When President Roosevelt died, we were shown a Berlin newspaper with large front page headlines that said, "The greatest war criminal of all is dead." But one morning, we woke up and, to our surprise, all the Germans had disappeared. We were there all by ourselves, right in the middle of the fighting. Some of the prisoners took off, but most of us thought it too dangerous, so we stayed where we were. Then after a few days, the Russian troops came in. As I say, there were Russian prisoners there, and I think the troops regarded them as traitors. They swept the Russians up in their ranks and went on to the fight for Berlin. I'm sure an awful number of them were killed. I think the Russians felt that if you didn't fight to the death, you were a traitor.

So there we were. The Russians brought in a cow or two and slaughtered it. I remember eating meat with hair on it. It was pretty rough being left, but we were on the east side of the Elbe River. The Americans had agreed they weren't going east of the Elbe. The Russians wouldn't let the Americans come get us. Then the Russians started to interrogate us. And I said, "Oh boy, now I'm going to be a prisoner of the Russians." You know, I'm convinced those stories about prisoners being carted off, disappearing into Russia, are true. I think that happened.

When did the Americans come in?

After about three weeks, the Americans succeeded in making an entrance to the camp. They brought several trucks, but the Russians wouldn't let them drive into the camp. They made them park about two miles away. So now we have the Americans arguing with the Russians all day long. I watched them argue from a distance.

Did it seem like negotiation, or foot stomping?

I wasn't too close to it, but I think it was mostly negotiations. At times though, I could tell the parties were getting upset. I think the Americans couldn't understand why they wouldn't let us go. Finally, at the end of the day, they apparently agreed to let us go, so we walked the two miles to the trucks. We traveled back across the Elbe River and drove to Magdeburg, Germany. There we climbed in planes and flew at treetop level to Nancy. Next we went to Épinal. Then we had another interrogation—this time from the Americans. We got deloused there and received clean clothes. They sent us to Camp Lucky Strike near Le Havre. We waited for about a week till we could get a ship, and we went to Southampton and then to New York.

Do you remember any individual fliers?

The pilot of the crew I was assigned to was Will Ten Eyck, a New Yorker.

He'd already flown a tour of duty and was now starting a second tour. He was really different from me. He was brusque, and very self-confident, and I don't think he liked me and I don't think I liked him. But after we got to England, we recognized the good qualities in each other and became closer. After just a few missions, he was taken from our crew and made a lead pilot. He was killed in a raid on Berlin some time after I had been shot down.

As someone interested in music and art, how'd you feel about being over there bombing?

I remember one bombing mission to Leipzig. For some reason, maybe weather, they decided not to bomb the primary target, so we looked around for another target. We ended up dropping bombs on Zwickau. It is right on the border of Czechoslovakia and Germany. I knew this was the birthplace of Robert Schumann, the great German composer. I had always admired his music so much and was shocked to think that we were bombing his birthplace.

Did it take awhile to get over it?

I think I sort of brooded about it, but of course there was nothing I could do. You know, I didn't think I was a superb navigator. I had some problems in training, especially with celestial navigation. It took so long to sight. I remember one night training flight (practicing celestial navigation) when the pilot asked me if we were near Sioux City. I was just completely lost. I looked down and said, "There it is." It was just some little town—it wasn't Sioux City, at all. However, when we got to England and were able to use that marvelous device, the "G" Box, I quickly gained a lot more confidence in my ability to pinpoint our location.

Hugh Boyd

HUGH BOYD

Hump Adventures

"I think I started to bail out over the Hump three times," Hugh Boyd says, stretching back in his large rocker. "I was never crazy about jumpin' in those mountains. You'd run a mountaintop up your ass."

Hugh Boyd flew the Himalayas in the China-Burma-India Theater in World War II. He completed ninety-seven missions over some of the most fearsome and deadly terrain known in the history of flight. Boyd adds, "Those ninety-seven don't include the sixteen 'Dear John' missions I flew—that I didn't record."

Boyd became interested in flying in Eastern Washington, when he watched his father and a pilot friend, Nick Mamer, fly about putting out grain fires. Mamer took an interest in Hugh and took him up in the plane several times. By the age of twelve, he had sparked a serious interest in flight. Still, when war came, Hugh, a ski racer who'd skied at Nationals three years, opted to sign up for the military as one of the ski troops. Then, with the announcement of the need for more pilots, Hugh reversed his direction and went to training in Cedar City, Utah.

Boyd is an open and candid person, a man of boldness and of depth. His wife, Bettylee, whose father was an early pioneer flier, serves up iced tea. Hugh rubs his hands together, and we are off on a great adventure.

What was it like flying the Hump?

It's a lot of varied experiences. You take off out of Chabua, India, in the middle of a tea plantation. It would be 130 degrees and ninety-eight percent humidity, no shade, and climb out to fifteen thousand feet, put your wooly suits on, and turn south and reach for Myitkyina, Burma. And, if we didn't land at Myitkyiná, we'd climb on out to the Charlie Course fifteen minutes out of Yenangyaung, where there's a mountain called Old Ta-li: "The 1405 you cannot force and you'll bust your ass on the Charlie Course."

Where did that come from?

Oh, that came from a little rhyme we'd sing when we were flying the Charlie Course over around Yunnan, which was Chiang Kai-shek's headquarters, and then we would go in and land at Kunming, unless we were being shot at. We got pinned down at Chungking once in awhile.

You got pinned down? What did that mean?

Rifle fire. You were getting shot at by the Japanese and you would land and get into those shit-kicking slit trenches that were always full of shit and everything, and stay there until the firing stopped, and then you'd get up and go someplace else.

Did you ever fear for your life down there in the trenches?

Why should you? You're dead when you started!

You experienced all kinds of natural phenomena over there—weather, monsoon rains, etc. Did you have hail?

Yes. As big as your head. I brought one airplane in and barely got it back to Chabua, India, which was my base on the plantation. The old operations officer said, 'We'll throw it off the revetment.' We 'twenty-sixed' that airplane. It wouldn't fly anymore. In fact, I was wondering how I got in there because it looked like someone had worked it over with a ballpeen hammer.

That sounds pretty bad.

Well, with the hail as big as your head, it looked all pockmarked. Sometimes two or three inches deep.

The windshield didn't break?

One time, yeah. I had a buddy that had it happen down there. He was checking out B-24s at Gaya, and he hit a buzzard. The buzzard went through the windshield, and a big sliver of glass went through and cut his jugular vein.

And killed him?

Yes.

How long did it take to fly the Hump?

The whole operation from Chabua on the Charlie Course took about eight hours and forty minutes, then we'd land and unload our cargo and take off again and come back on the Able Course, up around Mount Lichiang—that's a twenty-one-thousand foot mountain. And then we'd climb out to Fort Hertz, Burma. That's about opposite of Mount Everest, which is 29,500. One night I went into this cloud at 14,000 feet and came out at 29,500 feet on my back— went from thirty to seventy two below centigrade.

You went in at fourteen thousand feet.

Yeah. And it blew out all the oxygen tanks. It flipped me out, and I went right up the elevator in thirty seconds and came out at 29,500 feet.

The air forced you up that fast?

It was a vertical elevator inside of a cumulo-nimbus cloud and, if you go on into it, it'll take you right on up to the top. We moved to my co-pilot's and my navigator's oxygen. We were all sucking off of one mask and so I said, "Well, should we set up here and freeze to death or get the hell out of here?" So we dove down and just missed Mount Lichiang at about sixteen thousand feet, came out, and came on in. I blew an eardrum that time. We came back to Fort Hertz, and then on in to Chabua on the Able Course.

Tell me the story of how you got into the cloud.

I was climbing out of Kunming, and I got into a situation. Actually, this one Japanese plane had been bothering us. My buddy had shot one down with a .45 pistol.

Shot one down?

A Japanese fighter. He came up and tapped wings with us and my copilot shot him down—one shot of a .45 right off of the wing tip. So we were afraid some of the guys would be looking for us because we didn't have any armor. We just had a .45, that's all. The Japanese had .50s or whatever they were using that day. They could have shot us down if they wanted. But they wanted us to get our gas in and then come in to take us over, because we were flying gas and ammo and 88mm. mortar shells. So I ducked into the cumulo-nimbus cloud—I'd be going around it normally, but I was trying to evade this fighter. I ducked in there and I hit this updraft, and I went up. In thirty seconds I was on top of it at 29,500 feet.

What's the strangest thing you carried on the flights?

Madame Chiang Kai-shek's piano.

Her piano?

Yes. She wanted her piano so we got the word to fly her piano over to Yunnan. So we did. I flew celebrities like Jinx Falkenburg. Also, I flew a lot of the USO troops and most of the 88mm. mortar shells and gas. Forty-three fifty-five-gallon drums of a 130-octane gas that were leaking as we flew half the time.

Did you know of anybody that ignited it with a spark?

Well, we would go into these electric storms. One time I had a bolt of lightning come down and hit my right wingtip. It came in and fired all the cylinders in my right engine, came through and blew out my 'coffee grinder,' which was my loran radio, went out the left engine, fired all the cylinders in the left engine. It went off the left wingtip and burned a hole in solid aluminum three inches across. I had four drums leaking that time, and it didn't blow.

Did you think that maybe you had somebody on your side?

God was with me. I always had God as my first pilot, and I used to get it on the ground and say, "Okay, God, I'll park it for you."

Did you ever crash?

I started to bail twice. Once we had eleven inches of ice on the wings, and we were going into St. Elmo's fire on the props. We were ready to bail out— we were dropping 2,700 feet a minute. So the pilot—I was the co-pilot—and the loran operator bailed. The pilot took his hat off and laid it in the front seat, and he jumped out of the airplane. Just then the ice came crashing back on the tail of the airplane—off the wings. We just started melting. I had said, "Hell, I'm bailing out of here, too" just before the ice broke. When it did, I ran back and got in the left seat and flew the plane home. It took them thirty-three days to walk out.

The Chinese built the runways over there, didn't they? How did they do that?

Little buckets and shovels.

Did you see a lot of runway building going on?

Yeah. We'd fly right in, and the Chinese would try to lose their dragon. They'd get right in the middle of the way of the props and everything else, and we'd have to duck them. They figured they'd lose their dragon that way if they got in the shadow of the airplanes.

Can you explain that?

Well, the Chinese would lose their hex that might be on them. They'd lose their dragon. And a lot of them lost their *heads* while we were landing!

Did you hit any?

I suppose I did. I don't know. I didn't look back. You just have to land, get in and get it done. They wouldn't go get out of your way. They'd see you coming.

How would they do this?

They just got in the way of the prop. They couldn't see the prop because it was going fast.

What did you think when that happened?

I didn't feel very good. I got pretty sick.

Reversing this discussion, what's the thing that really stands out in your mind as your most treasured moment of your days piloting?

We got one of the spies, Henry Felton, out of China on his ass south of Chanyi. We had gone in and landed in a rice paddy. We blocked up the tail and the wheels, and we were getting ready to pull the chocks and he comes out of there at 4 o'clock on a Friday. He comes over the hill with about two Japanese divisions on his ass and dives into the airplane, and we pull the prop and get out of this rice paddy. We got him out of there. He was working for Bill Donovan of the OSS, the Office of Strategic Services, and he had a lot of information. He had been involved in infiltration.

Another time we went in there I took thirteen guys for the OSS, and they got General Wainright out of a Japanese prison camp. Wainright was the guy that McArthur left on Corrigedor. We were not even supposed to be around. We came back over the Hump at 7200 feet. I was the copilot on that. That was the lowest anybody ever came through the Hump. The CNAC or the China National Air Corps flew at 13,500 feet.

Just tilting through?

Coming through canyons and stuff.

How did it feel?

A lot of fun as long as we didn't hit anything.

What were the fliers' attitudes? Did you have to be sort of loose?

Well, everybody was in the same barrel. This one night we came in over Kunming and we were stacked up to thirty thousand feet—and this major, operating in the tower, flipped out and said, "Everybody let down five hundred feet a minute." He didn't mean that, but he said it. So I ducked out of there and headed for Chanyi. It was too much. Those C-109s,—which we called "C-1-0 Booms," were crashing into each other all over the place and blowing in the air and all kinds of shit like that. I went over to Chanyi, circled, then came back and landed.

Your relationship with the Chinese was good.

We treated them like brothers. But the grim humor of the thing was that line that went, "You kill a million Chinese that day and wipe out a hundred thousand Japanese, and pretty soon there are no Chinese."

The point to this?

There were more Chinese than there were Japanese. But we did kill them—

accidentally—and the Japanese killed them.

Did you see any real barbarisms?

I flew the Chins in one night. We had about two platoons of Japanese jungle fighters that came in to wipe out this one village. A guy named Sanders was the one that directed Chin activities. When we flew them in they decapitated two complete platoons of Japanese imperial jungle fighters without a sound.

Is that right? Who are the Chins?

That's a native of Burma. All they wore were loincloths, and they just lived in the jungle. They were fearsome warriors. We had a Cherokee who wove a beaded loincloth with a peacock on it. The peacock was their god. And we gave the Chins beaded peacock loincloths. That was their Congressional Medal of Honor.

How did they respond to that?

They loved it. Very great people. They were a very quiet people. They were just great, that's all. They moved through the jungle at night, no sounds, no nothing.

What kind of fighters were the Japanese?

Oh, some of them were pretty good. Some were mean and cruel. If we bailed out over the Irrawaddy River and, if we tried to float down to the bay, they tried to pick you off along the river.

Shot at our pilots as they were floating?

Yeah, or catch you, torture you or whatever. Some would cut your balls off, disembowel you, whatever.

Did that happen to anybody you knew?

Yeah. Because of these dangers, our fliers had something like six hundred miles of mountain range to cover instead of going down the rivers. You had to go up and over and up and over these different mountain ranges and walk out through the jungles to miss the Japanese because they controlled the rivers.

What did you think when you saw a Zero? Did you head for the clouds?

As I said, they would come up and tip wings with us. They wanted us to bring our gas in to our bases. They had those two or three divisions that would come in and take over Kweilin or Luchuan. So we had to blow up those gas dumps so they wouldn't get them. We were flying gas into Guiyang right in the curve of a river. We had to land with loads and everything, and

226

brake the tail wheel lock before we went over the cliff at the end of the runway. We had a four-thousand-foot runway and would stand on the brakes at the end of it, and ground-loop the airplane to keep from going off the end of the cliff—fly over Japanese lines—the Japanese were all around us.

That time when the Japanese pulled up beside you, did they hit the wing hard?

They just banged the shit out of it. My co-pilot's brother had been disemboweled on the deck of a Japanese carrier, so he had a lot of hate for the Japanese. He shot this one pilot right off our wingtip with one bullet—right through the side of his canopy.

You actually saw him go down?

Yeah.

How did he know his brother had met that fate?

He got reports from his mother and the navy.

You didn't have icing boots on the plane, did you?

No. The reason was the laminar flow of the wing. When we had the icing boot, it would break the ice out but leave rugged edges on the wings. So, the laminar flow wouldn't flow air over it very well—it just burbled—so we took the icing boots off and, when the ice stopped at about eleven inches of ice, at least the laminar flow of aerodynamic lift would go over the wings. Of course, that would mean 8.33 additional pounds per gallon of water and ice. The weight of the wing would bring the airplane down. Then, when we hit the warmer air, the ice would come off just like that. That time my pilot and radio operator bailed out and I stayed, the ice hit the tail of the airplane, the props threw the ice, and the airplane started flying again. But that had a better chance of happening than when you broke the ice off with icing boots.

What was the key to survival, if you crashed in the jungle?

Salt. We used to carry salt and morphine—in case you broke a leg. *Salt* was the thing that people in the jungle didn't have. It was like gold. You could trade salt better than you could morphine. Down there you would run into places where there were huge blocks of drugs—cocaine and stuff. The jungle people would try to trade you: they would rather have salt than cocaine because it made their food taste good. You'd get pretty dried out in the 130-degree heat, and the salt carried fluid in their bodies.

Did you guys ever have any fun over there?

A little. When we were going on a fireball run down through South America, we'd stop at Ascension Island; the British had Ascension Island. There was a mountain that had a runway cut in the top of it. We landed there one time for gas and our food hadn't gotten there yet, but the British had the radio on top of Ascension Island, up on the peak. They had all kinds of food. Their ship had just got there, but they wouldn't give us any. So we went down on this bay, which is right on the final approach as you come into the island. It's a nesting ground for sea turtles. We got a sea turtle, a five-or six-foot sea turtle, flipped him over, and took our bayonets out and cut steaks out of him. We barbecued him on the beach. The British charged us $3,800 for that sea turtle.

We went in to one British base one night and got half-snockered, went in and stole two six-by-six's full of cement—forty-pound sacks. They had just gotten a load of cement in and had built some bases with it. We had a contractor, I mean a good contractor, who was a pilot with us. We got an idea and developed plans for a ninety-foot Olympic swimming pool. Our contractor built it out of their cement. It had eight lanes for racing, and all that good stuff. We built it right between the bashas, number one and number two bashas, the thatched huts where we lived. Nurses from the 803 Aero-Vac Squadron and the 410 Field Hospital at Lido came over and we partied, had musicals. Ziggy Elman played trumpet, and on Saturday afternoon we had a musical right alongside the swimming pool.

When they evacuated Kweilin and Luchuan, I ended up getting the flight surgeons' Servel-Electrolux refrigerator as they were blowing the gas and stuff up. So I flew it back, and we had cold beer for the rest of the war. We were the only outfit that had cold beer. The nurses sure loved that cold beer. That thing was full of beer all the time.

You made a big hit?

Oh yeah. Major Whitenacks was the point man, and he was the last guy out of Chabua. We made him promise to blow the swimming pool up. We built a little box in the bottom of the swimming pool—when we built it. So they put a bomb in there and, when we left, he blew the swimming pool up so the British wouldn't get it.

Was there a rivalry with the British?

I don't know. They had their way of doing things, and we had ours. We called them a bunch of chirpers, just like the colonials on the plantation. They'd come over from England to make their pile and get snockered on rum, but they'd never go back because they'd stay and just drink rum or tea and gin—Hayward's Gin. They were plum red from drinking all the time. Tea at four every day. You'd get tired of listening to them. They were always chirping about merry old England. I guess they got tired of hearing us, too.

Did humor help to sustain you over there?

If you didn't have humor, you were dead.

What was the first flight like that you took?

I was flying out of Gaya, India, checking out. I'd been a single-engine fighter pilot up to then. I checked out at Reno on twin engines, but I had to go and check out on C-46s to become a first pilot, then as a flying copilot.

Anything you remember about it?

Just go out and load up with gas and start putting your suits on and climbing up and getting into humidity country, climb on out and you are dripping wet. You start out in your jock strap, let the sweat run down the crack of your ass.

Those were normal conditions?

That was every day. You'd climb up out and pretty soon you'd be thirty or forty degrees below.

So did you change outfits?

No, we'd just change clothes as we were getting out of there. When you got to seventy-two below zero centigrade, the Gantrol heaters would go out because they didn't have enough oxygen. So, at fifteen thousand feet you'd start pulling out your suits. First we had bunny suits of sheepskin, then later we got electric suits. The wires in the electric suits would break and you would half-freeze and half-burn up because the rheostats would kick up for half the suit that didn't work.

We'd be listening to all these different radios. I was a radio nut. We'd get Tokyo Rose and the BBC in London. Then there was the code machine. I could normally take about thirty-five words per minute on these code machines. I'd come back and say, "We got bombed, and we got the shit kicked out of us here, etc." The guys would say, "How did you know?" "I listened to the radio." They'd say, "We listened to the radio, too, and we didn't know that." I found you could concentrate yourself warm. When you are freezing your balls off, the subconscious takes over, and what I found out was I was reading code machines at three thousand words per minute in my subconscious mind. That's how hard I could concentrate.

I went to the lama's for eight days, and it seems my subconscious took over. I could walk across the world in my mind when I graduated from the lama's meditation bit. I was able to clearly move without a gap from my conscious to my subconscious: without a break. I remembered the code that was in the subconscious. I could concentrate so well, that it scared the shit out of me. So I left it alone.

You left it alone?

Like a cow peeing on a flat rock.

Was there anything that really bugged you about the planes?

When the props would run away. The Curtiss electric props. The fuses would blow on the Curtiss electric props and run away, and damn near shake the engines out of the mounts. When that happened, you'd get up to about 2,800 or 3,400 rpms. And when that happened, they wouldn't have any bite. No bite to the air. They'd go flat. You'd have to chop that engine and fly on just one engine.

The days of the props.

Yes. I was flying a BT-13 out of Sacramento, just climbing out, when the prop came off. It went zinging off into the sky. I was only 700 feet up so I landed it on a country road. This old farmer's wife let me use the phone, and I called McClellan Air Base. This weathered sergeant came out to get me. When I got back to the base, I got a call and this guy started chewin' my ass out for about an hour. He said, "How come you didn't bail out?" I said, "I was only seven hundred feet off the ground." He said, "You might not have made it." I said, "Well, I wanted to save the airplane." He said, "We got more airplanes than we've got pilots. We've got two million bucks in you," he told me. Then he said, "You could fly a barn door if you had to." Finally, he closed the conversation with "next time bail out." I asked the sergeant who and the hell was that? He said, "That was Hap Arnold."

Did you ever fly over the Burma Road?

Oh, yeah. I used to take General Palmer there. There's the Burma Road and the Lido Road. The Burma Road went through Myitkyina, Burma, Chuxiong, and into Kunming. The Fifth and the Ninth fighter outfits out of Italy came in one time. They were hot pilots. They had P-47s and P-25s. They were to bomb Chuxiong, which was loaded—it was a Japanese base—but they hadn't flown in jungles before, and they mixed up the navigation. So they bombed Baoshan, which is where the Chinese First Division had 125,000 women and children. They completely annihilated the Chinese division's families. So the Chinese First Division revolted and took over the Burma Road and closed it off and robbed all trains and all the ambulances and took all the morphine. They shut the Burma Road down on the Allies because the bomber pilots out of Italy didn't know their ass from third base about flying in the jungle. So we had to build another road, the Ledo Road, which came out of Ledo and out of Chabua, in the Assam Valley. As it was being carved out through the jungle, the jungle would almost take it over in a week. It would start growing back over, so I had to take two generals that built the road, General Tunner and

General Miller, and fly them over the road. We'd go hedgehopping through the Himalayas, so that they could tell which parts of the road needed fixing, and what had gotten washed out by the monsoon.

How low did you fly?

Pretty low. Five hundred feet sometimes. Being an old fighter pilot . . . we used to do that for fun.

It was easy to get trapped over there.

Yes. Once we landed in Zhenxiong. We landed there, and pretty soon the Japanese started moving in on us. We got pinned down for three days in a graveyard and had our noses in the slit trenches. Our saying was, "When you dip your nose in shit, keep your mouth shut." That experience was hairy. Bullets flying all over the place, hitting stones and the wooden grave markers.

How did you get out?

Some fighters out of Kunming came in, and got them off our backs.

Didn't you train with the Chinese?

Yes, at Thunderbird #1 at Phoenix, Arizona.

Any story there?

Most of them were generals and they were flying P-40s. They outranked everyone in the field. You couldn't fire them. Half of them weren't very good pilots to start with. Outside of their training, they were cracking up airplanes all over the place. They were a bunch of characters. There was one, I forget his name, he busted up about four P-40s.

How did they bust them up?

Just landing them. The P-40 had a built-in ground loop in it anyway. Unless you knew how to smooth it in, you'd ground-loop a lot. In other words, it had a narrow gear. It didn't have a broad gear like an AT-6 that even I could land on, but it had a narrow gear and you had to get it in. You could land on one wheel and drop the other down or just get her in straight. If there was a crosswind, there was a problem. You'd lose airspeed and just snap around.

Most memorable character?

There was a chief's wife. I don't know if she was the most memorable or not. But she liked me. She was a headhunter's wife out of Lolo, Tibet. We'd go in there for jungle indoctrination, through twenty miles of jungle, over the Irrawaddy.

How did you know they were headhunters?

Because they had heads sticking around on sticks.

Okay.

You know, they may have been romancin' me to get ready to use my head.

What else about the headhunter's wife?

She seemed to like me. She wove me baskets. I got some stuff down below in the basement that she made for me out of wood, and a blanket. I guess I gave my daughters the bags she knitted me.

Well, it sounds like you were between a rock and a hard place.

I think I got out of there just in time. (*laughs*)

Were you excited to go home?

Yes, absolutely. The British used quinine to prevent malaria and the only way you could get it was from the British tea planters. We'd go over to the basha around four in the afternoon and have tea and quinine. We also took atabrime as a service medicine therapy. But atabrime turned our skin yellow. As soon as it was time to go home, I quit taking atabrime because I knew my mother wouldn't have recognized me. I was completely yellow.

Marion Carl and a D-558-1 Skystreak, August 1947.

MARION CARL

The South Pacific Ace

Marion Carl was born in Hubbard, Oregon, in 1915, and attended Oregon StateUniversity. When he left Oregon State, he was a second lieutenant in the Corps of Engineers. He had taken four years of Army ROTC and aeronautical engineering, but in order to enter flight training, he had to resign his commission. In the period of a day or so, he went from second lieutenant to seaman second to private first class in the Marine Corps.

Thus by this circuitous route began one of the most remarkable flying careers in history. Joe Foss, the great Marine Ace, calls Carl "number one of all pilots ever." One has only to look at his many records and distinctions. Carl was the first Marine Corps Ace in World War II. He shot down eighteen and a half planes, the seventh most in his branch of service during that war. His records include the world altitude record of eighty-three thousand feet in a Douglas Skyrocket; he was the first Marine assigned to helicopter to hold the world's speed record at 650 miles per hour; he was the leader of the first jet aerobatic team, among others. He served in combat at Midway, Guadalcanal, and later in Korea.

Carl, who had two hours and thirty-five minutes of flight time before he soloed and distinguished himself in so many ways, retired in June 1973 as a major general. Carl is currently working on *Pushing The Envelope: The Career of Fighter Ace Pilot Marion Carl,* his biography, which promises more than a glimpse of his amazing life of flight.

You majored in mechanical engineering, aero option, in college?

It was actually the aeronautical option the last two years. There were only about four or five of us who did it. The others went to work for Boeing. I just went to flight training.

Did you feel like Odd Man Out?

No. And my engineering background didn't do me any good, particularly until I came back from my second tour during World War II and went to Flight Test in January, 1945. At the time when I was in Flight Test, I ended up being head of the carrier section eighteen months later. Flight Test was divided into subsections: carrier and noncarrier, in other words, all fighters and attack aircraft.

Your training meant somebody couldn't buffalo you?

Yes. I had about a dozen test pilots and almost that many aeronautical engineers working for me, and therefore I wasn't out in left field when it came time to review the work that these people were doing.

I took a P-80 aboard a carrier. It was the only air force airplane that ever had a hook on it. I made five landings, and it was the second time that a jet had gone on board. I was the first marine to bring one on board.

That sounds like rivalry?

They wouldn't let me be the first one because they wanted a navy plane and a navy pilot, so I ended up with my assistant taking it on board. He ended up taking a Phantom-1 on board. It was three months later that I took the P-80 aboard.

How did you feel about not being the first?

I couldn't blame them for that. Why use an air force—actually air corps— airplane to be the first jet to go aboard a carrier?

When that was over, I came back, and the project engineer who was working with me wanted me to do "rate-of-roll at five hundred indicated"— and then on down, four hundred, three hundred etc. I said, "No way. I don't think that airplane will hold together at five hundred miles per hour." I said, "I will do it at four hundred miles per hour," and I did it. That was the end of it until not long after that the airplane was transferred to another unit called Tactical Test. Only a short time after that, it was used in a demonstration.

We put on a lot of demonstrations at NATC Patuxent, because it's so close to Washington, DC, only sixty miles away. Normally, I was the senior one involved in these demonstrations, but this particular time, I was on the ground because it involved all the marine officers from the marine corps schools at Quantico as spectators. So I was on the ground, and this pilot came down across the crowd in this same plane. It was just on the edge of the Chesapeake, and he did a roll. I estimated he was doing more than five hundred miles per hour. While he was on his back, I noticed his nose was a bit low, and that he was going to have to do something radical, or he was going to hit that water. He realized it too and, instead of stopping that roll and getting his nose back up, which would mean a little bit of negative Gs, the ideal thing to do, he gave it full aileron and the whole plane came apart. It just turned into confetti, killing him instantly. That's just one of four instances in which people flying my project airplanes were killed.

That was tough on you?

That's one of the things that points out what experience will do for you. By this time, when I went to Flight Test, I'd already been out in the Pacific twice in what you might call two campaigns. The first time I was on Midway and Guadalcanal, and the next time I was squadron commander of that squadron and ended up on Vella Lavella.

Tell me about Midway.

I was in the only fighter squadron on Midway. See, my squadron, which was based on north island, had received orders to be transported to Hawaii to go to a field called "Ewa." This was before Pearl Harbor. We were to depart on the eighth of December, the day after Pearl Harbor. So we were loaded up on Saturday and as Pearl Harbor came along we shoved off on the eighth of December aboard the carrier *Saratoga*. We went directly to Hawaii where the *Saratoga* refueled. The *Saratoga* was there two days, one day longer than was necessary. We were then ordered to go to Wake Island. When we got within four hundred miles of Wake, Wake fell. All we had with us were a couple of destroyers. So we then diverted and landed on Midway, Christmas day of 1941. I was one of the few that stayed there for the next six months, until after the battle. Most of the talent was pulled out of the squadron and sent back to Hawaii to form new squadrons. In that period of time, we had four different commanding officers at the squadron.

As it turned out, I was one of the more experienced pilots. I had fourteen hundred hours by the time of the battle. However, we had kids flying there who had less than four hundred. They had come from flight training with very little operational training.

When did you get your wings?

I had gotten my wings on the first of December in '39 and gone directly to a fighter squadron up at Quantico. I was there six months and was sent back to the training command as a flight instructor, which was primary operations, where I taught aerobatics. I picked up quite a bit there. In fourteen months I think I averaged fifty or sixty hours a month of flying.

Did the young kids look up to you?

Oh, I don't know. I remember one day I took Joe Foss up for a flight—he was a student—and I had gone out and just taken a plane up by my lonesome. Once in awhile, rather than having to sit there and watch a guy fumble through the air, we'd like to take one up and fly it our own way. Now, on this particular day, I was walking up to a Stearman and Joe Foss came walking up too and asked, "Can I go along?" I said, "Sure."

When I got down, he was airsick and headed for the nearest bush to upchuck. I really wrung that airplane out.

Did you scare yourself?

Anytime I had a close call, but I forgot it overnight.

Give me a close call you had.

I had seven aircraft accidents: four of the planes were never flown again, and two of them were never seen again. I bailed out of them and they went into the water, one in the South Pacific and the other in the Chesapeake Bay. I also had three deadstick landings with jets: one at night, one in a rainstorm, and one of them, which should have been the easiest one—I broke the back of the airplane and broke my own back.

Where'd that one happen?

At Patuxent. When I got shot down in the Pacific, a Zero came up from below. I was driving back up to make another pass on the bombers and I never saw him until the next thing I knew, my plane was on fire, and I bailed out at twenty thousand feet. And in the Chesapeake incident, I was out doing some spin tests, in what's called an AF2S—the Guardian. It wasn't much of an airplane, there weren't many of them produced, but in this particular configuration it had radar on one side attached to the wing, and a fuel tank on the other. I didn't like the looks of the configuration. Also, it hadn't been tested at Grumman with that particular kind of external stores.

I had a chase plane. I also had them put a raft in my chute, the first time I'd had that done in a long, long time. The chase plane was a Beechcraft with two pilots in it. So I went out and did several spins and finally I said to the chase plane, "Well, this one's going to be a critical one." I was starting someplace between twelve to fourteen thousand feet. I said, "This time I'll leave it in for two turns before I take corrective action." When the nose came up, I knew that I had a problem. I couldn't get out of the spin. It was a spin to the left. And, on the Guardian, you have two seats, side by side, and the pilot's on the left and the radar operator's on the right. So, I tried to get out on the left side, which was the easiest normally, but the centrifugal force was so high that I couldn't make it. So I had to climb across that empty seat and go out the right side. Well, I bailed out so low that the chase plane reported that I went in with the airplane. Actually, the chute just barely opened and I went into the water. If I'd been over land, I'd have broken both legs. It just happened that there was a seaplane about to land just across the Bay at Patuxent. He aborted his landing and came across the bay and picked me out of that water. I needed that para-raft because the water was forty-six degrees.

What are your feelings about luck?

There's no doubt luck plays a certain part in it. If you run into a case of real bad luck, particularly in combat or flight test, it would have been different. I would have been one of those four that were killed, not the one that survived.

A lot of Japanese aces were at Guadalcanal. Did you notice a high skill level in those pilots?

Yes. You see, we were up against real tough odds over there. In the first place, there were days when we only had six airplanes, and yet our job was to go up and shoot down bombers, not fighters. So we always ended up in a fight in which they had the advantage. And they were top-notch pilots, because this was still the beginning of the war.

We knocked off a good many of them at Midway, when half of them had to land in the water because their carriers were no longer afloat. And, at Midway, we had some real tough competition. First, we were in those Wildcats, so the only way we could get away from a Zero that was on our tail was to dive. If we dived steep enough, they would break off. If you were in the dive and gave full aileron roll in a Wildcat—which would take it with no problem— we could outmaneuver them. The ailerons on a Zero were pretty large and, if they tried to give full aileron, they couldn't do it, they'd have to break off. But, the problem came if you didn't have altitude. Then you were in a hell of a fix. In fact, I picked off one Zero who was onto one of our guys, who was right down on the deck. The Zero was just sitting behind him, firing away at him. He would have eventually gotten him, if I hadn't been on the scene.

I had an incident only about a week after I got there at Guadalcanal. What happened was, I got my wheels down on the downwind leg. The first thing I knew, I got a bunch of tracers going past me. Here is a Zero had sitting back behind me, shooting away, and my gear is down. Well, I dived for the nearest antiaircraft battery, which is right on the edge of the field. They were right on the ball, and opened up. Meantime, I'm cranking up those wheels; twenty-eight turns of the crank to get them up. At that time, the Zero breaks off and heads for the open water—he was about a mile from there—and I take off after him with no hope of catching him. But he decides to turn around and make a fight out of it, and we meet head-on, just off the beach. He decides he doesn't like that head-on stuff, so he pulls up real steep. He would normally have passed overhead, but I pulled straight up and I got a ninety-degree deflection shot and blew him up right over the beach. That night one of the marines brought the oxygen bottle to me that was recovered. It had floated ashore.

What did you feel when you held that oxygen bottle?

Well, what I felt was pretty good at taking advantage of a guy's stupidity. If he'd have pulled up sooner, he'd have gotten away with it.

What were the most planes you shot down in a given flight?

I think the most I ever shot down in any one flight would probably have been two bombers and one Zero. I would only attack the bombers with one type of attack. See, I was normally always the flight leader. When we left Hawaii to end up on Guadalcanal, the commanding officer was John Smith. They had an executive officer named Morrell. It happened shortly after arrival that Smith and Morrell made major, and I was a captain. I had made captain just before the Battle of Midway. But I was a fairly junior captain, and I was number three in the squadron.

Well, Morrell got shot up and was evacuated. However, he did survive, so that put me at number two. It wasn't long after that that we started trading off as flight leaders. I was the leading ace in the squadron until I got shot down. I was always ahead of Smith, so we would usually take turns as flight leader, we had so few airplanes. We went in there with nineteen and it wasn't long before we had only six in commission.

So we'd trade flights, and so would the other officers, because we had twice as many officers as we had airplanes. So one flight I'd be the flight leader, and Smith would be the flight leader the next time. Well, I got shot down and was gone for five days before I got back. So, Smith was ahead of me by that time. He'd had some real good hunting while I was gone. He was now ahead of me by about three airplanes, and I never did catch up with him.

How intense was that rivalry?

Well, you don't really think of it as a rivalry. Each time you got out there, you did the best you could. If you try to get too eager and too aggressive at the wrong time, you get shot down. That's how we lost a lot of good pilots. You've got to use discretion and common sense or you're not going to live very long.

Any examples of that?

Yes, a fellow by the name of Joe Bauer. Joe Bauer was in the first fighter squadron that I went into Quantico with. He was a captain, and I was a green second lieutenant. And I promptly got on the wrong side of him. Most of it was my fault.

What happened?

I was in the squadron for six months and went back to the Training Command. When I came out of the Training Command, I joined a fighter squadron at North Island. When I did, guess who was the operations officer? Joe Bauer.

Joe Bauer was a very fine officer and a very fine pilot, and had the best reputation of anyone in the whole Marine Corps as far as I can find out. About two or three weeks after we got there, Joe says, "Okay, let's go out for a dogfight." We were flying Brewsters at the time. So, when I got into that cockpit, I cinched my shoulder straps as tight as I could, because I realized I was in for a fight. I found out I should have tightened them even tighter, because when the fight was over, I had two raw spots on my back when we came back in. It turned out I had fought him to a draw. From that time on, I didn't have any problem with Joe Bauer.

But, while we were there at Guadalcanal, Joe Bauer had a squadron. He was a lieutenant colonel, and I was a captain. He had his squadron down at Éfaté, and he came up and was real eager to get into a fight. He went to Smith and he said, "How about letting me fly with you today?" Smith said, "Well, you're going to have to talk with Marion Carl. He's the flight leader today." So here a lieutenant colonel comes and asks me for permission to fly with me. I said, "Joe, I'll be happy to have you. How about taking the second section?"

So we take off. We had a warning that the bombers are coming in. So we started climbing, and we ended up at about thirty thousand feet, which was about as high as we could get. Now we're sitting up there, waiting for something to happen. This was one of the very few times we had an altitude advantage. Then, we get word that the bombers had turned around and gone back. Well, normally, the fighters stay with the bombers; that's their job, to stay with the bombers. In this case the fighters decided to stay and came on in to Guadalcanal.

I'm just about ready to call everything off and get back to the field, when I see nine Zeroes down below me at about ten thousand feet. Normally, I wouldn't have said anything, but since I had a lieutenant colonel back there, I said, "Joe, we've got nine bandits below us." I think "bandits" was the code word we used. Anyway, no answer. I knew Joe well enough to know that he had problems with his radio, so I waited a couple of more seconds. I said, "Here we go," and we went down. When we got down there, there were eighteen Zeroes there!" The nine that I didn't see were under the cloud cover, so we jumped nine and it turned into a real fine brawl. Of course, I got one of them because I was the lead, and was on my second one when he ducked down under me. I had the trigger down on negative Gs, and I jammed all six of my guns. Well, by the time I got the guns unjammed to get back into the fight, the fight was over. So we had to go back to the field, and I noticed Joe was stepping pretty high.

I said, "Joe, how many did you get?" He said, "Four." Frazier, who was the top ace beside me, was shot down, bailed out and recovered. Frazier said a guy made a strafing run on him while he was in his chute. He only made one pass. And, of course, here's a lieutenant colonel on the first flight, and he's got four airplanes. I wasn't about to argue with a lieutenant colonel, so that was it.

The situation kind of bugged me over the years because I was not quite convinced that Joe Bauer, in the excitement of his first flight, got all the airplanes he thought he got, and that wasn't unusual. However, only several months ago I got confirmation of what he did. Fellow by the name of John Lundstrom is a Japanese history buff. He's got it all down on the computer, and he works for the Aviation Museum in Milwaukee, Wisconsin. He was down at Nimitz Museum last month when I was down there. I had talked to him on the phone prior to this and had asked him if he knew how many aircraft the Japanese had lost on this particular day. He said, "Yes," he had it all computerized. He checked and said, "They lost nine." I said, "We claimed nine." He said, "That's right." So Joe Bauer did get four airplanes.

I had already left Guadalcanal when Joe Bauer brought his squadron up, and he was pulled out of the squadron and made what was called "Strike Operations Officer." In other words, he was in charge of controlling all of the fighters and dive-bombers taking off as well as setting up the missions. So the thing was a lot better organized than when we were there.

He wasn't supposed to be flying anymore combat, but he went out on this particular day, and he got into the action. There were a lot of Jap transport ships that had come in with some air cover that were landing more troops on Guadalcanal. I don't know the details, but he got involved. Joe Foss was involved in this also. Anyway, Joe Bauer was strafing ships, and he got shot down. Whether it was by ships or another aircraft was never known. He got out of his airplane okay and was in the water. Joe Foss came over and saw him, and Bauer signalled him to go back to the field, because it was getting dark. They promptly launched Dumbo to go out and pick up Bauer, but once they got out there, they couldn't find him. That was that. To this day, they don't know what happened to him.

Did you lose a lot of friends in the war? And was the first one the hardest?

Well, the death that kind of hit me harder than any was a second lieutenant we had at Midway, named Corry. His home was in Santa Ana, California. I didn't know him that well, but he was one of those guys that you just naturally liked. He was a fine pilot. I took him up in dogfights to teach him what I knew on the subject. He was green at first, but it turned out he knew how to fly an airplane. He gave me a good, honest fight. Corry was one of three of us who went on and joined the squadron that went to Guadalcanal. The names of the three have stuck in my mind. We were in the 221, then came back to Hawaii to join 223. The names were Corry, Canfield, and Carl. Corry and Canfield were lieutenants; I was a captain. Anyway, we'd been out at Guadalcanal for just a few days, and Corry didn't return from a fight. We don't know what happened to him.

That impacted strongly on you?

It was one of those things I figured would happen to some guy I didn't like so well. At Midway, we had twent-five planes take off and only ten got back. Corry was in that fracas. In fact, of the twenty-five airplanes, six of them were Wildcats. I was in a Wildcat.

Did that have anything to do with the aircraft?

It's just the way the ball bounced as far as I'm concerned. If I would have had my choice, I'd have flown a Brewster because I had had only twelve hours in a Wildcat and I had over two hundred in a Brewster. Wildcats showed up just a few days before the battle.

Did you see any big Japanese ships go down?

No, we didn't get out that far. We only got out about thirty miles when we ran into incoming Japanese. There were three of us together. Here's another screw-up. For one thing, we had a bunch of fresh-caught lieutenants in the squadron, and the flight commanders and executive officers had only been in the squadron for less than a month. When we got into the scramble, we knew we were going to get hit, but we didn't know exactly when or from what direction. When we were on the scramble, there were seven Wildcats, but one of them was out of commission, so there were six. Captain Carey was a division leader. I had a section and a guy by the name of McCarthy had the third section, Corry was his wingman. Also, in that division, Carey was the division leader; I was a section leader, and Canfield was my wingman. Corry was McCarthy's wingman. We had a sixth one whose name escapes me. He was from Santa Ana, too.

McCarthy and Corry were up on patrol at the time the rest of us were scrambled. Just the two of them. McCarthy was shot down and never seen again. Corry survived. The other guy on the scramble—the one whose name I've forgotten—got screwed up and joined the Brewsters instead. That left only three of us. They sent the Wildcats out first because in Operations they didn't know that we had only three airplanes. Secondly, they thought the Wildcat was the best airplane, so they sent them out for what we might call the point. We had only three airplanes and, since radio silence was in effect, we couldn't tell them differently.

When we ran into the Japanese, we were at fourteen thousand feet—incoming flight was at twelve thousand feet. There were 3 of us and 107 of them, which included something like 25 or 30 Zeroes. You can imagine what happened. We were two thousand feet above the dive-bombers. We made an overhead, and I put Canfield up on Carey's wing and I was flying what you call "tail-end Charlie"—one plane in a separate section. Carey and Canfield then made the mistake of pulling out. They made an overhead and pulled out below the dive-bombers, heading the same way the dive-bombers were going. Then, just as I rolled into the attack, I saw all these Zeroes coming down. The air was full of them.

After completing my attack, I rolled out at 180 degrees and pulled out going away from the dive-bombers. The Zeroes didn't follow. It was intuition on my part because I figured it was the fighter's job to cover the dive-bombers, and they weren't about to follow me going the wrong direction, and they didn't. Carey and Canfield really got shot up. Canfield wasn't wounded, but Carey took a bullet through his knee, and both of the airplanes were wrecks when they got them on the field—they never flew them again. Carey, Canfield, and myself are still alive and well.

I got back and ran into two more fighters that were by themselves. The first one I should have had, but he was pumping me full of holes and I dove into the nearest cloud. When I hit the cloud, I threw it into a skid and cut the gun, and when he came out, he was ahead of me and below me. I pushed over and pulled the trigger at the same time, but my guns jammed. That was the first time I did that. I then went back to the field and watched what was going on, all by my lonesome. When everything had left except for three Zeroes, I clipped on the tail end of one and I shot him down just off the reef.

You got eighteen planes, overall. Is there one in particular that you remember more than others?

That one I told you about, the one who turned around and came back. A couple of thousand people saw that. I didn't have any trouble confirming that one!

You've held a lot of records. Is there a favorite?

Here's where experience comes in. For the rank, I had more time than any combat pilot, more flight time than anybody else. In the Marine Corps, about the only guy that could have competed with me was Joe Bauer, and he's dead. And, of course, Pappy Boyington had been eliminated, because he retired. Boyington was a good, aggressive fighter pilot, but I don't believe he shot down all the planes he claimed. My investigations into his record reveal that all of his record is suspect. So much depended on the claims, on the individual's truthfulness. He claimed three on the day that he and I traded fights down at Vella Lavella. Bruce Mathews, whom I had lunch with in Hawaii just last week, claimed one. I believe Bruce. The Japanese records indicated that on that particular day, the Japanese only lost two airplanes. Boyington claimed he shot down three of them all by himself. He was the tactical leader that day of forty-eight fighters, so you can figure that one out for yourself.

He narrowly beat out Joe Foss as leading ace.

By two airplanes. This shows up in my book in greater detail.

What about the world altitude record?

I was no longer in Flight Test when that happened. I had been out of it for about a year. The navy decided to go for full-pressure suits. The Air Force didn't have full-pressure suits, they were using partial pressure. I had a suit that was built to fit me. It was built by a company in Worcester, Massachusetts. The suit was tested in a pressure chamber up at Johnsville; it would only fit me. The Bureau of Aeronautics at that time was headed up by Rear Admiral Apollo Soucek. Soucek, at one time, held two world altitude records; one in a seaplane. The first one was about thirty-six thousand feet; the second one was about forty-three thousand feet. He was a real gentleman. Everybody that knew him well would admit that. Anyway, I was over at Quantico, Virginia, when I get a call from him to come in. He wanted me to test this suit in an actual flight, in a rocket-powered aircraft. I said, "Sure." I went back out to Edwards Air Force Base.

On my first flight I was dropped at thirty-three thousand feet, as I remember it. Normally, it was some place around thirty to thirty-three thousand. Then I had three minutes of fuel left at full power. You had four burners back there, and you lit them when you got clear of the other ship. Then you start heading up.

The first flight, I was a little too steep. Since you only have three minutes of fuel and you're moving so fast, if you make one mistake, you don't have any time to rectify it. You've simply got to be right on the flight profile set up by the aeronautical engineers.

I wasn't sent out there to set a new record. I was sent out there to test that pressure suit. The fact that I was going for a record was my own idea. I came up with that after I got out there. I didn't consult anybody. I just told the NACA group that, "Hell, I'll go as high as I can." But I did keep it to myself that I was going for a record. Anyway, on the third flight, I was right on profile and I knew it. I also knew that Bridgeman, who had the record of seventy-nine thousand feet, had told me that as soon as he ran out of fuel, he shoved the nose over. I didn't do that. I set up what I called a trajectory—a no-G trajectory in which I wasn't making any negative Gs or positive Gs. In other words, I was just doing it by the feel—by the seat of my pants, you might say.

When I went over the top, I was below stall-speed. If you don't have any lift on the wings, you're not going to stall. In other words, I was set up in the trajectory of a missile. My only concern was, when I headed over the top and came back down, would I establish control fast enough without the aircraft tumbling or something like that. But that never happened. So I came back down and, not having any fuel, I made a dead-stick landing on Edwards

Air Force Base. I gained four thousand feet over Bridgeman.

That was 83,235 feet.

In the Douglas Skyrocket.

Then you did a world speed record.

That was in 1947. Here again, a little experience helped. At this time I was head of the carrier section. I thought I was going to be the only one on this project. But, just before leaving, I was told that Turner Caldwell was going to be on the project also. I said, "What's he doing on this project? He's never even flown a jet before." Caldwell was chief of the fighter section in the Bureau of Aeronautics. He was senior to me, and there wasn't much I could do about it. I wouldn't say that Turner Caldwell isn't a good pilot; he is. He's a hell of a nice guy. I got to thinking about it. If I was in his position, I'd probably try to do the same thing.

So we got out there. This was August when normally the temperature was up there in the hundreds, but we had a cold spell. The next day, we knew the airplane was going to be ready. Now, who was going to fly it? Meantime, Caldwell is checked out in a P-80; I think he'd flown it three times. It was probably the only background and experience he had. On the other hand, I probably had more jet time at that time than anyone else in the navy or marine corps. Anyway, I said, "Turner, I'll make you a proposition on who flies tomorrow." I said, "We're going to have from seventy-five to eighty-degree temperatures tomorrow and, if you want to take it, fine. But I want to be permitted to stay as long as I want for a higher temperature." The optimum temperature for the best speed was 104 degrees. I also knew something else that Turner didn't know, which I'll bring up in a minute. Anyway, he said, "I'll take it tomorrow." One thing that influenced him was that he had to be back in Washington. He knew he could break the previous record, which was around 620 mph and was held by General Al Boyd, chief of Flight Test at Wright-Patterson.

Caldwell goes up and sets a new record of 640 miles per hour. After he left, I got together with the engine reps we had there. I think it was a Westinghouse engine we had in the plane. I said, "Look, we're not getting full power out of that. We're only getting 98 percent. We're getting 100 percent on takeoff, but we're only getting 98 percent coming across the lake bed." We were coming across the lake bed at about fifty feet on the three-kilometer course. We had to make two passes in each direction. I said, "I want you to set up the governor so I can get a full 100 percent rpm."

He said, "But that will give you 102 percent on take off—I can't do that."

I said, "Look, I'll control that rpm with the throttle, but I'll then have a full 100 percent."

He didn't want to do it.

I said, "Okay, I'll do it." I knew how to set up a governor.

He said, "Okay." He didn't want any pilots fooling around with his engine.

So that's what he did—he set up the governor. The additional rpm gave

(Left to right); Major John L. Smith, Major Robert Galer, Capt. Marion E. Carl, October 1, 1942, Guadalcanal. The men had just been decorated by Admiral Nimitz with Navy Crosses.

OFFICIAL U.S. MARINE CORP PHOTOGRAPH.

me about five miles per hour and the temperature, as it turned out, gave me about five miles per hour, so five days later I set a new world's speed record of 650 miles per hour. That meant Turner Caldwell had the speed record for five days!

You've flown a lot of planes.

My latest audit shows about 257 different models and types.

Do you have a favorite quirky plane you've flown?

I flew thirty-one different experimental aircraft. My first tour in Flight Test, we had a lot of experimental planes that never made it into production—the XBT-K, for example. I remember the F15C, which was built by Curtiss. It had a prop in the front and a jet in the back, actually in the tail. The Ryan Fireball was another one of those. Both were kind of quirky, and they never really did anything. We did not get involved in some of the things like spin tests in those airplanes—we just went out and flew them for their performance. It was like the project I had on the ME262. I made four emergency landings in a row in that thing. But it's easier to pick out the best than the worst. For example, the best prop fighter ever built was the F8F Bearcat, and I flew the P51, the P38, the P47. None of them would stack up against the F8F as far as I was concerned.

Why?

Because it had lots of power, and it was very maneuverable. A good fighter had very little stability built into it. It's almost neutral about all three axes. If you build stability into the airplane, the airplane wants to resist changes and resist being maneuvered. That's why all transports are very high on stability on all three axis.

When you were doing the first aerobatic team, what was the toughest thing about putting that together?

There wasn't anything tough about it. In the first place, I did it all on my own. The Corsair, a prop job, was a better fighter than the Phantom ever would be. The Phantom-1 was a little twin-engined airplane, and it was a very nice airplane to fly. Because it didn't have any military future as far as I was concerned, I was looking around for something to do with it. I was the squadron commander at the time and I said, "Hellfire, let's try some formation aerobatics." I started out with just a wing man, then with four airplanes. It turned out to be a real fine little airplane for this, because it was twin-engine. If you had an engine failure while you were on your back, you were not in a critical position. You still had fifty percent of your power left. This situation happened once up at Akron, where we were putting on an air show. Walt Domina lost an engine. I said, "Roger," and then I called for a loop. He stuck in there with that plane, and I cut back on my power. We still completed the routine, and he was on one engine.

What year was that?

That was 1948. What started this on an approved basis was that there was a flyover down at Camp Lejeune at a big change-of-command ceremony. I didn't know it, but my commanding general—my major general—was down there. At the end of the flyover, I had four airplanes, and I did a formation loop. When I got back, I got a call to see the general. That's the first I knew that he had been down there. I said, "I'm in trouble."

I reported to the general. The first thing he said was, "I liked that loop you did at the end of the flyover." He was an old-timer years before the marines had had an exhibition team. I said, "General, I can also do formation rolls." Those are the two basics for any type of formation flying. He said, "I'd like for you to put on a show." I said, "Well, General, we don't have any authorizations. I've just been practicing this on my own." He said, "I'll get it." Two weeks after we got authorization during an exhibition at Oceana, in Norfolk, Virginia. I was upside down in a roll, and my wing man and I came together. Of course, it's the wing man's fault, because I had the wing men on both sides and the one guy slid across right on top of me. He rolled across my horizontal stabilizer and elevator. This locked my controls. As it turned out, all he had was a groove across the whole length of his wing on the bottom side and it didn't affect his controls. But I had a problem.

I finally got it down. I had enough stretch in the control cables so I had enough control left on the side that was still undamaged, so I was able to sit it down on the NAS field at Oceana. I remember while coming in I had both feet behind the stick. I had to use that much pressure to keep the nose from coming up and going into a stall. It also turned out that when we checked it out, that the whole fuselage was twisted. And they struck the airplane, in other words, carted it over to the junkyard.

The worst landing you ever had?

That was when I broke my back. I'd taken off in an F9F5 to chase Bob Rahn, a Douglas test pilot, who was flying an F30 on a demonstration flight. I had just pulled up, and I was going away from the field when I felt a tremendous vibration in the engine. I thought I'd thrown a bucket—a turbine blade. I cut the power and headed back to the field. I figured I could make the field, but I misjudged it. I didn't keep my speed up quite enough. I had a full load of fuel, which affected things. So I made the field, but not the runway, and I hit in the dirt. I broke the back of the airplane and I got a compression fracture myself and spent ten weeks in a cast.

What did you think of being a marine in the navy?

Well, as things turned out, I would never have been permitted to fly as much as I did if I'd been in any other service. In the marines they didn't have any regulations like they did in the air force. They didn't have the type of system you had in the navy where, once you get above a carrier group commander, you don't have much chance to fly. In the marines as a group commander, and as a wing commander, I could fly. Nobody told me I couldn't. But in the air force you had to have a safety pilot if you had a star and, in the navy, only very few captains got to really fly—as far as tactical flying was concerned. That's how I piled up fourteen thousand hours while the average time for a fighter pilot was less than five thousand hours.

What was your proudest accomplishment?

I've never given that much thought. You see, I was the first marine ace; I was also the first helicopter pilot. I had the number one designation. I was actually the second one to check out in helicopters, but I was the first one to qualify as a helicopter pilot.

How did that happen?

This friend of mine over in the Helicopter Section asked me if I was interested in flying a helicopter. I said, "Hell, yes." So he gave me three hours of instruction. That's all the instruction I ever had in the helicopter. In Vietnam I flew over one hundred flights in Huey gunships, and I was a brigadier general. I also flew seven or eight fighter missions there.

You were also in Korea.

I didn't get to Korea until the war was over. That was primarily due to that accident I had. When I finally got there, they gave me a photo squadron, of all things. I'd been a fighter squadron commander twice, and I objected to being given a photo squadron. I said, "I don't know anything about photography." They said, "That's not the reason you're being assigned to that. The squadron needs an experienced squadron commander to straighten them out." I soon found why. We went to Taiwan and flew high altitude reconnaisance flights over Red China. Until recently, those flights were classified.

Any particularly interesting flights?

I didn't take the first flight, but I took the second one. It turned out that was the only one that was intercepted by MIGs. I was at forty thousand feet, and I picked up these two MIGs coming up from below as they broke into the contrails at thirty-five thousand feet. Of course, we had no guns in the photo planes. I had objected to this. I said, "Damn it, we're flying over Red China and we're liable to be intercepted." So here I am, a fighter pilot in a damned photo airplane with no guns. So, I turned right into them and hit them head on. I then rolled over and went straight down, speed brakes out, and my wing man followed. Boy, that ole crate was really bucking. When we got back to the deck, we scooted out and away. The MIGs never saw us again in the haze.

I was working for the Seventh Fleet with Admiral Price, who had his flagship in Keelung, near Taipei. I talked him into giving me two fighters. "Well," he said, "I can give you fighters, but I don't have any pilots there." So he actually gave me four fighters. From that time on, when we went across Red China, I was in a fighter. I let somebody else fly the reconnaisance plane. In fact, I didn't have any fighter pilots in the squadron. I was the only one. Anyway, we had radar on the Pescadores Islands. It was manned by the Taiwan Chinese. Of course, the islands of Quemoy and Matsu were also controlled by Taiwan, and that's the reason we were out there; we thought Red China was going to take possession of those two islands.

I complained about the Taiwanese radar operators because they'd get excited and I couldn't understand them. So they put a fellow on the scope by the name of Bill Hardy. Hardy was a fighter pilot who had thirteen airplanes to his credit. That solved it. We didn't have any problems with radar from then on.

In fact, I ran into Hardy a few years ago at a reunion in Mesa, Arizona. He came up to me and said, "You probably don't remember me, but my name is Bill Hardy." I said, "You're one name I'll never forget. Once you got on that scope, we didn't have any more problems."

How many flights over China did you do?

I think we flew seventy-some sorties over there.

Did you find out anything much?

We never got anything of significance, only enough to prove there was no build-up as they had expected, so we canceled the whole thing.

Joe Foss, the great marine ace, told me he rates you number one of all the pilots ever. What do you say to that?

I don't know why Joe would say that, but I appreciate it.

It's been quite a life of flight, hasn't it? What has flight meant to you?

Oh, I don't know. You see, there's an awful lot of luck involved in just having the opportunities. I'll say I didn't miss many opportunities. There was one opportunity I didn't know was there that I did drop the ball on.

Which was?

On the speed record in 1947. That airplane later went supersonic, and it was a straight-wing airplane. It was after the air force had broken the speed of sound by Chuck Yeager. I knew Yeager. I met him out there in 1945, as I remember. But it always bugged me because that airplane had broken the speed of sound for the air force. I said, "Why, if we had pushed it, why couldn't we have beat them to it?" So, a few months ago, I stopped by to see Ed Heineman, who designed the airplane—one of the top designers of tactical aircraft in the whole world—and I said, "Ed, why couldn't we have beaten the air force in breaking the speed of sound if we had put the proper push on?" He said, "We could have." And I would have been the pilot.

But otherwise, you don't have many regrets, do you?

No, I don't.

Bo Bowen on the right

JOHN H. "BO" BOWEN

Carrier Times

On December 7, 1941, "a date which will live in infamy," "Bo" Bowen was en route from a weekend home at Greenville, Mississippi. He was a freshman at Ole Miss on a football scholarship and had promised his father he would finish his freshman year before joining the military.

In the summer of '42, the navy sent Bowen to CPT Training at Oxford. He reported to Athens, Georgia, for preflight training. In mid-March he moved to Pensacola, Florida, then to Mainside, then Ellison Field, then "Bloody Barren" Field near Foley, Alabama.

Bowen took Operational Training at Lee Field near Jacksonville, where he was introduced to service-type planes, all one-seated fighters. Therefore, all first flights were solo. The pilots flew Wildcats at Lee Field, and in early September went to qualify in Wildcats aboard Jeep carriers around the Great Lakes.

After stays in Jacksonville, Atlantic City, Oceana, and Virginia Beach, Bowen boarded the USS *Franklin* in March of 1944. The ship was anchored off Port of Spain on its shakedown cruise. In May they simulated an attack on the Panama Canal, then cruised into San Diego Bay. They were part of the initial strike against Iwo Jima on July 4 of that year. On October 30, 1944, during the Lehte invasion, the *Franklin* was hit by one five-hundred-pound bomb and one plane. The ship returned to Bremerton and Bowen's group, VF-13, reformed at Fallon, Nevada, and was sent to Livermore, California. Bowen and his group were in the Hawaiian Islands when World War II ended.

After the war, the affable Bowen went back to Ole Miss and played football there from '46, to '48. He flew out of Memphis in the reserve until June 20, 1950, when he went to California, and boarded a ship. Home for Christmas, 1951, he went to primary instructor school. He was an instructor until he got out of the navy on July 20, 1952.

The final years of his flying career were served in the reserve and in Jacksonville where he flew jets. He quit flying when he couldn't get a berth in a reserve unit in Jacksonville.

In the old days you did 189 carrier landings. I told one flier about that and he said, "This guy must be one hell of a flier."

I did those on two tours of combat duty—one in World War II and one in Korea. I made sixty-three flights in Korea and, of course, when you got over there, everything was a carrier landing.

Tell me about your primary training.

I went through primary flight training in the "two-wing yellow perils." The "yellow peril" was a nickname given to the yellow Stearman biplanes that we flew in primary flight training. I had a real cocky instructor. I was his first student after he had had a crash from flathatting—you know, flying around low to the ground. Of course, I looked up to him as a little god.

One day he decided that we would go out to the circle, which was the place where we went up. The planes would come around and cut the engine. They would pull the throttle all the way off and see how close to the circle they could land. I had already soloed so this was further along. Anyway, he got out of the plane when we landed and went over to the edge of the circle with the other instructors. I was to make either six or eight landings. I did. I hit all my circles and was really hot! I made a low turnout like he had made, rather than go up to a thousand feet and come around. But the way we had headed meant the field was shorter. So I came over the place where he was, going wide open, with the wheels just barely bouncing. The last thing I saw was him going under my wing with his parachute. I landed and rolled on down to the end of the field, and I sat there. Then I taxied back slowly. When I got back, he got up on the wing to climb in and I said, "I guess I failed that one!" He growled at me and said, "Don't you ever say or suggest to anybody that you failed." He got into the plane, and he never said another word about it.

Why did he do that?

He would have probably fussed at me about it if I hadn't said anything, see? He said that because I was his student, and don't you ever suggest to an instructor that you didn't do well.

What was the hardest plane to learn to fly?

That probably was the Cub. I had only flown in a Cub once before. Some of the guys had flown a Waco and knew how to fly solo, but I went in really cold. It was at Lee Field in Jacksonville, Florida. I graduated at Pensacola at the field named "Bloody Barren." I got to fly fighters, which I requested. They sent us to Fighter Training in service aircraft, which was the Wildcat. We had a great instructor. In fact, nobody in our flight of six ever ground-looped a Wildcat. A Wildcat is a little Grumman plane with the landing gear about two feet apart, or so it seemed. The instructor made us look down the runway and not at those wings. What would happen sometimes was the wings would go down and then one would come up—resembling shock absorbers on an automobile. The wings were sequenced, and one wing would stay down. The flier would go to correct for the wing down, thinking the plane was turning, and it would make him ground-loop. But anyway, we never did have a ground loop. Very few people who flew them didn't ground-loop at one time or another.

It's hard to believe no one in your flight did it.

Yes. There was an instructor named Kirkpatrick. We were put into six-man flights and used the better planes for our regular training. For the first week or so—the first so-many flights—they just had us fly these planes around, not doing anything acrobatic or any fancy stuff because these were older planes, which had all come back from the fleet. They were antiquated.

We were coming in one day, and my engine started cutting out on me. This was during the familiarization stage. My buddy from Shreveport, Leo Bird, was flying with me. He said, "Remember this: remember your flaps; remember to get into the wind." He said everything he could to help me. From up there the engine cut out at about 1,200 feet. I had plenty of time to think and look and find a place on the ground to set down. But I wasn't used to Florida. I didn't know what those skinny-looking pines down there were. They looked like a bunch of switch willows to me. But when I got down there with them, they were like telephone poles.

Southern pines?

Yes. You see, after I got so low I couldn't turn anymore, I hit a tree with my left wing. It threw me sideways into a row of trees. The plane broke right behind me and I went out with the parachute. Now there is an armor plate behind the cockpit and you are supposed to have your shoulder straps behind a rod on the armor plate, which would hold you firmly in there. But my shoulder straps, for some reason, were not over that rod, and it saved my life, in that I went out clear.

It would have pulled you down.

It would have kept me with the tail section, which was hanging up in a tree. The accident cut me a hole in the shin, and I was unconscious for about five or ten minutes. My friend, Leo, was circling when a SNJ plane and a Cub relieved him.

When I came to, I was lying in a little bit of water—about two or three inches of water. So I got up and the first thing I did was pull my seat belt: I was already loose in it. I got up on this little mound. I heard something coming through the woods. I looked around and wondered what in the world it was. It turned out to be a twelve-year-old kid who had just joined the

Boy Scouts. He had his first-aid kit. I knew what I had in my first-aid kit—I had that iodine—that burning stuff. He had methyolate, which was gentler stuff, so I let this kid doctor me on my head and my shin.

I didn't have a thing in the world to give him for helping. So I gave him the piece of my helmet and my earphones. My helmet was torn in three strips, and my earphones were wrinkled. Anyway, that boy stayed with me until the truck got there. He was good company. He had seen me go down behind the trees and heard the crash.

What happened next?

We went to VF-13 in Atlantic City, New Jersey, in October 1943, and the squadron was formed. We flew out of Atlantic City for three months and then Virginia Beach, then we went on to the USS *Franklin*. I've got a little plaque here that says we are "plank owners." That means we are the original crew.

I want to tell you one thing. In that flight at Jacksonville, we had two marines in the flight with us. There were six to a flight, plus your instructor who flew with you every flight. These two marines—number one, being marines and number two, being Texans—were pretty big braggers. One day they told my buddy from Shreveport that the city of Houston was going to raise money enough to build a cruiser, and name it the *Houston*. My buddy says, "Look, you Texans, you can't do that. That's impossible." Well, it developed later that they got enough money together to build the *Houston*, and had enough money left over to buy a CVL, a Jeep carrier. Leo, my buddy, who told them they couldn't do that, ended up stationed aboard the *San Jacinto*, the ship built with surplus fundraising. So Leo had to eat crow. I don't know if he ever saw those two guys again.

What was it like when you were first over there?

When we first got out there, we did a lot of bombing. One of my first contacts was a Zero—up close. We, the fighters, were escorting the dive-bombers and the torpedo bombers into a strike on the Manila. We had three layers of fighter cover above the bombers and torpedo planes.

We had a couple of contacts with the air force guys. All of a sudden, a plane came putting right through the middle of us. I said, "Look at that dumb air force guy, flying right in the middle of our formation." Just as he got closer to passing me, I saw that big meatball on the side of the plane. It was one hundred percent poor recognition on my part. Most all of the Jap planes had radial engines, but this one had an in-line engine like the P-51 or P-39. I did a frantic last-minute turn, but he had gone on past so I stayed in the formation.

One thing of interest. We heard that the Japs rammed you and all that. I was going up, and my airspeed had gotten fairly slow because I was trying to climb to get something above me. I looked down and here comes a Zero, aiming right at me. I zigged to the right, he zigged to the right. I would go to the left, and he went the other way. He was trying to avoid a head-on collision as much as I was.

How did you find that out?

I realized it when he had me. See, he was coming down. He had plenty of speed. He was maneuvering. I was getting real slow going up. He elected not to make a head-on collision.

An apprehensive time?

Yeah, for real. I thought he had me. Anyway, I pulled around and another Jap came by me. I got on his tail and I followed him down—way below where I was supposed to go. I shouldn't have left the formation, but I couldn't make his plane smoke. He might have been dead in the cockpit. Finally, I smoked him, and I started back up, and my engine wasn't going to run. I'm sitting there, looking at all this dogfighting above me, way out over the Phillipines where there are supposed to be head-hunters. I'm thinking, "What am I to do?" The clouds were below me. The Japanese were famous for picking on a cripple. Do I dive into the clouds and hope I miss the mountaintops? What do I do?

I stayed down until we got to Clark Field; I couldn't gain on them. The weather was bad, so the group had to make an extra circle. My plane was going to quit running. When they made the extra circle, I joined up with the torpedo and bomber fliers. A Zero came through, and my plane was wobbly—no maneuverability at 125 knots. I just threw my nose out and squirted a round of 50-calibers, and he flew out of there.

There was a guy when we got back later who, every time we would go to the bar, would buy me a drink. He said that plane was headed for him when I scared it out of there.

We went into the dive on Manila Field, and I went down with the Torpedos beside them. When I went and moved my super-charger into neutral, it was running like a perfect engine. What had happened in the dive behind the Japanese, my supercharger had blown out. I put it in neutral for the dive. So I covered the Torpedos on the left rear side. I looked up over my shoulder and we were coming across the water real low, and this Zero was coming down on me.

I pulled around and made a head run on him. He would pull out, then I would go back down, and he would go down behind me, and then I would pull around too, and he would go up. Finally, I said, "I'm going to let him get far enough into this dive this time, and he won't be able to pull out." So I waited and sat there looking at him. But I waited too long. I let him get really down in there, and I pulled it around hard, and he got past me. So we got into what we call the scissors, but each time he got closer on my tail because the Zero is lighter and can outmaneuver you. I knew I had about two more times before he was going to be sitting on my tail. So I got as high as I could on the far side, and then I came back and put that thing right on the water.

I looked up ahead of me and there were three Hellcats, which I was also flying, and two Zeroes going around and around in a circle, down on the water. One of the Zeroes made kind of a split S. He was so low he made a maneuver that came back under, so that the Hellcats couldn't follow that close on the water. They would have hit the water. Then he came toward me. By this time I had forgotten about the guy on my tail. So I got right down on the water. He was looking back behind him to see what was following him. I got him in a head-on run. He had to have been killed by my 50-calibers because as I was about to lose my lead and go head-on, he kept the same turn and flew right into the water. His left wing hit it, and he cartwheeled. Then one of those three guys chasing those Zeroes took this Zero off my tail. I had gotten so into shooting that I forgot he was on my tail.

So they knocked the guy down?

Yeah, if they hadn't, I'd still be out there. That guy's name in that Torpedo 13 was Bob Freligh. We had a flight where a lot of the younger guys were flying—leading. The junior grades were division leaders, and the ensigns were section leaders. I was leading my division leader. He was flying wing on me that day. We went to the Leyte invasion.

As we approached the ships in the invasion area, the radar called. They had a Japanese strike coming in from the other side at ten thousand feet. So we went across at twelve thousand feet. That way we would have an altitude advantage. Radar said, "They're right in front of you at twelve o'clock. Right in front of you." We couldn't see them, looking down and around. All of a sudden, these Zeroes were making runs on us, coming down shooting on us. Instead of being at ten thousand feet, they were at fourteen thousand. We had a lot of dogfighting, a big dogfight. Willie Gove's plane got to smoking. Willie, my division leader, was flying wing on me. He had a rule that we wouldn't send a plane home by itself. I had to take him back, and I missed the fun of the rest of the dogfight.

What happened?

There was a lot going on. We had a replacement pilot that had just come out. A Zero got on his tail. He had just come out of training command where one person would get behind the other, and the front plane would drop the landing gear to slow down to make the one in rear overshoot, which is strictly taboo. So this guy drops his wheels. The Zero overshoots him, but in going by he shot out his hydraulic system. This boy couldn't raise his wheels.

There were P38s flying up above, but as I said, if they saw a likely victim they would make a dive on him.

Thinking he was a VAL Japanese dive-bomber with a fixed landing gear, the P-38s came down and shot a bunch of holes in this kid. This kid then started home and flew over, not around, the Leyte invasion ships and forces, which is also taboo. Also, he took some holes from the ships below. He landed on the carrier. He had Jap Zero holes; P-38 holes; and surface-to-air holes. He was shaking!

He didn't know whose side he was on, did he?

No. We turned the Japanese strike around. They called the coordinators and said, "We're checking out now. We are going back to the carrier." The guy said, "We got another strike coming in." So the pilot says, "We don't have enough gas. If we stay to intercept that, we won't be able to get back to the ship." The coordinators said, "The P-38s have got a field down there." "All right." So they stayed and intercepted. It was getting about dusk at that point, and they started to come in to land. For some reason, they couldn't land on the P-38 field. They had another field, a mud field.

The first guys that landed on the mud field got out of their planes and helped direct the other guys in, so they wouldn't get into the worst mud holes. The Zeroes, meanwhile, were strafing the fliers while they were getting out of their planes. A boy from Vicksburg was getting ready to step over on the wing, when he got nicked in the balls. The war stopped as far as he was concerned. That guy had his britches open, his balls in his hand, hollering. It turned out to be just a flesh wound, but he had a lot of blood on him.

Hollering what?

"They castrated me."

He still functioned after that?

Yeah, it was a scratch, a deep scratch is what it was. It didn't get below the skin.

Any other characters that you remember?

There was a great guy in the squadron—Deacon—he was a Harvard graduate. He graduated from flight school a little ahead of us ensigns. He was kind of in that middle gap, rank-wise. He was a really funny guy. He had a tooth he could flick out. That night the Japanese made a predawn strike, he found a big pile of something to hide behind. After the strike when it got light, he went out there and looked at where he had been. It had been gasoline drums. *He* got some gas!

We had a little guy named Brooksy. He had had a full tour before he was in our squadron, and now he was just winding up. He was flying and his gear wouldn't come down. They couldn't let him land on the mud field because then no one else could land. So they told him to go up and bail out. He went up, and we never heard from him again.

You never heard from him again?

No, we don't know if the Japs got him or if he didn't get out of the plane.

They didn't want him to land.

They didn't have any equipment to move him or his plane. Without wheels, he couldn't taxi. If he would land on the strip, then the other planes couldn't land. So they had him wait until last, but it had gotten dark by then, and they didn't have lights. So he elected to bail out rather than try to land in the dark.

Where was this?

This was in Leyte Gulf. This was the invasion of Leyte. The P-38s had a pretty good field, I guess. We weren't feeling too kindly to those P-38s, at that point.

I still don't understand why they wouldn't let the Hellcats come over and land on their field?

I wasn't there, you see. I had to take Willy back to the ship. It was just a mud puddle, I guess. They had difficulty taxiing at all. I imagine that the fact that we did the three-point landing—you know, with the tail down—would help prevent any nosing up. But they all got on and off the mud field all right.

The next day the guys—all young boys—were talking. "You going to give us a good dogfight in the morning? Yeah, we'll hang around. We'll take the early flight and then go back." Which they did. So they started back to the USS *Franklin*. Well there was a solid line of thunderclouds, a tremendous front. Usually you can go around these things, but this was one solid mass. I'd flown through it with Willy the day before, but these guys were trying to fly it all in formation. They were just sitting there. My buddy, Deacon, was leading the flight. Everybody was real tense, keeping that formation, and bouncing those planes. The guys looked over at Deacon who was leading, and he was yawning and putting his hand on over his mouth like he was bored to death. These guys laughed, and it relaxed them and the group got through. There was a guy named Winecoff who had come out as replacement pilot, only he was a full lieutenant. He had two thousand hours, which was a whole lot of time then, but he didn't make it back through the clouds. He was a well-qualified instrument man. That was terrible.

Other people who were lost?

Everybody has a station on the ship. The doctor's general quarters station is up right by the flight deck under the super-structure. Anyway, the doctor always went the same way to his station. He decided that if his station had been bombed that he needed to know how to go to the other one. He came out in the black dark an hour before sunrise, with no moon. The last step he made, he felt nothing was under his feet. He went off the flight deck, not the hangar deck. He went down and down and, on his way down, he got his whistle out and blew his whistle—he had it around his neck. He didn't have his life belt on. The guy hit the water going thirty knots, which is thirty-five miles per hour. Somebody heard the whistle, and so everybody got to looking for who was missing. The doctor was the only one on the ship who didn't have someone to report to. Finally, a destroyer stayed back and went around, waiting to pick up the survivor when it got light enough to see him. I guess they cut the screws so they wouldn't run over him. Well, they found him and it was Doc Moy. Word came aboard the ship that it was Doc Moy, and he was okay. Up to the carrier they brought the boatswain's chair. Doc Moy had the most chickenshit grin, if you'll excuse my French, that you ever saw in your life. The band was out, and the bandleader was a guy named Saxy Dowell, who wrote "Three Little Fishes," and they played "The Man Came Off." Absolutely, Doc was the most shitty-grinned person I ever saw in my life.

Any more embarrassing moments on ship or elsewhere?

We had a guy in our squadron named Johnny Johnson. He was a Hollywood stuntman before he joined the navy. On our first strike against Iwo Jima, he got shot down. He got into this rubber boat and a United States submarine picked him up. He bumped around the islands trying to get back to the USS *Franklin*. He ended up, I think, going all the way back to Hawaii. Then he came back to Saipan. He got tired of waiting to get on his ship, so he went on some clean-up maneuvers with the marines and got wounded in the arm when they invaded Saipan. He was nicknamed "Saipan Johnny." They put a tourniquet on his arm, and he came into the ship. He wasn't bad. He had lost some blood. He was a great warrior and went on to make admiral in the reserves after World War II.

One of our pilots, A. J. Pope, had the knack of being in the right place at the right time. He was making a carrier landing and received a "wave-off," requiring him to pull off and go around for another try. When he pulled up, there was a Betty, a twin-engine Jap bomber in his gun sights. He pulled the trigger and shot down the plane, which was slightly above the flight deck level. That gave him seven enemy downed.

What was the most amazing bravery you saw over there?

To be honest, in most instances, we were eager beavers. We wanted to be aces. We got credit for bravery—shooting planes down. I guess they were comparing us with an air force bomber flying over Germany. We did a lot of bombing and strafing because the Japs pulled back their forces then to the Philippines, getting ready. I guess the thing we did most would have been bombing. We'd come back—eight planes and a guy named Hudson, who was a wild man. We made these strikes, kept going around and around, one plane at a time, until we sank this destroyer.

During training we practiced bombing one plane at a time, in column. During combat attacks, we'd generally have several planes diving on the various targets. But Hudson led the trainer-type attacks on the destroyer until it was sunk. He was shot down and did not survive.

What about the USS **Franklin?**

I was on it the first cruise. It only made two. In fact, it wasn't out there very long. It got hit in March the second time. We got hit October 30 of '44. It went back to—

Bremerton, Washington?

Yes. I had pneumonia on that trip—flight pneumonia. I asked somebody what is flight pneumonia? Well, it's from breathing the oxygen, your lungs drying out.

Let's talk some more about the carrier landings.

After you make so many, they are not much more difficult than a field landing, except that if you make a mistake on a carrier, you are in trouble. You can make a mistake on a field landing.

I had a lot of rough carrier landings—as everybody did—but I never busted a tire. Most times, it isn't the pilot's fault, but if you hit a little too hard, you'd bust a tire.

The hardest carrier landing we did was when we were on the edge of a typhoon, early October of '44, I believe. The deck was going up and down the way a destroyer normally does (a big carrier just goes straight through the water). At the edge of this typhoon, those waves were so long that the carrier was even going up and banging back down. The signal officers would bring you aboard if you were right and the ship was at the middle. But if the bow of the ship was high out of the water, then if they cut you, indicating you should land, the ship would be going away from you, and you would go up the deck too far. On the other hand, if the carrier was at the bottom of its pitch, then the deck was coming up as you were going down. It would wipe out a landing gear. Signal officers would only cut you if you were in the middle, but there is a lot of timing on that.

I'll tell you the best carrier landing I ever had.

There were thirty-six of us planes who flew into Panama. The P-39s intercepted us as an exercise. But we went in and spent two of the wildest nights you ever had. We had the local cops after us. I made a bargain with them. I told them if they didn't charge me, I would get on that ship and never come back.

My division leader was Kelly Blair, an Academy man who had spent a lot of time on cruises, and he told me that there were more sharks in that water, just west of the Panama Canal, than he had ever seen in his life. Of course, a lot of ships dump garbage there—sharks learned that that was a feeding ground.

We flew out, and at that point, I probably hadn't had ten or fifteen landings. The signal officer on the ship gave me a "Roger"—which is "You're right." I received that "Roger" all the way in. He never gave me a signal until it was time to cut. Afterwards, you debrief with the signal officer—he'll tell you what you did right and wrong. He said, "Bo, you made a perfect landing! I've never seen you make a perfect landing before. And how could you make a perfect landing after all those two nights of drinking?" I said, "That didn't have a thing to do with it." He said, "What was it?" I said, "It was all those sharks." So that was my only perfect landing!

One old flier told me you had a reputation; he said you stayed upside down most of the time when you were flying.

Yeah, I liked it. I liked aerobatics and air-to-air. It's too bad we didn't get back to combat because we had a real good squadron going back. We also had a good one going out. There is the "Thatch Weave" that Captain Thatch developed. It's where two planes get on one side and two on the other, and they turn into each other and cover each others' tail. Looking at it, it doesn't look like it would be as effective as it is. We tried the technique around Manila when we were in the area of combat, and when we got back, I developed the thing further and found out we had just scratched the surface in terms of possibilities.

Can you explain that?

We went out with four planes and had someone else's division attack us. We won by using this weave. If we got the other plane in a head-on, then it was considered that we had won and he would have to pull up. Somebody would have to pull up or have a collision.

The movement of a plane is hard to describe. You have this one plane turning on the other and the whole air moves. We'd have a radius big enough to where you could get your full nose all the way around on the other plane. Then we would both turn to the same direction and then come back, either behind or forward. But we would always go back with the two planes covering our tail. The air force had a circle they would get into—a big circle—and anybody who broke that circle would have somebody on their tail.

The hardest thing to describe is that everything is moving. You have this plane turn towards this one (*gestures*), but that plane is not there when you get there; he has gone the same distance you have.

I had pneumonia and went to bed in Hawaii on the way home. I got back late, and they had already made the divisions up. My rank put me as division leader, but I told them, "Don't worry about it." I would fly with one group and then another group. I did a slow roll at four thousand feet above the ground, and a boy named Lezak fell out of the roll. He did a split S from something like 220 knots, and it killed him. He went in. They checked me out, questioned me. There was no charge brought against me, but I hated losing that boy.

What do you think happened?

What he did was try to do a split S and we were already at high speed. I got the rest of the boys together, and I really got after them. I went from a playboy to a hard nose instructor just with my boys. Just last week, one of them who retired, a boy named Schmedler, told me that I chewed him out one time. I didn't even remember chewing him out because he was a great pilot, but it occurred as a result of the other boy going in. I used to put them in a column and roll them over on their backs. I would tell them what I was going to do beforehand. Then I would hold it upside down, then roll it back, or roll over on our back, pull it down about thirty degrees, and then roll it back and come up. The idea is that you don't ever go all the way from high speed to start with. You don't do a split S from there. And the boy who was lost should have learned that before he ever finished cadet school.

A split-S is just rolling over on your back and pulling through all the way, but you do it from a lower speed or at a high level of altitude. You have got to know your plane, too. You see these guys at air shows that make these loops right off the ground. When they are coming down, they have to have so much altitude for a certain speed. We did that on overhead gunnery runs on the sleeve, but we were starting off slow and going straight down. You are supposed to be going almost perpendicular when you pass the sleeve, but you are up high enough that you pull on out and go ahead.

I went to sleep one time in an airplane in Jacksonville when I was in operational training. We were doing overhead gunnery runs. One plane was pulling a sleeve and you went down and shot at the sleeve. It was my time to do that. I always made a steep run, almost going straight down. I started pulling Gs and the blood left my head. When that happens, you get over and you grunt. I rolled over a little early so I had to push my nose back a little bit to keep from hitting the sleeve, which put me more or less going straight down. Well, I was sound asleep, and all of a sudden, I'm hearing this noise.

I'm thinking, "What's that noise? What's that noise?" But I couldn't see anything. It happened that that noise was my horn. On the Wildcat when you pulled your throttle all the way off and your gear was not down, it made your horn blow. That's what kept you from landing wheels up. That's what I heard. Fortunately, those instructors had taught us to trim those planes up pretty good. If it hadn't been trimmed up pretty good, I would have gone in and never known what had happened.

What was the biggest adventure you had in Korea?

The Korean War was a ten-year step back from WWII, except for the jets up high, and I wasn't in the jets. That's what I wanted: jets. And to go up and get in a dogfight. But we got the Corsairs instead of jets.

The one thing I got recognition for doing was when we spent our time knocking out little railroads across the sand pit. What we'd do is we would peel off and go down, one at a time like the training command, rather than coordinated attacks. The Koreans let us dive in there a few times, then they opened up on us. In one place you couldn't get to the target except from the west; you had to go down and turn. I didn't want to take the division in there, so I just decided I would do it myself—a grandstand play, I guess. I made a dive down to the right of the target and, after I got down below five hundred feet, then I turned and went through that pass in the mountains. As far as I know I didn't take any hits, but the way I went, a second plane would have been a sitting duck because the North Koreans would have seen how we were coming in.

I always worried about dropping the bomb or strafing my own troops. I had heard that had happened in WWII, but I didn't want to be part of that accident. I was leading a flight on this particular time, and I don't know whether we had the ADs with us or not, but we had Corsairs. I checked in with this coordinator, flying this little Cub-looking plane. He is talking to the ground, and then he's telling us where the strafing or rockets would hit. The minute we got there he said, "Come on in quick." They gave us some instructions. I'm already starting in my dive, and I'm asking this coordinator, "Where are the troops?" He said, "Go on in there and move it right on up that hill."

So we hit there and were strafing it. We would come around and this time we were having more than one plane going in at one time. We would go across again, and he would say, "That's good. Move it up on the mountain a little bit."

I said, "Where are our troops from there?" "Well, you are doing good, now move it on up. Come on."

Finally, we were out of 50-calibers—everything—and I said, "We don't have any ammo left. We are going to head back." Then I asked, "What kind of shape are they in down there?"

"You did a really good job, but we still got a little problem down there."

"I tell you, I'll just make a couple of dummy runs down there, and it will take them a couple of runs to figure out we don't have any more ammunition, and then another group will be there."

"Yeah, I would appreciate that."

So we went around and made the runs, but we only made a run to look. I got lower, but not as steep an angle as I'd been, almost parallel to the ground. On that first loop I came across the top of the hill. There was a bald spot there. I looked down, and these guys are stretched out on their backs with their hands on top of their helmets. I called that coordinator man and said, "Whose troops are on top of that hill?"

"Those are ours."

"Do you know that we just strafed and bombed within feet of them?" I must admit I cussed him out a little bit.

"Well, that's why I didn't tell you. I knew you would be too cautious. These guys had to have help, and we had to make you throw bombs up in there. If you had known that they were that close, you wouldn't have done near the job that you did."

This boy, Tom Davis, was flying wing on me, and he got a big part of his wing blown off. We flew our Corsairs into Kempo, the big air force base there. We didn't think he was going to make it. It looked like the wing was going to come off, but it had just torn all the flimsy stuff—it hadn't really gotten the main structure. This Tom got a ride back to the ship some way. When the plane was ready, this boy named Buck Dawson, who had a brother in the marines, asked to let him go get the plane, so he could see his brother. He went over there and asked where his brother the marine was. He got the name of the outfit. This helicopter pilot put Buck down by his brother's tent nearby. So he and his brother were talking, and he asked his brother, "Are we doing any good up there?" The brother said, "Wait a minute." He went next door to another tent and brought back pictures showing where they bulldozed a trench of bodies twenty feet deep.

What was the hardest thing about covering Guam?

It wasn't a real difficult thing. Honestly, I don't think we ever got the full benefit out of our air on that Guam invasion. We bombed it and made runs on it—attacked. Hours before the landing craft got there, they pulled us out. The thing that always haunted us a lot was that after they pulled us out, the air group commander spotted a tank in the bushes right where some of the landing craft were headed. Whatever did happen, we didn't know, but we didn't prevent it.

He wasn't able to communicate that the tank was there?

268

At that point the landing craft were almost there, and there were waves of them. There was a guy in the squadron named Magnuson. I think it was Eric Magnuson. He was an old top-hatter—the flying dive-bombers that were top-hatters in the early '30s. He was the oldest man and pilot in our squadron. I remember I wrote home and told my mother I didn't know how that old man could fly that plane: he was thirty-five years old! I was twenty or twenty-one at the time. I was on the flight when he got shot down. Here's a picture of him. He was a great guy.

We were getting our planes at Atlantic City, where they were being delivered. We were getting one and two at a time. A boy named Ginther came out to join up. He was involved in some sort of operation where he was overshooting all the time. He went up and somehow he got his tail in front of Magnuson's propeller and had to bail out. Magnuson managed to get the plane home with a bent prop. From then on, when they took off to go to a gunnery hop, everybody else went out. The leader would go out and make a turn and come back, then all the others would join him. They called that a rendezvous. Then they would go out as a flight. Magnuson wouldn't practice that. He got into that airplane and he pushed the throttle full forward. When they were able to catch up with him that was fine, but he wasn't going to let young ensigns fly into his prop again.

Any memories about flying cover on Iwo Jima?

The Iwo Jima to us was July 4 and July 5—and then later. I got a hole blown in the middle of my wing the first day. I was in a high-speed dive and this explosion—whatever—hit my wing. Something exploded on contact. It blew a hole in there about three feet in diameter, and it rolled me slightly. It hit in the right wing, so it rolled me to the left. I was afraid to pull back, so I eased it on around to where I was flying with my wings level, and then I started a very, very slow pull-out. The squadron was supposed to make their attack and veer to the right, then go out to about five miles and rendezvous. We would go home from there. Well, I couldn't make that turn out to the right because I was afraid of that wing. So I went out past that volcano at the bottom of Iwo Jima. I saw some stuff coming at me when I was down under three hundred feet. I could see the tracers coming at me, but they were behind me. (That's one thing about my high speed—they always underlead.) I pulled out and looked around and I said, "My goodness, it's raining." I looked above me and I said, "There is not a cloud above me." It was all shrapnel falling like rain. It turned out that I was the only one the whole island was shooting at at that point because the other aircraft had gone to the right. Then, the next day I got a part of my rudder shot off. Other than hoping that everything stayed intact, there was no drama to that.

What about the battles of the Philippines?

We were in the Second Battle of the Philippine Sea. I flew wing on Kelly Blair. There were two of us from Mississippi in the squadron. Jack Robbins flew with the skipper, and I flew with the executive officer—the number two in command. Kelly Blair chose me as his wingman. Why he did wasn't necessarily based on how well I could fly—it was the fact that he wasn't an experienced pilot. He had been in the floating navy and gone back through flight training. He was in dive-bombing training while I was in fighter training. I was ahead of him on the flying.

If Kelly would turn into the other guys out there, they would complain. "You turned into me!" I told Kelly, "Don't you ever worry about flying into me. I got as much rudder and stick and turn and throttle as you have. You can forget me." Well, that put a big worry off of him because he was leading flights with twelve or more people in them. The skipper too would be leading a flight with twelve. If Kelly got to sliding into the skipper a little too fast, that was trouble.

We did such silly things, you wouldn't believe. We would go out on a flight—we were preparing for combat—but none of us in my division had seen any combat at that point. So we practiced spotting planes. I never looked at Kelly straight away. I looked ahead always and relied on my peripheral vision in case he turned on me. It was crazy. I think it was on July 2, we were getting ready to go into Iwo and he spun into the groove, which is just before you land. He spun in, and the plane went below water, and he never got out. Kelly was my good buddy.

You mentioned the words "gung ho."

We had a guy who had been out there for a full tour of duty, full-time, when they decided to make him a division leader. He said, "Just stay with me and I'll get you home." He made good strafing runs—he made good bombing runs—he never got himself in a bad position—he was effective and he did a good job—but he wasn't hunting Zeroes, and I was hunting Zeroes. We went into either Guam or Iwo, and we were told for one group to hit the north field and one group to hit the south field, and then rendezvous out in the water and come home. We went to the north and there weren't any Zeroes there. The other group went to the south and caught the Japs taking off without the wheels up yet. Man, I was dying to run down there, but they made a rule that anyone who left their leader would be grounded, and I didn't want to get grounded.

I went back and I told Willie Gove, I said, "Willie, I didn't leave him. I did what you told me to do, but I'm not going to fly with him again." I don't know how I had the nerve to say that. This is nothing derogatory about the other guy. He had put in his time. He did his job.

Willie said, "I will let you know in a couple of days. Let me think about it." He came back and said, "Bo," apologetically, "Would you fly with me?"

"Would I fly with you? Man, I would love to fly with you."

So I flew with him the rest of the time there. I also flew with a boy named A. J. Pope and a boy named Willie Nigren. Nigren came as a replacement pilot when we were out there.

Willie did some great stuff. He flew over a Jap cruiser to dive on a Jap destroyer. At first it sounded like, "That's wild," but at second thought, it was a great strategy. They don't hit you too good coming in at that angle right over them. We didn't have any ammo that would have done anything to a cruiser, but it hurt the destroyer.

It was during this second battle, maybe the same flight, that we got off late for some reason. They sent our group out; four planes. There were planes from the other carriers out there, but we were not sent with the other group. We just went to the same place. When we got through and did all we were going to do, the four of us started back to the ship. All of a sudden, Willie, who did the navigating with the chart board, with the navigation board there in his lap, announced there was nothing there. No ship. So we set up a square search: you go this way ten miles, this way fifteen. You keep going in a square and making your square bigger and bigger.

We realized we were in that Pacific Ocean without a ship. So we went up to ten thousand feet and called the ship. Fortunately, it wasn't radio silence. We called the ship, but we couldn't get them from down low, so up we went with our Hellcats. Willie was leading us, and Willie called. The Hellcats that were flying combat air patrol over the carriers answered us. This was a high frequency radio and it didn't go over the curve of the earth, but up at ten thousand feet, they could hear us. They related the message and said, "Oh, yeah, we changed what you call point OBO or point option. That's the direction you go, but you zig-zag going that way." So they gave us a vector in, and we went in a little short of gas, but we managed to get back. We were the last four planes off, and they hadn't given us the change from what we had had in the ready room.

Pretty scary?

Yeah, I guarantee you, I would much rather have gotten hit going in at heavy odds with Zeroes than I would have fought the odds of finding a ship in that big ocean.

How did you feel when the USS Franklin was hit?

I had a little luck, I guess. It was my own doing because this was at the end of the tour of duty, and the young boys were beginning to lead more. Someone came by and wanted to know who wanted to volunteer to go cover some Jeep Carriers that had planes on them. There were FM-2s on that carrier. I went out, and the Zeroes didn't come while we were there. To start off, they asked us for volunteers, and I was one of the group that said, "I want to go." I think I was the last one off. I could have been the next to last one. I remember making the right turn you do to clear the deck of the prop-wash, and I looked over my right shoulder and saw there was an explosion behind me. But they told us to go on our mission, so I didn't even get to fly around and see what was going on and why. I can't understand why they would have sent us off and not told us to stay there and intercept anything coming in. But they sent us on up, and that was after the first hit—a kamikaze or a bomb.

Then we came back. They couldn't take planes aboard the *Franklin* or the *Bella Wood*. But the other ships, the *Enterprise* and the *San Jacinto* could. The *San Jacinto* was the one I told you about that they made out of leftovers.

Anyway, I landed on the *San Jacinto* and the reason I did was because my buddy, Leo, was on there. He was my good buddy. Everybody would prefer to land on the bigger carrier, but I landed on the smaller one. In fact, when I said I would go on the *San Jacinto*, they had plenty of volunteers for the big carrier.

You must have been feeling like a man without a ship after the landing.

I tell you, I don't remember any other emotion like this in my life, except maybe the first high school football game I ever stood up and heard them play "Star Spangled Banner." We came back aboard, and I rode that boatswain's chair from the *San Jacinto* over to a destroyer. I spent several hours on the destroyer and then went from there over to the *Franklin*. The next day, Admiral Halsey, Bull Halsey, came aboard and the band played "Anchors Away." I had stuff running up and down my spine like I never felt in my life. It was a crippled ship, but it was afloat, and that was real emotion. I never felt that strongly.

You made it through.

It really was in that first crash I had when I went out the side. People might think I made that up, but I had a guy flying around who witnessed the whole thing when I crashed. Let me tell you about him: We were coming in from hops, so they sent a Cub in to relieve the SNJ. So he went home and landed, then went to the dispensary. He sat there waiting, seeing if they had heard anything. See, I was unconscious the whole time he was there so he didn't know where I was. I wasn't in the wreckage. He was looking in the wreckage for me. I was out cold. I had been thrown thirty feet. Finally, they got in there with a four-wheel-drive ambulance and took me back to the same dispensary. They opened the back door of the place, and I was sitting in the back of the vehicle. Leo, my friend, had commented to somebody else that "Oh, Bo is dead. He wanted to go to the fleet so bad. Bo is dead." And they opened those back doors, and he looked up and here came this whole body out with only minor nicks that you could see. He came to hug me just as I hit the ground, and—as I hit the ground—I ducked. I went under his arms and just kept going because I wasn't going to let him make me cry, too.

You were young. You dropped out of school?

Yeah, I was at Ole Miss and in 1941 played on the freshman football team. It had more All-Americans on one team than I ever heard of: Charlie Connelly was a freshman; Barney Pool was an All-American too—at army and at Ole Miss; Leon Bramlet was an All-American at Navy; Doug Kenner was an All-American at Army. We had some others that made honors.

After the war I went up to Ole Miss. In fact, I wasn't through flying at the time. I called to see about going flying with the Flying Tigers over in China. They sent me the number of a lady to call, Madame Chiang, who was the mother of the "Bastard's Son" organization, which all the Flying Tigers were in. They gave me her number, and I called her up in San Francisco. She referred me to somebody in New York to call. When I got home, I tried to call them once in New York, and when I didn't get them, I went over to Ole Miss. They threw the boxing gloves on me, and I never did leave after that.

I got married that June 1946, and the Deacon came up to my wedding. I have painted him primarily as a Harvard graduate, but he was a Harvard graduate with kind of hayseed blonde hair. He was square-built, a blocking back in college. I mentioned the front tooth he could flick out. Deacon had the greatest sense of humor. I mentioned he was the guy yawning, coming back, through bad weather. Anyway, he was in my wedding. It was a dress white wedding, so he came in a seersucker suit. When he was about to arrive, the train rolled in, then left. It went down the road a hundred yards or so, stopped and let him off. Deacon stole the wedding. Everybody loved him. We called him Deacon, because his last name was Parsons.

Then, after the wedding, I didn't see him for awhile. In fact, I didn't see him for a good while. LSU and Ole Miss were playing in Baton Rouge. One habit we had was to dress in our football uniforms at the hotel there in Baton Rouge, get on a bus, and go to the football field. This was in '47. Connelly was our tailback; Y. A. Tittle was the LSU quarterback. This turned out to be a close game. We won by two points or something. So I had just dressed out and had come down to the lobby. I looked up and there was Deacon. I said, "Deacon, what are you doing here?" He said, "Well, I've been studying in the Episcopal Church. I was leaving Houston going to St. Louis and decided to look and see if you were playing." He saw we were playing in Baton Rouge and caught a plane and came by. So there he stood.

Coach Vaught of Mississippi had been an old navy man, too, you know, so we were able to put Deacon on the bus and take him to the football game.

He sat on the bench during the game. It turned out to be a great game, too. Incidentally, it was the game that Y. A. Tittle's britches came down while returning a Connelly punt after Jack Odom hit him at his belt buckle and nobody could tackle him.

Nobody could tackle him?

People kept missing him, and someone said, "What might he have done if he hadn't had to hold his pants up?" I said, "Well, someone would have knocked him on his butt because we didn't know how to tackle a guy that ran around with his tallywhacker in his hand!"

So, anyway, Deacon went back and spent the night there at Baton Rouge. The next day I got him on the plane. I didn't get to ride with him. I was on the first plane. I did pick him up at the plane and took him home with me at Oxford. The next day, Monday, he flew on to St. Louis. I saw him again on the way to Korea years later. I flew a plane from San Diego and flew up to Oakland, and saw him. And then he died. He had a brain tumor.

He was missed?

Yes, very much so. Knutt Weidman, from VF-13, flew out over the Pacific and spread his ashes.

What are you proudest of in your flying or military experience?

I'm one continuous regretful—regretful that I didn't shoot more. The proudest? I don't have one. It could have been when I shot down two planes in one day. The day I got the third plane I probably did the best flying I ever did in my life. It was that day when Willie's supercharger went out. We were up above the neutral where we needed a supercharger. His engine wasn't running: he was running like he had half an engine, half power. So I had to cover him. We were doing a kind of weave. I was having to cover him—you know, we were making the turn going away, and I would go away further and then cut across. We had the odds against us. In fact, I didn't know I shot down the plane I shot down. When we got back, A. J. said, "Willie, what about the plane you shot down?" Willie said, "I didn't shoot down a plane." Then he told me which one it was. The plane went on out, and I followed it away and cut across back. Then they said just about the time I came back, the plane blew up, and they thought I had seen it. That was the same time Eric Magnuson got shot down. We kept trying to get on into the clouds where they couldn't make overhead runs on us. They would have to come in flat instead. But we couldn't keep these guys under the clouds. They kept getting out there. We would have to go out there and run them off. I guess at the end of the war I'm sort of a frustrated ace. I only shot down three planes, but I loved it. It was a game.

Jeff De Blanc, VMF-112, Solomon, 1942

JEFF DE BLANC

Captured in the Solomons

With three years of college, Jeff De Blanc went into the military, first the Naval Cadets, then Marine Aviation. As a member of VMF-112, he served at Guadalcanal, where he and his fellow fliers would meet many of Japan's top Aces, including the likes of Junichi Sasai, Saburo Sakai, and Hiroyoshi Nishizawa. In November of 1942, De Blanc and eight of his fellow Marines made history. Each received the Medal of Honor on that day.

"How brave was Jeff De Blanc?" I ask.

"I made more errors than you can shake a stick at and I just got by with it," he says, his green eyes ablaze. "I'm not a brave man. I've just been fortunate to be at the right place, at the right time, and have survived. Anybody could have done it."

I gently disagree with him that anyone could have done it. He sticks to his guns, downplaying his own talent, courage, skill. There's no arguing with him, so I let it drop. So much for the great modesty of one of America's war heroes.

In the interview, De Blanc tells of his island capture in the Solomons, a profound experience that would forever affect the way he sees the world.

After the military years De Blanc taught school in the St. Martin Parish and worked as Supervisor of Secondary Education. De Blanc did his undergraduate work at LSU and received a Ph.D. from McNeese State University. At one point in his career, while teaching overseas in the international school in Brunssum, The Netherlands, he taught with Luftwaffe pilots, many of whose fathers had fought in WWII. The Luftwaffe pilots would come to El Paso, where they had a school, and De Blanc would sometimes hitch a flight across the ocean with them. "I felt a little bit like a traitor," he says. "The Maltese crosses were on the wings and everything." He laughs.

Jeff De Blanc carries on the warrior tradition, which extends for years across history. Relatives of Jeff's have fought in the Revolutionary War, the War of 1812, and the Civil War. Alcibiades De Blanc led a famous charge on General Howard's exposed right flank on Cemetery Hill at the Battle of Gettysburg. As he points out in *Once They Lived By The Sword*, Alcibiades was born in 1821; Jeff was born in 1921. Alcibiades received his appointment as full Colonel on July 2, 1863; Jeff received his appointment as full Colonel on July 2, 1963. Alcibiades was imprisoned in the Old Capital Prison in

Washington, D.C. where an exchange for ten Union soldiers gained him his release; Jeff was captured and traded for a sack of rice on Kolombangara Island.

The curly hair from his early photos is gone, but this inveterate tennis player continues to stay busy in his semi-retirement. He and his wife Louise's five children are grown, and he looks forward hopefully to a long life. After all, he explains, "My father died young at 82."

How rudimentary was your training?

My training was before World War II. The draft was coming on, and they needed pilots. They started a crash program called V-5 and hit the colleges to recruit. The navy required four years of college. I had had three years of college, and they dropped it to three years. They would give us 230 to 250 hours of flight time for our wings.

Do you remember your solo flight?

Yes, it was in New Orleans at an elimination base. After you went into the program in V-5, they ran you through ten hours of training. I made it in eight hours. This was to see if you had the aptitude for flying.

When they saw the war coming in Europe, they put in a Civilian Pilot Training Program (CPT) at Lafayette, Louisiana. They would give you three hours' credit for it. You took thirty-five hours of Piper Cub training. I had a real love of flying—in fact, when I first got into it, I had a real fascination with the handling of the aircraft. I was sixteen at the time. I'm a product of the Depression. In those days they had those magazines called "G-8" and "Flying Aces." They were all over the stands and sold for ten cents a copy.

Do you think you learned anything in your training as far as tactics were concerned?

Not exactly. They trained us in World War I tactics. When we got to the Pacific Theater, if you didn't develop your own set of tactics, I didn't think you could survive. At least that's the way I felt.

Can you explain that?

They had a Lieutenant Colonel Bauer there, who was killed later on. But I owe him my life, really, me and a couple of other guys. We were sent overseas with just 250 hours of flight time, no night flying, and just four or five hours of flight time in the fighters we would be flying in—Wildcats. Bauer told us, "Dogfight them. They're just paper kites." He meant that because the Zero could outclimb us and outmaneuver us, we needed to use our fire power. The Zero could not withstand the firepower from the Wildcat. It had six 50-caliber machine guns. The Zero had only two 7.7s in the nose and two slow-firing cannons. Bauer said, "If they come head on into you, you can blast them to pieces. If they're on your tail, don't worry about it. What they will do is open up on you. The tracers will go by your cockpit, or else they will hit the armor plate in back of it. When they stop that, they're going to open up with their two 20 mm, low-muzzle velocity cannons. Then, all you have to do is skid." I only had the opportunity to do this one time in a dogfight—to take advantage of what he said.

Describe that one time.

It was the January 31, 1943. That's when I got five planes in one dogfight. The action there was witnessed by rear gunners in the bombers returning to Guadalcanal, as well as Missionary Silvester on the island of Vella La Vella. There were two Zeroes coming in from the rear. I couldn't outrun them—I had to dogfight them. I was in their territory, so I turned into both of them. I hit one of them head on. He was diving off towards me, and I was climbing toward him. When a plane dives down, the pilot has to trim the airplane to fire properly. If the needle and ball is not centered, the bullets will go off target at a tangent. You won't hit what you're aiming at. They have to be perfectly level and stable before they can open fire. I thought he was going to ram me because I started firing on him, and he wouldn't get out of the way. I became frightened because my plane had slowed up so much from the firing that I couldn't control and maneuver. He was going to ram me. I held the trigger down and the Zero blew up. Then I flew through the pieces.

The other guy had passed me in the meantime, and I tried to get on his tail, but he had already pulled up because he had the speed advantage. He came down on me from a high altitude and at high speed—a high side run. I could see that he was going to overshoot because I was going slow, and he was coming fast. That's when I let him get on my tail. He opened up and fired. He was going too fast to slow up, and I skidded and dropped my flaps, and he went sailing past me. He knew I was about to nail him, because he froze on the stick and we locked eyes as he passed me to the right of my wing. He froze and went straight ahead. I got him with one short burst.

Any other images like the guy freezing at that stick in your mind?

A lot of that stuff is a little hazy after so many years, but that man's eyes—when he passed me—that's pretty vivid.

I saw he was a short fellow, and he had this fur cap—a Japanese fur cap. He was right up against the canopy. In other words, when he looked at me, he wasn't sitting straight up in the cockpit. He glanced left and put his eyes level with the cockpit rim, as he was looking toward me—and he stayed that way. I saw him fishtailing like mad, trying to stay in back of me.

It was the torpedo bombers who came to hit our fleet about forty to fifty feet off the waters. We had to dive through our own antiaircraft fire to pick them up below the level of the ship. I shot two of them down at this level after diving down through the antiaircraft fire.

I was in the same flight pattern, going in to our fleet, as the Japanese bombers were. In fact, I knew that when I cleared the fleet that there were other bombers in back of me. I did a wingover and came back and headed on into them. It turned out to be just one bomber coming out of the fleet. It didn't take me long to line up on him because I was in his flight path above him. That's when I opened fire on the head-on shot. I saw the right engine flare up and I saw the greenhouse—that's where the pilot is—and I shot him. At high speed, the two things, speed and motion, are mutually exclusive. In other words, if it doesn't move, you won't spot it. So I came down across the top of the bomber and looked down into the cockpit. This was at high speed, it was in a flash, and there were three men. Either the torpedo man or rear gunner reached over and pulled the pilot from the left seat of the controls. I can see it as if it were yesterday! I don't know if the man was dead or not. I assumed he was. I know two of them didn't move, but the third man did. I do remember that vividly. These images hold fast and linger.

Describe another plane you shot down.

Lieutenant Pool was a dive-bomber pilot, and I had to shoot over the top of him to get the Japanese plane in back of him. I'll never forget that one. When I shot, all of the brass free-fell below my aircraft and rained down on him, as I passed over him.

I forgot all about that when I pulled the trigger.

Well, they had developed a set of tactics. When the dive-bombers were very slow to pull up because the dive flaps were open, the Japanese would come in and shoot them down. So they decided that with every fourth dive-bomber that went down, they would send one Wildcat fighter down with them to be there. It was then that I came down with the last twelve. The twelve dive-bombers had already passed into this run, and I followed them down.

In the meantime, one of them was heading straight toward me—that was Lieutenant Pool and his rear gunner, and there was a fourth plane right on his tail, right below him, and Pool didn't see him. They were all in line with me so I had to fire over his head. I didn't feel apprehensive about it even though I knew that it would be a close shot, but I forgot completely about the brass from the machine gun linkage falling underneath the aircraft.

If you are going about three hundred miles per hour when the brass leaves the aircraft, the brass is falling at about three hundred miles per hour—because it is a free-falling body. So this is what rained down on his dive-bomber and almost knocked him down. I didn't know it until I got back.

So what did they say to you?

Well, we weren't on the same radio frequency, so I didn't know about it then. When I got back I began thinking, "I forgot about the brass." I worried about whether the guy could make it back, after having that fall on him. When he got back, he was furious. He said they could have gotten the plane. He thanked me for being on the spot, but he said he was going to turn his plane so his rear gunner could take care of it. I doubt it because the Jap had it right below the rear gunner, behind his tail, and was ready to boresight it.

Lieutenant Pool was killed later, wasn't he?

Yes, he was checking out in a P-47—a friend let him do it—and he flew it into a mountain on a hillside.

What was the hardest loss you experienced over there?

On the second tour over at Okinawa, they sent us down with a new type of fuse, a VT fuse. A proximity fuse. They put one-thousand pound bombs on our planes, and we were supposed to drop these bombs. Of course I wasn't a dive-bomber pilot.

The fuse man wired the nose fuse of these VT-bombs, but intelligence said, "Don't drop these because they are highly classified. It's a new type of fuse, and we don't want the Japanese to have it." They added, "If you have to drop it, drop it at sea and not at land." Finally, though, after our briefing, they decided to let us drop them.

They had twenty-two planes specifically to drop these bombs. On the way over we were going to meet with the army, navy, and the ordnance people who were going to wire the safety fuse wire through the nose of the VT fuse. That way it wouldn't spin and warm up and explode. But, when the wire would pull out of the nose fuse, it would generate three hundred turns and then explode when it was close to any object.

The Corsair has a thirteen-foot, four and a-half-inch diameter propeller. Imagine this bomb sitting in the middle of this Corsair's belly strapped underneath. Instead of being in line with the flight path, the wire would stretch from the nose fuse across to the right pylon. This was like taking a rubber band and putting it in the wind crossways. What happens is that when the wind gets faster and faster, the rubber band will vibrate at both ends. The same thing with the wire. What happened was that the wire would pull out because of the wind and, armed, it started to turn three hundred turns. Of course, then the bomb exploded, and the aircraft was blown to bits.

I was leading the flight, and we had ninety-six planes in all. Some of the planes had rockets, and we had bombs. Midway over there, two planes blew up in midair. We lost a fellow by the name of McCoy and one named Hale from our squadron. I first thought some antiaircraft fire hit us. Then I realized,

"Drop everything, drop these bombs!" I dropped mine and got so excited that I dropped the fuel tanks and everything else.

At the time we were three-quarters of the way over there, and we had the range to come back. We had four planes to a division; my plane and my wingman was one section. On his wing is my two section. His wing was Landsberg and Stephenson. So I looked over there and there was the bomb still on the aircraft. I gave a direct order to drop them. I don't know if they couldn't get rid of them or what. So I said, "Don't dive, stay up here."

When we finally reached the target, some were going to run out of gas, so we had to go ahead and dive. Since I was leading, I went ahead and began my dive. I had rockets beside the bombs. Somehow or another I made my dive under the plane, and I looked and saw the wire was still intact. I flew under the other guys' plane and the wire was still intact there too. I said, "You guys stay up here." They agreed. This is documented by everyone else because they held an investigation about it.

I went into my dive but these two guys, instead of staying up there, pushed over. They weren't halfway down before they blew up. When we got back, one aircraft wouldn't take off because of engine trouble, so they looked at the fuse and discovered the problem. We were dismissed of any charges. I never forgot that.

Why did they come down?

I don't know. They were pretty wild youngsters, to a degree—not wild, but they were the type of guys that figured nothing could happen to them. We had fifty people like that. But they just didn't stay up. They came down with it, and that was it.

Do you remember what you did that night?

Well, naturally, there was an investigation into the whole thing. It upset me terribly. We had a few drinks to wind down, but you never get over things like that.

Any other experiences you haven't gotten over? The Japanese were real close to the field you used at Guadacanal.

Yes, right on the perimeter. But the first two planes off would create a lot of dust, so the Japanese mortar man—we called him "Pistol Pete"— who was sitting back in the hills maybe two miles away, maybe not that far, would zero in on the dust. The last two or three fighters to take off would take off with mortars hitting the field. So you could count on us to get those two fighters off fast.

Was "Pistol Pete" that good?

Yes, he was good. He never shot anybody down, but he caused problems. When you first took off, you weren't sure if any scrap metal hit your controls or not.

Any other stories about taking off?

Yes, I was very apprehensive about taking off in the Wildcat. It was new to us. The propeller had an electric motor to change the pitch. I hated that damn motor. If you put it in manual instead of automatic, it would go into a prop pitch sometimes, but not all of the time. In manual you'd have twenty-eight to twenty-nine hundred rpms. A lot of the guys took off with the thing in automatic, but I always put it on manual so I could get max power. I had two of my friends, who had it in automatic, killed when they hit the trees. They took off at twenty-five hundred rpms, and that wasn't enough for them to clear the trees. Master Sergeant Guy Conti got killed that way.

When were you most frightened?

Outside of being shot down, it was when my engine failed in the morning. It was about four in the morning. Pitch black. We were supposed to take off and get to the eastern part of Guadalcanal. They figured they had some twin-engine bombers coming in to hit the fleet at dawn. It wasn't radar, it was the coast watchers telling us this. So four of us took off. As soon as I left the deck with full power, I started to lose power, with not much rpms, just a little. I had to hop on instruments because you can't fly in pitch black, you had to use instruments. After flying on the instruments to pick up altitude, we got a red warning that some Japanese aircraft was coming in. The ship in question started to maneuver and turned over at high propeller pitch. The South Pacific is very florescent as a result of the animal life. Whenever a ship turns over at full speed, you see the fish life. You can see all these lights. They look like thousand-watt bulbs. Once I spotted this, I became oriented with the earth, and I quit flying instruments. About that time I saw the needle vibrating, and I knew I had a leak. I knew my engine was going to fail, and that I wouldn't make it back. That scared me. We were far out in the ocean.

A few minutes later the engine did fail, and I could smell the rubber burning and the hot metal parts. I thought the only way was to jump, but I couldn't. I tried it three times. I trimmed it down to about 130 knots, which isn't too bad of a wind, and I got out to jump. I realized I couldn't jump because I didn't have my regular chute on. The day before we were in a big dogfight, and I saw one of the guys bail out and his chute didn't open. I watched him go down, pulling and trying to get his chute to open. I didn't know if mine would open. I stood on the wing for just seconds. I held onto the cockpit. I put my feet on the wings. Did I have a chute that needed to be repacked? I didn't let go to where the wind would blow me off at 130 knots.

But I got pretty frightened. That's when I decided, at night with no moon, to go in on instruments and land the aircraft.

You actually landed in the water.

Luckily, an air raid alarm sounded, which caused the ships to swerve with high-speed evasive moments. One ship really started maneuvering at about three hundred feet and the USS *Jenkins*—that's a destroyer—went straight ahead about two hundred yards, and it turned up so much animal sea life acting like thousand-watt bulbs. It looked like a football field lit up. So I kept the wheels up and landed in the wake of it.

Was there anything dangerous about landing in the wake?

No. There could be, though. But I had a wing tank, and I didn't think that my wings would dip. The engine was not turning over. Everything was still. So when I hit, it skipped and jumped because the surface tension is broken, but I had light from the waves which gave me three dimensions. Of course, a slick sea is very difficult to gauge heights for landing purposes.

You really didn't want to get on the destroyer?

Well, there are different breeds of me. I could not fight on a ship. There are certain people who are that way, and I'm one of them. I feel that there's nowhere to go. I guess it takes a certain individual to have a certain slot in wartime.

I have seen the Achie 99s, the Japanese dive-bombers, hit our destroyers. Before I could crank up my wheels, our destroyer broke in half and sank. So, I wasn't about to get aboard one. They wanted to pick me up before the air raid started and I said, "No way. I'd rather take my chance out here in my little rubber boat." In the water you have a chance of getting all your intestines all messed up because of the shock waves from bombs. It puts your intestines in knots and will cause a blockage and, of course, you will die. But, if you stay in the rubber boat, you won't be affected—nothing would go through your body. I would be parallel with the waves.

What did the guys on ship say to you afterwards?

They gave me a lot of static. They thought I'd been shot down. I said, "No, I wasn't shot down. My engine failed." They'd ask, "Why didn't you want to get on?" I said, "I wasn't about to get on. I don't like a destroyer." That brought on another round or two of laughter.

I was very impatient aboard their ship because I wanted off right away. They had to send me down to the engine room to keep me from talking, and to dry my clothing. Even with the air raid over, I wanted off. To put it another way, I was "nervous in the service."

You're clearly an individualist.

That's the way pilots are, don't you think? That's the way I feel. In my family we come from a long line of military who served in the wars over a long period of time. Different wars. But I've always felt that in a group of pilots, you can almost tell who's going to make it and who's not. It's just the attitude of the individual. A case in point: one guy wanted to bring a rifle with him in case he was shot down. Well, that's a negative attitude. Anything you bring in loose into the cockpit,—as soon as you pull four or five Gs, it (the rifle) is going to go through the cockpit and out of the aircraft. So a fellow like that is overcautious. I wasn't that brave, don't get me wrong, but after you've been in combat a few times, you develop a feeling that you can handle yourself.

Let's go back to the plane you flew through, the one that blew up.

That's the one that scared me the most. I was slowing down as I flew up toward him; he was diving and I was climbing. I figured I could fire and get him and bank to the right or left, or get away from the man if he caught fire. Unless he got me. But I felt that my 50-caliber could really blast him well before he could get me. He was firing two pea-shooters! When he opened up, he was out of range and I was more stable. He was diving, and he had to trim his aircraft before he could fire. By the time I got to about 130 knots, which is a little slow, I opened up with both 50s and this slowed me up that much more. From then on the plane went to ninety knots, just like that. At ninety knots you can't maneuver because the stick is very loose in your hand, and it goes all over in the cockpit before you can get control of the aircraft. At higher speed just a touch of the stick, which is very sensitive, will give you a change of direction. When his plane caught fire, he came straight at me. He was going to ram me. That's when I really became frightened. I tried to maneuver out of the way, but the wing wasn't responding. I just held the trigger down, and he blew up. I flew through the pieces.

How many seconds between him blowing up and you flying through?

I don't know. I started to open when he was about 400 yards away, and he closed in a hurry. The outer guns started at 350 yards; the midboard at 300; and the inboards, at 250 so that's a solid mass of steel at 250 and 300 yards. That's what I hit him with. I just held the trigger down. I imagine it was a fraction of a second from the time I became frightened and the time he blew up. I was lucky he blew up, and I was able to go through.

What do you think when things like that happen?

I think that some of us were made to survive and others were not. I don't know how to put that. I've been going on borrowed time since I started flying those airplanes. I've been lucky, that's all.

Getting back to Okinawa, that was the thing. That changed my whole life, the day the VT fuses blew up, and I lost the two men. It was a predawn takeoff, and I was the lead person in plane number forty-four. This is the God's truth. I had the aircraft number forty-four for the flight, was strapped in, tested out, going to the end of the runway. I revved up so I could clear the engines for take off. Suddenly, a jeep came from headquarters and told me to get out of the airplane, that I had another number. I said, "Well, hell, you could tell me that by radio. You don't have to have the number of the aircraft to lead. We can do this up in the air." The guy said, "No, this guy Hale is going to take it and you're going to take the other."

I cussed him out, I got mad, I put the brakes on. I got into the jeep and then into the other plane. Guess which plane was the first to blow up? Number forty-four—Hale's.

So what do you say to that?

Somebody is looking after me somewhere along the line. I'm a religious man, and I learned a lot of religion then. I have a son who is a priest. To survive that war, you have to remember this fact—and it is a fact—that I was sold for a sack of rice. That and the "number forty-four" incident changed my values in life.

You were sold for a sack of rice?

Yes. After I was shot down, it took me about six hours to swim in. I had been wounded, and I treated my wounds with the first aid kit that they had included. I was really adapted to the swamps in Louisiana. I was born and raised in the swamps, so I was very comfortable in the jungle of Kolombangara. I knew I could survive. However, I dropped the dressings I had all over the bottom of the jungle floor. The headhunters—I presumed they were because I talked to the coast watchers about it—had been tracking me from day one. They picked up all my debris. I came across a clearing which had a little hut. Of course, knowing the swamp, I knew if the birds were singing, everything was all right. The birds were singing there in the clearing. I figured good and well, that no one was in the hut.

I set up housekeeping there but on the third morning, when I awoke, the birds were not singing. I looked out and spotted this native standing in the clearing on the other side, holding a Bowie knife.

What did you think at this moment?

Well, I knew good and well that no man is going to stand in the clear unless there's someone in back of him, so I dropped my knife. I didn't have a pistol. I lost my pistol when I parachuted out. I was right about the numbers. They didn't say anything to me—they didn't speak English. they came forward, captured me and put me in a twelve-man rigger canoe. We went to a village deep inside the island of Kolombangara. There was another type of native there. These others were the same small height, wide-shouldered with Afro-hair, red lips from betel nuts, and red hair. This other group that had me had a bone through the nose and were a different breed altogether. They kept me in a cage with two people on guard.

I don't know if the people who kept me were headhunters or what, but I do know, from research years later, that they still had some headhunters around there in those days. Anyway, the following day, five members of a different tribe came in with a sack of rice and threw it down, and I was released to them.

The coast watchers bought you?

Right. A fellow by the name of Missionary Silvester.

The natives had planned on going on a raiding party to kill five Japanese from this barge. They found it practical for me to go along. I went along, but they killed the Japanese by the time I got there. I needed clothing because I was stripped to the waist. They had this Japanese locker with a uniform in it, and I put it on. That picture with the Japanese uniform on is in my den over here. They had a bottle of sake. We drank and I was feeling no pain when I got out of there. They took me from the island to where the coast watcher was stationed. It was a long trip. We left at night and how they navigated I'll never know, because it was raining and no stars were out.

We didn't reach the island at the proper time so the Japanese planes came low over us. The natives kept me covered with palm leaves over me so the Japanese wouldn't spot me on the bottom of the boat. When we arrived, I was told to get up in Pidgin English. I sat up and there stood this white man, calling me by name and rank. When he pronounced "De Blanc" in fluent French, I almost fell out of that canoe. I thought, "How can a man in a war zone come over here and call me by name." He knew all the other people I was working with. He was a missionary from England. I gave him all my Japanese weapons that I had picked up along the way, and I picked up a spear. He said, "You have a knife hidden on your body. The natives expect you to turn it in." I thought it would be mine. He said, "No, you're going to have to turn it in." When I did, all the natives shined big smiles. They probably thought I was going to hurt their missionary. After the war he said he would send it to me, but he never did.

John McKinny in his F4D Skyray. 1956, North American Air Defense Command

JOHN McKINNY

The Battle of Leyte Gulf

J ohn McKinny was playing a pickup football game in Long
Island, New York, where he had grown up. A friend, parked nearby, was
listening to his car radio. Suddenly, he yelled, "Hey, the Japs have bombed
Pearl Harbor." John asked him where Pearl Harbor was. Nobody there
knew where it was or, as John explains, "even what it was."

John immediately thought of the old World War I movies he'd seen,
depicting soldiers jumping out of trenches, racing across the field, hollering
"charge." He admits he couldn't see himself doing that. However, when the
opportunity arose to enter the navy flight training program not long after the
attack, the idea seemed a natural. After all, he had grown up around airplanes,
though he had never been in one, and had always wanted to fly. He had also
lived around some historic flight locations, including Roosevelt Field, where
Lindbergh took off for Paris and Mitchell Field, an army field.

In the interview John describes his experience in the Battle for Leyte
Gulf, one of the great sea battles and a major victory for the United States,
where three Japanese battleships, nine destroyers, and four carriers were
sunk. He was awarded the Navy Cross for his role in sinking one of the
carriers. He retired with the rank of commander. Following retirement from
the military, he continued to fly as a pilot for General Dynamics.

I flew for nearly forty years and, while in the military, was shot at on numerous
occasions but never hit. It was rather strange. I made the same runs, participated
in the same strikes as other pilots, but never received a bullet hole in my
aircraft. Others had control surfaces blown off, all kinds of things.

Anybody ever tease you about that?

No, no one ever did. I don't know that people remembered that much about
that kind of thing at the time. I didn't realize it myself until later. There must
have been others in the squadron who were not hit, but the majority of them
had been.

You flew at Iwo Jima.

Yes, our baptism of fire occurred on the fourth of July, 1944, at Iwo Jima. We
were operating off the USS *Franklin* in Air Group Thirteen. I was in Torpedo

Squadron Thirteen. Our first strike at Iwo involved bombing the runway, anti-aircraft positions, and buildings. I think the *Franklin* was positioned about one hundred miles east of Iwo.

It was just like a Hollywood movie scene. Of course, we didn't know what to expect; about three-quarters of the squadron had never been in combat before. There had been planes in there ahead of us, probably two hundred planes on that strike. Approaching the target I saw everything you see in the old movies: parachutes, planes spinning down, flaming, anti-aircraft fire, etc. My target was a gun emplacement. The gunner nearly had me boresighted, as I could see those things coming up at me real slow at first. Then all of a sudden, whistling past beneath the cowling of the airplane, a steady stream of them. I figured that if I changed my dive angle, I'd miss the target. I don't know whether I hit it or not, but I know that if the gunner had raised his gun one inch or so he would have had me for sure. I followed those tracers down to his location and released two five-hundred-pound bombs, then retired to the east, rendezvoused with the others, and flew back to the carrier. Everything was fine.

We landed aboard the straight-deck Essex class carrier; they didn't have angled decks then. When we landed, we had to retract the tail hook, fold the wings, and taxi forward in a hurry because of the approaching aircraft about thirty seconds behind us. So I landed and taxied forward.

Following engine shutdown, you are expected to get out and run into the island structure to safety to avoid any aircraft bounding over the barricade. But I couldn't get out of the airplane. All of a sudden this whole battle scene, which had taken place about an hour earlier, just hit me. It's strange. While the battle had been going on I wasn't especially frightened, just awestruck! It wasn't until I was safely on the deck that my feet started trembling on the rudder pedals, and I just couldn't get out of the airplane.

What happened?

One of the flight deck hands had to help me out.

Did you have any other delayed reactions?

No, that was the only time. After that, I knew what to expect.

Did you know how important Iwo Jima was?

No, that was the first we had heard of it. That was the first time it had been attacked; many months before our marines landed there. But the anti-aircraft fire was rather intense.

Where was the worst anti-aircraft fire you saw?

Chichi Jima, an island north of Iwo Jima. That's where George Bush was shot down.

Did you know George Bush?

No. There were a great number of people in the class. He flew TBMs in the Torpedo Squadron identical to ours. The anti-aircraft fire we experienced at Chichi Jima was the heaviest land-based anti-aircraft fire I've seen anywhere. It was heavier when we hit the Jap fleet units later, however.

We hit the Japanese fleet units in the Battle of Leyte Gulf. One of the fellows in my squadron was shot down on September 1 over Chichi Jima in withering anti-aircraft fire. The harbor was shaped like a bowl with guns on the mountainsides all the way around. This meant they could send up a cone of fire. In fact, one strike was called off because we had lost so many planes during the initial phase of the attack. So we went back and attacked it again later. George Bush was shot down either that day or the day following. Both Bush and the other flier I mentioned were rescued by the same submarine. In fact, this friend of mine was with Bush on the submarine for nearly a month. I understand he was invited to Bush's innauguration but couldn't attend because his wife was ill at the time. He has remained a friend of George Bush to this day.

When was the Leyte experience?

October 24 and 25, 1944. We were with Admiral Halsey's group, the group that steamed north to hit the Japanese carriers and other fleet units that had been sighted off the northeast coast of the Philippines. There were four carriers with several cruisers surrounding the carriers, and a number of destroyers protecting the cruisers. This was the most intense anti-aircraft fire I've ever experienced. It was a cone of fire, a cloud. It seemed impossible to be able to fly through it safely. I figured it was full of lead.

Did you want to turn around and go home?

No, you go through a lengthy training period and perform automatically. I was the junior officer in the squadron and flew wing on my leader. There must have been two hundred planes on that raid, and we were positioned toward the end of it. It was to be a glide bombing attack. We each carried two one-thousand-pound armor-piercing bombs. We had been briefed to make the attack from west to east because our own carrier was located to the east of the combat area, one hundred miles or so. So we were to retire eastward to the rendezvous point, following the attack. Well, that was great except that wasn't the way it turned out. There were so many airplanes in the attacking group. They were flying around in a circle, peeling off one after the other. We, at the tail end, were advancing farther around the circle all the time and ended up attacking instead from the east to west.

I flew through a small cloud formation and, when I broke out of the cloud, the only thing I saw was one aircraft carrier. I just eyeballed this vessel and dropped two bombs. My flight leader—who had dropped his bombs before he pulled up to look back—said he saw one of mine hit just inboard of the deck edge. It blew up inside the ship while the other landed close to the ship and blew up in the water, a near miss. I was awarded the Navy Cross for this action.

So you actually sank the carrier.

Not alone. I only assisted in its sinking. I understand United States submarines assisted also. Our planes sank all four carriers and a number of other ships. The fact that we made this run in the wrong direction resulted in our having to turn around and fly back through this stuff again. Our aircraft, TBMs, once leveled off—big lumbering things—were probably going all of 140 to 160 knots. But the strike turned out okay. We did lose some people though, and that is always sad.

You never got hit at all?

No.

Did you have anybody that you really admired over there?

Yes, my flight leader with whom I flew the entire time we operated in the Western Pacific. He was a lieutenant JG when I first joined the squadron as an ensign, and he was promoted later to Lieutenant. He was from Pennsylvania. I'll never forget his name: Frederick Wistar Morris Janney, Jr. As the junior officer and pilot in the squadron, I thought this gentleman was God Almighty. I followed him everywhere, through every one of our missions. Of course, I deeply admired every one of our pilots and aircrewmen and especially our commanding officer, Lawrence C. French.

There had been a number of planes that had made emergency landings at Tacloban, on the island of Leyte, where MacArthur had landed. We received orders to fly in there, six of us, to pick up these pilots and bring them back to their respective ships. However, when we got there, we learned that there had been a mix-up in communications, and that some other ship's planes had already picked them up. While we were refueling, an army colonel came screaming down the runway in a jeep and told us to get the hell out of there, because the Japs were coming.

We jumped into our planes and took off, and promptly ran into a horrendous storm. Really rough weather. Just terrible. I stuck with that leader of mine—I stuck with him like glue—bouncing all over the place. I noticed that he was headed downward in a graveyard spiral, which is kind of dangerous, especially if you get close to the water. We pulled up at maybe eight hundred feet, beneath the storm and in torrential rain.

After we had returned to the ship, I asked him what he was doing in a graveyard spiral that close to the water. He said he didn't even know he was in a spiral. He thought he was flying straight and level, but his gyro-horizon had tumbled! He was actually headed straight for the ocean and hadn't known it! He would have flown right into the ocean had the cloud layer been much lower. Being a young ensign, I figured he knew what he was doing.

You flew the Pacific for how long?

Until November 1944, when we took a kamikaze hit into the flight deck, through the number three elevator and down into the hangar deck. It exploded and killed a great number of people. The ship retired to Bremerton, Washington, for extensive repairs. Our squadron was later reformed at Alameda, California.

Where were you when you were hit by the kamikaze?

I was in the officer's ward room, several decks below the flight deck. I didn't know what had happened. They had closed the watertight hatches so that we were unable to move around the ship after that.

The thing I thought was rather disconcerting was that the ward room served as an emergency battle dressing station during general quarters. It was here they brought the wounded. And so you would see these horribly burned people lying on the tables at which we were to later be served dinner. It was a pretty miserable sight. The explosions knocked out all kinds of power, and we didn't get the word down there, though we were relatively safe.

How many planes hit the Franklin?

This particular time just one. He carried a bomb which he didn't drop. He just flew straight into the after elevator, down through the flight deck, into the hangar deck. The flight deck in those days was made of teak wood. Nowadays, they are all steel. The Zero and its bomb actually blew up in the hangar deck, causing catastrophic damage.

Did you lose any fliers that were close to you?

Every one of them was close. I've often said that I felt closer to those fellows at that time than I did to my own brothers, and I consider my brothers to be very close. That is to say that I think I knew more about each of those people than I did about my own brothers. It was pretty rough losing any of them.

How do you remember those fliers now?

I thought every one of them was absolutely fearless. I thought I was the only one who was frightened out there, but I'm sure they all were. However, we performed as we had been trained in spite of circumstances.

Any weird airplanes you've flown over your career?

I guess the F4D Skyray, a jet fighter made by the Douglas Aircraft Company, might be considered weird in a way. It was an impressive-looking aircraft, with a modified Delta wing and, at that time, back in the early and mid-50s, it held the world speed and climb records. It was a great airplane to fly, but a rather unstable gun platform—so it didn't last long.

What else did you fly?

Just about everything the navy had, with the exception of helicopters. While stationed in Miami in 1943, I flew the SBC-3 and the SBC-4—Curtiss dive-bombers. They were identical in appearance, but the SBC-4 was a newer version in which the wheels, flaps, and cowl flaps were hydraulically operated. The SBC-3 had a manual system for the gear, flaps, and cowl flaps, and was considered out of date by everyone.

There were several instances in Miami wherein SBCs were ditched at sea off the coast for one reason or another, mostly as the result of engine failures. The aircraft, a biplane, had flotation gear between the wings which automatically inflated to keep it afloat for some time following a ditching.

Instructors would approach the ditched aircraft in a boat and shout at the pilot, "Is that bird a three or a four?" If the pilot advised that it was a three, the instructor would stab the flotation device, allowing the aircraft to sink. One way to dispose of obsolete aircraft!

You were involved in air intercept operations, weren't you?

Yes, I was stationed at NAS North Island in a Jet All-Weather Intercept Squadron. Mostly we chased Air Force B-36s. I don't remember ever scrambling on an actual unknown myself, although other pilots had. It was a standby situation twenty-four hours a day, seven days a week. SAC would send up the B-36s on unannounced training missions to see if they could be intercepted. We would make a run on them and take a photo for proof of the intercept.

What was Search and Rescue like?

Another of those standby operations. MATS (Military Air Transport Service) had a regulation that was strange. This was back in 1954–55, prior to the jet transport age. If a MATS passenger plane flying across the Pacific were to lose one of its four engines, it was still capable of flying at about 230 knots. They weren't really in trouble at all. But they operated under a rule whereby they were required to call for an intercept. So we would take off from wherever we were stationed—then Wake Island or Kwajalein—and head out to intercept them. This might be as far as six or eight hundred miles.

A fully loaded UF, which we flew in this type of operation, following take-off seldom attained a speed of over 120 knots, so we weren't really going to be an awful lot of help to them. The idea was that, in the event one of those aircraft had to ditch at sea, we would home in on them by electronic means and drop needed survival gear. Although the UF was an amphibian, by regulation we were not permitted to land in the open sea. The strange thing, of course, was that they were in better shape on three engines than we were on two.

You never had to throw rafts?

No. There was never any real trouble.

I flew one of those UFs from Kwajalein to Honolulu and refueled at NAS Barber's Point. From there I was to ferry the plane to Alameda, California, and then on to NAS North Island. The aircraft had a large fuel tank in the cabin, in addition to the regular tanks in the wings and pontoons, for the trans-Pacific flight. Instead of flying directly to Alameda, the meteorologist advised that were I to fly a northern route, I would pick up some horrendous tail winds about halfway. So I took off, headed out on the northern route and, after a number of hours, noticed that our fuel supply was approaching the minimum allowed, arriving at a point called ETP, which is the "Estimated Turning Point." If the fuel supply is below a predetermined amount, or an engine is lost short of that position, we'd have to return to Hawaii. If we crossed that point with sufficient fuel and both engines still churning, we would continue on course. ETP was based on winds, fuel consumption, and other relevant information.

We headed north but failed to pick up the expected tail winds. We crossed ETP with barely sufficient fuel and had to continue on course. The fuel was getting lower and lower and still no tail winds. Then, all of a sudden, we encountered tail winds close to one hundred miles per hour: they were about an hour late. At this point, I wasn't sure we were going to make it, so I called the Coast Guard in San Francisco and requested an intercept. It would fly along with us in case we went in. I was happy to see that bird! It was winter, and it would have been mighty cold in the water. Anyway, the pilot flew formation on us the rest of the way in. And I landed in Alameda with three gallons in one tank and five in the other. That was it. That might have been good enough for one lap around the track, maybe!

Not a lot of people realize this, that the navy was involved in the Berlin Air Lift.

Yes. In 1948 I was flying R5Ds (DC-4s) out of Honolulu. I took a trip one afternoon to Moffett Field, California, a routine passenger flight. I was to turn around immediately at Moffett and head back to Honolulu at 4:00 am. While filing a flight plan at the Operations Office at Moffett, we were handed a message that advised, "Don't come home. Proceed to Rhein-Main Airport in Frankfurt, Germany." As you might imagine, there was a lot of scurrying around for charts and things. I had no clean laundry or anything. So off we flew to Germany. Half the squadron (twelve R5Ds) subsequently were transferred to Rhein-Main from Hawaii.

Any interesting things happen over there?

Twice I landed without ever seeing the runway, and had to be towed off the runway, which meant that the plane only three minutes behind me didn't get to land at all, and had to return to Rhein-Main with its cargo. Once when I broke into a clear spot while approaching Templehof, I looked up and saw a Russian propeller-driven fighter alongside. He waved, climbed a little higher, and made a sort of high-side run on us—and that was it. It was kind of spooky.

You were a sitting duck—if he attacked.

Yeah, we were unarmed. Just pilot, co-pilot, and flight engineer, and a planeload of cargo.

Once, as I was letting down for an approach into Templehof, I broke beneath the overcast and, lo and behold, there in front of us was a barrage balloon. It was at our level, but we had plenty of time to avoid it.

Explain how you felt.

The Russians did things to upset us psychologically. They never shot anyone down, or any such thing, but they pulled all this psychological stuff, such as launching the barrage ballons on the end of cables into areas where they knew they'd be seen. As far as we knew, they never located them where we couldn't see them—where the weather was bad—but we didn't know that for sure. It just made you think, made you wonder what might be in that next cloud ahead.

How big was the balloon?

I saw it for only a couple of seconds. I'm guessing it was somewhat larger than those advertising balloons you see sometimes.

Did you ever feel any rivalry between the air force and navy over there? Any snide remarks like, "What's a navy guy doing here?"

Oh yes. They kept records of everything we accomplished. VR-8, the squadron I was assigned to, stood number one from the time we arrived in October 1948, until the airlift ended in June 1949. These standings reflected flight time, cargo tonnage delivered, aircraft maintenance, turnaround time, aircraft availability, etc. There were a great number of air force squadrons involved, but only two navy squadrons of twelve planes each. All were competing with one another. VR-6, which was our sister squadron from Guam, was number two. The air force naturally chose not to advertise the fact that the navy was involved in the airlift and, especially, that two navy squadrons were numbers one and two in the standings.

Any parting shots? Any feelings about the career?

I consider myself extremely lucky and grateful to have been able to serve in the navy as an aviator, and to have followed that up with a flying position in the business world. I thought it was the greatest thing in the world to have a job I enjoyed as much as I did flying for all those years.

You couldn't get enough of it?

Yes, that's right. But then, all of a sudden in 1980, I just felt as though I had had enough. I haven't flown an airplane since.

Can you explain that?

No, I can't. I would love to fly aerobatics in an old Stearman or something similar, out there in the toolies, but no more airways flying for me! I don't know. It just got to the point where it suddenly became boring. Progress in aviation I guess means being controlled more and more all the time. You no longer have the opportunity of flying off in any direction you feel like, as we could in the past. Of course, to the kids today, this doesn't mean much because they are brought up under all this positive control from the start. They find it quite normal.

What does flight mean to you?

Mostly serenity. You know the old saying, "Flying involves hours and hours of tedium, interspersed with seconds of sheer terror." That's the way it was, certainly. But most of it was relaxing and serene.

Jack Yaeger, Jr. explains to his crew chief how he shot down two planes.

JACK YAEGER, JR

Nagasaki Overflight

J ack Yaeger Jr. is descended from old-time Florida pioneers, including "Watermelon Eaton," who experimented with mint and cherry flavors in watermelons. Jack himself is an original. He is a natural Southern-style storyteller, and has plenty to tell.

A member of the 318th Fighter Group of the Seventh Air Force, Jack saw WWII action through the Gilbert, Marshall, Marianas, and Ryukyus campaigns, from Hawaii to Japan. He served twenty-one months in the South Pacific and became an ace.

"One thing I thought might cause me to wash out was when "Seahorse" and I were each flying out of Carlsbad, New Mexico, practicing nightflying, and we got lost." It seems Jack and his friend ran into a snowstorm and lost their bearings. Suddenly, Jack spotted an airliner and decided to follow it. He kept trying to call the plane but to no avail. Finally, when he came out of the snowstorm, he found himself in Blythe, California. "Seahorse" had kept going and had flown on into Mexico. Jack didn't wash out, but the close calls of one sort or another kept coming. Perhaps his most compelling story is when he tells of having to write a letter informing a friend's mother of her son's death.

During one of the reunion meetings in Tallahassee, someone asked Jack to stand up. Jack stood up, albeit reluctantly, and explained that he had nothing much to say. One member of the audience said, "We don't care about what you have to say. You were the youngest pilot in the squadron. We just wanted to see what you look like now." Today, this mild-mannered Southerner looks fit and fine. He is married to his second wife, Elinor Whitney-Yaeger, and they live in Tallahassee.

How did you get into the military?

I was right out of high school, but at this point, in the early stages, you had to have two years of college. I had none. Every time I could save up enough money, I'd go out and take flying lessons while I was in high school. And I had gotten my pilot's license before I graduated from high school. And so they set up a review board of about twelve officers out at Dale Mayberry Field. I went out and talked with them and met with the board. The board had gotten all my transcripts of grades from high school and had scrutinized them.

Was that intimidating for a high school kid?

No, not really, because I realized they were doing this to possibly let me escape having the two years of college so I could get in. And so they started entertaining me with all these questions, trying to see what kind of guy I really was.

Some of the money that I made to take the flying lessons came from working at Wakulla Springs during the summer months as a lifeguard and a pier captain. As a result, I ended up making some underwater movies for Grantland Rice. Then they had the Tarzan pictures, and I was able to work in the Tarzan pictures and dove out of trees, doubling for Weismuller. Then they blacked four of us up, and we would paddle out into the springs in a dugout canoe, and Johnny would turn it over and kill us. Oh boy, when they learned that, it got them. They quit asking me questions about me and started asking questions about all these things. "You knew Johnny Weismuller?" "You dove out of trees and stood in for him?" And oh man, they just went wild on all that, asking me about the movies.

What else did you tell those officers?

They were also quizzing me about the Grantland Rice underwater movies we made. You know how they used to put on newsreels or short subjects for people to watch while this transition was going on? That was when they would put these Grantland Rice highlights on. We had one where we had an underwater picnic with the girls sitting around with baskets underwater, and we're smoking cigarettes. The cigarettes were just white sticks with little black tips on 'em, and we'd have a mouth full of milk, and we'd look like we were taking a draw off of the cigarettes and we'd blow the milk out in the water, and it'd look like smoke. The review board was really interested in all of these things. And finally, they approved me. So when I graduated from high school, I phoned 'em and told 'em I was ready to go, but all the flying schools were full so they told me to go on to college, and they would call me when there was an opening. I was in college two months, and they called me up and sent me to California—Santa Ana, then Ontario.

Any stories about training?

One thing is that everything was done alphabetically. Zimmerman and I would be the last to do anything. If we're getting passes off the base, we're the last ones to get the pass. If it was a night flight, we'd be the last ones to take off. Everybody'd be asleep when we'd get back, but when we were at Luke Field, we were checking out in the old P-40 fighter, and we were with a bunch of Chinese in our class. Evidently, the government had sent Chiang Kai-shek a bunch of P-40 planes, and they didn't know how to fly 'em, so they sent these guys over to learn how. At that time, you had to just get a good cockpit check in a P-40 and learn what all the instruments were. They'd blindfold you, and you'd have to put your hands on the instruments and tell 'em what they did and the name of each. Once you went through all of that and a class of instruction about how they flew, they'd just send you out on the runway, and you'd take off and learn how to fly. No instructor could go with you. The day that I had been passed to go out and check out, I was taxiing out and got on the end of the runway. They'd cleared me for take-off, and when I was in position they started yelling at me to "Get off the runway! An emergency landing is coming in. An emergency landing is coming in." And I looked out across the desert and here came a P-40. Smoke was a boiling out of it, and it was down low to the ground. Then it hit out there about three hundred yards off the end of the runway and blew up. They called me and said, "You're now clear to take off." I thought, "My God, I'd rather wait until tomorrow!" But, I took off, and I went up and I flew it around, and I did a few rolls and loops and came back in and landed. I found out that that was one of those Chinese boys who only knew two speeds in an airplane—and that was the engine cut off and then wide open—had crashed.

The Chinese would stand around nodding their heads and bowing and smiling, as if they understood everything the instructor was saying. He would lecture for about fifteen to twenty minutes and then he would say, "Do you understand what I'm telling you?" And then all of them would shake their heads, "No." That instructor was about to go wild, trying to teach those Chinese boys how to fly.

But when we were training in Pecos, Texas, we'd take rolls of toilet paper and throw 'em out of the plane, and they would unroll and unroll and make these long streamers and so then we'd fly down, pull up, and chop it all up with our props. Confetti would fall all over Pecos, Texas. One day they put a notice on the bulletin board: "Damn it, if we catch you doing that anymore, you're going to be court-martialed." Of course, we'd do it again the next week.

There's only one railroad coming through Pecos, going on down to El Paso, and there was one train that came through there at night. If we had a night flight, one of the guys would drop down right on the railroad track and turn one night landing light on, as if he was another train coming, and fly down the track right straight towards that train. The engineer would slam on the brakes, thinking it's another train coming. He'd come to a stop and then the guy would zoom right over top of him, and he'd have to crank it up and start going again. And that's another time they were going to courtmartial us if they caught us.

Sounds like you were some pretty wild characters.

Well hell, we were a bunch of kids, you know? A bunch of children with the big, fine playtoy. (*laughter*) When were flying out of Phoenix, we found the military had marked the Grand Canyon on our maps totally in red—we weren't supposed to fly over it, much less down in it. But of course, that's where we would go fly. We'd go down in the valleys of the Grand Canyon and just fly around and zoom around those curves and, all of a sudden, another plane would be coming from the other way, and you'd just barely miss each other. Then they'd have it on the bulletin board. But we had more fun looking at the Grand Canyon that way.

What was your most sobering experience early on? Did you have any scares or anything?

We were down at Makin in the South Pacific, in those old P-40s. We hadn't been there long before they sent a marine outfit in with Corsairs to take our place and took us back to Honolulu and gave us brand new P-47s. Spudoni and I. "Spud" we called him—was one of the test pilots taking these planes up and checking them out. The last thing you did was get up to about thirty thousand feet and put it into a power dive and come down and make damn sure the wings were going to stay on the damn thing. One day I had finished the whole check list on it, but I was going to thirty thousand feet to make the power dive. I got up to about seventeen thousand feet, and the engine caught on fire. I cut my switches immediately and cut the engine off and put it into a power dive. I was out over the ocean, going back towards the airfield without any power. I called them on the radio and told them to clear the field, that I was coming in a dead stick landing. The plane had caught on fire and was hot, but I had to turn the engines back on. So I was coming in off the end of the runway—coming in short. There were just a bunch of rocks and crap out there, and I reached over and I hit my switches on the engine. Thank God, the engine caught right away and lifted me up just enough. I landed on the end of the runway and just as I sat down, there was one hell of an explosion. Fire was all over the left hand side of the thing and all around the engine, and so I dove out onto the wing on the right hand side to get away from the fire. As I did, I tried to grab the leading edge of the wing, but I didn't quite make it and I started sliding off the darn thing, and I fell off on my back doing, I guess, about seventy miles an hour. I had a jungle pack on, and a one-man life raft, as well as a parachute. Fortunately, I just slid along the runway on all of that until I slowed down and started rolling over and over. I'd skinned up my elbows and knees and that's all. Afterwards, I was standing out there on the runway. I'd taken my parachute off, and this captain pulled up beside me in a jeep. Since I was just a young yardbird lieutenant in the squadron, he said in a nasty tone of voice, "Well, what did you do wrong this time?" I told him. I said, "I saved my damn life. Is that upsetting to you?" Boy, I was scared, upset, full of adrenalin, but it made me mad. He said,

"Well, throw your parachute in the back and let's ride down there." The fire trucks were down there putting the flame out. I said, "I wouldn't ride a damn inch with you." I mean, I just knew I was going a get court-martialed for the way I was talking to a captain. So I walked on down there, and he had driven up. By then they'd gotten the fire fairly well out. The left leading edge of the wing was blown wide open, from the fuselage all the way out to the tip. Also, rivets were blown out of there where the gas fumes had built up. And the captain looked at me. I glared back at him, and he shook his head, got in his jeep and drove off. And I didn't have a thing to do with that captain the rest of the time I was in that squadron. He would try to be buddy-buddy with me, and I would half-ass respond, you know?

Let me tell you what they did to us. We got those P-47s and none of us had ever flown them. So they took one of the best pilots out on a carrier, and they had figured out on paper that if there was a headwind of twenty miles an hour, and the carrier was traveling twenty knots, that they could catapult the P-47 off—if it had half the ammunition in the machine guns and half the gas load. All of this was on paper. So they took one of the older pilots with lots of experience out there and shot him off, and he made it. So then, they loaded two of those small carriers with our planes and took us to Saipan for the invasion down there. The whole plan was that the marines were going to go in and take the airfield, which was just a grass strip that the Japs had there. Then they'd call the carriers, and the carriers could shoot us off and we could come in and land, get all squared away, and give the marines air-ground support for the rest of the campaign on the island. And so you—you talk about a scared bugger! Never been catapulted off a carrier in my life, none of us had. We were all scared. And they shot us off, and all of us got airborne and we went in and we helped the marines. It just happened that a high school friend, George Taff, was in that marine outfit, so I was with George through the Saipan, Tinian, and Guam invasions, giving his outfit air support. If they ran into a cannon in a cave, or in a mountain, that was giving 'em trouble, they'd get us to shoot rockets in there and blow the thing up for 'em.

What was the toughest part of doing that support?

It wasn't bad at all because we'd practically take off and make a circle. They'd already told us what they'd wanted to do, so we'd know whether to load up the rockets or to have bombs or delayed fuse bombs or just what. The worst thing is the fact that we were working so close that we didn't want to drop on our own troops. We would get them to shoot a smoke grenade over into where the Japanese were for us to hit that area, but then they got smart. When one would drop on them, they'd shoot one over into our troops, so we worked out a situation where we would lay out these yellow panels in front of our troops. They'd tell us how many yards ahead of them the Japanese were located, so that way we would not shoot into our own troops. Finally, we would put one of our pilots up there with them because he knew what we could do, for sure. Also, we were the first outfit to use napalm.

Any problems handling that?

Not too much. We didn't know enough about it to really get scared, until we got to Okinawa for that invasion. We'd have a guy who would have an engine failure and couldn't get off and have a load of napalm. He'd blow sky high.

Did you lose any friends that way?

Two. This one boy could have possibly been horribly hung over. He had gotten a notice from his wife that he was the proud father of a baby bouncing boy, and he proceeded to get good and drunk. The next morning when we were taking off, almost a predawn take-off, he had his engine sputter just before he was getting his airspeed, and he crashed on the end of the field. His napalm just incinerated everything. You couldn't even hardly find bones of him. It was such a horrible thing.

He was a new one in the outfit. But Spudoni, who was a test pilot with me, was testing planes one day. He came down, and I came down at the same time on the power dive. We'd done all our checklists on the planes and had climbed to the altitude. We were coming down. Now, the P-47 had what they called a red line on the speed indicator. When you were in a dive, you damn sure didn't let that plane go over that red line because it would hit compressibility and none of your controls worked. You might use your trim tab when you get down lower, closer to the earth where the atmosphere is a little heavier, or you might be able to work it out and get it out of that damn dive. Usually you couldn't. But we peeled off, and when I leveled off, I looked around for Spudoni, and I couldn't find Spud anywhere. I called him on my radio, and I called him some more, and he didn't answer. I was getting furious as hell, so I called our tower; and my radio was working, and they answered. I asked them, "Have you heard from Spud anywhere?" And they said no, so I came on in. When I landed I saw that he wasn't there. He hadn't come in. Finally, a transport plane had heard our conversation about it and had seen a P-47 coming down, hit the ocean and blow up. We went to that location and tried to find something and couldn't find anything, but evidently he hit compressibility. Boy, when he hit the ocean he would have gone to whatever bottom was there.

Spud and I had gone all the way through flying school together. His mother wasn't wealthy, but anyplace we would move in training, she would get an apartment or a room there, so she could see Spud on the weekends. Spud's father was dead. Of course, we had had dinner together many times and chatted, and I knew his mother extremely well. When it was obvious he was dead, the squadron commander asked me to write the mother a letter, being as I knew them so well. I'm telling you that's the hardest thing I have ever written in my life, then and now, writing his mother trying to tell her that her son was dead. Now, you felt like getting drunk. We didn't have much liquor, but I found some that night, and I got drunk after writing that letter.

What did you tell her?

I started out talking about the war and how dangerous it was, and how so many of the guys had been eliminated due to the enemy, and also there was a certain number of pilots just because of the mechanical breakdown of the planes. I told her we had flown the planes so long that they were worn out. Some of them had been shot up and patched up—all this routine trying to build up a situation in her mind as she read the letter. Then at the very end, I said, "Spud was killed and I hated to write you and tell you this. I knew how much you loved him." I had to fight tears all the way through it, and right now I'm getting teary-eyed just talking to you about it.

Everything was done alphabetical, so Zimmerman and I and Spudoni and Warton and Wardlow were always the last ones to get to do anything. So we got our wings and our commissions as second lieutenants from the air force. Then they told us to report to the auditorium where we'd get our new assignments. So we all went to the auditorium, and we were sitting there and they said the first thirty men were going directly overseas into a combat unit in the Pacific, which had lost quite a number of pilots. So the officer started on the list: Zimmerman, Yaeger, Warton, Wardlow. This time they started at the bottom of the list. They had never done that before anywhere. It was always alphabetical.

What were you thinking then, the luck of the Irish?

I turned around to Warton, because his dad was a general at the Pentagon, and I said, "Does your Daddy really like you Warton—what with sending you straight into combat?" (*laughter*) But then they said the rest of the class was going for further training at Dale Mayberry Field in Tallahassee. Now here I am being sent overseas, and the rest of my class is coming to Tallahassee, my home town!

Later, I'd get letters from those buggers. I had told them my mother and dad's phone number and address. They would write me and say, "Well, we stopped by to see your mother and dad the other day, and they made us stay and have dinner with them. Afterwards, we went over to Chi Omega sorority house. All of those girls knew you." I'd get those letters, and that would infuriate me. They're out there chasing girls, and I'm gettin' shot at every day. So I finally wrote 'em and I said, "Don't write me another damn thing about Tallahassee. All it does is just make my morale slip down." (*laughter*) And they quit writing me, thank God. But most of those guys later went to England.

Talk about one of your most difficult situations.

I got pretty well shot up on one of the missions, and because the Japs had hit our airfields, I couldn't land there. This was down at Okinawa. Our field was over on the little island of Ie Shima. You could almost throw a rock and hit Okinawa across the bay. And the Japs had hit it, so I had to land over at the marine airfield at Okinawa. I started to put on my brakes—I had already jettisoned my canopy, in case I had to bail out. I was coming down the runway and lasted until I got on the ground. I put on my brakes to slow down because it was an awfully short airfield with a bunch of boulders at the end of it, but I didn't have any brakes. My hydraulic system was gone. So I went off the end of the damn runway, and I flipped over upside down on all those boulders. Since I was so excited, I grabbed my safety belt and just pulled it, which turned me loose. I fell down on those damn rocks, but my hand was up there in my throttle quadrant and got hung there. It cut one of the tips of my fingers off. It also cut my hand and my thumb up pretty bad. There were three marines sitting over there watching me falling there underneath on all those rocks, and they were laughing like hell at me, saying things like "Look at that dumb ass."

The one thing about Tinian, which was right across the bay from Saipan, was that we could fly in support of the marines there more often, about three missions a day, whereas before we'd fly about four or five hours to get to a target, hit the target, get shot at, and come on back. When we're attacking Tinian, we'd just take off from Saipan, circle around, do exactly what the marines wanted us to do, and come right on back. If they wanted us to drop napalm, if they wanted us to bomb something, or shoot rockets, or just spray something, then we could just circle and land. We didn't even have to gas up, just put on whatever was necessary for the next mission.

Still, those three missions were a lot.

Not really, because we were so used to sitting in that damn plane, like going to Iwo Jima or Truk—a seven hour mission. It felt kind of sporty, just go over there. Of course, we lost quite a few guys. We lost some planes. We lost more planes than we did guys, because they could make it off an island and bail out, if they weren't hit bad.

Do you remember a story of a guy who had a great escape and bailed out?

Well, I was one of 'em. Let me get through with this. We'd fly about three missions a day as long as it was daylight, because we couldn't support the marines at night. Of course, there wasn't much activity going on at night, except to stay dug in and listen for Japs. We had flown an average of, each one of us, about fifty missions from Saipan to Tinian. Some general back in Honolulu saw that we were flying three missions a day and he said, "They shouldn't get credit for a mission. That short hop over there and back." We were getting shot at just as much as if we'd flown seven hundred miles. Some of the guys had been shot down, and I was one of them, but he said, "For every three missions they flew, we're only going to give them credit for one." And you talk about a bunch of boys wanting to kill a general. Oh boy!

Jack Yaeger Jr. and his new P-38.

So what happened on that?

Nothing. That's the way it stuck.

How many missions did you fly in toto, *and how many did you actually fly?*

Well, I flew 117 that I got actual credit for, and I ended up with about—I'd say—twenty out of the fifty missions; I got credit for twenty, but it was never put on my damn record.

So you really flew about 147 missions?

Right. When the war ended, my squadron commander had 270 damn missions. But my classmates that went to Europe, they flew thirty missions, and then they got a reprieve and sometimes got to come home. When you went to the Pacific, they didn't have any rotation plan at all. Once you went, you were there. You might get ten days to R and R to Australia or ten days to Honolulu, and that's all my squadron commander was authorized to give.

On one mission we were flying up the Yangtze River to Shanghai to hit some Jap subinstallations that they'd built there. They gave us a map of a big red area off to the left of the Yangtze for us not to fly over. We were all curious. We thought maybe it was that some of our prisoners were there in a concentration camp. But I was flying up the river, and I looked over at that red area. It was this big industrial complex. On top of one of the metal-topped buildings, it said Sinclair Oil. And I thought, *my God, the oil companies can tell us where to fly during a damn war.* Also, they gave us $10,000 in Chinese currency in case we were shot down, but boy, as soon as you got back, you had to give that $10,000 back.

Tell me about being shot down.

Well, I was hit in the engine, and my plane got shot up. I was trying to get off from Tinian and make a big circle and come back to our field on Saipan, and was climbing for a little altitude. I had been down shooting rockets. I was climbing for altitude in case it did quit, so I would be able to bail out. I had made a big circle around when the engine started sputtering and trying to quit, so I bailed out. When I did, I hit the tail assembly of the plane. And, of course, I had a jungle pack on and a one-man life raft and a parachute, and these things once again cushioned the blow for me. However, it did crack a vertebra in my darn back and broke three ribs. If I hadn't had all that equipment, it'd probably done me in. With the parachute open, that didn't help me too much with my broken ribs and cracked vertebrae. But I was sitting out there about nine miles off of Saipan in a one-man life raft, reading the survival manual, which I hadn't read, trying to memorize it in case I lost it. Suddenly, a flying boat found me, a PBY, and they started circling and finally they threw out a big raft for me. It had lots of additional food in it: K-rations, C-rations, flare guns, and sea dye.

When the plane left, I thought, "God." The sun was just dropping, and it was getting late in the afternoon, and I thought, "What in the hell. I can't paddle this big raft nine miles to shore with the wind blowing against me."

And it was blowing, and I found out later that the PBY couldn't land because the waves were too high. But just about twilight, I saw something breaking waves and coming towards me. I didn't know if it was Japs or whether it was some of our people, and I had my damn pistol out. We had bird-shot also for our pistol so we could shoot a seagull, or something to eat, if we were out and not found. I switched the bird-shot out of there and put regular bullets in it. Then I could tell it was a torpedo boat, one of ours coming towards me. The PBY that had circled me had given them the proper vector to come to me out there. The boat loaded me up, then radioed a ship that had a doctor on board. They stopped and let me off, and I went on board the ship, and the doctor examined me. He taped me up a little bit and said, "Son, I got something in my medical cabinet here that will help you a lot." He unlocked it and reached up on the top shelf and handed me a fifth of rye liquor. He said, "Now take about three good straight shots of this, and you'll feel a hell of a lot better." I said, "You're my kind of doctor."

Later on, I found out another coincidence, that Tom Massey from Tallahassee was one of the crew members of the PBY that circled me out there. Furthermore, on the ship they had stopped with that doctor on board was Buppy Fain, an engineering officer. Buppy died here about a month ago of emphysema. Everytime I turned around out there, there was always somebody from Tallahassee. Also, in the outfit that my friend George Taff was in, the marine outfit, was Governor Holland's son, Lindsey Holland; I had known him in high school. He was a captain in the Marine Corps out there. One time I had a day off, and so I went over and saw in the church bulletin where he was; they passed out names through the Saint John's Church bulletin. Stompy Parker, who was a dentist here and a good friend, was a dentist in the navy. When we took Guam, he was sent to Guam. At that time, our squadron had an old man who was a horse doctor of a dentist and stayed drunk most of the time. Every time he worked on anybody's teeth, boy, he ruined 'em, so I would get in my plane and fly to Guam to get Stompy Parker to work on my teeth. Every now and then, he'd catch a navy plane coming up to Saipan and visit with George Taff and me, and then he'd spend a day with us.

I went over to see Lindsey on my day off. We'd fly seven days, and then we'd have a day of rest. Then we'd fly seven days and have a day of rest, sort of a rotation type of plan. And Lindsey did not drink. It seemed that there was an old custom he told me that the Marine Corps from centuries back would give each marine in combat an ounce of liquor a day or every other day to help keep diarrhea down. Sometimes, instead of doing that, they'd just give the officer a fifth every now and then, and he'd put it in his foot locker. I was telling him that George Taff and I were having to pay some of the navy boys down there at the harbor $50 for a damn fifth of liquor that they paid

$1.45 for—Four Roses. And he said, "Well, why don't you take this footlocker full of liquor back over to your place, and you and George enjoy it?" Well, when I drove up in the jeep and had that footlocker in the back of the jeep— it was pretty heavy—there were three men who had come to see me there who were from Tallahassee. One of them was named Rhodes. He lived one block from my mother and dad. The other one was Mackie Davis, who was an electrician in Tallahassee and lived down on Meridian Circle, and the other was Governor Collin's brother, Arthur Collins.

So the three of them helped me unload the footlocker full of liquor and put it in my tent, my old pyramid tent that slept four people, but only three of us were in it. And so I broke out a bottle, and we all sat around in the tent and had a drink. I'd go off on a mission, and I'd come back and the three of 'em would be sitting in my tent having a drink. When the last bottle was gone, I didn't see any one of them until the war was over, and we were back in Tallahassee! At home, I went to see each one of them and took each one a fifth of liquor. I said, "Now, I see what my friendship really was. You'd all come to see me as long as I had liquor, so I brought you a fifth of liquor over here and let's talk."

My friends in the navy served as electricians and were sent out there to help install the biggest radar station the U.S. had ever constructed, to be set up in Saipan. The main purpose of this new sophisticated radar station was that our old radar would not pick up Japanese planes coming in on the water, right down on the deck, but this thing would. It could pick them up twice as far as our regular radar, and right down on the water. It was a beautiful thing, and it was supposed to be installed before the first B-29 ever came to Saipan to protect those expensive planes that were built primarily to hit Japan from Saipan and Tinian. Nonetheless, Tokyo Rose told us when the first B-29 left the United States and landed in Honolulu! She told us the name of the first pilot, the co-pilot, and the engineering officer on board each one. Now, that's how sophisticated their spy system was. She then told us when they landed on Saipan and that we had over a dozen B-29s there, and that they were going to come and blow them up.

Well, Peyton Yon was the post office manager and before that he was in the hardware business here in Tallahassee. His brother had flown B-17s in Europe, and he had finished his missions, and when he came back to the States, they put him in the B-29s and he learned how to fly them. Then they sent him to Saipan. Well, Tokyo Rose had told me that P. L. Yon was the first pilot on the B-29 coming to Saipan.

They had taken our airfield and had made it three times as big because the bombers were coming in. They had moved us across Magician Bay to another small airfield that they had built for small fighters to take off. But one day I went over to our old field to see P. L. Yon, and he said, "Well, how in the world did you know I was coming in over here?" I said, "Tokyo Rose told me." He said, "You're lying." And then I told him what the situation was and some of the other guys in my squadron confirmed the fact that Tokyo Rose had told us.

One time I had just gotten back from a mission, and I was taking my parachute out of the plane and had it over my shoulder. I looked across Magician Bay, and I saw all these damn airplanes right down on the water. There was a cliff there that dropped off from the airfield the B-29s were on, and the enemy was coming in right on the darn water. They shot up over the end of that cliff and started strafing those B-29s. Well, I made a run for my plane. There hadn't been an air-raid signal, but we were being attacked, so I jumped back in my plane. And one of the guys was taking off that had not been on the mission. He too saw what was going on, and just as he was getting airborne, coming off our little airfield, a Jap plane flew right around in front of him. His wheels hadn't fully gotten in place, and he started shooting at them. He didn't quite have flying speed but, when he started firing his guns, he began loosing flying speed. He shot the Jap down, then barely was able to pull up and get some altitude. But we chased those darn Japs all the way to this little island of Pagan, where we had been hitting them. But we kept it neutralized. The island was between Saipan and Iwo Jima, and we chased them way on past there. Eventually, we shot down just about all of the original thirty or so, except for about three.

Shortly after that, the guy I just described was taking off on a predawn mission when it was still pitch dark. His engine started acting up, and he had to make a forced landing on Saipan. Now, there's nothing level on Saipan except where our two airfields were. The rest of it was mountains. He saw some light, and he landed in that area, right in the middle of a marine area. He had gone through a warehouse and come out the other side of it! His plane had started burning. He ran back through the tent area yelling and screaming and waking the guys up and telling them to get out of there, because that plane was gonna blow up any minute. It was on fire and fixing to get really bad. And, to make a long story short, he ended up under psychiatric care and in a mental institution for a long period of time until he got straightened out. Due to being in the psychiatric hospital and everything, he decided he wanted to be a doctor and he decided to go to college and medical school. He was at High Point, North Carolina, practicing medicine.

What was it that emotionally upset him so much? Was it just the pressure?

Well, we were under lots of pressure. We had had a bonsai raid from the Japs. They came into our tent area, chopping with their sabres and everything. We were throwing hand grenades into them, and it was sort of a bloody mess. Just as he rolled out of his cot, a Japanese had chopped his dad-gum folding cot right in two with a sword. The cot was made with a wood frame with canvas in between. If he'd been there just two seconds longer, he'd have gotten cut in two.

Our guard system wasn't too good at that time because we didn't know about these things. We were having to learn the hard way. One of the boys, named White, who was sort of very quiet—his father was a minister—was standing out there in the open and he started throwing hand grenades and cussing them. He never used profanity, but now was using every word of profanity that's ever been invented, yelling at them and throwing the hand grenades. He got all kinds of decorations. In fact, he killed most of them. And there wasn't a whole bunch. It was about twenty men. All of them were drunk, stumbling around as if they all drank a bunch of sake before they came in for a bonsai raid like that.

You were an ace. Tell me about some of the planes you shot down.

The first one I got was when I was taking off with my plane, fixing to go up to Amami Oshima, which is a Japanese island that still had the enemy on it, that we tried to keep neutralized. It was between Okinawa and Tokyo in Japan. We were going up there and Stumpy Snider was going up there too with his flight. We planned to strafe some installations that photo recon had picked up. I looked up and saw a Japanese plane coming in on Stumpy Snider's flight out of the sun. We always attacked them out of the sun, and they attacked us out of the sun. Stumpy, I'd have to explain to you, loved fighting that war. He was an ace more than twice already, and nothing bothered him. He thought that your time, when it comes, is coming no matter what you're doing. That was his theory. And he wasn't worrying about getting shot down at all.

I yelled at him, "Stumpy! Stumpy! A damn Jap is coming in on you. One's coming right in on your flight right now out of the sun!" And he laughed. Nothing bothered him. He laughed and he says, "Don't feel like the Lone Ranger. Look at your tail." And I looked back and a Jap had closed in on me and was just starting to shoot, although he was not quite in range enough of me. We went into what we call mutual support, and that's when your flight turns straight into the other flight, head on. You shoot the Jap off of his tail and he shoots the one off of your tail, head on. Actually, that's what we did. I got the one off of his tail, and he got the one off of mine. I hit the other plane straight in into his engine and it blew. It dropped down a little bit and, of course, I had to get out of his way, because I was going straight at him. I pulled off to the side. Just as I pulled off to the side, he blew and so man, I really pulled off to the side. And then as I pulled up, I saw the one Snider shot burning and hitting the ocean.

There was a picture of me showing my crew chief how I shot a plane down. This article was in all the major newspapers. I don't think it showed up at the Tallahassee Democrat, but my aunt happened to be in New York City and picked up the New York Times, and there it was. Good propaganda.

But one time when I was with Stumpy Snider, we were coming back from a mission on Japan. There was a downed pilot at Amami Oshima, this island that we were going to hit that day. They called us—they'd heard us talking—and we were heading back, and getting close to Amami Oshima. They said, "Hey, we've got a pilot down out in the bay at Amami Oshima. The flying boat is gonna fly in and pick him up, but we need for you all to come in here and strafe the beach area where the Japs have this installation of guns and machine guns. That way they couldn't shoot at the seaplane when it lands to pick him up." Well, Snider's flight went in ahead of mine and he finished strafing. I started strafing and when I pulled off, I looked up and I saw Snider with the flames shooting out from underneath his plane. And I said, "Snider! Snider! You're on fire!" He said, "Hell. You don't have to tell me. All the damn hair is burnt off my leg. I'm going to get as uninvolved in this damn island as I can. And if you don't come back and pick my ass up, I'm gonna swim back and whip yours good." And he bailed out. We sent a PBY up there, and they picked him up. He was in that one-man life raft, part of our equipment. He had blisters underneath both arms where he had been lying down and using his arms to swim while trying to stay away from the island. Meanwhile, the wind was blowing him into the island, and the Japanese were sitting up there on the beach shooting at him, which gave him lots of incentive to swim fast. The PBY landed and picked him up. When he got back he said, "Those son of bitches almost got me, didn't they? I guess my time hasn't come."

I got shot up there at Truk, and I need to tell you about that because that was the dirtiest, nastiest thing I have ever done to anybody or group of people in my entire life. Truk is one of the islands that Yamamoto used as his get-together to hit Pearl Harbor. Saipan was another part of that same thing, but it's seven hundred miles from Saipan down to Truk.

That was a big battle down there. The navy had sunk quite a few ships down there, though we didn't need Truk. We just kept it neutral. When the photo recon boys would pick up some activity—some submarines would be down there—we'd fly down there from Saipan. With a belly tank we'd have just enough gas to get there and back. We'd have to go right in and hit our target and get the hell out of there. This one day my plane was dive-bombing the subs that they had spotted. The other guys dropped napalm, or they were shooting rockets. And I was coming in on my dive-bombing run. They're shooting tracer bullets at you, 20 mm, and about every third bullet is a tracer. Tracers look like oranges floating up towards you, but slow, because of the distance between you and the bullet. You can usually just move over, but you don't know where those other bullets are.

I saw the bullets coming up. Just as I moved over, the 20 mm hit the cowling of my plane and blew a big hunk of it off. This let lots of wind pressure come into the accessory section between the cockpit and where all the engine stuff is. The wind blew a bunch of that metal off, and a piece of it flew by and broke a hole in my canopy, and another piece came loose and cut the top of my vertical stabilizer off. But it worked fine. Right in front of the cockpit a big piece of metal had blown up, so that I had to stretch my neck to see in front of my plane. Also, it had cracked the cylinder and a little bit of oil was leaking. The plane flew fine. It just looked like hell with the engine sitting out there and all the metal blown off behind it. And so the squadron commander told me over the radio, "Hey, Yaeger, there's no way you're gonna have enough gas with all that wind resistance to get back to Saipan. There's no way you're gonna be able to do that. You'd better head to Guam."

So I struck ass off to Guam, and the rest of us—nobody else had gotten hit or anything—went back to Saipan, all fifty-four planes. There I came into Guam, landing, and the dad-gum meat wagon was following me down the damn runway. The fire truck was right behind it, and the oil was leaking, although I hadn't lost hardly any oil to speak of. Still, the propeller had painted the side of the plane with oil. It looked like hell, but it flew fine, except I had to use lots of power because of the wind resistance on all that open area on the plane. When I pulled off the runway and stopped, I stopped right beside a transport that had just come in from Honolulu full of brand new pilots from the States. I was getting my parachute out of the plane, and they all started crowding around looking at my plane and finally one of them said, "Man, it must've been rough up there today." And I said, "Yeah, we were hitting Truk, and I was the only one got back." The whole squadron, see, had gone to Saipan, and I was the only damn person there. And they started looking at that plane and said, "You were the only one that got back out of fifty-four planes?" I said, "Yeah." I said, "It's tough out here." And I turned around and walked off, and you should have seen the eyes in those boys' heads. They wanted to jump back on that transport and get right on back to Honolulu.

Did you ever tell them the truth?

I didn't. That's the reason I said that's the worst thing I ever did to a group of people in my life.

I'll tell you something that Snider pulled, the guy that didn't think he was gonna ever die. Snider and I got involved with some Jap planes, and they were attacking us just off of Saipan. Snider shot down three of them, and I shot down a couple. As a general rule when you come back to the airfield, you'd come in real fast, low on the field, and pull up and you'd roll for the number of planes that you'd shot down. Snider'd shot down three. The squadron commander could hear the fight on the radio and what was going on and everybody talking to each other and yelling to each other, "Look out here comes one," and all this crap. So Snider came in and made the traffic pattern and landed and the squadron commander said, "Stumpy! I heard you. You shot three planes down and you didn't even roll."

He said, "No, it was overcast, and I didn't see any sense in rolling. I just came on around and landed."

"Well, by God, you should've rolled at least three times."

"Well, let me tell you something, Colonel. Republic can build all of those damn airplanes out there on an assembly line, but they can't build another Snider on an assembly line. And so I didn't roll."

And he turned around and walked off, and the squadron commander just had to laugh.

Did you ever think, "I shouldn't be in this business. I'm accident prone."

Well, no, because all kinds of things were happening to the others, and I was just one of the fortunate ones at the end of the war to still be alive. Out of all of the pilots, there weren't but four of us alive.

Out of how many?

Four out of thirty that went overseas together. And I was one of them. I've always said that the good Lord must be looking after me. The reason I say that is when I was at Leon High School I broke my nose, and a broken bone went right up underneath my skull and cut an artery. They couldn't stop it from bleeding. They turned Leon High School upside down to see if they could find somebody else's blood that would match mine, because I had bled my uncle, my Daddy, and everybody else to death. They couldn't give any more blood. They phoned Johns Hopkins, and two specialists flew to Tallahassee since I was too weak for anybody to carry me up there. The specialists stopped it from bleeding.

Having gone over with all of these boys and being just one of four that got back was something. We buried the rest that we could find; some we never even heard from again—they just disappeared over water, flying all those missions. It wasn't unusual for somebody to be not accounted for. If you got back, you felt lucky. Still, some of our boys in our squadron got shot down over Japan, and we were told if you could possibly do it, bail out over a Japanese airfield where some of their pilots are stationed. For Godssakes, don't bail out over a town, or they'll kill you. If they haven't got something else to kill you with, they'll stone you to death. And three of the guys in our outfit bailed out over an airfield and were prisoners of war. The Japs had surrendered already and damned if they didn't chop their heads off anyhow before we could get up there and get them.

You hit Japan as well, didn't you?

Well, I can tell you when we first started hitting Japan, we were hitting their industrial areas where they were manufacturing bombs, ammunition, guns, and tanks. That was our assignment. We also were hitting the subs and ships. We hit the railroads that were going into these industrial areas and blew out the bridges, so they couldn't get supplies. After we had hit an airfield and strafed it, we'd blow up their storage tanks of gas. We'd have a free hand. Once we had a mission to blow up a bridge, we had a free hand at anything we saw that we ought to hit on the way back home. Trains were something they wanted us to hit, because then they couldn't carry supplies to their industrial plants. So we would pick out targets, and if we saw some Jap planes, we'd shoot them down.

One day, while we were up there, we ran across a bunch of planes that looked like our Stearman planes, training some pilots. And they had one little machine gun in the back on a swivel, reminiscent of WWI. We set up a traffic pattern and shot them down. There were eighteen of them. Somebody would shoot one down and say, "Damn it. It's my turn to shoot one down." We shot them and their instructors down, but they wouldn't give us credit for them. They said they weren't army planes.

One day we were going with a bunch of napalm to Japan and went through a front, and there were about thirty or forty kamikazes. You could tell the way they flew because they didn't know how to fly. They'd been taught to take off. They didn't have to be taught to land one. They weren't supposed to come back. They didn't know anything about how to fight in a plane. They barely knew how to fly. We started climbing and went back through the front. As they would come through in about twelve or fifteen minutes, we shot down thirty-four of them. We were taking turns doing it.

How many did you get from that?

I got three of mine by actual fighting. The rest of them were just individuals that we would spot coming home from a mission. As for the kamikazes, I got only one of them that day. We got in an argument about who was going to shoot one down next. There were some of the guys who hadn't shot any down in the war, so they were given a sort of priority to go ahead and boost their number and morale too. Still, it wasn't too uncommon to run into the kamikazes. The kamikazes would not mess with us, except if our planes were in bunkers, any place they saw something lined up in a row.

Now, one night we had a Jap transport plane land at Yontain Airfield on Okinawa, and I'm a son of a gun if Japs didn't pile out of that thing, and start running all around, trying to set planes on fire. One of those bonsai-type raids—but it came in a plane. The plane slipped in there late at night around midnight.

That sounds insane. You were there when that happened?

No, that happened over on Okinawa. We were at Ie Shima across the bay. When that happened, we had communication back and forth over there all the time. They called us and told us, "Well, this was what happened here, so you all be careful and keep an eye open because it could happen over there."

So did they get a lot of them? Did they shoot a lot of them?

Hell, they got all of them. They were so drunk. They were wondering how the pilot even was able to fly down there at night because he was all soaked up with sake. The kamikazes sank fifty-four of our destroyers in one month! And those boys caught hell.

So were you thinking of that, and revenge, when they were coming through the clouds?

You'd better believe it! A real good friend of mine at Leon High School who went into the Marine Corps was the first Tallahassee boy to get killed. He was killed on Guadalcanal, and when I shot my first Jap down near Pagan Island, I said, "Goddam it, I got you for Phelps Long." I was thinking about him when I was shooting him down.

Didn't you see the big bomb blow or something?

Yes, I sure did. Let me tell you this before we go too far. When I was going to Japan and napalming industrial centers and blowing up railroads and bridges and all of this, we were not lashing out at the civilian population at all. Now one day, they, the photo recons, came back with some pictures of a big red brick building that was building plane jet engines for airplanes that they had gotten from Hitler. After we had been hitting all these industrial places, we started dropping napalm and burning towns, and that is when the B-29s started dropping their fire bombs on the towns. We'd come in with napalm right on the top of the trees and sew napalm all through that area, and let it burn right on into the big firestorm. You're at the treetop level, and as you come in on a street just before you turn loose the napalm bombs, you could see people running. You could see the children, women. You could see the old people. You could see soldiers. You knew when you'd land, you'd have burned 'em up.

Was that tough on you emotionally?

Emotionally it hurt, but then you'd stop and think about Pearl Harbor and the sneak attack, and you hoped maybe this will make Japan quit fighting, and the war will end. You'd have to really talk to yourself about it. Anyway, we went up to hit this factory up there that was building, we had been told, jet engines. Nearby was this red brick building just big as life—there are very few brick buildings in Japan, especially red brick ones. So we lashed at that thing with napalm. We totally set it on fire. That evening we listened to Tokyo Rose, who was almost comical sometimes. Once she had told us at Saipan that they had rigged up the island, and as soon as they got ready to, they had fixed it so that they could set off all of their explosions planted underneath and sink it. That happened right after we had an earthquake. I guess she was depending on the earthquake to scare us, thinking they were blowing the island up or something.

This time Tokyo Rose told us we'd hit a schoolhouse, the red brick building we'd hit, and we had killed six thousand children. Initially, we figured that was just one of her ways of making us feel bad as usual, of hurting our morale. But photo recon went back up there, and they came back and said, "You didn't hit the red brick building. It's three miles up the road." So we figured we must have hit the school house. And then we knew it the next time we went up there. We were up there with another group of planes, and the Japs would pick ours out with our stripes on the tails, to identify us. We were the 318th Fighter Group.

So you figured what?

When we'd go up there on a mission, the enemy would jump on us and not mess with the other guys with different stripes on their tail. They'd pick us out because we'd burned up that schoolhouse, and they were getting revenge. So we changed the color of our stripes on our tails to black and white.

Any stories about flying in Japan?

Photo recon had picked up three airfields over in Korea where the Japs had hidden a bunch of planes, anticipating the invasion. At the time we were tearing up their airfields and their planes on the ground. One day we were strafing an airfield about fifty or sixty miles from Nagasaki when we saw this explosion. The explosion produced a huge glare, even with dark goggles on. It was terrible, like somebody took your picture with the flashbulb right in your face.

We pilots started talking about it to each other. We'd hit Nagasaki three or four times before. They said, "God, look over there. That was a big industrial center." And, "Something blew up over there in Nagasaki. Look over there, man. It must've been one of those big powder plants that made bombs." We could see that column rising up in the distance, and so when we started back home, we decided to fly over there to see what in the hell happened, not knowing a thing about atomic bombs. When we got to Nagasaki, we flipped over to just cameras only and started taking movies of it. We flew all around the damn explosion, as it mushroomed out. We were talking to each other about it saying, "God. Look at this."

You didn't have any clue, did you, that this was the atomic bomb?

None whatsoever. When we got back to base, they had heard us talking on the radio about it and knew we were up there fiddling around. When we landed, there was a group of men from Special Services there with these little boxes. They started running them all over our airplanes and all over us. We didn't know what the hell was going on. They were geiger counters which suggested we might be radioactive.

Were you?

No, not at all.

At how many thousand feet were you, when you flew over?

When we were done strafing over there, we always climbed for altitude, in case we got jumped by the Japs. But as we went over to Nagasaki, I guess we were up to about 10,000, maybe 15,000 feet by the time we reached Nagasaki. And those guys from Special Service took all of the film out of our airplanes and hauled it off with them. Luckily, one of the guys happened to take a picture of it with his 35 mm personal camera. He kept it hidden, and we took it over to our lab where we had our gunnery film processed and made prints of the pictures he took. The picture was taken just as the column mushrooms down.

Do you still have that?

I've got a copy of it. I had it in an album at one time. When I got home, it was still such a big secret until they showed the tests at Bikini. So I finally dug my picture out and showed it to my mother and father and family—the damn picture of the bomb that was dropped on Nagasaki. I had it in a picture album, and when my wife and I got divorced, she took that album. When I got my albums back after she died, she had cut them up in fury. Not only that, there were just tons of other pictures that I'd loved to have kept. Then too, some of the pictures were gone, and some of them were cut up in the album. She was bad about drinking. I know that she must have gotten drunk one night. and because she was pissed off at me, she was getting even.

In one instance, a photographer that was just standing there took pictures, showing all of these islands that we had taken, being marked off with a big "X." The words were spelled real big: Tinian, Siapan, Truk, Guam, and Iwo Jima. The picture featured a big "X" mark by each island. I was standing in that picture in a half-assed profile with Spivey and others. That picture was destroyed. It was published in all the newspapers in the U.S.A.

The Japanese called down to Okinawa and Ie Shima and said they wanted to surrender. They were told to paint one of their bombers white and put green crosses on it, so we wouldn't shoot them down when they came down to surrender. The next day they wanted to bring two planes. We said, "Hell, if you want to quit, you can bring twenty, but be damn sure you paint them white with green crosses on it, so we won't shoot you down." Well, they wanted to put a general in one and an admiral in the other. They said they had them painted. We said, "Take off." They landed on Ie Shima and handed over a sword and a bouquet of flowers and surrendered. We impounded their crews.

You were right there?

Oh yes.

So now we're close to the end of the war.

Broward Taff of Tallahassee was in the army air force, flying four-engine bombers. Broward and his whole outfit landed on our airfield on Ie Shima, and set up their tents, down from our tents where we had our area. We were getting ready for the invasion of Japan. About two more weeks passed, and then here came a smaller bomber outfit of B-25s. In it was George Watts from Tallahassee. His tents were set up down past Broward Taff's tent. So when the Japanese flew down and landed and surrendered, there was Broward Taff, George Watts, and I, all from Tallahassee, watching them surrender. We put the Japanese on another plane, and they were flown down to General MacArthur in Manila to make formal surrender plans in Tokyo Bay at a later date.

Any stories or details about putting them on a plane?

About the time the Japs came back from Manila and left and went back to Japan, I started hounding my squadron commander. I asked if the three of us could fly to Japan. He told us that he did not have the authority to authorize that at all. I had been his wingman when I first came into the squadron, and then I was his element leader. Then when I got a flight, he said, "Your main job when you're in my flight is to keep the damn Japs from shooting me down."

Finally, after hounding him, he said, "Let me tell you something. You all can go to Japan, but you aren't gonna take a pistol with you or anything. You're not gonna start the damn war over again. If you get up there and get in trouble and they courtmartial you, I'm gonna tell the courtmartial, with my hand on a stack of bibles, that you are AWOL, that I did not know you were even going up there. You all just went out, got in your planes, and took off. I tried to stop you and I couldn't." And he says, "I ain't defending you in any kinda way. It's gonna be your own little red wagon."

So the next morning we took off and flew to Japan. We couldn't find an airfield we hadn't already torn up around Tokyo, but we did find one at Yokahama that was half-assed fixed. We parked our planes and got side-by-

side and started marching towards an old torn-up hangar, where some Japanese were sitting on a bench out front. We didn't know if we were going to get shot at or not. When we got fairly close to them, one of them stood up and bowed. And when he did that, the rest of them stood up and bowed, and so we walked over. They were nice. They weren't jubilant to see us, but they were nice. We had these little talking books that we always carried with us in case we were shot down. The books had the English word and then the Japanese word spelled out, so you would point at a word and communicate. And I got it out but hell, they could speak English! And we told them that all we had was aerial maps, that we needed to have a road map of how to get to Tokyo. One of them got a piece of paper and drew us one. We then told them

Jack Yaeger, Jr. with his P-47

that we needed transportation to get there.

This little old vehicle they had looked like a jeep, but it was German-made. They gassed it all up for us, and we took off and went to Tokyo. We pulled up in front of the Imperial Hotel in downtown Tokyo, the one that Frank Lloyd Wright designed, and we walked in. Everybody was bowing and scraping, and they didn't want any money or anything. They showed us to a room, and we had a meal there that evening. I asked the guy who was waiting on us in English if they had any scotch liquor. He said, "We got a basement full of it. We had tons of it given to tourists visiting Japan from America way before the war. Japanese don't like scotch liquor." He brought us two fifths of scotch.

Later, we were on a train, traveling around seeing Japan, and a young boy in a uniform, not a military uniform, sought us out and started talking to us. He was in Princeton University, and his father was ambassador to Brazil. He said that just before Pearl Harbor was hit, his father was sent notice to get him out of Princeton University and get him to Brazil and then come back to Japan. He said, "When we were on our way back to Japan is when they hit Pearl Harbor." He took us under his wing like a tour guide and showed us Japan, all the points of interest we hadn't blown up, and we had a wonderful time.

How long did this last?

It lasted about fifteen days. We were in the Imperial Hotel in downtown Tokyo, when General Douglas MacArthur steamed in on the *Missouri*. In fact, we were looking out the window of the Imperial Hotel watching it. The war had ended.

DEAN DAVENPORT

"Doolittle's Raiders"

Dean Davenport and seventy-nine other pilots flew a mission that has become the stuff of legend. Known as "Doolittle's Raiders," the group was under the command of Jimmy Doolittle when it took off from the USS *Hornet* to bomb Tokyo during World War II. Dean Davenport was one of the co-pilots.

Dean Davenport was born in 1918 in Spokane, Washington. When his father, who worked for the Oregon-Washington Railroad and Navigation Company, was transferred, the family moved to Portland, Oregon, where he was introduced to flying.

This short gentleman—slightly taller, he says, than Jimmy Doolittle—has the infectious habit during the interview of breaking into a kind of snicker before he tells a humorous incident. It's as if he's ahead of things and rehearsing it in his mind.

Davenport returned to the United States after flying with Doolittle and began flying fighters. He's flown a range of fighters, from the P-40 to the F-106. The Tokyo raid was his one and only B-25 mission. He went on to become head of Tyndall Air Force Base and was also division commander of the Thirty-Fifth Air Division (NORAD). He retired a colonel in 1969. Despite several strokes, this hearty soul keeps on going and busies himself with golf and gardening in Panama City, Florida.

Where'd you get interested in flying?

A long time ago I lived in Portland, and we had a little airport there where an old barnstormer named Tex Rankin used to come. You could give him two dollars for a ride. So I thought that was the greatest. He took me up and did a little aerobatics and landed, and I said, "Boy, that's for me!"

How'd you get into "Doolittle's Raiders"?

After getting out of flying school, I was assigned to the first B-25 outfit, in Pendleton, Oregon. We had gone to Chamberlain Field in Minneapolis to get our planes modified. We were staying at the Nickolet Hotel in Minneapolis when we were approached. Someone said, "We want some volunteers for a "mission." We were given just a little bit of detail. So I decided to volunteer.

No idea what you were doing?

We did a lot of speculating, but none of us really came up with the right answer. Most of us were speculating that it had something to do with the trouble along the Panama Canal. Then when we went to Egland Air Force Base and started training with short-field takeoffs, it became clear to us that we must be doing something weird. We still didn't know. About this time, the Old Man, Jimmy Doolittle, got us all together. He told us to stop guessing and, by all means, don't guess out loud.

You might happen to be right.

Yes, you might tip the whole thing off. We were told not to mention what we were doing, or to speculate why we were doing it. We could talk to ourselves only. We were also told while at Egland that if we were approached by anyone who wanted to know what we were doing, or wanted to speculate on why, we were to get his name and turn it over to the air police.

Did that happen?

I understood that some of the guys got the name of one guy and turned it over to the air police. I think this person was interned until the end of the war.

What were your impressions of Jimmy Doolittle?

He was an extremely dynamic man. When he started talking to you, he had you right in the palm of his hand. You knew he knew what he was talking about. He was the leader. In fact, if you would interview all the guys from the Tokyo mission, you'd probably find that they'd follow him anywhere.

Favorite Jimmy Doolittle story?

I remember when we were getting ready to go on the mission, there was a strange feeling around there. And some of the guys started growing beards. One day Jimmy got us all together, and he said, "I never could understand why anybody would cultivate on his face what grows wild on his ass." The next morning everybody was clean shaven.

What' was next?

After training at Egland we went to Alameda Naval Air Station. There they loaded our B-25s on board the carrier, the USS *Hornet*, with the use of cranes.

Lose any planes?

No, we didn't. My gunner was a young kid. He ran around saying, "Damn sir, these guys are going to break our bird in two." I said, "No, they've done this before. They know what they are doing."

So then they lashed the planes down on the deck. After completing all this, they pulled out into the harbor and said, "Okay, you've got the night on the town. You be sure to be back at such and such a time." So we went to the top of the Mark Hopkins Hotel in San Francisco and had a little party. We didn't have much of a party, because we were a bunch of second lieutenants and didn't have that kind of money. We got back at the dock in time to catch the last ship to the *Hornet*.

On the ship we had to be schooled a bit. For example, when we came on board, we had a time finding our living quarters, which is a job in a carrier. There's a maze of ladders and small hallways, and most of us got lost and had to ask help from the navy types.

Next morning we set sail and were up on deck. After we went through the Golden Gate Bridge, and got out into the wide ocean, I was fascinated by watching the task force join in. The force seemed to come from all directions. "Another carrier. Oh, boy, here comes another carrier. Now we've got an auxilliary fleet." Then a big tanker and a bunch of destroyers. It was really something to watch.

We were finally out to sea, and the Old Man got us all together in one of the ward rooms. He said, "Okay, now, I know you've done a lot of speculating. Some of you may have guessed right, but I'm going to tell you exactly what "we're going to do." That's when he told us we were going to bomb Tokyo. Many of us had pretty-well guessed it by that time. Then he laid it out. He said, "I'm going to tell you that you have a fifty-fifty chance of not making it. We have spare crews on board. If any of you feel that due to family matters, or whatever, you would like to back out, nothing will be thought of it." He looked out at us and said, "If any of you feel you should not go on this mission, due to some reason, just hold your hands up now. You'll not be thought ill of. But do it now, before we get any further."

Did anybody back out?

I recall at least one crew that backed out. After we started getting maps and briefings, and had our targets and whatnot, somebody asked what if we get hit over target and have to bail out. We had a navy commander, an intelligence type who had been at the embassy in Tokyo. He said, "I advise you not to bail out." The Old Man said, "If I get hit over the target and am given the choice, I'm going to find the best target I can find, and I'm going to dive my airplane straight into it." Fortunately, we didn't get hit over Tokyo and have to dive our planes into anything.

Describe your take-off from the USS Hornet.

Our crew was the crew that took off with our flaps up. Fortunately, we got away with it because there was so much wind across the flight deck.

On the flight we had two five-hundred-pound HE's on board, and we

327

dropped those on industrial targets. We also had two five-hundred-pound incendiary clusters on board and we dropped them in residential areas where they figured they'd start fires. Then we got the hell out of there.

How bad was the flak?

Moderate flak. Not too intense. Our gunner said, "Hey, look at that puffy stuff around us." I said, "Hey, Dave, that's flak!" As you can see, the crew was rather uninitiated! We did see some fighters above us—some Zeroes—but they never made a pass at us or anything. I have always felt that they were probably on a training mission and didn't see us, or weren't even armed. They sure as hell would have seen us. They were right above, maybe twenty-five hundred feet.

So then you had to get down in Japanese-held China? Was it a good calculation, do you think?

It was Murphy's Law—anything that can go wrong, will go wrong at the most unexpected moment. There was a plane that was supposed to come from India up into China, carrying a beacon to help us to land on a safe field in free China, but it crashed. Of course, we had kicked off early, which left us short of fuel. So we just scrambled for what we could. Running out of fuel, we elected to ditch our plane on what we thought was the mainland, but actually was an island right off the mainland. Fortunately, the Chinese guerrillas that picked us up hated the Japanese. If we had landed someplace else, it could have been a Japanese encampment, but we lucked out.

When we landed, we got up on the beach. I had a pistol and a shoulder holster. I took the pistol out and watched. The Oriental man that came down fairly close saw I had a pistol. Then he went away. Pretty soon he came back with a bunch of his friends and a rifle. I said, "Oh, boy, here goes the shootout in the O.K. Corral." So then this guy got right in front of me and held the rifle over his head. He then put it on the ground and held his arms up. He surrendered to us. Then he came down and made some more friendly gestures. By this time he had an interpreter with him, a guy we called Charlie. He was actually named Chou-Lee. He said, "We know who you are. You're in friendly territory." So he took us to the mainland on an old Chinese junk. The Chinese moved us through what they knew were safe routes. I asked this old guy, Charlie, who spoke a little English, how we were going to avoid the Japanese. He said, "Japs no come out at night. Japs scared to come out at night." Apparently, his guerrillas had them afraid to move around at night. They began to gather us together so they could move us as a group. They moved us by sedan chair—that is a chair sitting at the end of two poles—and ricksha. While we were moving, we came on a village. It was toward dusk, because we almost always moved at night. We saw this big skull and crossbones.

Above the skull and crossbones was the picture of a rat. I made a couple of inquiries and found out that the village was quarantined. It was bubonic plague. We made a long detour around that village and didn't come anywhere near it.

When we were on the road, we were met one day by a rather disheveled woman who spoke to us in English. She explained to several of us that we were being taken to an English mission hospital. And I talked to her at length.

In 1992, Bryan Moon, who wrote *Born Free*, had a reunion for us in Minneapolis. He got us together and the reunion was written up in an Australian newspaper. Lo and behold, I heard from that missionary that I met on the road to Dr. Chen Shenyan's hospital. She now lives in Australia and is now a deaconess in the High Episcopal Church. Deaconess Mary Andrews is her name now. Back then she was just a little old missionary at the hospital.

What did she say?

She just wanted to tell us who she was. We have been writing back and forth ever since. But I would never have envisioned that I would hear from that little missionary on the trail. I later realized the reason she was so disheveled is that she did not want to draw any attention to herself, in case there were any Japanese around. So she looked like a coolie. It would have probably been suicidal to be recognized.

Three of your pilots landed at Japanese-held airfields and were executed. Did you know any of those men?

I knew Dean Hallmark, who was one of the men executed. He was a friend of mine, because we had the same first name. We got to know each other that way. Dean was a big, strong guy, strong as a bull, who didn't take any nonsense from anyone. I have a hunch that some of those little Japanese tried to manhandle him, and he probably put them on the ground, so they executed.

You had that injury, didn't you, on your leg?

I had sores on my leg, and maggots had gotten into them. I left my wound open, which was the smartest thing that ever happened to me. Ted Lawson, another member of our mission, had similar wounds in his leg to what I had, and we made a mistake: we bandaged it. We bandaged his leg and gangrene set in. By the time we were to the mission hospital, he was in bad shape. He had to have his leg amputated there.

How accurate was the movie Thirty Seconds Over Tokyo?

It was pretty accurate. It had better be, because I was sent to Hollywood to be the technical advisor on it! When they were making the movie, they had to make some carrier take-offs. They took a dock out there in the harbor and made it look like a carrier. Then they put up a false island, etc., and towed a B-25 out there, and I flew it off the dock.

Was that hard?

No, it was an empty B-25 with just a little fuel in it.

How do you look back on the Tokyo raid now?

At the time it was something that had to be done, but for the amount of damage we did, it was a rather stupid stunt. Still, it had to be done to get the Japanese off our backs. It did take a lot of pressure off us in the South Pacific, when they were forced to pull back a tremendous number of forces to protect the homeland.

Do you think you've got the credit you deserved?

Oh, more credit than we deserved. After all, there were a lot of other people in the war that did a lot of things, too.

Francis Agnes (In Sailor hat front row, third from right) five days after surrender. On American rations from air drops.

FRANCIS AGNES

From the Bataan Death March to the Prison in Japan

Francis Agnes was born on 28 April 1922 and was raised during the Great Depresson. He spent his early years in the cities of Haynes, Hebron, and Zap, North Dakota. In 1937 the family moved to Wenatchee, Washington, where Francis graduated in 1940 from Wenatchee High School. When he graduated in 1940, Francis Agnes went to work picking apples.By the latter part of September, he realized he couldn't go to college on the money he was making in the orchards, so he decided to join the military. On October 4, 1940, he went to the city hall in Wenatchee, Washington, and enlisted in the army air corps.

After a short stay at Hamilton Field, he was alerted that he'd be going overseas, destination unknown. He sailed out of San Diego Harbor on the USS *Washington*, which was still a luxury liner. He found conditions remarkably to his liking. He and his squadron lived four persons to a stateroom and were fed, all the way across to the Philippines, in the first-class dining room. "Our squadron was first class all the way," he says. This idealized preface to military life changed radically when Agnes was captured by the Japanese and forced to join thousands on the infamous Bataan Death March, where seventy-six thousand Americans and Filipinos were driven into the Bataan Peninsula in one of the most tragic and terrifying episodes of World War II. Only fifty-four thousand completed the journey.

Agnes was imprisoned in prison camps for forty-two months in the Philippines and in Honshu, Japan.

After the war he went home but found he needed the support and solace he had found in the military, so he returned to the service. He worked at Galena Air Base (now Fairchild Air Force Base) in Spokane, then went to Scott Air Force Base as a flight engineer on B-25s and B-26s. He was commissioned a second lieutenant, then went to Shephard Air Force Base, Parks Air Force Base, and served for a time at Nouasseur Air Force Base in North Africa as a maintenance officer. Agnes retired from the air force in 1961 as a captain. "Don't take anything for granted," he says, "Appreciate everything," reflecting back on his experiences in the war.

Today, Francis describes himself as "a died-in-the-wool" ex-prisoner of war, trying to help other POWs and other veterans. He is a member of the Governor's Veterans Advisory Committee, works with the National Cemetery Commission out of Tacoma, Washington, and is past National Commander of the American Ex-POWs. "I try to stay busy," says this man who's witnessed both Bataan and Hiroshima.

After that trip overseas, you must have been thinking military life was pretty good.

We were thinking this was the greatest thing since bottled beer. You had somebody to wake you up in the morning, who would announce that breakfast was being served. On the way, of course, we had to stop in Hawaii for a couple of days. There they off-loaded national guard and civilians, and from there we went on to Shanghai. In Shanghai we took on civilians, mostly women and children, who were being forced to leave. From there we went to the Philippines.

We arrived at Nichols Field in the Philippines and, after about a year, moved to Clark Field. Then, a week before Pearl Harbor, we went on alert at Clark. At that point we were not allowed off base for anything. The day before Pearl, we were allowed to go to the barrios or cities around the base. On our return to the post, some other fellows and I were met by MPs at the gate and told to go to the squadron, that Pearl Harbor had been attacked. At that point I went to the field and worked on my airplane. I was assistant crew chief. The crew chief had gone back to the squadron area to get some rest. Come morning several of the squadron planes had flown on a reconnaisance mission. They had encountered some bombers, pursuing one of the enemy out to sea and one near to Camp Baggio. By that time the planes were out of fuel, so they came in and landed. We checked them over and refueled them, so they were all ready to go. This is now around 9:30 to 10:00 AM. I was relieved of my duty at that time to go back to the squadron area and get breakfast and take a rest, then come back down.

While I'm up taking a rest, somebody comes in and says, "We've got a new flight of B-17s coming in." We go running out to take a look and see these planes have the red rising sun on them. At that point in time we didn't know what to do. Should we go to operations, headquarters, or where? I was standing there, and I witnessed a flight preparing to take off in response. The flights always took off in threes. Anyway, this time a bomb hit the center plane, and the other two planes went up with it.

The thing that came to my mind was to find a place to protect myself. I went to a wooded area behind the base. When the attack had quieted down, I and two other fellows with me tried to get back to the base. We were told "no," that everything was under security, so we spent the night in the woods. The next morning I could hear voices downstream. The three of us got up and went to the area where we heard the voices. Members of our squadron, the first sergeant and the CO were standing in the middle of a big circle of men. We walked up and the sergeant looked at me and said, "You're dead—

you're not supposed to be here." Well, I was the deadest GI you've ever seen! I guess what happened was somebody grabbed a pair of my coveralls and got killed on the way. Somebody ran by and saw my name on them and reported me dead.

We received instructions and went back to the operations area and saw all the damage. We still had three planes that could fly. We maintained operations at Clark Field and did what we could to repair and make additional planes flyable that had been damaged. We finally put together a total of five planes. The pilots flew strafing and bombing missions out of Clark Field on Japanese landing parties at Lingayen Gulf and Tarlac Bay until December 25, 1941. On December 25, we were told to retreat back to Marveiles on Bataan with four planes, which would act mainly as observation planes. At that point we were required to pick up rifles and become flying infantrymen. This was a shock. Why should air corps men carry rifles? Still, we needed the rifles to protect our country and ourselves, though we were not put on the front lines and maintained our operations out of Marveiles until the night of surrender.

How did your surrender transpire?

Our commander had gone for food and supplies to the island of Mindanao, so the acting commander called us together on the evening of April 8, 1944, and told us that in the morning, we were going to be surrendering. He told us to take what supplies we had and also to break our sidearms into pieces, so no one could put them together, and then throw them into the jungle, which we did.

Then all of a sudden, we heard the tanks and the troops coming down the dirt road. We went forward and surrendered as a group. Otherwise, we probably would have all been shot. We had to surrender. We were outnumbered, overrun, and we had no supplies, ammunition, or anything else. We were fighting with World War I ammunition. Maybe every third round would go off properly. We had taken some of the 30-caliber machine guns off of destroyed aircraft. The machine guns had tracer bullets in them, which was kind of enlightening. Every fifth round would light up, so you'd know you were firing in the right direction. The Japanese took us down to the airfield and they took an American flag, tore it up, threw it on the ground, and stomped on it. They told us we were through fighting and wouldn't fight anymore.

How did you feel at this point?

I thought the world had come to an end, personally. You just didn't know what to think. We'd had all these rumors we'd been living by: that help and food were on the way, that ammunition was on the way, and now the Japanese were there.

You were in the Bataan Death March?

We were at the beginning of the Bataan March. The Japanese marched us about as a unit, and then we joined another group of people. That's when we began to realize that the less material items you had, the better off you were, because the Japanese guards would harass you and take whatever you had, whether a ring or a watch. Anyway, as the Japanese congregated us in groups, they began to realize the numbers were greater than they had expected. They put us in these open areas with guards walking around us. The sun was beating down. We didn't know where we were being taken. We weren't allowed food and water. I remember one instance when I stopped and was sitting there, and I heard this voice. It said in English, "You're on the wrong side again." I looked up and it was a guard talking to one of our soldiers. Apparently, the two of them had gone to rival schools in California and had played football against each other. When the Jap said he was on the wrong side again, he was saying that his team had beaten the other guy's in college. That was really tough to hear.

What was the most terrifying thing that happened to you?

There was a lot of shooting of people, for trying to get water out of sinkholes with bodies lying in them, or for trying to eat sugarcane. The most devastating thing I saw was when I looked over and saw this one American digging a hole in the ground. He was digging it quite deep. All of a sudden, this guard made the guy get into the hole, and the guards forced other Americans to bury him while he was still alive. I didn't know then if I'd ever get out of that mess. It really takes the wind out of you when you see somebody doing that sort of thing to another human being.

If you had a buddy you were walking next to, and he fell and you tried to pick him up, you both got shot, or bayonetted. Being bayonetted is even worse than being shot, when somebody actually runs a bayonette through someone when they're helpless.

Did you lose any close friends on the Bataan March?

I lost some close friends on the march, but mostly I lost close friends in the prison camp. I can't think of anybody's name that died on the march, but I can think of several fellows who died in the prison camp. Two guys who died, Holmes and Prosser, I chummed with quite a bit. They pretty much gave up. Holmes gave up through cigarettes. Everything he got he traded for cigarettes. Prosser traded everything for brown sugar that was bootlegged into the camp. Actually, they both intended to get rid of themselves. I guess that's why I don't smoke now.

I saw individuals actually attack guards. Of course, they wound up dead. We would be unloading one of those small ships, in a detail of twelve or fourteen men. Then we'd go by the galley where there would be a tub of rice with a cook standing over it, and because of one's mental state, men would reach in and try to grab some of the rice. You know what's going to happen. You're going to get the hell beaten out of you.

Didn't the Bataan March last six days?

It depended on the individuals. It might have lasted seven or eight days, or even twelve days. On the first day, it was pretty chaotic and the guards didn't have too much control. You could pretty much mingle around during the evening or nighttime, and they couldn't stop you. I recall the first day. I think Ernest Loy was with me, and we managed to run into some Filipinos, who had some canned abalone. We traded them something for it, then managed to get off into an area where we could do some cooking. They were allowing some of the men to do some of that along the way. Anyway, I don't know if you've ever tried eating boiled abalone, but you can chew it forever and it will never go down.

The next morning I saw that when the groups were moving, you could go on ahead in the evening. Maybe there would be some food up there for you. I used that strategy and soon parted from the people that I knew. I felt there was no need to sit idly in the sun and cook myself to death. So I actually got to the front of the line, so to speak, and went from Marveiles to San Fernando in four days.

Four days instead of six?

Yes. This was a matter of not staying with the group you started with. When I got to San Fernando, I received a bowl of rice. In the meantime, somewhere along the way, I had scrounged some things, but there had been no supplies. I was weak by the time I got to Camp O'Donnell. I started having a high fever. Then for about three days, I'd feel fairly good. I had heard that there was another camp with a hospital called Cabanatuan. Camp O'Donnell was a place of death. There was only one water spigot in the camp and very little food. Though there were thousands of us there, the guards controlled that water spigot. They wouldn't let it run all night or all day. This is where they brought all Americans and Filipinos.

There was a detail going to Cabanatuan, so I got on this four-by-eight boxcar for the trip. We were standing, just as tightly packed as possible. Ventilation didn't exist, except for a few cracks in the top. At Cabanatuan, they processed us and the guy looked at me and said, "Are you sick?" I said, "I sure am. I think I've got malaria." So he sent me over to the hospital, but the poor doctors were working as hard as they could but had no medication. A young corpsman working there asked me what I had and when I told him, he gave me a box of pills, which to this day, I think were APC—aspirin and codeine. He said, "Take one every four hours." Luckily, it wasn't malaria, it was just high fever, dengue fever, so after about a week, I started getting my strength back.

An officer asked if I would take this detail down and put a tarp over this building where they were going to make a mess hall. I went down and stood around while this detail put up the tarp. I wandered into the mess hall and talked to this sergeant there who was cutting sweet potatoes. I got a job cutting vegetables and greens but got fired the same day. A friend of the sergeant took my place. I looked around and saw that they cooked all these vegetables in these fifty-five-gallon drums. I volunteered to do the clean-up on them, so they set me up a place in a shed, so I could heat water and wash them there. My thought was that there were always scrapings and leavings in the bottom of the containers. By washing these containers I would be able to acquire additional food from the bottom of them.

How long did you work there?

Quite a while. This area was where they split wood for the fires for the kitchen. It was right on the pathway from the lower part of the hospital, which was called Zero Ward. The people who went down to that area almost never came back out alive. They died of dysentery or malaria, or whatever. I'd be there working and watching and people would be carried out on slabs—a hundred or two hundred a day, or more when I first started. The day when there were only ten slabs went by, we all cheered. We figured things were getting better. You would watch individuals carrying others out to the grave, and then the next day, you would see those exact people being carried out on a slab. Sometimes though, the slab-bearers were so gaunt that when they went past, you could hardly recognize them.

At the prison camp in Cabanatuan, all of us were Americans. It was here that they put us in ten-man squads and if one person escaped from the squad, the other nine got shot. You had to do one of two things: you had to escape with someone escaping, or you had to stop them. I was with a pretty good group, one that wasn't anxious to escape. We did have to witness the shooting of squads. This took place outside the gate. The prisoners would have to dig graves and then kneel in front of them and face a firing squad. They'd march all of us down there to watch. This is what happened when one person escaped.

How were your spirits in the camp?

We were still going to make it out of there, but you had to be careful and you had to walk a straight line, or you were not going to make it out. I was in this camp about eighteen months, from April 9, 1943, until September of 1944. At that point they moved us to the duty side of Cabanatuan. We were assigned to a detail, and they told us we were going to Japan, but they didn't tell us we were going to be slaves. We thought maybe things would be better in Japan, maybe there would be more food. What we found was total slavery. We worked in a steel mill, with some working on the firing pots, other in the machine shop. All of us had to work unloading ore and coal ships, loading and unloading pigiron, working in the hot slag pits, coal yard, coke yard, or slurry pits.

Describe your day.

We'd start before sunup. Somebody would go to the mess hall and get the rations for the first two meals, usually a watery soup made out of rice that was less than a teacup. Then you'd get less than a cup of rice with radish or seaweed in it. Next you'd be marched to the mill, where you'd be turned over to the mill guards to work. You might go down into the hold of a ship to unload it. You'd be expected to unload whatever was in that hold. Or you'd do your regular job. At the end of the day about sunset, you'd be returned to the camp. You'd be served a meal, which might be a small bowl of soup and half or three- quarters bowl of rice. We'd put in anywhere from ten to twelve hours a day. Not all of that involved working. You had to walk to the mill and back, five miles each way.

What was the worst thing you saw in these work details?

There was this fellow who had the symptoms of spinal meningitis. We knew the disease was in the camp. Several POWs had died from the disease. Anyway, this fellow had backaches, neck aches, all the symptoms. I was one of six who were to hold the arms and legs of this fellow while, the doctor went in there without any anesthetic or anything for pain and tapped the spine to take the fluid off. This fellow was a pretty big man, and he was hard to hold. He had to be held really still, because of the nature of the operation. That man managed to walk out with all of us when we were liberated.

I especially remember Lee Garner from the camp. He just passed away. He was always fighting with the Japanese for food for the men of that camp. He did another thing. In the camps the men started trading rations, especially those who were unloading the ships. They would get into the storerooms and (I shouldn't use the word "steal," but I will) they would steal food and carry it back to camp. They would trade it to some individual for future rations. The individuals who were doing this didn't realize that they were trading away their lives. Finally, they'd be so in debt that they owed a whole week's ration food, and they had none coming in. So Lee, in his wisdom, and the first sergeant, took these men and put them into what they called "bankruptcy." In this, they had to pay something to the individuals with whom they had traded, but they still got something to eat. My personal opinion is that they saved a lot of lives by doing this.

Lee had to go to the warehouse and pick up supplies with the guards. On this one trip he went in and found these barrels filled with silk worms. They had been treated with soy sauce and other things, and to be used as food for the animals. So Lee told the Japanese that he'd like to take some back and feed it to the prisoners. The Japanese thought it a big joke and gave him a number of barrels. He brought the barrels back and made soup out of the silk worms. It became a big trade item. For example, you could trade one bowl of that—with one bug on top—for five cigarettes. The soup had a lot of protein in it, and made a huge difference. In fact, I visited with Lee before he died, and he told me he had received a citation from President Truman for his initiative with the silkworms.

What was the worst thing you had to eat?

Nothing is "worse" when that's all there is to eat. When we were on Bataan, we lost 40 percent of our body weight. I think the worst thing I had to eat was a monkey that was roasted over a fire. You look at that, and you think you are eating a baby. That was the worst.

Talk about the transition to home.

I was a service man returning home. Everyone I had gone to school with had moved out and left the area, but it was very difficult. I couldn't stay home. I went back in the service, knowing that if I had any medical problems resulting from prison life the military would take care of them. Furthermore, no one believed you. They would say, "You were a prisoner? So what?" So I quit talking about it. I couldn't talk about it at all until 1981. I was working for Employment Security in Spokane, where I worked for twenty years, when one day my wife saw in the paper that a group of prisoners was meeting out at the VA Hospital. I said, "Oh, that's another bureaucratic operation." And that's the way I left it. I came home one evening and saw my wife getting ready to go somewhere. I asked where she was going, and she said, "I'm going to that meeting." I said, "Well, wait till I get my second wind." So I went there with one purpose and that was to see Sam Grasio, who was a prisoner friend. It turned out they wanted to start a chapter of POWs in Spokane. So I spoke up and said, "Well, you have to have some by-laws." As it turned out, I helped to write the constitution and ended up being the commander of the newly-formed organization!

Was it easy to talk about the past yet?

It was easy in the group. I wasn't the only one who had similar guilt feelings, "Why me?", and this sort of thing. Then I left Spokane and moved over to the Seattle area and became more involved. Then I got involved with the National.

From then on talking about it hasn't been a problem. I know there are still men out there who won't go to meetings, but they should, so they can talk to each other, and their wives can talk to each other. They can find out they're not freaks.

Did your confidence come back?

Oh, yes, undoubtedly. After getting into the group, I chaired the national convention of the American Ex-Prisoners of War in 1984 and was elected a Northwest National Director. In 1990-91 I was elected National Commander of the American Ex-Prisoners of War.

You saw Hiroshima blow, didn't you?

I did not see Hiroshima blow. I saw the result of what happened. We were at the mill. They rushed us off into an area behind the hills. They did that any time a B-29 flew over. It was from there that we looked up and saw this big black cloud going up into the air. Needless to say, the only thing we'd ever heard of was a 500-pound bomb, so we figured in our infinite wisdom they'd hit an oil refinery or an oil dump that had caused all that black smoke. When there was an all-clear, they took us back to camp and when we got back there, the first sergeant told us that there had been a horrible bombing of Hiroshima. He said one bomb had killed over one hundred thousand people. He said he had been told this by a Japanese interpreter, Tahara, who was pro-American. This interpreter was an older man, in his late forties or fifties, who had been living in the U.S. The Japanese brought him back to Japan on the pretense that his folks had died. He was to be drafted into the army. Then they found out he was too old for the military, so they made him into an interpreter. That night it was very quiet in camp. The guards were outside the camp and never bothered us. Usually, they would have been inside getting a head count and hitting us for no known reason.

The guards finally deserted you, didn't they?

They had a conference there in the camp. We were in the Osaka area. Some of the officers from the other camps, as well as the Red Cross officer, met there and said that a surrender would be signed. When they left that day, the guards also left. So we formed our own guard set-up for the camp security. Then an American plane, a B-29, flew over and dropped American food and clothing. That's when we knew that we would be free.

What's the most indelible image of the war?

One of most indelible images, I think, was of that first day when we got attacked. Our squadron commander got his plane off the ground and shot down three Zeros. Another thing that sticks in my mind involves a guy named

Anderson, whom I thought was the greatest pilot there was. He went out on a patrol mission. On this particular day, he was on his way back, and a Zero hit him and knocked him out of the sky. While he was coming down to the ground, the Zero circles around and strafed him in his parachute. I think that really typifies the war—when they kill a helpless individual.

You saw that.

Yes, I and several of the men from the organization witnessed the incident.

You don't have nightmares anymore?

No, I really don't, not like the others claim they do. I do wake up sometimes and I'll be thinking of it, but I won't be dreaming of it at all.

Don Conley

DON CONLEY

The Marine Flier

Don Conley sits cross-legged, chatting. He is a serious man with a wry wit that catches you off-guard. Don has a gray beard that he announces he is just "cultivating." The mustache part of his hairy countenance looks a little darker—perhaps closer to the color his hair was while he was flying for the marines years before, during World War II and in Korea.

Conley graduated from flight school as a naval aviator, applied and was accepted as a marine second lieutenant in the United States Marine Corps. He went to Jacksonville where he trained in Scout Bombers (SBDs), and from there to Cherry Point, North Carolina, and Eagle Mountain Lake, Texas. He was assigned to combat air groups and ended up as a pilot replacement in MAG-32 on Mindanao. From the base near Zamboanga ("where the monkeys have no tails in Zamboanga," as a song of the period went), he flew close air support. He was recalled to active duty in 1952 and assigned to the Marine Transport Helicopter Group, whose mission then was to determine the capability of the transport helicopter in known or anticipated combat situations, such as Air-Vac, in moving troops ship to shore. It was also during this period that he met actors Humphrey Bogart and Lauren Bacall while flying the photographer for segments of the film, *The Caine Mutiny*. At one point in the interview, while talking about a "confrontation" he had with tough guy Bogart, he postures like the late movie great.

I was inspired to fly in 1927, when the famous Charles Lindberg flew over Wallace, Idaho, in his *Spirit of St. Louis*, the ship he'd just returned from France in. He was taking the plane from the East Coast to San Francisco, and Wallace was on the northern route he flew. He circled Wallace once and went on his way. Our school emptied itself on the playground, and we all stood out and waved to him. Of course, I'm sure he could see us. That's when I decided that I wanted to fly.

We're jumping ahead a little, but helicopters were pretty new, weren't they, when you started flying them?

When I started flying, I was helicopter pilot number 305, and so there weren't many helicopters out there because there weren't many pilots out there. And one of the pilots in our squadron took the HRS out in a field right off highway 101, just south of Newport Beach, and did what we called helicopter gymnastics. That's bouncing, vertically up and down. That was the yo-yo maneuver—swinging back and forth as though the helicopter was on a large swing, turning on a point, rotating right over the same spot on the ground. The helicopter was probably fifteen or twenty feet above the ground. Then it would turn in the opposite direction and then swing forward and back. These were preliminaries to all the maneuvers done now. But the pilot was performing these right alongside the highway during a busy afternoon. I remember I happened by and saw two to three hundred cars stopped dead in both lanes. People were out of their cars—some of them standing on car roofs—watching. The helicopter was new to the civilian side and new to us in the military. That occurred in October or November of 1952.

I just about got in some trouble when I was in Hawaii, on the island of Oahu. Our squadron was based on the north side of the island of Kaneohe. Because the helicopter was relatively new, we rewrote some of the regulations. One was how close to the surf or beach the helicopter could fly. We had flown out to the surf, and the citizens swimming with their families were concerned that the helicopters were too close to their children, who were swimming and playing there. Their theory was that that wild-looking machine would just come apart, and the parts would hit the children. So the rule came out to maintain two hundred yards distance from any populated beach. That was Hawaii. In California, we flew the surf almost anytime and anyplace, and no one seemed to care.

This brings me to the trouble story, the famous apple-core incident. One morning on the first flight—I'm flying right side, which gave me responsibility for the aircraft—our plane was identified as the plane from which an apple core was thrown. It seems one of the citizens of a small town north of Honolulu saw something coming from a helicopter. He stood back and watched it fall—and it was a good shot—it hit him right in the head! And, of course, he complained, and justly so. Well, did the apple core come from our airplane? Of course, as commander of the plane, I denied it, knowing at all times what the other occupants were doing every minute. In fact, I'm certain the co-pilot didn't throw it out, but that's only ninety percent certain. The crewman was reliable. If he said he didn't, he didn't.

The investigation showed that the crewman probably did not, but the co-pilot could have. That morning in the officer's mess a big bin of apples was available at the exit to the mess hall for the taking—for snacks. So it's conceivable that the co-pilot took it and ate it and threw it out. Anyway, we were able to clear the airplane I was flying. But that caused a new regulation restricting us from flying over that part of the island at any time, at any altitude.

So you were cleared of the apple-dropping, but was there any stigma against your reputation?

My reputation was unblemished.

How about the apple?

(*laughs*) That wasn't the only area that was restricted to us. There was an area close to Bakersfield where a nudist camp was in operation, and it took just a short time before that area was completely restricted. Obviously, it was possible for a helicopter to come in and get a good view of camp activities.

And blow the volleyball away?

(*laughs*) Remember we're talking about the early '50s, so helicopters were not new, but the numbers were. We probably had twenty to thirty helicopters in our squadron. And you can be sure we explored every possibility of where to fly or how to fly before it became a violation. In the beginning it was any place there was air.

You did close air support during World War II. Tell me about that.

Close air support —as we did it—was terminated with a one-thousand-pound black bomb on a designated target. A target perimeter was generally less than one hundred yards, so the drop would have to be relatively accurate. The target was given to us by people on the ground, by radio, using map coordinates. They also used smoke bombs. They would direct us by radio or by colored panels, usually florescent red. We would be given a direction from the panel to the target. Most targets weren't visible from the air. They were, for the most part, strategic. I remember one drop was made at a camouflaged ammunition dump. The first bomb did no apparent damage. I went in there second, and my bomb put a black plume up to ten thousand feet in less than ten minutes.

Close air support sometimes left an on-station flight of three planes without a target. Each flight stayed on station for a period of time. This was affected by gas load and the distance the area was from home field. When relieved by another three-plane section—and still not having been given a target—our section moved into enemy country, just looking for something that we could dump our bombs on. We didn't find anything so I chose to dive on what appeared to be a one-hole outhouse. A direct hit.

The reason we had to get rid of our bomb was the danger of landing at home field with a bomb still attached to the plane. Another pilot tried to get rid of his bomb. As we flew back from the target to home field, we suggested how he could try to get rid of it. But he was unable to relieve himself of the bomb. So, with preparation, he was given clearance to land. "Preparation" meant moving everything that could be damaged so the plane could land.

Anyway, the pilot made a beautiful landing, and one hundred yards after he touched down, the bomb dropped off. The tail was badly damaged when it bumped over the bomb. Fortunately for everyone, the bomb did not detonate and was defused right on the runway.

Didn't the enemy disguise the scene on close-air flights?

Yes, we seldom saw anyone. The enemy was skilled at camouflage and just flat-out hiding. I remember one day the section I was in was over a Japanese airfield that was clearly surrounded with anti-aircraft guns and emplacements. The guns looked inactive. We circled over the field for a period of time and then left the area. When we were relieved, the section that followed us took up station where we had been. The anti-aircraft suddenly started to fire at them, and one of the planes was shot down before they could return fire. The planes dropped a couple of bombs and got out of the area. That was just the luck of the Irish. We assumed that the Japanese were just getting irritated with the airplanes flying around. They finally decided to try and get a couple of them.

What was the SBD like?

The speed was so ridiculously slow in relation to the other aircraft the United States had that we were usually not hit by ground-air fire. The SBD was led several hundred yards. The enemy just felt that if it had the United States insignia on it, it should be going over two hundred knots. The peto-tube is a three-quarter-inch to one-inch diameter tube that extends from one leading edge of the aircraft about twelve to fourteen inches. It's there to pick up the pressure that is translated onto the instrument panel to the airspeed indicator. Of course, the tube itself is pretty close to the lowest level of the aircraft in flight. Whenever one of our pilots would make an exceptionally low recovery, he would say "It wasn't until I pulled out of my dive that I realized there was seaweed on my peto-tube." Any recovery under fifteen hundred feet had the possibility of high risk, especially if a one-thousand-pound bomb hit the target and exploded. The material from the target area would catch up with the SBD and do some damage. It's possible to bomb yourself down, if you dropped a bomb under fifteen hundred feet.

Did they say that, or did you?

I think I said it first, but that grew out of a dive I made in a SB2C, when I was still in training.

What happened?

The field we were operating from was twenty-four feet above sea-level. I remember those numbers very clearly because I was impressed with that. It was common to set the altimeter at zero. On most sea level fields that we took off from, my altimeter setting was zero, although I was actually twenty-four feet above the water.

I remember it was a practice dive on a floating target several miles out of North Carolina. I made two dives and decided that it wasn't my day. It's possible to make six possible dives. On my first two dives, because of the unusual diving speed of the aircraft in relationship to the SBD, and before I released, I got my altimeter needle below zero twice on recovery, which meant that I was somewhere between twenty-five feet and water. This is coming out of ten thousand feet. I thought about sitting quietly on the ground and thinking about what I'd been through before I tried it again. But I went out the next day and the day after and the day after and dropped probably thirty or forty bombs without getting that low again. The gunner who rode with me in the SB2C enjoyed those two dives a great deal, apparently. When we walked from the plane to the ready room, he pounded me on the back and thanked me for such a great flight—the greatest in his life. Of course, when he said "the best in his life," all I could think of was "you have no idea, young man, how close your life came to ending on both of those dives."

Any other time you were frightened?

Almost every time I dove, I had a reason to be. I'm far from a brave man. Whenever I saw any junk flying around my aircraft, I got a little frightened.

You did some bombing on Mindanao, didn't you?

The field I was stationed at was just out on the southern tip of Mindanao. One of our jobs was to target area routes, probably fifty miles offshore. There was just a rock, a very small island. The island had an observation deck on it—a short one, but it was a place to get rid of a bomb—maybe just for practice.

On one occasion the three planes in my group had a little 50-caliber left and went in to practice on the tower. During this, one of the boys in the flight went into his circle. When he did that, he felt some slugs coming into the sides of the aircraft. He looked across to see where it was coming from, and there was a Japanese soldier on the small tower with, probably, twin 25-calibers, firing at the planes as they returned for a second pass. The soldier would disappear to a safe place. Being fired at, we decided this wasn't going to help the war effort at all, so we went home and recorded it in the session. Sometime later a landing party found six Japanese, who had been there for six months. They were just waiting the war out and getting upset that people were shooting at their home. They didn't have transportation off the island. There was nothing on this rock that would float.

What about relief tubes as well as peto-tubes? Any relief tube stories?

The SPD had a relief tube. That's, of course, an apparatus that would allow the pilot to relieve himself, to urinate while he was in flight. It was easy to use and not always used. It was required after using it to make a note of its use on the post-flight sign-out sheet. This sheet was filled out by every pilot upon returning from any kind of flight. There was no penalty for using it but, if you used it, it was necessary that the ground mechanics flush it out for the next flight. On one flight a pilot in my section dove and, when he rolled over into his seventy-degree dive, the trapped urine from the flight before him came out of the tube where it was trapped and out into the cockpit, out into his face. He was, needless to say, upset.

You did some flying for **The Caine Mutiny**.

This was in 1953; I was in a transport helicopter team in Oahu. They asked if a helicopter could carry a camera from broadside and do overhead shots of the ship being used. I volunteered to pilot for the film. The flying itself was relatively easy.

After the film crews were finished in Hawaii and were leaving, the producer invited all the military crew who were involved in the film to a cocktail party at the Royal Hawaiian Hotel. Two of us went—pilot and co-pilot. We had taken turns flying. So we decided for the pride in our branch of the service—the marines—that we'd wear our uniforms. The wearing of uniforms in our off-duty hours was not required at that time. Anyway, we went to the party and there were probably 150 other military personnel there— a couple of admirals and a few captains. We were the only ones in uniform. So this makes a couple of marines stand out.

Lauren Bacall was at the party, and she thought a couple of marines were kind of cute to spend some time with. So my buddy—Dennis Kegin— and I spent the entire party trading stories with her and enjoyed the few hours very much. When the party was breaking up, Humphrey Bogart came to get his wife. She stood up and staggered a little bit—she had had a few scotch-and-waters—and introduced us to him. He looked at me. He was just a little guy, five-five or so, and he put his nose right up to my nose and said, "What did you bastards do, get my wife drunk?" He sounded like he was in his John Dillinger character. I said something dumb like, "Yessir."

Any other glamour moments?

Nothing very glamorous. I remember going to Twenty-Nine Palms. My job was to fly the infamous General Chesty Puller around an area that was being considered for a marine artillery base. We waited three hours for Chesty to show up. He finally arrived in a car and obviously had had a long wet lunch.

I was trying to help him climb into the helicopter, and he was having trouble locating the kick holes in the side of the fuselage. I started to guide his foot into one and had my hand on his heels, and if he didn't kick back at me and look down under his armpit and say, "Take your hands off me, son, I can do it!" He was certainly crusty. I guess that's not glamour—that's crusty.

Do you remember the first bomb you dropped in combat?

The first real bomb? My first combat flight turned into a flight of opportunity. The leader of the flight was a captain and an executive officer. He knew that he had a brand new combat pilot flying with him. He didn't hestitate to let me know, every chance he got. The target of opportunity was a bivouac area for Japanese troops. It was located on a lagoon, a pretty good-sized body of water.

The captain made his approach over the water, which I didn't like. It was a flat dive, more like you'd do for skip bombing rather than dive bombing. So the close on the target was considerably faster. The first time it was obvious that I had over-shot the target, so I decided not to release. We also had a little bit of resistance—people were firing at us. It was pretty exciting. So I didn't release, and I pulled up into our formation to leave the area. The captain ordered me to go back and drop the bomb. I wasn't excited about that, but I went back and dropped. I overcompensated and the bomb hit the water about fifty yards from the shore and about fifty yards from what I was aiming at. It was a pretty lousy drop.

When the flight returned, there were probably about twenty-five of us in the mess hall, eating a late dinner. The captain seemed to wait until everyone was there and then he stood up and looked around and said, "Who was that pilot that missed the target this afternoon? I don't think I know him." I'd been in the squadron less than twenty-four hours. I put my hand up. He insisted that I stand up so everyone could get a good look at me. He was not a typical marine pilot in my opinion. There were very few who used their rank and position to embarrass people.

Did you ever break procedures in communications?

Probably never. We never broke radio silence at all. On a training flight out of Fort Worth, Texas, three of us had gone up above the overcast and had just played around in the clouds for probably a half hour after we had dropped the bombs. When we came down through the overcast, none of us recognized the terrain. But one flier had a map in his airplane and was able to look at it while he was flying, and he located where we were. To get on the radio would be a mistake because our transmission would be picked up by the control tower at Eagle Mountain Lake, where we were stationed.

What the three of us had done was specifically against regulations. So now we were doing everything by hand signals. But the one guy was so excited when he found out where we were that he opened the canopy and the map flew out of the aircraft. From there he flew from memory. Lucky he had seen enough map to get us back home.

Another one out of this squadron: I came back from a gunnery training flight, and on this kind of flight is an opportunity to do roll overs, snap rolls, and just some traditional maneuvers. When I landed, the ground man recorded that I lost my life raft, a two-man inflatable life raft. It seemed it had fallen out of the compartment behind the gunner's seat.

About two hours later, the mayor of the town of Bridgeport, Texas, telephoned the base, telling us they had found a two-man life raft in the middle of Main Street. I didn't get in any trouble, but we all were very happy that no one got hurt.

How were you looked upon when someone got killed and you replaced them?

That's what I was when I made my first lousy bomb drop. I think there were four of us who came into the squadron as replacements. We were replacing pilots who had come into the squadron when it was organized three years before. The four of us were the first replacements. It took awhile to become accepted.

Why do you think that was?

It wasn't personal, but I always felt the people in the squadron could see me taking the place of one of their long-lost buddies who had been killed, and they resented the fact that he had been killed, and they probably felt that no one could take that person's place. And I agreed, no one could. But someone was there to try to take this person's place, and that someone was me! What it seemed to do was drive the four of us closer together, and we did have each other to look to. And, in a combat situation, most men looked for all the support they could get.

What made you a good pilot?

To begin with, probably the same thing that made an American pilot potentially the best pilot in the world. Our culture, social, and economic system put almost all of us in the driver seat of an automobile. Almost all of us who flew in World War II had been driving an automobile since we were ten or eleven years old. We had mind/motor coordination well in place; we had a head start. Education, too, was a reason.

Any stories about when you first came under fire?

I remember the first time I was shot at. It was by a United States navy unit, something a little bit bigger than a destroyer but smaller than a cruiser. I was sent up out in the Gulf to train gunners in anti-aircraft. A nearby base had B-

26s, which were designed to tow targets, which is nothing more than a huge cylinder of canvas, thirty or forty feet long. Occasionally, I would go out of our area and put the SBD right down at the surface of the water and fly broadside toward the side of the training ship. When the plane would get close, I would just pull up close to the mast and then down and out of the way. I wasn't the only SPD pilot doing that. The people on the ship got tired of it. One flight I was going in, and they put a couple of anti-aircraft rounds into my SPD.

How did you explain that?

I didn't admit a thing. I don't think anyone knew who was flying the plane.

Were you frightened when that happened?

You bet I was. I didn't fly into that ship again.

Remember the last days in the service?

I was released in August '45 with eight or ten pilots and sent to El Toro to train for carrier duty for the invasion of the islands of Japan, which was scheduled for November 1, 1945, but the war ended abruptly in August of 1945, so I didn't become part of that carrier squadron.

Ever regret that?

No. Certainly the experience I missed, but the end of the war was a blessing for me.

Do you remember where you were when the war was officially over?

I was at home on ten days' leave. The first thing I did was wire El Toro and ask for an extension of my leave. I believe I got another week, then I went to El Toro and flew TBFs—torpedo bombers

Do you miss flying?

Yes, I miss the kind of flying that was available then. Anything less than those experiences wouldn't begin to be worth the trouble.

Ann Darr in AT6 (advance trainer), Sweet-water, Texas

ANN DARR

With the Women's Air Force Service Pilots

In 1977, President Jimmy Carter signed veteran's status for the Women's Air Force Service Pilots, thus ending a long and arduous odyssey for this group of fliers. Ann Darr was one of those who served the United States as a WASP.

When a member of the Women's Airforce Service Pilots was killed, when her plane crashed, the government refused to pay for the body to be sent home. To Ann and her WASP fliers this was a shattering experience and one, she relates in the interview, that she couldn't talk about for years. She would later come to grips with the experience and, in the 1970s, was part of the group that testified before Congress in an attempt to receive official recognition.

One thinks of writers, such as Ernest Gann, who has written well of flight. In a sense, Ann Darr is to poetry about flight what Gann is to novels. She has written about her flight experiences in all eight of her books, most recently, *Flying the Zuni Mountains*. Hers are poems that, among other things, celebrate the experience of flight and of those who have flown.

Ann Darr is an introspective woman with piercing blue eyes and the active mind of an artist in free fall with ideas and feelings. In her writing, flight remains central to her life.

How did you become interested in flight?

My mother died when I was three. I was told she went to heaven and I knew the only way I could get to heaven was to fly. I had a myth that I would fly to heaven under my own steam. When it turned out I could learn to fly at the University of Iowa—when I got there—the myth turned into reality.

What was the program like at the University of Iowa?

It was the Civilian Pilot Training Program (CPT), and I took ground school work in the Engineering Department and flying lessons at the Iowa City Airport.

Did you get college credit for it?

I got college credit for the ground school work, but not for the flying. I got up at 6 AM to do the flying before my 8 AM classes.

Did people think that was kind of strange? You would come rushing into the class from a flying course?

Yes, because they thought I was dressed oddly.

How were you dressed?

In boots and jodhpurs.

What was the most interesting thing during training?

Shall I say the tall handsome man that I fell in love with? I was always in love with somebody, especially teachers.

This was your trainer?

My pilot instructor. The instruction was given in a Piper Cub plane. One early morning, after we'd been practicing take-offs and landings, he hopped out of the plane and said, "It's all yours."

So you remember that solo?

Do I? Yes, indeed I do. I found myself singing at the top of my voice.

You were singing?

Yes. I say in a poem someplace, "I learned I sing when I'm afraid." One of my flying buddies, not long ago, read that poem and scoffed at the idea that I was afraid. I wasn't afraid of flying, but I didn't think I was ready to go up by myself.

Do you remember what you sang? "Go Down, Moses?"

That I don't remember at this moment. but it wouldn't have been "Go Down, Moses" under any circumstances! It was probably, "Up...up...in my flying machine."

What was next?

I graduated from college, went to New York and started working for NBC.

Then the war interrupted that?

That's right. Pearl Harbor came on December 7, 1941, our first anniversary. I had been married on November 7. My husband was in medical school and, of course, signed up for the Navy immediately. In January, 1943, while I was working for "'The Woman of Tomorrow" program on NBC, I went to cover a fancy shoe show at Bendel's.

I ran into the other young woman who was writing copy for the radio show. We'd been sent to cover the same event by mistake. She was in a great state of excitement. She said, "I just have to tell somebody what I've done. I hocked some of Grandmother's jewels she left me in order to take flying lessons. I've just found out about the organization called WAFs." "Isn't that the British women pilots?" I asked. And then she told me there was an American group of women fliers named after the WAFs and she was going to try to get into the group as soon as she had enough flying time.

How much was that?

The original requirement was 250 hours, but she learned that they had lowered the time to 45 hours. She thought it was because they had found that pilots with 250 hours had more trouble learning precision flying.

Precision flying?

Yes, in the Army you had to learn how to land on a dime, or to hold a specific altitude for formation flying. Pilots with 45 hours could be taught more easily than some of those pilots who had much more time and were set in their ways.

So what happened when you heard what she was doing?

I was so excited, I shouted, "I've got 45 hours." She was dumbfounded when I told her. She didn't know until that moment that I could fly. Somehow, I just hadn't told anybody at the office.

So what did she say when you told her you flew?

She was agog and said, "You can get into the WAFs!" For whatever reasons the organization of the WAFs was kept quite secret, or it certainly wasn't advertised. I don't know to this day why that was the case, unless it was prejudice against it from the start. And it must have been partly that or it wouldn't have taken us so long to get veteran status.

Did you see some prejudice early on?

Yes, we did, unfortunately. It was at the bases where we were sent. The male pilots—some of them—were not eager to have the women pilots around. Some of them simply thought women couldn't do anything as well as men. Some thought it was too dangerous a job for women. Mostly, though, it was a matter of ego, I believe. As it turned out, our record for flying was better than the men's. Anyway, there were twenty-five thousand young women who did everything they could to earn enough money to get flying time so they could apply. There were over eighteen hundred who were accepted. One thousand and seventy-nine graduated.

And your friend from the show?

She washed out.

How did you feel?

Sick to my stomach. She called me up the night before I was to leave New York for Sweetwater, Texas, where we were to be trained. In fact, this is a point I want to bring out. All of the women who were accepted into the program had to know how to fly before they were accepted. This was not true of the male flying cadets. They were taken in on the basis of physical and mental health—which we were judged too—but we also had to know how to fly.

Anyway, my friend was back in New York City. She telephoned and said, "I have washed out." I thought, "If she can't make it, nobody can." She was a bright, competent, an extraordinary young woman. She had made it through basic training, but had not been able to handle the larger planes. I believe she eventually qualified to teach male cadets in primary trainers, but I'm not certain about that.

So how'd you feel?

Glum. I thought, "What's the use of trying, if she couldn't make it, what chance have I got?" However, I got on the train and went to Sweetwater, Texas. I was picked up at the station in a big old truck that they carried us around in. I arrived at Avenger Field.

Avenger?

It was named that because it had been turned over earlier to the training of young British pilots. In fact, when the first class of WAFs arrived from Houston—their earlier base—the British cadets were just finishing up. This was before I arrived.

There were, of course, three phases to training: primary, secondary, and advanced trainer planes. If we failed, we washed out. If we passed, we were thrown into the pool that was at the gate of Avenger Field under a big Fifinella sign.

Fifinella sign?

Yes, Walt Disney drew it for us—a flying woman in helmet, boots, wings—our own flying symbol.

Disney actually drew it?

That's what I understood. One of the women of our class had worked for Disney as a cartoonist. I always thought Fifinella looked like her; maybe she was the model for it. Anyway, Fifinella is still our emblem. We have it on our flight jackets and stationery and the like.

What about your class?

The course was set up so that first, we were in primary trainers, PT-19s; then we went to basic trainers, the old BT-13; then to advanced trainers, the AT-6, which was fast and had a lot of horsepower. Our particular class was the first one to go directly from the PT-19 to the AT-6, skipping the BT-13. This was done to see if we could do it. We were guinea pigs. When we were successful at it, that procedure became the standard way of doing it for men. After the war, I understand, cadets went directly to the AT-6 for all pilot training.

How about the planes that you flew? Any that you especially remember?

My old BT-13 rattled and thumped when you put it into a spin. It sounded like an egg beater. We took instrument training in the BT-13s after we had jumped the primary. That was when we flew under a hood so we couldn't see out.

They actually trained you that way? Under a hood?

Yes. Until I learned to do it right. It was one of the scariest things. Of course, we were also training, at that point, in the Link trainer, so we could learn to do this on the ground in a simulated version. That's when we learned how good our pilots—friends, other women—actually were. Some of them were good; a few were not so good.

Talk about one that wasn't so good.

Someone once gave me a figure as to what our altitude was and she was off by a hundred feet. It was very startling. She was not aware that she had given me the wrong information.

How'd you manage to get out of that one?

I didn't fly with her again and I do believe she washed out.

What was the living like there?

The typical life of Army Air Force training. We lived in barracks, six women to a bay, a long row-house with bathroom facilities in between. A big room that served as living room, bedroom, study room. We got up to reveille and went to bed by taps. We lived by regular Army rules and regulations, but we did try to have as much fun as we could.

We were not allowed as WASPs to socialize with our instructors, though as I remember some WASPs married their instructors after graduation. On special occasions, carloads of male pilots would be brought in from the base at Big Spring for a dance. Once, I won a dance contest with a wonderful young dancer I had just met that night. Then they took the men back to Big Springs. I never saw him again. In fact, I don't even remember his name.

Later on, when we were sent to the Advanced Training Base in Stockton,

California, we lived in the nurses' quarters and were not really welcome.

What happened?

There was conflict with other women. The nurses didn't think the pilots were their equal. There was a competitiveness that made us uncomfortable. We were "wild women" because we flew planes. At least, that's how they seemed to feel.

Do you still keep in touch with any of your old WASP baymates?

Oh, yes, of course, we have reunions. I haven't been able to go often, but I've kept track of several of the women I was closest to in Sweetwater. Mary Cooper Cox—she had so many hours when she came into our class she practically took the whole flying course flying upside down while the rest of us were taught flying right side up. Marg DeBolt from California was another special baymate who is remembered particularly for her creative excuses for not getting up when the bugle blew. She's still flying her own plane on the West Coast. A young woman from New York, Cecily Elmes, a debutante, I remember for being very generous with her wardrobe. Once, when my husband came as far as St. Louis to visit me before he sailed for the South-Pacific, she loaned me some of her best civilian clothes to go meet him.

We were really very supportive of each other. Living in such close quarters we needed to be. Especially when bad news came from overseas or one of us flunked a check ride. We were like a big family of sisters.

What happened when you first lost a pilot?

That was the hardest of all. When one of our women crashed and burned in a trainer plane, it was as if we had lost a member of our family. We grieved, then we went back to the flight line.

We realized that this was war, this was no game we were in. That was the reason I was there. I wanted to do something for the war effort. I could fly—this was something I had—a skill that I could give my country. By this time, we knew what a dreadful situation it was in Europe. We knew the Holocaust was happening; we knew there was no certainty that we were going to win the war.

Who were your flying heroes?

Lindbergh had been my idol. "Lucky Lindy flew all alone in a little plane all his own." Remember that old song? No, you're too young. I said in poems about sitting at my grandma's player piano and pumping away and singing—alternately singing and playing my brother's saxophone. There were several songs about Lindbergh when he flew.

And you knew them all?

ANN DARR

Oh, yes. And Amelia Earhart, of course, was a dream woman as far as I was concerned.

Do you remember where you were when you learned the news that Amelia Earhart had been lost?

No, oddly enough, I don't. I do remember walking out into the front hall of my house and seeing on the floor the Des Moines *Register-Tribune* that had been delivered by the paperboy. The headline read "Wylie Post Crashes in Alaska." That moment I do remember. I can still see it.

Did Amelia Earhart show you that women could fly?

Strangely enough, I knew I could do that. I knew that a woman could do that. I didn't know that being a woman was going to be a problem as far as anything I wanted to do was concerned.

But did you find it a problem?

In the actual WASPs, yes, I did. Once, when I did a cross-country from Sweetwater to California, I had barely made it over the mountains at El Paso when I set down my plane for an emergency—there was so much oil on the windshield. When I walked into the ready room, they made me account for every instrument reading before they would even go out and look at my plane. When they did go out and look, they said, "What kind of plane are you being sent off with? This is in terrible shape."

Did you fly an inordinate number of clunkers?

I can't put blame on anyone. We were flying everything we had and everyone was working hard around the clock.

At Stockton, my job was to test planes. After a plane had been flown a certain number of hours, it had to be tested, all the instruments, the condition of the plane itself. Or, after it had been in an accident, the condition of the plane was checked. Or, after a plane had been in an accident and repaired, it had to have a check flight.

Where'd you go from there?

From there we were sent to Las Vegas to be checked out in the B-26s we missed in Dodge City, Kansas so that we could tow targets in the Gunnery School.

Gunnery School?

We towed the targets in B-26s while B-17s flew beside us. In maneuvers, what we did was tow this big sleeve behind us. The B-17s flew alongside with training cadets operating from their positions in the nose, the sides and the tail. First, they trained cameras until they had their reflexes under control so they could start firing, and stop so they wouldn't shoot down our own planes.

After they learned that control, they used live ammunition, which had been dipped in red or blue or yellow wax so their accuracy could be checked. You see, after a shooting run, we would drop the target on the ground and the ground crew would retrieve it and check it out. The colored wax left color around the hole in the target. Red, yellow, blue, very colorful. We used those discarded targets for bedspreads, curtains, everything.

Wasn't it scary flying targets? Did you ever get hit?

I was too intent on keeping that plane at a specific altitude—on course. I never got hit, but there were crashes. One plane went down with a WASP co-pilot. Both the pilot and co-pilot were killed. The pilot's body was sent home, but we had to take up a collection to send home the WASP.

The military wouldn't pick up the tab?

Correct. We were being paid by the Civil Service, although we were flying under military orders with military rules and regulations, military punishment. For example, we were dressed down if we didn't salute. Everything we did was military, but they said we were Civil Service, so the Army wasn't responsible. Civil Service said they weren't responsible, so we took up a collection among ourselves to send her body home.

That was pretty devastating?

I was so hurt and angry about the situation. I just didn't want anyone to know it for years.

You didn't?

My own country wouldn't. I was ashamed of what they did. I didn't want to admit even to myself that we were being so humiliated.

When did you finally come to grips with it?

Only after the war. Are you aware that we were disbanded before the war was over?

No.

We were told that we were being disbanded because more male pilots were coming back alive from overseas than they had expected. We flew over six million miles and did it all extremely well, and we were being disbanded. We flew every kind of aircraft they had from PT-19s to B-29s. Anyway, we were dismissed in December, before the end of the war in June.

You never refused to go up because a plane was too dangerous?

No, I didn't. Once we flew UC-78s back from Stockton to the factory in Texas. Regulations said we had to have a pilot and a co-pilot but we flew solo.

The UC-78s on our base had wings damaged by wind. They were not strong enough and needed to be reinforced. The Army wanted all of that model to go back to the factory, so we made the trip. I don't remember how many planes were in the group, maybe twenty. I didn't want to do that trip, but didn't feel I could refuse. I would have preferred to have had a co-pilot along for that lengthy trip from northern California to Texas.

I think the idea of flight, which you've explored in the poems, is interesting. Flight is really one of life's great metaphors.

I think human beings have been wanting to take to air since their eyes first lighted on birds. You can't see birds flying without wanting to join them. Flight is my metaphor—a personal metaphor—for flight in all of its meanings, from the power dream—rising and flying with one's own power—to the Phoenix rising from the ashes, to flight as in "running away from."

You actually have one poem about running away from home as I recall?

Yes. It's called "Orders."
> After I ran away from home and came back again
> My Papa said, Go if you must, but mind three things:
> Stay away from water, stay off of boats and don't
> Go up in an aeroplane. So first I learned to swim
> Then I learned to sail, and then I learned to fly.

Your father is in another flying poem of yours along with other of your heroes. Can you tell us about that?

I knew a flying poem was going to surface at some point or other after those years. It happened when the invitation came to put my name in a time capsule for the dedication in Texas of Hangar Nine where many of the famous fliers learned to fly.

That was exciting.

Yes, when the mail arrived, it was like a switch turned on! I sat at the typewriter and wrote for hours—pages and pages. It was as if all of the flying experience finally took off and was flying under its own steam.

It's evident the flight experience as a WASP has been an important part of your life.

Yes, indeed, it created friendships that last to this day. It gave me confidence that I wouldn't otherwise have had. Even with the mistakes I've made, I've learned from those. Maybe one learns more from mistakes, but the triumphs were rewarding too. When those silver wings with the diamond in the middle were pinned on me, it was as if I made a success of something I started out to do.

You were active in the WASP *recognition movement weren't you?*

We were told not to get in touch with our Congressmen and we were supposed to "act like ladies." So we didn't fight it when we should have. When they said, "Go home, you're finished here," we went. It was a terrible time for all of us. We were being dismissed as if we had not done a good job—which we had. Yes, I became verbal later on. There was a quote I remember well: "The only reason I'm listening to the testimony of you WASPs is that I owe Senator Goldwater a favor."

Somebody actually said that?

Yes.

What year was that?

1977.

But you were finally recognized.

Yes, what we got out of it was recognition and a burial place.

How about concluding with a poem.

Here's one, called "Gather My Wings."

GATHER MY WINGS

There is a part of me that looks
forever for a level land
where rows of grain run
straightway to the wind.

Once you have trained
these senses, they stay trained
and though I have no need
for landing, forced or free,
this noticing is part of me,

makes me check imprecisions of an eye,
correct for choppy heartbeats,
hear a whipping tongue as dangerous.
I must go out and gather in my wings.

Once prepared for landing forced,
one lives too much alerted.
One listens for a twitch of snake.

Art Degenhardt. Belgium—1945

ART DEGENHARDT

From The Ninth Air Force To Flying Korea

W hen Art Degenhardt joined the military in February 1942, he anxiously anticipated getting into action. In those days, however, when you qualified for the Army Air Corps Pilot Training Program, you had to wait for an assignment. His friends gave him a farewell party nonetheless, but as circumstances had it, Art watched the fellows who had come to his farewell party go ahead of him to the war. Some nine months later the military had a spot for him and he went to Nashville, Tennessee for the first phase of his pilot training. After some further delays, he went through Basic, Primary, and Advanced training and got his silver wings at Marianna, Florida on Jan. 7, 1944.

Art served as fighter pilot with the 109th Tactical Recon Squadron; the 67th Tactical Recon Group of the 9th Air Force, retiring as a Lt. Colonel. I approach the interview with curiosity about Art Degenhardt. He has cautioned me by phone before our meeting that he doesn't like to talk about the dark side of the war years. In the latter part of the interview, I get to the reasons why.

A vigorous man, Art leans down hard on the arm of the chair, as if at various times he must emphasize some specific point. His blue eyes blaze as he recounts the feelings he has about the war years. After 26 years of serving in the air force, Colonel Degenhardt retired in 1968.

When did you arrive in Europe?

I arrived in Liverpool shortly after the D-Day invasion. Someone said, "we'll put you in a C-47 and fly you into Paris." I said, "You've got to be kidding. The Germans are there." They said, "It's been liberated." We landed at Versailles. We were responsible for supporting the Third Army and the Third Army had just got through liberating that part of the world and we eventually moved up to Belgium to support the First Army. We were assigned to front-line support and provided such things as reconnaissance, artillery adjusting and weather reporting.

What was the toughest thing about your job over there?

My kids ask, "Dad, what was the best time of your life?" I say, "I hate to tell you this but WWII, because you felt like you weren't going to live through tomorrow, so you'd enjoy today."

The British liberated Belgium and I—along with two other fellows—was among the first American troops allowed in Brussels. The British were there, and they didn't want Americans, because we had more money. Their monies were frozen in England.

I was fortunate enough to have served to the end of the war, and they sent me to Paris on VE Eve. It was announced the war was going to be over the next day, so I celebrated VE Eve in Paris. I flew out of Paris the next day and was in London on VE Day, so I celebrated the end of the war in two major capitals of the world.

What were the celebrations like?

The one thing I didn't like about France. I couldn't get across the main boulevard in Paris. The city was jammed with people and aircraft were flying overhead shooting off flares in celebration. The French were saying, "Yankee, go home." There was a whole group of them, saying, "Yankee, go home." I was hearing this on May 5, 1945. I guess there were a lot of women being taken over by the Americans and they wanted us out. However, I enjoyed getting into London. They were very appreciative of the fact that we had come over and helped them end that war.

Let's talk about the dangers of Recon work.

One of my associates, Lt. Thompson, flying at three hundred feet doing Recon work, got too to close the enemy and one of the Germans threw up his helmet. It got caught in the intake scoop of the P-51. The Lt. had to bail out of the airplane because it overheated and the engine shut off. That was one of the bad features of the P-51. First of all it was an in-line engine, not a radial, so that if you got hit, as I did one time, it knocked out half your engine. You only had half the power. When Thompson turned upside down in his aircraft to try to drop out, his aircraft caught on fire. He opened his canopy and the flames blew in—he had his gloves off —and he had a heck of a time undoing his safety belt. Later, I saw him in the hospital and he was all bandaged up—his face and hands. The war was over for him. On many occasions we were so close to the front lines that when we'd take off we'd need to take a sharp turn to get out of there so we didn't get hit by enemy ground fire.

I was flying the lead on a flight deep into Germany. We understood there was no power flowing through the power lines. I was flying with a fellow named Galuption. We came in real low—buzzing—but I kept telling Galuption, "Be careful, high tension wires." Since he was a trainee, I stayed up above a little, keeping an eye on him. I'm so busy insuring that he didn't get into trouble that I flew into those power lines. It ripped my wing, my vertical stabilizer, and damaged the hell out of the spinner on the prop. But

I managed to get back home. The Commander chewed me out for not flying low enough. My crew chief had just put a nice new spinner on the prop. The commander made me clean the paint off the replacement spinner—as a punishment.

Because we were so close to the front lines, we had an Army Intelligence officer who would interrogate us when we got back from each flight. Sometimes we'd see something we thought wasn't important, but it was important to him. He would take this info and relay it back to the front lines. This one particular day I was coming back in "Babe's Flash," my airplane—I called my wife "Babe." We were coming down at a low level, buzzing the highway—another fellow and myself—and I was in the lead this time. When you look at the front end of a P-51, it looks like a German ME-109. I didn't know at the time, but it's true. So we were just tooling along at low level and finally got back and landed our planes. Nothing unusual. The next day some captain came up and said, "Who the hell was flying UX-V yesterday?" I said, "I was." It seems that he'd decided to take a break on his way to the front lines to urinate along the side of the road, when he saw what he thought were these two ME-109's coming down the autobahn, and he jumped right into the ditch where he had just urinated! I was only a Lieutenant then. He was madder than hell at me.

We had six 50-calibre machine guns and the armament men would occasionally reset them up. One day they told me, "You will want to fire your guns today to check for alignment." My primary mission was checking and reporting on enemy activity, to find out what the enemy was doing. We kept being told that we weren't out there to shoot down any other birds but rather to bring back information. I was returning from a mission and when I crossed our lines, I realized I had forgotten to shoot my guns, so I told my wingman to stand by, that I'm going to find a haystack and shoot these things. I went across the lines and found a haystack and I started pulling the trigger, diving into this haystack that was almost two stories high. The haystack had an anti-aircraft gun in there and started shooting back! I hightailed it back out of there and reported the enemy gun to our intelligence people.

What was your most unsual reconn mission?

I sighted several train movements at dusk. One time when I came back, the anti-aircraft was shooting at me. I thought I was on my side of the lines, and I was. But because I was coming back at twilight, they asssumed I was enemy aircraft. We always had someone who'd come in and shoot us up at dusk when they knew we weren't moving. We had been warned to be careful when coming home at twilight, but it was still a surprise. I saw more 4th of July fireworks on that night than you ever saw in your life.

You mentioned earlier you got hit.

Yes, I was flying on a recon mission over the mountains of Germany. All of a sudden flak hit me. I hadn't been in the war long and nervously hauled back on my control stick so fast that the engine stalled on me. I found myself heading down to mother earth from 5,000 feet and trying to get the thing started. All I could see were the mountains coming closer. I thought, "What a helluva place to die in!" But I hit the primer and all of a sudden the engine started for me at about 2,500 feet. Of course, the mountain range was very close when I pulled out of the dive.

I got hit by an ME109. A guy named Turner from Boston and I were flying. It was toward the end of the war. By that time, there were few good pilots out there on the German side. They had by then put 15-year-old kids in the cockpit to fly. The better pilots were put into the jets— the ME262's. Anyway, we were just tooling along. You got to the point where you felt pretty cocky, because there was not much enemy in the air anymore. All of a sudden, these guys came out of the sky. My wingman says, "You got a bandit coming at you"— and by the time I broke away I had one on my tail. He hit me with his 37mm nose cannon. I lost power when he hit me the first time. We had an understanding that if you wanted to bail out you'd just pull back and drop your wheels and they wouldn't shoot anymore. I didn't know where he was because there was no more firing coming at me anymore, so I pulled up to see what was going on. All of a sudden, I saw him on my tail. I turned around to look, and Boom! he had blown up. Turner had kept on going all the way around and had finally got behind this guy. The German pilot had been so determined he was going to get a victory that he forgot about his tail and Turner came around and blew him up.

Now the question was whether I had enough power to get back to home base. I didn't. So we landed at a P-47 base, which had a longer runway and was close by. Because of the traffic we landed in a crosswind. Because I knew I didn't have the power, I concentrated like hell and I landed that bird. Halfway down the runway, however, it stalled on me. Meanwhile, Pat Turner was up there doing a slow roll, indicating he had a victory —he had shot down an enemy aircraft. After the guys towed me off the runway, Pat came in. But he was so excited he forgot to allow for the crosswind and when he hit the runway, he lost control of his aircraft and started going off the runway. We had control towers and trucks out there and he literally ran right into a truck. He got out of his bird, ran away, and both the truck and his airplane blew up. I always said we got one ME-109, but we lost a truck and two aircraft—because my aircraft was 86'd—disposed of.

Another time I was working with the 3rd Army at the front lines. We had to adjust artillery for them because their little Cub planes couldn't see out too far. I looked down and saw four big cannons sitting in a field and one in the center. So I started calling back commands to adjust our artillery. Our guns were maybe 15 miles back. I was sitting up there telling them how close they were. "We got one...two... three...four. Then I said, "Let's get the one in the middle." About that time the one in middle got me. It tore all the fragments off the end of the airplane, but there was enough left to fly back home. I was really shocked. It turns out that the reason those anti-aircraft guns hadn't fired sooner at me was because they were very short of ammo.

How long were you there?

My tour was supposed to be 50 missions, but some colonel came along and said, "We're running short of pilots. We're going to have to jack your tour up to 75 missions." Because we were at the end of the tour, we had someone new as operations chief. He was flying his friends, so we older men were having a hard time getting those extra missions in. Some were pretty bitter. By the time I got 74, they said I could go home. They scheduled us on a B-17 out of England as passengers. Then they said we had to go to Paris on temporary duty. We were told, "You P-51 pilots, we want you to film wartorn Europe." I flew one photo mission and we asked, "Hey, why are we doing this, when these johnny-come-latelies are supposed to be in the Army of Occupation? Why don't we go home and let them take over this stuff?" Somebody agreed and we were out of there again.

We went back over to England. We said, "Okay, we're ready to go now." They said, "We have to let these recent arrivals go back first because they've got to go to the far east and fly in the Japan war." I sat there for two months trying to get my ass out of England. Finally, I got on a B-17. I'm just a passenger along with three or four other guys. We took off, but before long we were landing. Somebody says, "I think the pilot's lost." We landed in a Spitfire field in Scotland, and sure as hell, the pilot leans his head out the window and says, "Where are we?" The guy tells him where we are, and they find it on the map. Then the pilot goes to taxi out and he hits a wing tip, so we had to sit out there and patch this wingtip. We still had to cross the ocean and I'm thinking, I hope we can get across all right. We landed in Iceland. Then we find out we're not going to go into New Hampshire as scheduled, but we're going to be landing in Bangor, Maine. It seems they were having a big celebration there and wanted to show off a WWII aircraft.

We got out at Bangor, and nobody talked to us. They talked to the pilot. I saw this little Piper Cub. I walked over to it and put my foot on a tire and looked in the cockpit, and some kid—he must have been ten years old— spoke the first words I heard on coming back, "Get your goddamn foot off that tire. I spent all day shining it." (laughs) They were the first words I heard coming back from combat. Welcome to America.

When did you go to Korea?

I went to Korea five years later. They told me they would put me in the B-26, which was the Martin Marauder, also called "the flying coffin" or the "flying cigar." However, the B-26 I flew was an A-26, a follow-up to the A-20 converted to a B-26. Several of us, together with a navigator, picked up B-26's in Hawaii

Art Degenhardt with the B-26 he ferried to French Indo-China. Jan. 1951.

to fly them to the French in Indochina. We left Hawaii in January, 1951 to navigate across the Pacific, island-hopping, following a B-29. Somewhere between Hawaii and Johnson Island, one of my associates, an Irishman, made his bird take a dive down and begins to fly upside down. That's the first time we knew that the B-26 could fly upside down. We're watching this and screaming, "All right, what's going on?" We went down to see, and what we found was that the co-pilot was drinking a bottle of whisky and the pilot wanted a drink. He said, "No, you're flying." The pilot responded, "If I can't have any, you can't have any." He turned the bird upside down so the whole bottle of whiskey emptied into the cockpit. At Johnson Island, that cockpit smelled of Scotch.

What was the toughest thing about flying in Korea?

The runway had a mountain at the end of it. We had two guys flew into it. As soon as you took off, you had to fly to the left or right to avoid it. That was the only spooky thing to me. I was at Taegu.

On one flight I got lost over Korea. Our weather was socked in. I figured if we couldn't land back in Korea, we could land in Japan. When we took off, there was a thin layer of clouds. The weather forecaster had forecast strong crosswinds. My navigator/bombardier didn't allow for the winds. He said, "Let's go back to Taegu and start over again, so I can figure out where I am." I turned up the radio. My radios were dead. We tried to dogleg it back, based on assumptions, but we basically had no idea where we were. The next moment I thought we were flying over Manchuria. We started telling everyone we were in trouble by announcing "mayday, mayday, if you receive us, we have lots of gas." I still didn't know where we were. Our radio operator in the back of the bird said, "I've got some alternate equipment." But none of it worked either. We kept flying around and, finally, we saw this great big, bright light coming up over the horizon. The navigator said, "That's Tokyo over there." So I headed for Tokyo, but just then the moon came up over the clouds. It wasn't Tokyo, it was the moon. So we called for help again. Next, we had a P-61 "Blackwidow" Nightfighter come up. He must have been disgusted: he gave me this prop wash—turbulence. I started following him down. Just as we pulled through the clouds, which were at a low-level, a beacon light flashed in my eyes. I hauled back on the wheel and pulled back up through the clouds. I didn't know where we were. I didn't know what he had down there. I knew he wanted me to follow him. He had all the equipment on board. It turned out one airfield was on one side of a mountain and there was a beacon on top of it. We made a second approach and when I broke in under the clouds, I circled and I was wondering where the damn runway was. When I saw this runway, I leveled out too high. All of a sudden, ka-boom, we dropped about twenty feet, and landed. Right then, my radio began blasting like all hell. Everything went on at once. The radio operator in the back was busy turning volumes down too.

We reported that the reason we were there was because we had lost all radios, so of course they sent a radio man out. He said, "Ground checks okay, can't find anything wrong." We stayed overnight. Back in Korea the next day, the commander accused us of screwing off by going to Japan. He asked if we had just gone over to get a little rest and relaxation. "No, Sir," I said. "Well, we couldn't possibly find anything wrong with your radios." We never did find out what had gone wrong.

What were conditions like in Korea?

We lived in tents. It seemed like we were always downwind from the Koreans and the food they would let get moldy. Bad weather, deep mud, mucky rain.

I had to fly a night flight, so I tried not to disturb the other six guys in the tent. I started getting dressed in the dark—longjohns, suntans, flying gear, and I was about to put the jacket on, when I felt this pain and I squeezed the hell out of my left arm. I turned on the light now, and began to strip my clothes off. I got down to my first flight suit layer and a mouse fell out of the sleeve. I was running around now trying to find the flight surgeon to find out if a mouse bite was deadly over there. When I found him, the C.O. just told me, "Get airborne!"

On many flights we would have great delay in getting a landing clearance because the jets were permitted to land first. I had a navigator named Cone, a major who had been around for awhile. We used to call him "Ice Cream" Cone. One day we came in to land, and they kept telling us to circle. We had a radar altimeter so Cone suggested we go out over the water and bust through the overcast, using our radar to get to sea level. We broke out at about two hundred feet and chose to follow the coast to land at Pusan Airfield in Southern Korea. When we got there, Major Cone said, "I can get us back to Taegu. We can fly on the deck up the river." There are all kinds of instruments now, but the original one was a needle-ball airspeed. If the ball went off center, it meant you were skidding this way or another and the needle would show the degree of turn. He said, "I'm going to give you a needle-ball turn." We then went flying up the river on the deck. He would say, "Turn right now, or turn left now." I could see mountains and trees on either side. The top of the mountains were in the clouds as we came up. Finally, we landed at Taegu. He said, "I forgot to tell you. I've done that before, but there were two planes then." I said, "Oh." He said, "Yes, I did it with a bigger aircraft—a C-54. The other C-54 cracked into the mountain." That was probably the best bit of flying I ever did. When he called, "Turn right now," you didn't sit there and say, "What?"

In Korea they jacked our number of flights up to 75, too. Again, a colonel came in and said, "We're running short on pilot replacements. I hate to tell you this, gentlemen, but you have to fly 25 more missions." I said, "I got screwed in WWII and I'm not going to get screwed now." I had already had my 50 missions in, so I scheduled and flew eight missions in seven days. Meanwhile, the other guys who were also eligible all went over to Japan on rest and relaxation. I was told that if I flew the extra 25 missions, all eligible crews would have to also. They asked me to also take R.and R. in Japan, and if they couldn't change the policy, I would be scheduled to fly the remaining 17 missions in 17 days or less. When I returned from R. and R., they said, "You can go home." So I only had to do 58 combat missions there.

Any problems coming home this time?

Yes. We landed in McCord Air Force Base in the middle of the night, and the fellow says, "You're a little late—it's going to be tough getting transportation out of here. There is a train that's leaving—if that'll help." So I got on the phone and I spoke to my wife in Coeur d'Alene, Idaho. I said, "Can you meet me in Pasco, Washington? I should be leaving here at three o'clock in the morning." I took the train, which was an old coal train. When I got to Pasco, I was all choked up with coal smoke. I had one son who fought in Vietnam. When I hear they didn't get a welcome home, I think, coming home from Korea, "Well, neither did I. Except for my lovely wife and at that time, two little sons. That was welcome enough for me."

There are certain things about WWII you don't want to talk about.

I lived the highlights. I turned my mind off about the blood and guts.

Do you think you got more blood and guts or internalized it, or what?

When I came home, my cousin, Artie, who was born and raised in New York, was telling all the miseries and all the death that he saw over there. The more he told, the more I could see the agony and pain on the faces of my relatives. My people did want to know what it was like in Europe, so I started telling some of the funny things. I found that the more Artie told the other side, the more I got off the subject of blood and guts. I saw some horrible things over there that would have upset my family quite a bit.

Because you were German?

Yes, because my mother and father both came from Germany. Later on, my stepfather also came from Germany. Then during my second tour in Germany, we were an Army of Occupation. You had to wear your uniform. I went down to where my stepfather came from, Neustadt, which means "New City," and this female relative would have nothing to do with me, because the American pilots had strafed up the town that she was in, and all there were were women and children. It was supposed to be a safe town. I tried to explain to her that when you're flying at high speeds and somebody's shooting at you, if you see someone moving around down there, you're going to squeeze that trigger. Our people didn't know there were women and kids down there. Anyway, the rest of the family all accepted me, but she never would accept me as a military man. I was that fighter pilot that shot at her.

Frank Potter surveys the tarmac

FRANK POTTER

The Berlin Airlift

F rank Potter welcomes me to his comfortable ranch-style Spokane, Washington, home. Once inside, he shows me the view of his backyard where a host of birds spirit their way through the air.

After graduating in 1945, Frank went to instructor school where he taught in the French program for several months. After that, he ended up in Japan where he flew throughout the Far East—Hong Kong, Shanghai, Guam and the Philippines.

The Berlin airlift started in June of '48 and Frank served there, both as group supply officer and as pilot. When he wasn't searching for an airplane starter or some other item, he was flying. The airlift, which flew in 1.7 million tons of food, machinery, and supplies, revolutionized air traffic control.

Next, Frank served in the Strategic Air Command, flying a mish-mash of planes from the C-45 and B-17 to B-29s, B-36s and B-52s. He instructed in all of them and was a checkrider in the B-52. He later moved into the DCO (Deputy Commander of Operations) job and was promoted to full colonel. He served as Deputy Base Commander at Minot, North Dakota, for a year and a half. Colonel Potter retired from the service in 1969.

Where were you when the Berlin airlift began?

I was in Japan when the airlift started. I'd just come back from a trip to Okinawa. I parked the airplane about three or four in the afternoon on a Thursday, and some of those maintenance men said, "Go home and pack your stuff. We just have a couple of days' notice to get ready and leave." We left our wives in Japan, and they stayed there while we were in Germany.

Do you remember what went through your mind when someone said, "You're going to supply a city of over two million with everything it needs for survival"?

It almost seemed like trying to dip the lake dry with a bucket. But once you got there and got to seeing it, you could see that stream of airplanes coming in. You could stand on the runway and you could see one coming in there. "There's another one, here are five of them halfway down." You could count six or seven planes just at one time, all in the process of landing. And here are fifteen or twenty landing and already being unloaded.

What was your favorite plane to fly?

If I had to say a favorite, I'd say the B-52. The jet flying for many reasons is by far the least complicated. It's much faster, things happen faster, you go faster. The jet engines are much more simple than the engines we'd have, like, on the B36 where you had the superchargers; the high superchargers, the low superchargers and, of course, mixture controls and anti-icing controls, and all of this stuff that was required on them. For example, with a B-36 you'd come back to base at twenty thousand feet, and it would take you an hour to get on the ground. Before you could retard the engines and start down, you had to go from high blower to low blower or no blower; you had to put the carburetor heat on and you had to go to auto rich and all of these things, which you had to do in the proper sequence. And then the airplane was limited in the speed of the descent that you could take anyway. So it would take you an hour to get on the ground. But with a B-52, we could come back at thirty-five thousand, just pull the throttles to idle, and down you come. Our standard rate of descent was four thousand feet a minute. So from thirty-five thousand to ground level was just over eight minutes. And you had to run three checklists from the time you started down, to the time you touched down so you were busy. It was fast, and it was fun.

You flew B-29s. Did you like them?

Oh, it was a good airplane, but it was quite a bit slower and a prop job. And it wasn't as reliable. We left Guam one time, and I think I was number five to take off and it wound up I was the only one that made it all the way home. For various reasons, the others dropped off here or there.

What was the B-25 like?

It was a two-engine model, and it was noisy. It was the only one that I'm aware of that did not have what we call a "collector ring" on the exhaust, and it was just like a motorcycle. The exhaust exited from each cylinder, and it was extremely noisy. Most of the time they run a collector ring and collect all the exhaust and exhaust it on the outside away from you so it's much less noisy. After you'd come home from flying for six or eight hours, you couldn't hear anything for a day or two. Of course, back in those days we weren't so cognizant of the fact that loud sounds cause loss of hearing; we didn't even use the earplugs. And you didn't use helmets or anything like that. You just had a headset, and we'd usually put it over the ear that was next to the engine and leave the other off so that we could talk. In the B-52 now, you wear the helmet, where it's impossible to talk, almost so you talk everything over the radio, through the innerphone to one another.

What were the flying conditions generally like in the Berlin Airlift?

A lot of fog, a lot of rain. We had some snow. I don't think we had over two inches, so snow was no problem. You've heard of London fog. Well, you have it all over Europe like that. The fog did shut it down a few times. I've seen the fog so bad you couldn't see ten feet in front of you. When it got that bad, it did close down, at least from our base. But usually they could run from one of the other bases.

What was the layout of Templehof Airport?

Templehof was right in the middle of the city, and the main building is a big crescent-shaped building. It must have been six hundred to seven hundred feet from one end to the other. And, of course, the building itself has about seven levels. It was a Messerschmidt factory during the war and when the Russians liberated Berlin.

We had two runways and you could land and just taxi in to this ramp. They had this great overhang. Sometimes you'd be under this overhang, sometimes you wouldn't, but you'd taxi right up to this main central building. As you got in near your parking place, the engineer with you would open the door on the lefthand side and before we ever got out of the cockpit, they would have a truck backed up and the Germans would be onboard, tossing off the bags of coal. Gosh, they would unload you in six or eight minutes. It was fast.

How many people would be unloading?

There must have been ten to fifteen on each truck. I know it surprised me. They didn't run around in circles where one guy would grab a bag and run back over here and say, "Excuse me." Instead, they set up a chain line and then, after unloading, they sent in a couple of women sweepers, and they'd sweep it out. There usually would be a half-bucket or sack, sometimes even more, of coal that had been spilled. So instead of us carrying it back home, they would sweep it out and onto their truck.

As soon as we landed, we'd get out of the airplane and at first you had to go into the office to get your clearance back. Then General Tunner, who was in charge, changed that. We would have the weather briefing jeep and the clearance officer would come out to the airplane. So almost immediately you'd have the two briefing officers there, and they would tell you, "The weather's the same going home" or whatever weather word they'd have, and the other guy would sign your clearance for the way back. The maintenance people would also be there if we had any problems. If it was something they could fix, then fine. If it wasn't, then you went on home. You always tried to go home with whatever the trouble was. If it was a light out, they didn't worry about that.

By the time you got that done, the Germans would be done unloading.

So you'd just jump back in and take off. Then they started bringing a little snack-bar truck around. It had hot dogs, hamburgers, coke, coffee, cigarettes, which you ate while you were getting your clearance. I'm sure your time on the ground wouldn't average fifteen minutes. And what struck me as strange was that we had to pay for the hamburgers! In those days they were probably only a dime!

What did you think when you saw the Berlin Wall come down?

We were there in October, 1989, less than a month before it went down. Let me tell you this, when we first learned the wall was going up, I said right then that we ought to knock it down. We had the atom bomb. The people I associated with thought we should have gone in there and taken a couple of tanks, and the heck with them, knocked it down. But we didn't.

When we saw the wall last, the uprisings in 1989 had just started. After we got home and it started, my wife and I watched TV for two or three days seeing the wall being torn down. My wife would say, "Look at this. Look at this." I think we were happier to see that than if we found out that we won the lotto. No, it was unbelievable because when we were over there in recent years, we had no idea it was going to happen. We were hosted by a German couple in their mid-fifties, so that would put them about fifteen, forty years ago. That was one of the questions they asked. From our standpoint, did I think the wall was going to come down? I told them, "Yes," I thought it would. But I had no idea it would be coming down within a month. I guessed ten or fifteen years. I told them I figured the people are going to tire of it and just flat not put up with it any more.

Air traffic control was revolutionized by the Berlin airlift, wasn't it?

Never before had there been such a concentration of aircraft into such a small area. The bombing raids of Germany during the war were spread out, and so were the airplanes spread out—in formation. And, of course, they didn't land, so that wasn't a consideration. However, the Berlin airlift landings required different kinds of spacing both in time and altitude to bring you in from seven thousand feet. You see, Berlin is practically sea level. I think it's 174 feet elevation. So to bring you down they'd step you down, and when you hit this particular point, they'd drop you to five thousand. The guy at five would drop to three, the guy at three would drop to one, etc. That had never been done before. There were not that many commercial aircraft flying at that time that required that, even at O'Hare.

What was your toughest landing?

We landed a B-36, I think it was with two engines out and with some of the hydraulics out. But I've never had any tough landings, nothing that we couldn't handle.

380

When we first got to Japan, we set up the airline for the Pacific area out there. There were no civilian airlines flying so we set it up. Well, I was flying the two-engine C-46 at that time. On a lot of the flights, you would burn your fuel from one tank and when that tank went empty, you would go to your next tank. The gauges were never completely accurate that they would indicate zero. They were always off a little bit. So we would always set up the tanks so that you run an engine until it coughed before you changed to make sure that tank was empty. Then you would change to the other. Just like running out of gas. And we were always hauling twenty-five or thirty people in the back, and sometimes we'd tell them we were going to do that. Sometimes we'd just be ornery and let them think we were out of gas. They'd get kind of excited!

Another thing that used to happen in the props—in the B-29 and in the C-54 when you were flying lower in very moist air and relatively warm temperatures—was St. Elmo's fire. The B-29 nose is round and has a lot of metal strips between each of the windows, and the St. Elmo's fire would just jump from one metal strip to the other. And then I've seen it on the props. There'd be a circle of maybe three feet like a pinwheel. Completely harmless. You might have it for three or four minutes, and then you'd pop out of the clouds, get out of the moisture, and it'd be gone.

Was there much to setting up the airline system in Japan?

I got there by mid-'46, so we had people all over Japan, Korea, Okinawa, Guam, the Phillipines, and many of the smaller islands, like Iwo Jima, etc. So we had a regular schedule set up. We'd run one trip a week to some of the spots; others might get a trip a day. I think we ran a daily, plus two or three others, into Korea. We had more people there, requiring more contacts and more people moved.

Because of the newness of this, we had limited air traffic control, except in the landing field areas. Mostly, en route, you were assigned an altitude, and you stayed there. There wasn't enough traffic to cause too big a worry, and we all knew what traffic we had out that we might see. Anyway, we always had radio contact with the people in the control towers on the airfields. You'd call them, telling them you would be there at such-and-such, and they'd give you the landing weather. This would give them a few minutes to clear the runways, in case there was work going on. It was a very primitive system, compared to today, with many airfields having only two or three landings a day. However, those fields where training went on were a bit busier but still light compared to today.

Was it ever hard to switch from one type of plane to another?

I think this is more true when you go from fighter aircraft to a heavy aircraft.

I was in heavies all the time. I have flown little airplanes like the Cessnas and the Pipers. I never really enjoyed them. I was used to at least two engines or four engines, or something like that. It's an entirely different type of flying.

It was hard for you to fly the lighter ones and feel comfortable?

Yes, it was. I belonged to the aerial club for several years. You could rent an airplane and go flying for a couple of hours. I took the kids and June up but I never flew enough to really feel comfortable in smaller planes. You see, in the really big airplanes everything is systems. You have to know the hydraulic system so in case a gear doesn't come down you have to know how to get around that system and get your gear down. You have to know your fuel system because you have several tanks. You have to burn your fuel so your center of gravity stays within the limits of the airplane, everything like that. So everything is systems, and you have to understand them. But in the little airplanes, it's not really that complicated and I never had any schooling on the little ones.

What's it like flying the big planes?

With the big bombers when you're heavy, if you got into the cumulus type clouds that had quite an updraft in them, you could feel it, you'd sit in there and bounce. But for the most part it's very steady. But now with the jets you fly high enough that you're above the clouds, most of them, so it's just like sitting right here. The only thing that you're fairly cognizant of is the wind going by the airplane because, you see, you're flying almost Mach one in these jets, and you can hear the wind and all the pressurization inside. Like in the 747, they pressurize the aircraft; if they're flying at, say, forty thousand feet, cabin pressure is at 7,000 feet. They do that by compressing air—by pumping more air into it so it feels like they are blowing up a balloon. You can hear that rushing of the air all the time.

Any resentment about setting up the airlines in Japan?

Well, that's the thing that surprised me. I got into Japan just very shortly after the war, and it surprised me that the people there accepted us as readily as they did. Because I thought there would be a certain amount of hard feelings, but I saw hardly any of it. The emperor told the people that they'd been beaten, and that the Americans were going to be there, and that they had better treat them nice. And they did.

Did you have a most memorable flight?

I was going to fly a C-46 to Okinawa, so we went down and got to Operations about daylight as we were supposed to. When I went to the airplane to make sure that it was loaded the way you wanted it—the stuff tied down, etc. (the pilot would do that before he went in and got his clearance)—there were two or three jeeps parked around the airplane with machine guns. I got onto the airplane and there were a whole bunch of boxes, marked "toy dogs." And they were all fifteen or eighteen inches long and about eight inches high and about eight inches wide. And I think we had four-thousand-some pounds of toy dogs. But when we went in to get our clearance—that's when you find out how many passengers you have—we only had one passenger. It was an officer-guard—a military policeman who was a commissioned officer—from General MacArthur's headquarters, from the GHQ in Tokyo, which was most unusual because that was the unit that was set up to guard MacArthur and the headquarters buildings in Tokyo. So it was most unusual to see them out in the field like that. But he was the only passenger. Anyway, we took off on the flight, and that's when he told us that it was money. It was greenbacks. This was when Mao Tse-tung ran Chiang out of China. Just before Chiang went to Taiwan, we took out all the greenbacks. I had 75 million dollars of greenbacks on my plane. There was another load the same day of 150 million. We landed on Okinawa and while we were still on the runway, a jeep came in behind us with a machine gun. And, just before we turned off, a jeep in front of us with a machine gun came up. Back in those days, and I guess it's still true, the pilot had to sign for the load. You had to sign that you had so much load. So I consider that at one time I had 75 million dollars!

You could have written a check!

It was all mine for about eight or ten hours! And, of course, flying over the ocean like that, especially in a two-engine airplane, if you lost one engine or if one engine quit running, the priority was to get the airplane back. You dumped the cargo and tried to save the airplane. So I said to this young guard, "What's going to happen if we lose an engine and I have to throw this stuff off." He said, "I'll stand back there and take the number of each box. They're all numbered. I'll just mark down the boxes, and you throw them out." It's just paper!

Any other unusual incidents?

When we first went to Japan, we went to the north island, Hokkaido, and while letting down through the clouds, our pilot tubes froze up. That's where you get your airspeed indication and your altimeter indication, etc. We let down, and as I remember I had the heaters on, but obviously one of them wasn't working and froze up. And I can remember that that caused me some moments of anxiety because you depend on those instruments so much, like your airspeed when landing. But before we got on the ground we got into warmer air and it thawed out. I can remember how tickled I was to see the airspeed come back and indicate about where it should be. But then you go back to the rpm and the manifold pressure and you know, at given rpm, a given manifold pressure should give you x miles per hour so you go to that.

Any memorable fly-bys?

In 1959 I had a B-52 out in the Pacific. We were out on a special mission. We were on Guam, and it was toward the end of November, on the Philippine independence day—their Fourth of July—and they always had a big celebration out there in those days, and we had all the American forces fly over. And since we were out there in a B-52 and it was new then, we got to lead the American forces across Manila. The Philippine Air Force flew over first. We left Guam and flew to the Philippines—It took us five hours or something like that—and let down in the "soup and salad" and came out. Manila sits right on a big harbor, maybe thirty miles across, and there's a large spit of land that comes out on the far side. And we let down to this spit and came across the bay there. We went across fairly low and quite fast and, of course, the B-52 makes a tremendous noise down at that altitude. So we came across, and I can remember seeing thousands of people lined up along the runway. I had the three-star general who rode with me in the jump seat, between the pilots, who thought it was great. It was the first time he'd been in a B-52.

You were in the Strategic Air Command. How was that duty?

We were the only ones with the atomic capability. It was the only force of all of our forces that had that capability. So much of our work was done in that area. Friends of ours in other commands—Air Defense and Matériel—made fun of us because we worked harder, we worked longer. We always had a closed base where civilians couldn't go. A lot of training bases let civilians just drive on and off any time they wanted. But we always had a closed base, where it took a pass to get on base, and it took a very special pass to get on out to the airplanes. You always had armed guards at the airplanes. We worked a lot of weekends, but that was where the promotions were. You got promoted faster in SAC. You had the possibility of getting promoted faster there anyway. So it had its compensations.

How long did it take you to move up?

I was a captain in 1958 and a major in 1959, then a lieutenant colonel in 1960, which is really unusual.

We would lose a few who didn't want to put up with it. We were separated from wives. And some of the wives wouldn't put up with it. So it took its psychological toll. It was a hard life.

Were you on alert during the Cuban Missile Crisis?

Yes, we were on alert most of that time. It was hard because you never knew what was going to happen. But the way I understood it, I think we were closer to going to war then than we've ever been. From noon to evening any day, that could have gone from naughty to real naughty.

How stressful was it?

I didn't miss any meals. But because of it you always ate the meal because you weren't sure you were going to be there for the next meal. I don't think the general public were ever aware of how close we came to going to war. And it would have been a nuclear war.

What was it like when you first went in the military? Any old, fond memories?

A lot of marching! We'd march down to the training field, then march back. So pretty soon they needed a bugler. I had played trumpet in the high school band. I didn't know the calls, but I volunteered and became the bugler. Then, when we trained, I'd ride in the truck and the rest of them would have to march. You know the old story about "don't volunteer for anything." But I didn't do that. I either volunteered or worked my way onto the honor council— we took disciplinary action over such things as oversleeping or not making your bed. I had two or three jobs like that. I figured it was better to make yourself more useful than the average person, and I kind of followed that throughout my career. It paid off.

Lee Strunk

LEE STRUNK

The Great In-Between

Lee Strunk is a slim, grey-haired man with a quiet strength to his demeanor. He has spent his time in recent years selling real estate, playing golf, and tending to his home in Central Florida.

Lee was a senior in high school when World War II started. He enlisted in September of 1942 and was sent to Floyd Bennett Field. He went in as a radio striker and received his radio rating. Then he tried to get into the scouting squadrons, VS34. When he succeeded, he qualified as radio gunner. At that time, he served on radio duty—midnight to eight am. Then he had an early morning flight, which he remembers was "awfully hard to stay awake on,"—after all night duty. On those flights, he would scout for subs for the convoys as they left New York for England or Russia.

Lee completed Navy Flight Training in February of 1944, then Flight School, then Dive Bomber Training. He speaks of some of the dive-bombing experiences in the interview. Soon Lee found himself assigned to Carrier Air Group 15, Pacific Fleet.

Strunk later worked at the Naval Air Test Center in Johnsville, Pennsylvania, did Night Attack Squadron work—VC33 of the Atlantic Fleet—and spent time at the Philadelphia Navy Yard and Navy Test Center.

This air veteran of over thirty years moved to Florida in 1966, and later received a permanent retirement order in 1973. Though he never got to fly combat in the major flight venues of World War II or the Korean conflict, Strunk symbolizes the hard-working competence of many who were prepared to serve anywhere, but did not get called. One senses from him a tinge of sadness, or maybe regret, edging his words as he talks about his career.

Remember your solo?

We had, at Lafayette, Louisiana, what was called WTS, Wartime Training Service. I had soloed and was flying in maybe my third or fourth flight. We had these Piper Cubs that we'd fly on a grass field and a strip. We'd land and come to a stop and change the trim tab and go on again. Well, one of the guys in my class, who was the last one to solo, was ready to do his first solo, first takeoff. At about that time, I had flown over and landed. As I rolled out to a stop, I heard this plane behind me. The pilot had tried to take off and had forgotten about me. He couldn't see until he raised the tail up. And then when the tail came up, there I was right in front of him. So in his very first take-off as a solo student, he attempted to fly over me but didn't make it. He hit my plane. At that moment I had just happened to have looked out the side. I remember the landing gear going by my face a few inches away and I ducked, and it took the whole top of my airplane off. I don't know how close I came to the prop. He went way up in the air and hit nose-first out there somewhere. I went out and pulled him out of the wreckage and asked him if he was okay, and he said, "I guess that does me in, doesn't it?" Those were the first words he said.

Did he get put out of the service in those days?

Strangely enough they took him out and trained him specially. He was a little bit leery about flying after that. Later on, he did quit.

What was it like coming along after the war? You've got the pilots coming out of the war, right?

Yes, I finished right at the end of the war.

How did they look at you guys, or were there any attitudes or relations?

They were looked on as upperclassmen, I guess you'd say. I became a dive-bomber pilot at the end of '45 and early '46, and a lot of these guys had flown in the Battle of Midway and had Navy Crosses and things like that. In fact, my old skipper was in the Battle of Midway and got a Navy Cross. And one other guy in my outfit was a Navy Cross guy and hit a carrier at Midway. A lot of guys were combat-decorated people. No, we were just a bit greener, and they trained us. They would be the section leaders and the flight leaders, and we'd be the wingmen. But we had a lot of respect for the ribbons. Occasionally, they would open up and tell us things about it.

I guess one of the most colorful guys was our skipper of Air Group Fifteen. One of the last skippers I had was Tex Conatser. He was pretty well known throughout the navy. He was a colorful guy. His carrier was hit at Coral Sea when he was the duty officer in the ready room. A bomb came through and took out some of the ready room very close to him. It didn't explode. It was a delayed fuse bomb that went off down in the ship and did a lot of damage to the ship. They got the *Yorktown* in, and they got it ready in very short order and back into the Battle of Midway, which was maybe a week later.

You've flown in some pretty rough flying conditions. Can you talk about the worst wind condition you've flown in?

The carriers we flew from were off the West Coast, the Pacific Northwest, and once in 1949 we had one heck of a bad storm. I was on *The Valley Forge. The Boxer* was alongside of us, performing some war games. At that time, we flew in fifty-eight knots of surface wind, I guess it held around that. I remember a strip off the teletype: fifty-eight knots. The admiral sent down word "congratulating" all-weather pilots. I don't believe any carrier ever operated near that again, as far as we could ever find out.

That's over seventy mph, right?

Pretty close to that: fifty-eight knots, I would believe, converted to miles per hour, would be very close to that. Almost hurricane conditions, and they sent out six AD Skyraiders—I was one of them from *The Valley Forge*—and six from *The Boxer.* We were out four hours for anti-submarine patrol. Mountainous seas. The ship was taking water over the bow, and when we started to taxi up, we couldn't deck launch because of the water. Whenever we'd hit one of these swells, I saw guys knocked over up ahead, just knock them right off their feet. They'd see one of these waves coming, and they'd signal with the deck handlers to hold the plane. The water would hit them and come on by, and then we'd inch up to the catapult. Once at the catapult, we'd wait until the sea was right, and then they'd catapult us away. That was pushing the boundaries right to the very limit. I never heard of any carriers operating in fifty-eight knots of wind.

Why did they do it then?

I don't know. They were doing a lot of things after the war just to see if they could do it, I think. And I believe that was one of them, just to see what limits they could do. *The Boxer* hit two barriers, as we understood, trying to land. their eight planes, two of them hit the barriers. And that night, two were torn lose from their tiedowns and went over the side. That's how rough the seas were.

I lucked out. I was the first plane aboard. The first two got waved off, and I thought I'd be out here all day if I didn't get on board in the first pass. I then went up to watch the rest of the show. We eventually got everybody safely aboard without any of the eight planes being damaged, but it took around forty-five minutes, which was an unusual length of time to get eight planes aboard.

Were they running out of fuel there toward the end?

No, that plane, the AD Skyraider, would carry a good bit of fuel. We had plenty of fuel, but nowhere to go. I mean, if the engine quit, ditching would be a completely useless thing. There's no way in the world to survive in that kind of mountainous sea.

Were you scared a little bit?

No, strangely enough, I was always very confident in my flying. However, after the landing—and I never had that happen before or since—when they brought me out of the gear, I didn't realize I was under any stress. I wasn't even thinking about stress. I was just kind of relaxed, I thought. But when they taxied me forward, I had difficulty holding the brakes. I couldn't hold a steady brake. That's the only time that ever happened to me, and I didn't realize it at the time. Mentally, I didn't think that I was that keyed up. But the conditions were so that everybody was keyed up. They didn't send out any fighters, just eight attack bombers, dive-bombers, for anti-submarine.

What was the hardest thing about doing that antisubmarine drill there?

Anti-submarine to me was always monotonous. You'd fly looking at ocean for long periods of time. Most of the anti-submarine planes were bigger planes with sonic buoys and all kinds of things like that, multi-engine or land-based planes. But, carriers can do it, too. And today they have very sophisticated anti-submarine planes.

Do you remember any other experiments that would seem to get a little out of hand, or that seemed to be pushing the limits?

I went through one such experiment. I was temporarily awaiting assignment at the Philadelphia Navy Yard, when they wanted to test this ground-level escape system called "The Martin Baker Seat." They needed somebody to volunteer for that. It was a way that you could actually eject at ground level, and it was very powerful stuff. So I said, "Yeah, I've got nothing to do; I'll do it." So they cranked that thing up. It was a pilot seat set up with a tall boom— a kind of ratchet effect. And they calculated that the shot would be about a fifty feet high, almost twenty Gs on the thing to get to where I would be and to stop at fifty feet. It was higher than that, and when I tried it, I went seventy-three feet. They had triggered the thing using old black powder, and I almost hit the top of the bubble; they had miscalculated. That was very marginal stuff. It was like being shot out of a cannon. And I didn't black out, though it was well over the twenty-G mark. I think that with twenty Gs they figured I would have gone fifty feet, and instead I actually went seventy-three feet. I could have gone over the top of the thing, or it could have broken my back or something, with that kind of powder shot.

Well, afterwards, they took me back to sickbay and did x-rays again to see if I'd broken anything, and I guess it would be that I didn't feel any after-effects. It's just that quick. If it'd been a slow shot at twenty Gs, I wouldn't have known a thing when I got to the top. I was a dive-bomber pilot for a long time, and we pulled seven and a half Gs on pullout. When that happened, you might grey out a little bit as you reached the horizon, but then you're releasing the pressure a little bit. On the other hand, if you held twenty G's pressure for any period of time, you'd first lose your vision, and then you could actually be out of it.

Any other stories about pulling a lot of Gs?

Well, as I said, the dive-bombing thing was a 7.5-G pullout. We'd start at ten thousand feet, then we'd go straight down. We'd pickle our bomb at three thousand and then take a 7.5-G pullout, which would put us out at 1,000 feet.

Once in a while there would be structure failure, or the pilot would misjudge and crash. In my very early training there in Jacksonville, the SB2C, in the old Curtiss Hell Divers, one of the guys in my flight went in. When that happened, I had just started training dive-bombing. I hadn't been out over half a dozen trips. When this one pilot lowered landing flaps instead of dive brakes, the flaps tore off, and the whole thing started coming apart on him, so he crashed, right on the target.

You had quite a few landings?

I think my last navy report was something like 385.

Do you remember any landings in particular that were beyond the ones you've talked about that were pretty rough?

Well, night work is pretty tricky, all the night landings are. And then, of course, my job as a landing signal officer was bringing people aboard during the old paddle days, and later on, during the mirror signal days. I worked both ends of it. It was easier on me to land on board than actually have to wave somebody aboard. The stress factor seemed to go up quite a bit when I had to wave the guys at night. In daytime with a pitching deck it wasn't bad. But with a nighttime pitching deck you'd have two or three LSOs out there: one watching the bow of the ship, and you're on the fantail back there, where you can't see the pitch too well. So, the guy's telling you the bow's coming up now, and you try to time it. So you cut him so the ship wouldn't be falling away too fast, or it wouldn't be coming up to hit him.

How many hours do you have?

I believe altogether I have somewhere near nine thousand, over twenty-five years as a navy pilot. Four years before that, at the very beginning of the war in '42, I flew as air crew—they called it radio gunners at the time—flying convoy duty out of New York for the anti-submarine unit VS34,, where all the merchant ships were leaving. That was an experience. There must have been seventy ships or more at a time that would leave. And we would escort them out as far as our scouting planes could fly and return.

At nighttime all the lights in New York City were blacked out. People drove with parking lights. My first flight, in fact, was a night flight over New York, with the OS2U scouting plane. I hadn't even been checked out on the airplane. We flew over New York with all these searchlights shining on us. The group was flying formation at the time. And this was my first introduction to navy flying. I started immediate training to try to qualify for radio gunner and become a permanent crew member.

Was there really the feeling that there might be somebody out there?

Oh, yeah, the submarines were very active at that time in 1942. We were losing shipping along the coast, yes. This was the OS2U scouting plane. We had a little bit of armour. In my back seat I had a .30-caliber machine gun. The pilot had a .30-caliber that fired through a synchronized prop and carried two depth-charges. With many planes out there, it was enough to keep the submarines submerged. In fact, the subs usually would wait till about mid-Atlantic, where planes were out of range, and then do their damage.

In those days, frequencies were very limited. We had big box-like discs with one frequency. And those old planes were very cold. We had these old sheepskin things that looked like Admiral Byrd going to the North Pole. And even dressed like that, it was cold in there. But it was pretty exciting for a seventeen-year-old kid; that's how old I was at the time.

I was a senior in high school when the war started, and I enlisted in September 1942. After "Boots," I was sent to the Navy Yard in Brooklyn. Then they sent me to Floyd Bennett Field. They put me in as a radio striker, and then when I got a radio rating, I did my best to get in to an airplane business, into the scouting squadrons there; VS34, I guess it was. Well, I got into that and got qualified as a radio gunner. I'd be on radio duty, say, midnight to eight. On about 6 a.m. they'd pull me off for an early morning flight. It was awfully hard to stay awake after all-night duty. A lot of shipping. The ships would all leave together in large convoys for England or Russia. In October or November of '42, they lost I think the largest shipping tonnage of the whole war for a one-month period. A lot of submarine activity at that time.

When did you move to Florida?

In '66 I left the Philadelphia area. My favorite station for duty was what they called Johnsville, Pennsylvania, in the Philadelphia area of Bucks County. And it was research development stuff. I flew as a projects pilot. I did two years there and when the Korean War started, I was recommissioned. I flew half my career as an enlisted pilot.

There weren't too many enlisted pilots.

No, there weren't too many.

How did that happen?

About twenty percent of their pilots were supposed to come from the fleet and be enlisted pilots. After I got my wings, I was just starting carrier landings on the old *Ranger,* and I was a first class (AP), and they sent us out for carrier landings on the *Ranger*—CV4. The carrier was due for its 82,000th landing—a special occasion. They had the air boss on the *Ranger* join the pattern to make the landing. They had the cameras set up and the cake baked for the event. They planned a big celebration for the ward room. However, something went wrong, and he got waved off. Instead, I made the landing. So they ran out and began to take pictures of me. I got out, dungarees and an old cloth helmet and a Mae West. Someone said, "It's not supposed to be yours, that was supposed to be the air boss." Anyway, they apparently had to go through with it.

I went to the ward room to cut the cake and get the pictures and all that kind of stuff. On my third landing, I had made the 82,000th landing on the *Ranger*—the old CV4.

Your own fifteen minutes of glory.

Yeah, that was my fifteen minutes.

But you didn't fly in the Korean War, did you?

I flew, but I was in VC33 most of the Korean War. The *Bennington* went to Korea and we put a detachment on the *Bennington.* I missed that, but my qualifications put me on the next ship, which was the carrier *Roosevelt,* and we deployed to the Sixth Fleet in the Mediterranean area. So if I wasn't sent to the Med, I would have been in a combat situation over in Korea. Just one of those things, a game of chance. Whenever you qualified, you went where they sent you, and I ended up in the Med. Great flying over there. I had three years of Pacific duty, but I liked the Mediterranean much better. We'd fly a couple of days and pull into port for a couple of days. That was a real great place to be for a six-month cruise.

You continued flying when you moved to Florida.

That's when my ears started having trouble. I had to kind of give up flying. I had trouble before I left Philadelphia. I got so sensitive to engine noise and things like that that I had to have special earmuffs. It finally got so bad I finally gave it up out here at Sanford. That's when I got out. I did a total of about twenty-seven years. I've still got to this day a very severe tinnitus ringing in the ears. The hard-of-hearing part's not that bad, although it's a part of the problem. It's the ringing that drives me crazy sometimes.

What was the most primitive thing you used for earplugs?

At that time they didn't pay too much attention to it. But later on they became more aware of the problem. They found out that all their people were becoming very hard of hearing and it was straight old noise explosion that was causing it. So now these guys on the flight deck all have what we call "Mickey Mouse" sound suppressers and things like that. In my day on the flight deck, guys didn't have those things. At least, the flight deck crews were the first to start it, but a plane captain may be wandering around there without any protection. We had old cloth helmets early on there, and they didn't do much.

Did you ever wish that you'd gone to Korea?

I would like to have gotten in combat, because I trained for it. I was usually about 90 to 96 percent combat ready. What we called combat ready was bombs, rockets, carrier landings, special weapons delivery, etc. My whole career, when I was on carriers that is, was for training to be combat ready. We had combat readiness at times up to about 96 percent, which was very high. These qualifications had to be redone all the time. So I never got a chance to really use it. I don't regret it, but at that time, yes, you train so long for something that you are kind of anxious get involved with it, show what you're trained to do. I never ended up in a combat situation. One time I helped try to sink the *Pensacola*, one of our own ships. I guess that's the nearest thing to it.

Tell me about that.

That was one of the Bikini test ships, and they towed it out to sea to sink it out there out in the Western Pacific somewhere off of Honolulu. So they buttoned it up real good, battened down all the hatches, no fuel anything. They gave our air group a shot at sinking it. They let the fighters first strafe the heck out of it and cause a few little fires. In my group were the dive-bombers. We had the heavy stuff. I had two Tiny Tims, the biggest thing they made at the time, something like twelve hundred pounds of warheads. Somewhere between a bomb and a rocket—they would shoot like a rocket.I could spend awhile on carrier stories. One time we launched to Saipan. We were going to be on the beach, practice flying for I awhile. So I went out on the bow with the folks from the Antietum to watch the planes take off. They'd take off right over your head. Here came my group. Suddenly, this member of my group in a SB2C just fell right in front of us there. The slipstream hit me and the pilot went on and hit the water. It was a very good friend of mine. The ship was closing in on him. I just saw him throw his shoulder straps back as the ship crunched the plane. It made an awful smash.

The helmsman only could guess which side of the ship the pilot went down. ue turned the ship, but the wrong way. Strangely, my friend survived, though his crewman didnt. What occurred was that my friend, the pilot, had not popped his Mae West jacket. His crewman did pop his, though, which wasa fatal mistake, as it worked out, because they found half of him|floating later where he had gone through the screws on the ship. My friend said that by not hitting his Mae West, the suction drew him below the screws. At that point he popped his Mae West and he came up in all this choppy water behind the ship. He was taking on water pretty bad. A destroyer picked him out and he was back on board in short order. We went into Guam that night and had quite a few cool ones at the club. How he escaped we would never really know. Normally, he would have gone right through the screws.

How deep did he go? You'd think it would have burst his ear drums.

It could have. I would guess he went forty or fifty feet. I never heard him mention any permanent damage from that incident. But he was killed later on, flying in a small civilian plane.

When I was up in Lakehurst doing catapults (I'd been a dive bomber for years), one time I came over the field at high altitude and got clearance to land. If there was nobody in the way, I'd a dive from high altitude. This time I rolled over at 10,000 feet. Here I was goinq toward the ground and the controls seemed locked. I pulled real hard and could feel the stick give way a little bit. I instantly realized it as the feeling of autopilot engaged. I released the autopilot.

I later realized that I had a radio navigation book stuck up on the windshield and when I rolled over, it fell out. I hadn't noticed it in the dark. When it did fall out, it hit the autopilot button. If I'd been pretty green, I might not have recognized the problem. But it did take a nip out of my ulcers before I realized what happened.

We lost a number of people in night carrier squadrons because it was tough flying. We'd go to look for bad weather. We'd have all this low-level flying, too—maybe 12 hours at a time of lowlevel flying. Anyway, we had this fellow flying in the El Paso area who went out and got into weather. Ee climbed to get out of it and got up around 20,000 feet. He still didn't clear the weather there, and didn't get on the instruments in time to really get stabilized. By the time he did, he had vertigo. So the first thing he knew was that the plane was in a graveyard spiral.He was disoriented and couldn't get the plane out. With thecentrifugal force, he felt he couldn't bail out either. After heSstopped fighting it, the plane started flying by itself andrecovered by itself. And he recovered below the mountains,belowthe peaks of the mountains.

How do you explain it?

The AD Skyraider had good stability and if you'd let it go, it would want to fly itself, it seemed like. The plane wanted to level out, I guess. I can't fully explain it. He was in a graveyard spiral. He told me after (I was his senior instrument training officer) that he'd just numbly waited for a crash—he couldn't do anything about it.

You knew this guy quite well?

Yeah, he was a young pilot, an ensign. He quit after that. He wouldn't fly anymore. We had a lot of guys turn in their wings in that outfit. Nobody blamed them, either, because it was very tough flying. Some guys just weren't up to it. We never heldthat against them. If that had happened to me, I believe I wouldhave given up, too. The thing is that a plane recovering by Sitself is really amazing. He said it recovered at 4,000 feet and the peaks were 5,000 feet on each side of him. Everything went in his favor. Everything had to, on this pilot's lucky day.

BETTY WOOD McNABB

Flying Civil Air Patrol

Early in her flying career, Betty Wood McNabb decided she was without promise as a pilot. Nothing she seemed to do met with approval from her instructor, or her husband for that matter. While on her way to the airport to "bow out gracefully," a huge tractor-trailer truck slid out of control and came right at her. Betty aimed for the ditch to escape him. The driver of a large logging truck followed her into the ditch, spilling logs everywhere. Enormous logs flew in the air, some only inches from her head. No one was physically injured. Betty proceeded to drive to the airport and when she saw her airplane, she says she hugged it and "got up into the nice, safe air."

With the arrival of the Hill-Burton Act (1948), many small hospitals were built around the United States. The hospitals needed guidance in many areas, so Betty Wood McNabb became a consultant for the Georgia Department of Health Administration and flew about assisting them, principally in the area of medical records. During her travels she has landed her planes in all forty-eight contiguous states.

Ms. McNabb has obtained ratings for multi-engine aircraft, single-engine sea glider, CFI-I (aircraft instructor and instruments), and ATP. Over the years she has owned seven airplanes. Presently she flies a Grumman Tiger. She was the eighth woman in the western hemisphere to have flown through the sound barrier, in an F 100F Super Sabre. Her public service side shines brightly in the work she has performed as a member of the civil air patrol (forty years) and the coast guard auxiliary (twenty-five years). She is also a member of Angels Flight, which flies ill or injured patients to hospitals. She has served as president of the Ninety-Nines, Inc., the association of women pilots, and is a member of the United Flying Octogenarians, Inc., the American Yankee Association, and the Grumman Aircraft Owners' Association.

Betty Wood McNabb graduated from the Florida State College for Women in 1930 and a year later graduated with a master's degree from the University of California in Berkeley. I ask her if she took physics or anything that might have helped with flying? "No," she says, "I didn't. I can't put two and two over yet," the spry eighty-one-year-old says.

To this woman whose history reaches through her father Frank Wood to the first flight at Kitty Hawk, the Coast Guard recently offered an aviation award in her name, "The Betty Wood McNabb Aviation Award."

Have you inherited your love of flight from your father?

Not really. I learned to fly without having any reason for doing it, except my job. I was working for the state of Georgia. The roads were terrible in those days, and I had to drive. They were red clay. I got stuck. I got flat tires, and I was by myself and it was dark at night. Oh, I didn't like that at all. I thought I have either got to learn to fly or give up this job, which I was enjoying very much. So I learned to fly.

What was the job like?

I was a health records consultant for the state of Georgia, and I had to get up in the morning and leave the house at five. I got home at seven at night. My husband got to the place where he was saying, "And who might you be?" So I thought, "Well, I can't do it this way." And you know that Georgia is the biggest state east of the Mississippi River.

What did your husband think of your flying?

My husband would have had a fit if he had known I was learning to fly, so I didn't tell him until I soloed. It was my money—I mean, I was working. I figured he wouldn't go anywhere with me in the plane. But when he found I had spent that much, he said, "Go ahead, finish. You are a nitwit." I said, "No, I just can't drive those horrible roads in Georgia anymore, and I love my job." I was right. He didn't fly with me for a long time; then I think he built himself up. One day I heard him on the phone—he was consulting for the state of Georgia education people—he said, "Bill, I'll come if Betty can bring me, but if she is too busy, I won't be able to make it." After that I took him everywhere he went.

Your father has a place in aviation history.

Well, he was at Kitty Hawk.

Tell me about that.

I think it's kind of interesting. His father had gotten him a job he had to worry about, and one day he sent his son—my father, Frank B. Wood—to Washington, DC. In those days you couldn't call and say, "I'll be over at such and such a time." So Dad went to DC., where the people he wanted to see were having a meeting. Dad was just sitting there, mad as a wet hen, trying to decide what he would do for the next two days. All of a sudden he heard someone holler to him, "Hey Tudy, Tudy." Why they called him that, I don't know. "Tudy, what are you doing?" The man was Barney Oldfield, who was famous at the time for bicycle races.

Oldfield and Dad had known each other for many years. Barney said, "What are you doing? You're not doing anything? Well, let's go down to Kitty

Hawk, North Carolina. I need to get a much better bike. My legs are too strong and I keep busting things." At that time, of course, the men who were doing the airplanes were also makers of racing bikes.

So the two men got into an automobile and headed to Kitty Hawk. Of course, Kitty Hawk is on an island and, in those days, they didn't have much of a bridge. That didn't matter because the car went bad, so they got in a horse and buggy and went on their way. When they got there, they saw some people, including the Wright brothers, messing around. Barney told Wilbur and Orville, "Hey, you two, when you get through with what you are doing, will you make me a stronger bike?" They said, "Okay, but that will have to be when we get back home. Come up here and help us get this thing up on top of the hill." So Barney and Daddy helped them get it up there. Daddy even did something or another with some of the inside parts that weren't working.

After the Wright brothers flew, Barney and Daddy got in their car, which had been fixed, and headed back to Washington, DC. Dad had to go back and tell these people why he wasn't there. It turned out there was a reporter there that had been at Kitty Hawk but had apparently not seen Daddy, and he asked, "What do you think the Wright brothers are going to do with that thing? Do you think it'll ever be any good? Do you think people will dare to get in it?" Daddy said, "Yes." The reporter said, "What's going to make it work?" Dad said, "What's going to make it work is that they'll give it to the military, and they'll make it work."

The Wright brothers actually did go to the military, didn't they, and begin selling them?

I'm not sure. Daddy thought that is what they would do. When they invited us to come to the fiftieth anniversary at Kitty Hawk, we decided to go. There were a lot of people that just didn't believe that Dad was there. Anyway, Daddy stood up to the questions of the people who were running the fiftieth. Finally, he said, "This does not look like the place where I was. It was much closer to the water." The man said, "I guess you were there. It's all been pulling in, pulling in." The particular little hill that they were using for the ceremony had moved over the years. Nobody ever asked him questions again. Knowing my Dad, I don't think he would really tell a whopper. That's the story of Dad at Kitty Hawk.

When I went down to Kitty Hawk the next time, there was a picture of three men, whom they didn't know, but they put it on the wall. One of them was dead; one of them was Dad.

Any other things that your Dad told you about Kitty Hawk?

No, oddly enough, he didn't tell us much about it until he got this letter saying, "Mr. Wood, would you come to the fiftieth anniversary?"

That would have been 1953, and you just started flying a couple of years earlier. How did you go about learning to fly?

In those days I lived in Albany, Georgia. All you did was get a man who was an instructor, and he did the whole thing. I went to Chicago in my little Aerocoupe. Of course, we didn't have any radio or anything like that. I just went by IFR. That means, "I Follow Railroads." I went anywhere I wanted to. Finally, I put my airplane in every state in the United States, except the two that aren't hitched on.

You've flown in all but Alaska and Hawaii?

Right, and I would like to do that. I started with Florida and with Georgia, of course. Medical records work was just kind of growing up in those days, and I had apparently grown better at it than the rest of them, so I went all over the U.S. doing medical records for other states.

One day I stopped in Arizona at just a little airstrip. The wind was blowing strong against me, so I stopped. I didn't see a soul. I got out of the plane and there was a little old house, little old building there, and I walked in. There was a little old man there. I said, "I'd like to have some gas, please." He said, "Well, we don't sell car gas at all."

"I don't want car gas. I want fuel for my airplane."

"You do? Well, all right, but your pilot will have to pay for it."

"Well, all right, here she is. I'm the pilot."

"Oh, you are?"

"Go out there and see if you see anybody there."

He did. He walked right out and looked to see if I was actually telling the truth, then he came back in and was so embarrassed. He said, "I just never happened to see a lady pilot. I'm going to remember you. And I want to know what your name is." He apologized and said, "Here's your gas. You don't have to pay for it."

Any other stories like that?

I was coming from the West to the East Coast. It was horrid. It had been raining, and I was afraid to be out in it anymore. I thought, "It's getting toward dark. I'm going to spend the night right here." I landed and went in, and the man said, "Where did you come from?"

"Wherever it was, I have forgotten."

"Well, you'll have to get out of here, we're going to have water."

"I can't. It's bad to the north; it's bad to the east and everywhere else. I've just got to spend the night here with you."

"Well, all right, you will make a nice person to have around to talk to because no one is around and no one can get to us."

He found a place for me to sleep. The next day he said, "You can't go yet. You are going to have to just sit here and do nothing."

"What?"

"That's what you do when you fly. I got some things we can eat. I've still got the phone, but it's apt to go." Then he said, "Excuse me, I have some work to do." He had to do some typing, but he said, "I can't use a typewriter, but I'm going to have to."

"No, you don't."

"Why?"

"Well, over the last forty years it seems to me I might have used one. I'll do your stuff for you."

So for three days I lived with that man. We did his paperwork and ate up all his food. Finally, the weather got good enough so somebody could get in.

Where was that?

Probably Arkansas, but wherever it was, he was a real nice man.

One of the times when I flew my little airplane to Chicago, I had a problem. There was a little place where you could stop there, and I never figured out why they did it that way because it was always against the wind. I managed to put the plane down there and tied it down. When I got through with my business there, I came back to find my airplane halfway full of water. Water had come from the bottom. It took hours and hours to get that thing dry enough for me to go again. Everybody in the place tried to get this little plane clean and dry and make sure it was going to fly, and somehow we did get home.

Tell me about your solo flight.

I was always scared the first two years I flew. When the instructor, John said to me, "You are ready to fly, aren't you?" I said, "No, not yet." I made him let me have two more days. Then, when I got into that plane, I thought, "Well, let's just play like John is here." So in the air I talked to John the whole time. We didn't have radios in those days. But I did all right.

You talked to someone who wasn't there.

Yeah, I played that he was there.

What did you say?

I said, "John, what do I do now?" Then I thought what he would tell me. Of course, I knew how to fly, but I was just scared about the whole thing and going by myself.

How long were you actually scared?

For two years. I found out that if you treat the airplane the way it should be treated, it will treat you all right, and I've been doing that ever since.

One time I was taking a bunch of teachers down to go to a seminar. It was all teachers and they were old to me. All of a sudden we got into bad weather—terrible weather—and we climbed and climbed. Pretty soon all these old folks but me and one other girl got sick. So the two of us ran back and forth with boxes and things for people to get sick in. You know, I was amazed, but those things happen. I can stand an awful lot, even as old as I am. I can stand stuff better than ever, better than most people can. I don't know why.

How many hours do you have in the air?

Nine thousand three hundred and forty-two.

You've got it down, don't you?

You bet. I was wanting to get to twelve thousand before I had to quit, but I don't think I will.

Any forced landings?

Just one. We had been up to Atlanta. We came out and all of a sudden the plane began to sputter and cough, and I said, "Suzy"—I had a girl with me who was a student pilot.—"find me a place, we've got to find a place, I've got to get on the ground." Me hoping, and she looking. All of a sudden she said, "Oh, hey look, there's Atlanta and the airport." Their airport then, of course, is nothing like it is now. So I landed in the airport without any radio and without telling anyone anything. I just looked to see if there was a place I could get in on. When I got that airplane on the ground, in about three or four minutes, it quit cold.

Do you remember any unfair competitions you were in?

Yes, I actually do. It was a powder-puff derby. Women were not allowed to fly in bad weather—I mean, real bad weather. You'd have to wait. I was coming in to put my airplane down, and coming right at me through the clouds and trees—four or five airplanes saw it—was the woman who had won many, many races. She came in through the white clouds. Thick, I mean, thick clouds. You first saw her nose, then you saw her come out. She was in ISR weather, and she wasn't supposed to be. She was absolutely wrong.

She was trying to get a jump on you?

She did get it.

By coming through the clouds instead of straight down?

Yes, unfortunately, even though there were several people who saw it, not just me, they decided not to do anything about it. She later got in a bad place and was killed. I think that kind of shows you that she was used to being bad during bad weather. I mean, she just did what she wanted to. I don't. I'm scared to death to do things that you are not supposed to do in an airplane.

Did your Dad tell you any stories about WWI?

Daddy was in charge of airplanes in WWI. He had to see that they were working all right, which he did. He talked a lot about them. One of the stories isn't about an airplane. It's about the surveillance balloons they sent up. This was in France, and they used it to spot airplanes coming in from Germany. Anyway, Daddy and the balloon man were up there looking. All of a sudden somebody came in that they didn't see and shot them down. They both landed in a tree. They weren't high enough to kill themselves. Daddy broke a leg.

They had a bunch of balloons, about twenty-five of them, near the beach here, and they told me to come at five o'clock in the morning so we could have a run in the balloon. There was a man in the balloon, who just didn't know what he was doing, I don't think. In the first place we didn't take off from the beach, which we were supposed to. The weather was not right for it. I knew that myself. Then I was surprised to have the head man say, "Oh, we've been waiting for you because we knew you would have all this information on what the weather is doing." I said, "I do, because that's the way I live. You know how to find out, don't you? You don't start along without knowing, do you?"

"No, but when we knew you were going to be here, we thought we would ask you. You did get the weather, didn't you?"

"Yes, and I can tell you people what you can do. You have two alternatives: you can either go to Cuba or to the other side of the United States. You cannot go where you want to go. Look at the weather."

"Well, we thought that was going to happen, but we wanted to ask someone else."

They took the balloon over to some place where we could get off from the right direction. It was real, real hot, and we were on a level place, with no trees around for a ways. So we floated, and the man apparently didn't know that when he was getting over trees, he was going to be cooler and he was going to drop down. Well, I wasn't a person who knew that much about balloons, but I knew *that* much. So because of his inexperience, he went down into the trees three times, and every time he would do it, he made it out, thank goodness. He'd say, "All right, put one hand over your head, your face and head, and hold on with the other. You're going in again."

We would go into those trees, but he finally got it out. He then said, "This is a big thing for anybody to do—but me doing my first run— "Mrs. McNabb, you are a pilot. Is there any place I can get this monster down on the ground?"

"No, I can't tell you much because I don't fly fifteen feet off the ground."

Then I remembered. I said, "I know there is a little place over there on the right. You can go that way if you want to." It was wet and we got to this place, a messy place full of water, which I knew would be there. I noticed two other balloons were in there. He crashed in. We just got to the edge of the trees and went right into the place.

He said, "Don't move, don't move. We will get out all right," just as the balloon came flat down with us in the middle. He said, "Don't move until I tell you." Well, I was on top of all of them. He was underneath me, the other man was next, and I was on top of him.

Finally, the man running the aircraft said, "Mrs. McNabb, if you get off please, the other two of us could get off." (*laughs*) You know, the other man—I never found out who he was and never saw him again. When I looked around, he was running as fast as he could away from there. I'm sorry to say the guy tore up his balloon, but we weren't hurt at all, which I thought was remarkable.

Did your Dad fly?

He had never flown the birds that he took care of in France, but he always wanted to. He used to go with me many times. One time he said to the man who had been my instructor, "Hey, do you think I could possibly get up and down in this airplane?" I was fifty or so at the time, and he was eighty. The man said, "Yes, sure you can do it, if Betty will let you." Well, I certainly had to let him. He helped me pay for the airplane. So Daddy got into the airplane. He wasn't trying to do it, really. He was just trying to get familiar. He certainly didn't mean to solo. But one of Dad's cronies came in one day and saw him getting out of the airplane—he didn't notice that Dad was in the right seat not the left —and he said, "Fine. You old fool, are you trying to learn to fly at your age?" Daddy said, "Why not?" He got in and went right to the man and said, "Look, Joe, do you think I could possibly solo?" Joe said, "Yeah, if Del will let you; if Bets will let you." I said, "Well, I have to. He helped me buy the airplane."

He'd help you buy another, maybe.

Yeah. I don't know what they do now, but long ago you were supposed to take three runs. So he made three. He did a good job. Then he made another, then he made a fifth. The instructor got on the horn and said, "Frank, Frank, what's the matter, why don't you get on the ground?" Well, you know, the FAA doesn't really like people to swear. Daddy said, "Hell, no, I'm not getting on the ground. I've never had such a damn time in my life. I love it. I'm going to do a whole lot of these. Don't bother me."

That was at age eighty.

That was at age eighty. He kept going as fast as he could, six or seven, then he got on the ground.

How did you feel when he was up there?

I knew he was going to be fine. I loved it. He was the cutest man in the world. He lived to be ninety-two. At eighty-nine he was still coming with me in the plane.

What about the earliest time with planes and with your father?

I remember that, years before, we had seen a barnstormer in a field. Dad was taking us from school to home and he saw an airplane in a field. I was eleven, and my brother was seven. Daddy said, "Hey, let's look at this airplane." So we walked over to see who this man was. He had his nose under the hood and was working on the plane. The man turned around. You know how he felt: "Go to the dickens! Who in this place is going to know how to fix this?" It was one of Dad's people from World War I in France.

This same man stopped in Albany once and invited my Dad to go for a ride with him. So Daddy did, and when they came back the man said, "Anybody you have that would like to fly?" Dad asked, "Are you going to go anywhere near Tallahassee? My daughter is there, and she would love to have a ride with you." So he stopped. I think he had some business there. He looked me up and said, "Hey, would you like to take three or four of your friends to Pensacola? I'm going over there and could take you if you could get yourself back."

I said, "I'll do it if I have to walk." It was terrible trying to get everybody's permission to do such a terribly awful thing. Goodness, getting into an airplane! We had to have a chaperone. Have you ever heard of anything so silly? So we got a chaperone. That was Tallahassee in those days.

The chaperone was a lady who taught geography, and she was scared absolutely to pieces. She had never been up before. She held both hands together with her eyes closed, praying all the way there. Now, of course, the flight takes a short time now, but it took quite a while then. It was just a beautiful day. He took us over the water. We four or five girls were just going crazy. We got out and, as our chaperone stepped out, she said, "Thank you, God, for getting me out of this place in one piece." Just then, she fell and broke her ankle. Wouldn't that be a note? How could we not laugh? We just died. We had to get away from it because we laughed so hard. It wasn't anything to laugh at, but I still laugh at it.

Do you remember the first plane that you saw crashed?

Yes, it was just a little airplane, and it was down in the trees. They had a plane down in Florida. They looked and they looked and they looked, and they called the Florida and the Georgia people in to help. Finally, a man found it. He called and said where it was, and he landed his airplane on the ground and said both the men were dead. He got back into his airplane and could never find it again. He couldn't find it. We didn't have loran then. They sent me out with a policeman who knew his way around. I am on the left side, and we are going around one of those little bunches of trees. Then all of a sudden, I saw it. I said, "Look, there it is." The two people on the other side and doing nothing didn't see it, and I did. They said, "I don't believe it. I don't know what you saw, but it was junk." Well then I started flying, looking for it again, and we flew and we flew and we flew, and we couldn't find it. Then, all of a sudden, I saw it again. So we stayed right there until we got people there.

The reason I guess why they couldn't see it was the wings got stuck up in the air, and the two men in the airplane were still in it, and they were sitting down there and the way it looked was just like some junk. It didn't look like anything and didn't show any sign of being an airplane.

You are a member of the Ninety-Nine?

Yes, I was president of it for two years, and I enjoyed it. Back in my day, I kept complaining to the girls that all they were doing was having lunch, and I wanted us to do something that would be good for aviation. So gradually we did. We do a whole lot of things. Most of us are either in the Civil Air Patrol or the Coast Guard.

Ever feel a little sad that you spent the first half of your life not flying?

You bet I do, and what I feel worse about is that I know it isn't going to be much longer that I can fly. I just don't know what I'm going to replace it with. I don't think about it anymore than I have to. I know at eighty-one I'm going to have to quit soon. I'm losing weight, losing words, etcetera. I don't think my reactions are slow because I can still pick things up before they hit the ground. But I just think it's not going to be a good idea for anybody this old to keep on going. I might hurt somebody. I just won't do it. I don't know what I'm going to do. I've loved it so much for so many years. Thirty-nine, to be exact. I've even been in the races, but I've never won.

What happened?

One time I beat fifty-four airplanes in a race. Don't ask me how many I didn't beat. That was fun, and a very good thing for us women.

What does flight mean to you?

It means so much. I can't tell you what, except that I love it. When I am in the air, it is like nothing else. I think I am closer to the Lord.

Paul Poberezny

PAUL POBEREZNY

"The Homebuilt"

The basement of Paul Poberezny's Hales Corners, Wisconsin, home in 1953 birthed an organization that would significantly affect the history of American aviation. That organization, founded by Paul Poberezny and a handful of other aviators, marked the beginning of the Experimental Aircraft Association (EAA), an organization of home builders of aircraft. Since its humble beginning, not only has the group inspired the homebuilt airplane movement but it also has honored and kept alive much of America's rich aviation history. The EAA, led by Poberezny's vision and genius, focused its efforts on family-oriented aircraft building. The organization's success is attributed to sponsorship of one of the world's largest and most successful aviation events. The annual EAA International Fly-in Convention. The Fly-in originally organized at Curtiss-Wright (now Timmerman) Field in Milwaukee, Wisconsin, now operates from its permanent site at Wittman Regional Airport in Oshkosh, Wisconsin. Recently more than 800,000 people and 12,000 airplanes gathered for the seven-day event. As of 1998, EAA's membership exceeded 185,000 individuals from over one hundred countries.

Paul Poberezny has flown over 386 different types of aircraft, including more than 170 homebuilt airplanes. Paul has designed fifteen airplanes, including the Baby Ace, a high-wing, open cockpit plane; the Super Ace; the Pober Sport, a low-wing, single plane; the Pober Pixie; and the Pober Jr. Ace, and Acro Sport I & II. Paul has logged more than thirty thousand hours of flight time in a variety of aircraft, from homebuilts to military jet fighters, bombers, and transports. He has also served as editor for EAA publications for the past thirty-four years. A collection of his regularly featured article, "Home Builder's Corner" (which he's written since 1953) is considered a home builder's bible.

Paul continues to speak to congressmen, regulators, and others to defend the rights of amateur aircraft builders, sport and general aviation enthusiasts.

Did you build models when you were a child?

Yes, I did. I built model airplanes—Comet models—out of orange crates, using a hatchet. I used nails to nail the wings on and nails for landing gears, when I was seven years old.

What was your favorite that you built?

I built the Curtiss-Robins with my third grade teacher, Mrs. Shebel, out of a Comet airplane kit. I also built a Little Dipper and a number of the Cleveland models.

The very crude ones I built were just plain pieces of wood nailed together. My family was poor. My dad had come from Russia in 1911. My mom was from Arkansas. We lived out in the country outside Milwaukee. As a child, I thought airplanes—real ones—were flown by little men. I had no idea of the proportions. I remember I built one for my girlfriend—my high school sweetheart. It had silver wings.

So you've really lived a life of flight, even from an early age.

I've said the word "airplane" every day of my life since I was five years old. I'm seventy-six now.

Did anyone think, "Oh boy, does this guy have a one-track mind?"

Yes, the neighbors did. I used to go up and down the gravel road making noises like an airplane. We lived between two cemeteries—the Jewish and Catholic ones. The road between them was called "Ghost Alley."

There was a two-and-one-half mile walk from town, and one day I got home from town, and my mother told me a plane had landed down by Pleasant Valley Park. I went down there about nine at night. I could see it in the shadows there, and I was scared. I walked home and got a blanket and went back and slept under a wing. I got up in the morning and went to school. I couldn't wait for school to get out so I could go see it. I went home after school and my mother said they'd taken off. That was the first plane I ever saw.

Were your parents worried about you?

No, that was a different time, when parents didn't have the fear many do today.

How many models did you build before you got into the big airplanes?

I'd say a couple hundred. I converted a chicken coop into an airplane factory and made very, very crude models out of wood. I remember taking wheels I found at the dump from a wagon or a coaster. I nailed them up on the wall, making a pulley and rope conveyor line. I took clothesline and put the models on a production line, which led from one end of the coop to the other.

When you got married, did your wife know what she was in for?

Everyone accepted what I did. By the time I got married, I was already pretty much involved in flying, and she accepted it. In high school one of the teachers, Homer Tangney, started up an airplane club. He had an old Waco glider, and he gave that to me for sixty-seven dollars. I bought airplane dope and fixed it up and made wood repairs, read books on how to fly, and taught myself to fly. My neighbor, an old school chum, took an old Whippet automobile that he had and pulled me into the air. I did 2,800 flights in it between 1937 and 1940.

Where did you make your flights?

I made them in a field near our house. The most memorable flight was the first. I was pulled up into the air about one hundred feet up, so I thought. I pulled the release for the rope, but I was actually only twenty-five feet up. From that I learned to keep the nose down. Another time I got up in the air about two hundred feet and couldn't release the tow rope, which was hooked around a bolt on the glider-release mechanism. I had to dive down and put it on its skid. I missed the car and snapped around and hit the ground about one hundred feet ahead of the car. It didn't do any damage but it was pretty scary. My dad was driving the car, but he didn't understand the seriousness of it. It didn't damage the glider, but it bent a couple of tubes. A lot of kids came down and some neighbors. I had assembled the glider in our front yard and pulled it down the gravel street to a field about a block and a half away. After my first flight, everybody was standing around when I landed. It didn't bother me. I wasn't thinking about them. I was thinking about how it had been a pretty well planned flight and was just concentrating on getting everything ready. Something I remember even today from sliding through the grass is the smell of cut grass and alfalfa.

Whenever you cut grass, you think of that first flight?

Yes, because it's that same good old smell.

Did you have an American Eagle?

Yes, but my solo was in a Porterfield—a 1935 model—in 1938. Ben White, a milkman, also a flight instructor at Waubesha, Wisconsin airport gave me instruction. I flew that, a kind of blind airplane—a high-wing plane with a radial engine in it. It was quite a thrill, more like a real, real thrill, being in a real airplane. I flew that, and then my dad went to the bank and borrowed $250 and bought me an American Eagle. The plane had been used in barnstorming. I flew the Eagle until World War II. During that time I learned to be a mechanic, and I met a lot of farmers from forced landings.

Tell me about forced landings.

I had one on take-off. The engine was cutting out bad. I looked for a place to land. About a mile away next to a tavern there was a down-sloped field. I side-slipped and ground-looped it at the bottom of the hill. That was pretty doggone hairy. Another forced landing occurred up at the high school. I had skipped high school that day. Anyway, I had put another engine (a Curtiss OX-5) in the plane because the one I had wasn't running too well. Eddie Holpher and I put the plane down in a ditch to make it easier to slip the engine on. For the test flight, I took off from a farmer's field and flew over toward the high school. The engine lost power, and I landed on a field near West Milwaukee High School. Then I walked over to the high school to use their phone. I called the tavern next to the farmer's field to see if I could get a hold of Eddie. Unfortunately, the first fellow to show up when I landed in the field was the truant officer. He was also a police officer. He was on a motorcycle with a sidecar. The officials there wanted me to take the airplane apart because they said it was too dangerous to fly it out of there. So I asked the officer if I could start the engine anyway and taxi over closer to the road. He said okay, so I swung the prop, and it caught and started right up. I'd probably been on the ground an hour and a half. The engine problem seemed to have gone away, so I opened the throttle up and took off and flew. I got to my field about four miles down the road, and it started cutting out again. I landed in the farmer's field where I kept it and still had a little power. I found I had a little hole in the expansion tank; water was squirting back into the magneto. So we fixed that, and I continued to barnstorm.

There were two other friends who had airplanes. One had an American Eagle, like mine, but with a short nose. The other was a three-cylinder American Eaglet. One guy was six feet, six inches tall and you should have seen him stick out of that little cockpit. We used to go out and circle the town, cut the engines, and land. People would come out and pay us fifty cents or a dollar, or a five-gallon tank of gas. Gas then cost fifteen to eighteen cents per gallon. We'd have fun and get paid for it. Many of the farmers used to invite us in for dinner. In fact, a good number of the farmers were actually pleased that you landed in their field. Today, if you did that, you'd be sued.

I bought two Waco 10s and flew them to Helena, Arkansas, where I was stationed teaching Aviation Cadets to fly during the war. One time I had nineteen forced landings on the way from Milwaukee down to Helena. I had carburetor problems, water pump problems, a broken rocker arm, carburetor ice, among other things.

You must have gotten a little paranoid after all those forced landings.

No, it didn't bother me.

What about military flying?

I didn't have the education so I went through the Army Glider Program and got my glider wings. Then from there I left the program and went to a program in Helena, Arkansas, and instructed aviation cadets. From there I took a commission as a service pilot. Most people don't know what a service pilot is. It's a pilot who has had civilian experience and met the requirements and earned a military pilot's wings and ratings. But it's not the same pilot's wings as the regular air force has. It was a pair of wings with a "S" on it. Flying before the war you got a direct commission.

Once, taking off out of an auxiliary field, I got up about four hundred feet and made a left turn in the pattern. The student was giving it too much rudder. I was nineteen and a half. All of my students were older than me. So I hit the opposite rudder too abruptly, and the airplane snapped at four hundred feet. The next thing I knew I was looking at the ground. I eased it out, but I must have come twenty to thirty feet from going in. I've tried to duplicate that many times at a high altitude. I still remember the ground coming up. As for my students, I didn't wash out any. Also, I took two or three student washouts from other instructors, and I taught all of them how to fly. All of them graduated primary, basic, advanced, Army Air Corps Flying School.

So you salvaged those washouts?

Yes. There's a lawyer in Washington, DC, whom I see occasionally. I padded his flying time. The rule was that if you didn't do a solo ride by the time you had twelve hours, you'd wash out. When he got to eleven hours, I took him on as a student. This one student had a little over eighteen hours of dual when I soloed him. By golly, when I ran into him years later, he told me he ended up flying PBYs in the South Pacific for the army air corps. He had quite a military career.

What did he tell you?

He was pretty thankful.

It must have been the patience that helped those fliers learn.

Well, it's a love I still share from flight. The enjoyment that I have held for flying all these years, and I always wanted other people to experience the same thing that I've enjoyed myself. To be a success in anything you have to first love people, then you have to have a cause. My cause has been aviation and people. Over the years I think I've learned more about people than I ever did about airplanes. I founded the EAA forty-two years ago.

Tell me about starting the museum.

Of course, I've always been interested in building airplanes. Then I started a little museum in a one-car garage. I'd go to the airport as a young guy and pick up any kind of stuff I'd find laying around. All kinds of junk. I'd bring home a bent wheel, or torn fabric, other parts of an airplane. One time I brought fabric with blood on it from a Great Lakes that crashed and two pilots had been killed.

Tell me about your first meetings of what would be EAA.

Of course our first meetings were informal back in 1948-49. They were held in my garage, where I built planes for fun. I had been building a Taylorcraft (much modified for air show work), then a Baby Ace, an old design that I modernized, that *Mechanics Illustrated* did run an article on. Seven fellows older than I came to the meetings. Most were active in flying in the thirties. They included Irv Miller, who was sort of the father of the homebuilt airplane in the Milwaukee area. He liked his booze and was a good designer. He worked for Miller Brewery. A heck of a nice guy, a sort of idol to all of us. Fred Miller, owner of Miller's Brewery, was member number 150 of the EAA group. He was a wonderful man. He was killed in 1957 in an airplane crash in Milwaukee. Anyway, I had these informal meetings in my garage shop, then I had to go to Korea. I was with the 176th Fighter Squadron. I did their test flying and maintained my combat readiness. I was qualified in all six kinds of airplanes on the base. When I got back home, the guys said, "Let's get the club going." I said, "You guys didn't even hold a meeting while I was gone." So it occurred to me to send out penny postcards. I did, and thirty-two people showed up on January 26, 1953, in the old Curtiss-Wright Airport.

Anything unusual about the first meeting?

Yes, probably the most difficult thing was deciding on dues. I wanted five dollars, the other guys wanted two dollars.

Tell me about your Korean War experience.

I flew the C-47 and the Mustangs. Probably the most interesting thing they asked me to do was to take the C-47 up to a little strip on the 38th parallel. The strip was three thousand feet long and you'd come in over the ocean, brake, then turn around and take off in the opposite direction. I had taken two weathermen up there and dropped them off. They would radio weather information from near the 38th parallel—the front lines—then someone else would pick them up. Anyway, we were getting ready to leave just before dark, when my right engine wouldn't start. My co-pilot, who'd been there for seventeen months, said we had to start because it would be destroyed by the North Koreans by morning. So I primed the right engine, yelled to my co-pilot to put the switch on, and swung her prop down.

Hand-propped?

Yes, I'd done that many times. Everybody on the plane couldn't believe it. So we got back to the base, and I was asked to demonstrate it. To do that it had to be the standard engine—the P & W, 1830-92—with the lower compression. When I got back to the States, I demonstrated it again. I even had to do it once, flying out of Norton Air Force Base. I took that plane up to Hill Air Force Base, and they wanted to know how I got it up there without a starter!

I've done a whole lot of hand propping in my life. It's a lost talent in this age. I've done it with one hand. Just get the prop in the right place, prime it beforehand, get the gas vaporized, and listen to it go "bang, bang, bang."

Let me tell you another experience from Korea. I had been real sick and had gone to Clark Air Force Base for rest and relaxation. I had gotten real bad sunburn on a Philippine beach, where MacArthur had come ashore on his return to the Philippines. I also had a bad cold. So, when I got back to Clark from the mountain retreat, the humidity was 100 percent. Well, I took off, and when we hit one thousand feet, we had engine trouble, so I turned around and came back. I lay around base operations and told my other pilot I was pretty sick and when they were done, that they should come and get me. About three hours later, they did. I got in the C-47 and stayed in the pilot seat until we reached our cruising altitude, then I went back and laid down. At one point I got up and walked up front and sat down in the co-pilot's seat. I looked at the fuel gauge. We were pretty well down. So I said, "Didn't you refuel?" "No, no, the navigator says it's only a five-hour flight." I think holy gosh. We continued on, and the navigator didn't know where we were. It was getting towards dark. We call NAHA air base at Okinawa, but their direction finder was out, so they couldn't get our location with a DF steer. We were going to have to belly the plane in the ocean, while it was still light. Then I saw two jets. I called the tower to say there were two jets nearby. The tower gave us their position, and we got a steer from that. We'd missed Okinawa, so we turned left 130 degrees and headed right toward the island. It was a wonderful feeling to see the lights of Okinawa. We were almost out of fuel. One of many close calls.

I was going to ask you if there was any time you were flying that your mechanical skills paid off.

Actually, there have been so many that it's hard to think of one. Flying the F-89 Scorpion, I had twenty-six engine failures in that. I had a time flying that. Just over a year ago, I was flying a B-25 when the landing gear wouldn't come down. After a struggle with that, I got the nose gear down—the left one, not the right one. I had to land her, but I sustained minor damage, really. All the fooling around I used to do with airplanes helped. I'd challenge myself against the airplane.

So that challenging was beneficial.

Oh, yes. Most people drive the airplane. When you just drive, so to speak, under normal conditions, it's okay, but if you're into a situation where you really have to match your personal abilities against the problem, it pays off always. I always tried to fool around with an airplane to get to know its best performance. With the B-25, it was a runaway propeller: no way to maintain directional control, no way to get it feathered. I knew the rate of descent was two hundred feet a minute. Fortunately, I tried to get the crew to bail out, but they wouldn't do it. We had just about made this little airport, but my co-pilot put the flaps down without my asking him to, and we landed short. I went through the fence and out onto the runway and stopped it about fifty feet from another fence on the other end. My feet were shaking on that one!

Did all those crashes ever indicate to you that maybe you shouldn't fly?

I've seen many dead bodies in the sixty or so years I've been flying.

Was there ever a loss that you commemorated?

Yes, the first one. In 1960 a couple of good friends crash-landed at the airport and partially burned. We dragged them out of the wreckage. Father McGilavrey stood with me and gave me encouragement to continue my EAA work.

I considered myself as one of the family, when I could be with strangers in situations like that. Many times I've gone to see widows or contacted them by phone, arranged to get the body sent home.

What are you proudest of, in terms of your flying?

I'm proud of the effect EAA has had on general aviation throughout the world and of the family traditions and the family environment: the high moral standards we've tried to set forth in our organization and in our chapters.

How would you like to be remembered?

As a good human being. There's so much we could talk about. Maybe for the nondenominational chapel that was built here at the museum complex at Oshkosh. Also, I'd like to be remembered as a pilot, not an administrator.

If you could only be remembered for one thing?

It would be as a person who can come up to anyone, a man or woman, and give them a hug, or a kiss on the cheek, and very rarely would that someone withdraw, because they know I'm someone with an affection for human beings. I guess hugs are part of the old-country way.

Abe Kardong tries on the old SR-71.

ABE KARDONG

Flying the SR-71 "Blackbird"

Abe Kardong played football for the University of Minnesota, but was side-lined with pulled hamstrings. That, along with limited funds and a lack of motivation, led to his decision to enlist in the air force. His duty as an intelligence specialist at MacDill Air Force Base caused him to shift direction again. Each morning he had to roust out the second lieutenants who had failed to show up for duty. He observed that while he was paid eighty-six dollars a month, these men made more than three hundred dollars plus "bennies." It dawned on him that one did not have to be a superman to attain officer rank in the military. From this, Kardong went on to earn two commissions and two sets of silver air force wings, first as a navigator and a year later as a pilot.

Despite his lack of academic credentials, he managed a twenty-six-year career that included flying some of the most sophisticated aircraft alongside some very colorful and talented aviators. His "dumb luck," as he calls it, placed him with some outstanding crew members, which made possible several "spot promotions" in the Strategic Air Command and an early promotion to colonel in Southeast Asia.

Kardong retired from the military in 1978 but continued to fly as a corporate pilot for some fifteen years before his second retirement. When I first contacted him at his lakeside home south of Spokane, Washington, he could scarcely speak. In a croaking whisper he told me that he was only two days out of a month's hospital stay, in which he had received chemotherapy for leukemia. Two weeks later for our interview his voice had returned, and he was filled with the enthusiasm and optimism that seem to be a basic element of professional aviators. It was obvious that he didn't intend to let something like leukemia cramp his active lifestyle. He commented that the hospital time had caused him to miss his goal of three thousand miles on his mountain bike for the year.

In his forty years of flying, Kardong flew more than fifty makes and models of aircraft, from Piper Cubs to ultralights made of canvas and wire, from 747s to triple-sonic spy planes. His flight time—13,700 hours—isn't a lot as aviators go, but at thirty-five miles a minute? Let's begin at the beginning.

After a year as a navigator at Smoky Hill Air Force Base in the KC-97 tanker business, he trained at Bartow, Florida, in the PA-18 Super Cub and the T-6 Texas. A checkout in B-25s and B-29s found him in North Africa at

Wheelus Field, Libya, in Tactical Air Command. There he towed targets for air-to-air gunnery, providing him the chance to check-out in jets. It also gave him an opportunity to work for and fly with a number of aviation's most skilled pilots. Colonel Robin Olds, a triple ace from WWII who would later shoot down four MiGs in North Vietnam, was his first squadron commander. Olds was followed by "Speedy Pete" Everest, the first man to fly Mach 3 in the X-series birds at Edwards Air Force Base. The world-famous Douglas Bader, a Royal air force Spitfire pilot, who flew thousands of combat hours on artificial legs, would sometimes drop in and drink with the guys at the "O" Club. Both Bader and Everest were avid hunters and, as resident expert, Kardong was assigned as guide for many African bird hunting trips, as well as sorties to the mountains of Turkey to hunt the wild boar that destroyed the crops of peasants.

Kardong's luck held good as the rickety old B-29s of the weapons center were replaced with brand-new Martin B-57 Canberra twin-jet bombers. A fully aerobatic airplane, it held more than five hours of fuel and had a spacious bomb bay that held more Heineken beer than a squadron could drink at one party. The frosting on the cake involved being checked out as an instructor pilot, which meant many trips to the continent for high-priority supply runs. Nothing like having your own private jet, a pack of credit cards for fuel, and all of Europe to ravage. Pretty heady stuff for a twenty-three-year-old country bumpkin.

Where were you sent after completing your tour in Libya?

Much to my chagrin, the buggers sent me back to SAC to fly B-47s at Lincoln Air Force Base, Nebraska. The B-47 was a six-engine, swept-wing, Boeing plane with a crew of three. Most airplanes are a sheer joy to fly, but the B-47 is the only one of more than fifty types I've flown that I really hated. The bird hated me right back. I had an engine failure on take-off on my first solo flight! Good thing I had a light load on a cool autumn day. It was a ground-loving, underpowered SOB. I was so unhappy with the B-47 and Nebraska that I gave serious thought to getting out of the air force blue.

Would it have been United or TWA or Pan Am?

It would have been something more interesting and lucrative. I interviewed with China Air Lines. They did have a legitimate passenger airline, but it was widely known that it was one of a number of CIA storefront setups. I was offered a job flying C-46 cargo planes throughout the Orient with a Chinese co-pilot. Guaranteed, nonboring work for big pay for a new operation called Air America. However, several things made me decide to stay in the blue uniform, including the fact I had just been promoted to the lofty grade of captain. Also, we had just returned from almost three years of overseas living.

At the time General Dynamics at Fort Worth was test-flying the sexiest-looking four-engine Mach 2 delta-winged airplane I'd ever seen, and I was in love. The Kardong luck was holding. I was crewed up with the best and brightest crew guys in the whole 307th Bomb Wing. My co-jock, a double-E graduate of the University of Nebraska, actually understood the fuel system and the electrical wiring. Jack Haley would in later years become chief of flight standards for the presidential flight at Andrews Air Force Base, the most prestigious instructor pilot position in the free world. My navigator and radar bombardier was Bruce Bradfield, who could put a four-megaton nuke in the glove compartment of a VW van eight of ten times. Because these guys were so good, we were nominated for select crew in less than a year. We were granted spot promotions to the grade and pay of major. Life was good. It must be said that these very temporary promotions were valid only as long as Bradfield's bomb scores were good, and Haley helped me pass my flight checks, and we stayed together as an integral aircrew—S-45, to be exact.

But you said you also flew the B-58 Hustler. Didn't that cost you spot promotions?

I never claimed to be smart! I was lusting for speed and fifty thousand-foot altitudes, plus Bradfield wanted to go to the University of Nebraska to complete a degree. As a result we gave back our beautiful gold major's leaves and went our separate ways.

Where did you go for Hustler checkout?

All applicants had to show they could handle a fast delta- wing craft, so we were sent to Air Defense Command F-102 interceptor school for four months of fun. The airplane was an absolute piece of cake to fly and land, a real vacation after two years of B-47s. Then it was on to Fort Worth to fly the Mach 2 Hustler.

How did they compare in complexity?

It was several magnitudes above anything in the inventory at that time. We were dealing with an entirely new realm of flight: high altitude, high mach-number cruise. I must emphasize the word "cruise," because all the other fast birds of that era only dashed to Mach 2 for a very brief time. Our airplane got so hot from Mach 2 cruise that we would burn off the paint and decals. That was just one of the myriad of engineering challenges that the GD engineering guys had to face.

Was the Hustler a success as a nuke bomber?

Yes, it was, but at a considerable cost in lives and dollars. Only about 119 were ever built, and some 20 were lost in the test program. Most of the very serious glitches were fixed before I flew the bird, but she was still a very sexy lady you never took for granted. A sheer joy in skilled, capable hands, but treacherously and fatally dangerous to the unprepared.

How did that program treat you?

The luck of the draw was still with me. I had another excellent crew. My nav/bomb, Paul Cornett, a CPA by profession and an IRS field agent in another life, was one of the best in the outfit. Charlie Levis, my defensive systems operator, was an ex-marine enlisted man who managed his way into the Naval Academy. These fine men did excellent work, made crew S-56 sprout gold major's leaves for all of us. Tragically, some twelve years later, I would be present over Mi Loc, Vietnam, when Levis was killed in an RB-66 with a direct hit from a Russian SAM 2 missile.

The Hustler was a fast, high flyer. What else was different about the airplane?

Not only was it nearly three times as fast any other bomber and most of the fighters, but it also had an escape capsule to make ejection at thirteen hundred miles per hour possible. This bird set many speed records: Los Angeles to New York roundtrip in four hours, twenty minutes, for one. It captured all of the major aviation awards and trophies at the time: the Bendix, the Harmon, and the Thompson. It also won the oldest of them all, the Louis Béleriot, which was first awarded for a powered flight across the English Channel. The men that flew this slick machine into the aviation history book were a talented, colorful group. They included "Dutch" Dutchendorf—who was one of my checkout instructors—Hal Confer, Robert "Grey" Sowers, and Joe Cotton. They made the machine into a weapons system that served our country well. Dutch had a long-haired teenage son that really gave him fits, skipping school and such. The only thing that interested the kid was his guitar and music in general. He wrote a few songs and sang backup with a few groups. Then old "Blue Eyes" Frank Sinatra recorded one of his songs called "Leavin' on a Jet Plane," and the kid was on his way. Dutch ended up working for his long-haired son, John Denver.

Why did you leave the Hustler unit and give up another Major spot promotion?

There were whispers about the existence of a secret super-fast airplane, and some of our officers were disappearing to fishy-sounding assignments in the third sub-basement in the Pentagon. Information was very closely held, but President Johnson finally revealed the "RS"-71, a quantum leap from even my beloved Hustler. I didn't misspeak, the President did. He said it wrong, so for awhile we had to call the plane the "RS", instead of the SR-71. When I heard about it, I started looking for a pilot's job at eighty-nine thousand feet immediately.

How did you manage to get into this small group without the sheepskin that the air force seemed to require for officers?

I was never known for my subtle approach or my excess amount of patience, so I picked up the phone and called the SR Wing Commander, Colonel Doug Nelson. The conversation was brief and went something like this: "Colonel, you don't know me from Adam, but I'm a Hustler select crew commander and instructor pilot, and I want to fly higher and faster, if it's all the same to you. I must tell you up front I don't have a degree, and I know you're looking for heavy engineering backgrounds."

I was shocked when he said, "You're wrong, Abe. I do know who you are, and I'm aware of your reputation. I'm hiring pilots not college boys. Please send me an application directly, don't bother with SAC Headquarters. I'll send them an info copy." I was stunned. A year later, I found out that Doug Nelson was a "Mustang" like me (a non-degree, former enlisted man). Nelson and I became good friends in the years that followed, and I was delighted to watch him rise to the rank of two-star general. He was obviously a superb judge of talent and character! Seriously though, the group of flyers he assembled at Beale Air Force Base, California, was unparalleled. Just to be sure that no one slipped through the standard selection process, all applicants had to survive the astronaut-selection physical and psychiatric evaluation. This involved a ten-day stay at the School of Aviation Medicine at Brooks Air Force Base in Texas. Many did not survive this screening and not only were not selected, but were grounded from all further military flight. I slipped through the net yet another time and reported to Beale in early 1967.

What was it like to fly the Blackbird?

There were still a lot of hoops to jump through before they turned you loose with a billion-dollar airplane. After a checkout in the T-38 white racer, there were hours of hooded instrument practice and an intensive aircraft systems and performance course taught by the Lockheed engineers who designed and built the bird. The air force only had two SRs at Beale so far, so we spent many hours in the flight simulator. Thank God the airplane flew much better than the sim, but it was a good way to learn the systems and smooth crew coordination. My luck was still with me. My nav/RSO (backseater), Jim Kogler, was a 6'5" pro with an intellect to match. He managed to make me look good and kept me out of serious trouble most of the time.

Tell me what made the Blackbird so different from other aircraft of the time.

Just about everything. The flightsuit, for instance. As you know, sea-level barometric pressure is 14.7 but decreases to only 0.5 at sixty thousand feet. Without a pressure suit, the gasses in the blood would boil out of solution, and this would spoil your whole day. The David Clark Company made two custom full-pressure suits for each crew member. It was said that these cost $200,000 each. Nothing about this program was cheap or off the shelf. It took a bit of getting used to, particularly if one tends to be claustrophobic. The suit saved many lives during high-altitude, high-speed bailouts. Our fuel, lubricants, along with just about everything about the air frame, were unique. Some areas of the plane would reach temperatures of more than a thousand degrees on a cruise leg.

How fast and how high could this bird fly?

Now that it's been declassified, we can say that 3.2 Mach, or about twenty-two hundred to twenty-three hundred miles per hour was our cruising speed at an altitude of eighty-five thousand feet (sixteen miles). Some fighter planes can attain Mach 2 speeds for a very brief time, generally less than ten minutes duration. After that they need a very rapid landing or air refueling.

Is there a sensation of speed?

Not really, flying at those altitudes. In our rural areas, the country roads are usually laid out in one-mile squares. These roads are flipping by at the rate of thirty-five per minute. The sky tends to take on a deep blue-black color. Some claim to be able to see the curvature of the earth; I sure couldn't. It's eerily silent in the hot cockpit, as you climb the cruise climb profile. All missions are flown in a constant climb, as the fuel burns off and the 3.2 Mach is maintained. The profile flown for climb and descent is roughly analogous to the flight of a large artillery shell. At cruise speed, the SR-71 would make the trip from Spokane to Seattle in about six minutes, thirty-five minutes to Dallas. This machine is such a perfect design that it gets its best miles per gallon at its highest speed.

Wasn't there a slight problem during your SR-71 tour of duty?

You could say that. After a fairly uneventful year in the program, we did experience one memorable event. That year, in September of 1968, there was a Friday the Thirteenth. At the very stroke of midnight on the thirteenth, I managed to run over a black cat with my Mustang convertible, just outside the main gate at Beale Air Force Base. The next month, October, the tenth month, on the tenth day, at ten o'clock, I released the brakes of aircraft #977 for take-off. Just about ten seconds later, I was on fire and about to rotate at 190 knots. As my nose rose past ten degrees of pitch, the left engine exploded, and the bird pitched and rolled violently. I spiked the plane onto the runway.

The left wheel rim failed and threw shrapnel into the left engine, causing it to explode. Being the eternal optimist, I figured that I had seven thousand feet of runway remaining, a brake chute, a jet barrier, and my consummate skill as a pilot to save the day. The brake chute deployed into the stream of fire from the burning left engine and melted instantly. The brakes on the "good" side of the bird failed, followed by the failure of the jet barrier. My nav ejected and was successful. A minor compression fracture of the spine kept him off the flight schedule for ten days. I flew two days later after an overnight hospital stay.

What did the accident board find to have caused the problem?

They said it was a material failure of the magnesium left wheel rim. As for me, I have no doubt it was that damned black cat, wreaking revenge on me. I continued to fly the SR-71 for another three years and then volunteered for flying in Vietnam.

Abe Kardong's Rebuilt SR-71 at its final resting-place in Seattle's Air and Space Museum.

What did it feel like to by flying secret missions?

There are situations that I can't discuss even to this day. The Russians were obsessed with their inability to bring down an SR. Billions of rubles were spent to counter the Blackbird, and fortunately, they were not able to touch us. A Russian trawler stayed at Okinawa to monitor our takeoffs to flash warnings [of] impending arrivals. In 1977 a Foxbat pilot defected from his home ba[se in] Iberia, landed in Japan, and asked for asylum. Victor Belenko was his [name.] He said his entire unit was there for one reason: to bring down an SR. N[everthe]less, we flew around the Far East with total impunity. Hundreds of SAMs [were f]ired at us, and none even scratched us. We had a saying, "Yea, though [I walk] through the valley of death, I fear no evil, for I am at eighty-five thou[sand a]nd climbing."

Yea[rs late]r, after I had retired, I spent some time in Russia and drank copious [quanti]ties of vodka with some Russian officers. One young man named [?] [h]ad served as a SAM 2 battery commander. He volunteered that the [SAM] was very inaccurate and difficult to maintain. I said, "I know a bit abo[ut you]r SAM 2 missile." He said, "Yes, it's a piece of crap. It couldn't hit anyth[ing." I] said, "Yes, I know. That's why I'm here."

Wh[at was] your job in Vietnam?

Officially [I was t]he commander of the Twentieth Tactical Air Support Squadron (Twentie[th TASS).] It was the biggest "little" unit in the war. We were a forward air contr[ol oper]ation and known as FACs. We would find targets and mark them wit[h whit]e Pete rockets and put in air strikes (F-4s, A-6s) or whatever was ava[ilable f]rom any unit—navy, air force, or whatever. It was a very dangerou[s but t]hrilling job. My little unit had sixty-five O-2 Cessna Skyhawks and fort[y O]V-10 Broncos, and 1,100 men, of which about 100 were pilots. M[ost of t]he pilots were "brown-bar second balloons," fresh from pilot school. T[hey w]ere full of pee and vinegar.

Nin[eteen s]eventy-two was a very bad year. We saw the introduction of the SAM-[7 heat]-seeker missile into the war. It was extremely accurate and usually fl[ew righ]t into your exhaust pipe. I had three of them fired at me, one of which [missed?], but I managed to out-turn the other two. The average line pilot wou[ld fly t]hree days and have the fourth day off. This was every day, for 365 d[ays a t]our, except for a two-week R and R. The guys renamed it I and I. It s[tood fo]r intercourse and intoxication. FAC work, though, was hard, miserable[, dang]erous, and thrilling work. Unfortunately, it was also totally unnecess[ary. I s]ent home thirteen young men in aluminum flag-draped boxes who neve[r had a] chance to see their grandsons.

I un[derstoo]d a daughter of one of your men contacted you recently about her fathe[r.]

Yes, one [of my k]ids, Steve Bennett, got the Congressional Medal of Honor. In fact, I hav[e a pic]ture of his widow getting the award from General Brown. At the time, [the wi]dow had a little baby. Years later, I get this call—this was three weeks ago from—this little baby. She said, "I've been looking all over the U.S. for you. Tell me about my dad." This was quite an experience.

Steve was in a "troops-in-contact" situation and took a SAM-7 missile. It blew off the right engine of his OV-10. He had a marine in the backseat whose parachute had gotten shredded by the missile. In the OV-10, you can't selectively eject. In other words, if the front-seater goes, the backseater goes first. So Steve could have parachuted out and saved his own life, but he would have killed the backseater. Instead, Steve elected to ditch the OV-10 out by one of the ships off the coast. The airplane could not be ditched safely; he knew that from training. To make things worse, Steve had one gear hanging off the aircraft from the explosion, as well as one engine shot off. Sure enough, it didn't work. Steve was killed in the ditching.

I got a call from an officer, who started to chew me out. He said, "Colonel, what the hell's the matter with your people? Don't they know how to eject? Don't they trust their survival gear?" I said, "Look, I have a lot going on here. I don't have time to argue with you, but yes, they know their survival gear. But this guy stayed in this airplane and in so doing saved this marine's life. And if you don't mind, I have better things to do." And I hung up on him. This was a three-star general. The next day, another general, Dick Cross, called me up. He said, "Did you say that this guy saved this other guy's life?" I said, "Of course. I know it for a fact." He said, "Are you sure?" I said, "Yes, I was at the debriefing." So he says, "Okay, put him in for the big one." I said, "I don't know what you mean." He said, "The Medal of Honor. Can you handle it?" I said, "You better believe it."

From Da Nang after my tour ended, I managed to get a tour with the Royal Thai air force in Bangkok—by far the cushiest job I ever had. One of my primary jobs was playing golf with the Thai Air Marshals. It was just too good to last. I was promoted to full colonel and shipped back to the Blackbird program at Beale as chief of the eight-hundred-man maintenance operation. I found out it was much easier to break airplanes than it was to fix them. After two years, it was back to Kadena as the unit commander. Eighteen months later I was sent to SAC at Omaha. I retired from there after twenty-six years.

Give me the emotional context of the conversation with the flier's daughter. It must have been pretty touching.

Well, yes, it was, particularly since I was coming off chemotherapy, and I couldn't give my phone number without sobbing, it seemed. It was very touching, particularly in the sense that Robert McNamara had released his book, where he said the whole Vietnam thing was a farce, yet he kept sending people over and kept the war going.

We all knew it was a farce, and one of my basic duties as a commander, which was absolutely ludicrous, was demotivation of my troops. This involved the following idea: "Fly at reasonable altitudes, and if you get down in the grass, these SAMs are going to pick you off. You're not going to win the war by getting that one extra truck out there, it would be stupid. Your job is to fly your missions, do them safely, and get that ticket home. One year, and you're home free. Stay alive. That's your job."

I understand you had an interesting find on the Internet.

Yes, we were discussing Blackbirds on one of the aviation bulletin boards on Prodigy one day, when someone chimed in, "By the way, you're a big hero over at the Air and Space Museum at in Seattle."

"What do you mean?"

"Well they dug up your airplane—the one you crashed—and they've rebuilt the nose section. For a donation to the museum, you can have your picture taken sitting in the cockpit."

I was amazed. I said, "No, they didn't dig mine up. I know exactly where it is. It's buried there at Beale Air Force Base at the end of the runway."

Then another message chimed in: "Oh, no, it isn't, Boss, I helped to rebuild it. We found the production numbers when we deskinned it. It's your plane."

Another voice, that of a reporter, chimed in. It was coming up on twenty-five years from the October 1968 date when I had crashed. He asked if he could get in touch with the museum to see if we could set up something. I said, "I don't give a damn."

So they had a Blackbird Week at the Museum on the twenty-fifth anniversary of the crash. I got to slip back into the very same cockpit—one that had literally risen from the grave.

What are you proudest of?

I guess I am proudest of the fact that a country kid from Minnesota got an opportunity to rub shoulders with a lot of aviation greats along the way. I got to meet some really fine people and sneak in the back door of some really nice programs—the B-58 and the SR-71, in particular. They were real hot, fine machines. The military didn't inspect my pedigree very carefully. I guess that's how I managed to get in. The military people were gentlemen enough to say, "Hey, if you can hack the program, you're one of us." As a consequence, they allowed me to kind of help write a few pages of aviation history. That to me is a wonderful thing.

I'm also proud of the fact that I've got four grandkids. I've lived long enough to see the flesh of my flesh. A lot of people don't realize how important that is—the fact that we're all occupying space here and in one instant we can be gone. The only thing that's going to live after us is not the damned

Mercedes or Rolexes or the fine whiskey. What's going to live on is the kids and hopefully they're on the right side of the law, gainfully employed, and solid citizens.

You have cancer. Does that make you think of these things more?

Yes, to an extent. I just got into the leukemia business three months ago, and I'm in remission. But I've always been one who felt that on any given day, if I had to check out, that it's been great to that point. I think I've tried to live as if one day it is going to be our last. There's not a lot that I've missed along the way. I've tried to take advantage of the things that were offered; I've had a hell of a good life. Besides, there are a lot of worse things than dying—I know that. I've watched a lot of good men die. And dying well is almost as tough as living well. When you've looked the Man in the eye and escaped or survived, or however you look at it, four or five times, you start asking the question, "Why? Why on earth am I still here?"

JIM SHIVELY

The POW: Life at the "Hanoi Hilton"

F ive years and eight months is a considerable time in an average person's life. But for pilot Jim Shively the five years and eight months he was a POW in North Vietnam seemed an eternity. Shively was shot down in a flight near Hanoi and spent some of his time incarcerated at the notorious "Hanoi Hilton," a prison camp the French had used earlier. In the interview he details his soulful, courageous life as a POW.

Born in Wheeler City, Texas, in 1942, Shively graduated from the air force Academy in 1964. After completing his master's degree at Georgetown University, he trained at Williams Air Force Base, flying T-37s and T-38s. From there he got an F-105 assignment, went to combat crew training, then on to Vietnam.

I asked this easy-going, articulate man if he ever regreted volunteering for duty in Vietnam, and he answered no, without hesitation. Perhaps this equanimity, in the face of his physical and psychological torture by the Vietnamese, enabled him to survive and even to maintain his sense of humor. At times in the interview he chuckles, perhaps with a sense of irony. The point is that he is still able to smile. Shively returned home to Spokane, Washington, where he became an attorney after graduating from Gonzaga Law School. He married, and he and his wife Nancy have four daughters.

How many missions did you fly in Vietnam?

I think I flew around sixty-eight or sixty-nine. I'm not exactly sure which mission I was shot down on.

Talk about your early missions and how you got started.

Generally, they started you off with easy missions. For example, the first five would be classified "Route Pack I." For air ops, North Vietnam was divided into seven "Route Packs": I through XI Alpha and VI Bravo. Route Pack I was the most southerly part of North Vietnam. Pack VI-A included the area around Hanoi and north; and Pack VI-B was the area around Haiphong and north.

The target was dictated largely by weather. If it was good in Thailand, it was usually bad in the northern parts of Vietnam—Hanoi, Haiphong, and that area—so we couldn't really get there. In early January of 1967, we were assigned targets around Thai Nguyen, which is just north of Kep Airfield, and those were really hard missions.

Any dogfights?

Only one time was my flight actually engaged in a dogfight. There were other times when others were engaged but not us. The dogfight resulted when we were on a mission to another airfield, which was southwest of Hanoi. During the run-in on the target, we could hear the Wild Weasel flight. Wild Weasels were F-105Fs, two-seaters, with an electronic warfare officer in the backseat with special radar detection gear. Their job was to keep SAM sites busy, while the attack flights hit the target.

The Weasel flight had been jumped by a MiG-17. The MiG was on the Weasel flight lead's tail, and they were in a series of high-G turns to avoid getting bit by the MiG's guns. As a result, both aircraft were on the deck at a very low airspeed. We had lots of airspeed because we had just completed our target run and our bombs were gone. The F105F and MiG just happened to be out in front of us as we came off the target.

My flight lead, Major Dennis, fired a sidewinder at the MiG. The sidewinder didn't track properly and kind of did a barrel roll around the MiG. That alerted him to our presence. We could tell because he unloaded. You could tell he unloaded the Gs on the aircraft. When you turn an aircraft at a steep bank, it requires a lot of Gs to maintain level flight. If you release Gs and roll wings level, pull nose up, you can look behind your aircraft. We couldn't see where he came from. He was real slow, and we were real fast, so we were rapidly passing him. We just pulled the noses straight up till we were out of airspeed, but we had lots of altitude. We pulled the noses back down, and the MiG was right there below us.

How many flights deep into Vietnam before you got shot down?

Probably twenty-five or twenty-six. We used to mark our missions on our hats. We wore "Go to Hell" hats, and we marked all the missions on there. We marked Pack VI missions in red. After a hundred missions, your tour was over. Pack VI missions were marked in red because that was the area most heavily defended. Always lots of anti-aircraft fire there, always SAMs, sometimes MiGs.

Do you still have the hat?

No.

What happened to it?

I didn't have it with me when I went down. I don't know what happened to it. I never saw it again.

Tell me about the flight you were shot down on.

That flight was on one of those days when we escalated the war in North Vietnam. We were, for the first time, hitting targets in Hanoi proper. Our target was a railyard on the outskirts of the city. Both F-105 wings (one based in Ta Khli, the other in Khorat) hit targets at the same time. Generally we were hitting targets in the city at the same time, so it was a major effort on that day. Those in Ta Khli and those in Khorat also began to do things differently—we each used different tactics. At our base we liked to go in in flights of four, spaced two minutes apart, at a moderate altitude. Khorat's attitude was different, in fact just the opposite. They went in in a group as in World War II formation bombing, in groups of twenty. Their belief was that with the jamming pods on, it would suppress the surface-to-air missile capability. We were lead flight that day, first flight on. We hit a railroad marshalling yard just on the outskirts of Hanoi. My flight had the flak suppression mission. Our job was to quiet the anti-aircraft artillery positions. I was hit, probably by 37mm or 57mm AAA, but the plane did not go uncontrollable. It kept flying straight and level. But it just wouldn't respond appropriately to any stick movements. If I tried to turn, no matter what I did, the plane overreacted, so I elected just to keep my hands off the stick. I then tried to restart the engine.

About how high were you when you went out?

I was pretty low. I really don't know. But I saw the airplane impact and explode about the same time my chute opened, so I was pretty low.

Did the enemy pick you right up?

I wasn't up very long, but I had time to look around. I could see I was coming down in a rice paddy that was about four or five hundred yards from a village. And in the village I could see people standing out under the trees, watching me, watching the action going on. My major sensation was the noise. When you're in the cockpit, you don't hear the bombs, you don't hear the shells exploding, you just hear radio transmission. It's very quiet. In the chute it's real loud: bombs are going off, surface-to-air missiles are exploding, all sorts of noise. I could see that some people in the nearby village were watching my parachute descend, and I knew they would come out to get me as soon as they could, so I tried to direct the chute away from that village as much as possible. As long as the air raid continued, the villagers stayed in the village; they stayed under cover, under the trees. As soon as the air raid was over and all the airplanes were gone, they came. I came down in a rice paddy. Chest deep in water and mud. Virtually impossible to move with any speed. I was still in the paddy when the aircraft had all left. When people came out of the village, they found me very quickly. There were four men in

435

the semblance of uniforms, who carried AK-47s. They kept the village people away from me. Had it not been for the military guys, I have no doubt that the villagers would have killed me.

After capture in the rice paddy, I was taken to the village and put into what was probably the schoolhouse. No one spoke English. I was tied with arms behind my back and stripped except for jockey shorts. Someone put cloth bandages around both forearms. (My forearms had been cut during ejection.) They opened a window in the building and let villagers walk by to look.

After about thirty minutes, the four military types blindfolded me, and we began to march along the dikes between rice paddies until we came to a road. We continued to walk until a military truck came along. Those four turned me over to the soldiers, and they put me in the back of the truck. Next, we drove along until we stopped at what I believe to have been a SAM site. All of the soldiers got out of the truck.

What was going through your mind?

Actually, I think you're kind of in a state of shock. Because everyone got off the back of this truck, this canvas-covered truck, and I just sat there and it got kind of quiet. Then somebody spoke to me in Russian, because he asked my name. I had a year of Russian language at AFA, so I could understand him. I was thirsty and tried to ask him for water but couldn't remember the word. He left. But we parked again and this time it was quite dark; it was late at night. After the stop at the missile site, we drove off again and continued to drive until we got to Hanoi. Again, everyone got off the truck but me. I was still tied and blindfolded. Someone came up to the truck and asked me in English what airplane I had been flying. I told him my name and my rank and serial number. After he hit me in the nose, I no longer felt like this was happening to someone else. Then I realized the full impact of my situation. Then we had this very scary parade through the streets of Hanoi. And I was afraid for my life in this little parade.

You were still blindfolded?

No, they took the blindfold off for the parade. I wasn't marched through the streets, but what they did was take a little wooden stool and fix it to the truck bed, so it was fairly stable. They left me tied and also tied me to the stool. They lifted the canvas off the truck—it was a flatbed truck. The stool was fixed to the bed of the truck. An armed soldier was positioned at each corner of the bed. Then we drove slowly through the streets of Hanoi.

The street was lined with people, both sides, and was crowded. People were shouting, and they agitated them with the bullhorn. Suddenly, people began to throw things, like stones, bricks, vegetables. They're, of course, hitting you, and you can't do anything because you're all tied up. The truck is going very slowly. It looked to me like the people got out of control. Of course, there were soldiers all along both sides of the street, with their bayonets out, forming a line the people were supposed to stay behind. But the people would start surging forward, and they actually started climbing onto the truck. And these four guys on the truck would be banging people on the head and shoulders with the butt ends of their AK-47s, knocking them off. But the sheer numbers were just getting to be too much for them. I thought, "I'm gonna be dead. These people are just going to climb up here and just beat me to death, because they can't possibly control all these people." And when it got to that point in time, the driver of the truck, who was just putting along in low gear, would accelerate. Everybody would fall off the truck, except me because I'm tied to the stool, which of course is fixed to the truck bed. Everybody would fall off and would scramble and get back on. And they'd drive away from where all the people were really upset. We'd then come to a little calmer stretch, and then the driver would slow the truck down, and we'd go through the whole cycle again—a number of times.

How many times do you think you got hit by things?

I don't know. A bunch. I kept thinking to myself: "This is a stupid, dangerous game these guys are playing." Because, you know, sometimes when you step on the gas, instead of accelerating, the truck would hesitate, or it could die. I said to myself, "If that happens, I'm done for." Fortunately, it never happened.

You were imprisoned in the notorious "Hanoi Hilton." Describe it.

It was real imposing, a scary-looking place. Of course, it was built by the French. Big, thick, tall walls with rows and rows of broken glass along the top and finished off with razor wire. Double gates.

In the courtyard, I was blindfolded again. My arms were still tied as they had been since capture. I was then led through a gate or door and into a corridor of some kind. We walked a long way, going through a number of doors. Each door would have to be unlocked to enter and was locked again after we went through.

In the interrogation room, the only furniture was a small desk-like table with two straightbacked chairs on one side and a stool on the other. The table had a purple table cloth. One light with a shade hung from a long cord from the ceiling. There was a concrete floor without a covering. The floor was dirty and had a lot of rust-colored stains—blood stains, I presumed. The walls were also stained. Some iron bars were lying against the wall along with some rope.

They sat me down on the stool and took the blindfold off but left me tied as before. I sat there a long time alone. Very hot with lots of mosquitoes. Finally, two North Vietnamese officers came into the room. Only one talked to me in English, and he would confer with the other in Vietnamese.

What were your first hours like in there? Did you think you were ever going to get out?

I was beginning to wonder. They were very good at setting me up psychologically. We drove into a fairly attractive-looking courtyard, French colonial style, with flower boxes around and green, shuttered windows. I said to myself that we must be going into this deepest darkest hole. We finally got to where we were going, and I learned later when I got to know more of the layout of the prison, that we hadn't gone very far. We had just walked around in circles. The walls, instead of being stuccoed or whitewashed, were real rough. It looked like the plaster had been applied by hand on one side of the table.

They started asking questions and we went through the "name, rank, serial number, and date of birth" business. They said I was not a prisoner of war, the first reason being that Vietnam has never declared war on the United States nor had the United States declared war on Vietnam. Therefore, the rules of war don't apply. Secondly, "we didn't sign the Geneva Accords—were never signatory to it—because we were subjugated by the French at the time." Thirdly they said, "because there is no state of war between Vietnam and the United States, you're nothing but a criminal, and you will be tried for these crimes." Then they said, "One of the first rules is that you will answer all the questions that are asked." I refused, and they said the whole thing again. Then they gave me a second chance. I again gave name, rank, serial number, and date of birth. They said I would be punished for refusing to answer. They then left the room; I sat there for a good long time.

Then they let you think about it.

Yes, they let me think about it for a long time. And then, eventually, the torturers came into the room. They beat me around a bit, and they handcuffed my wrists together. (I still had my arms tied around behind me.) Then they put this U-bolt-type thing on each ankle and ran an iron bar through the U-bolt's eyelets. I stayed lying there. They'd spread your legs out—just push them apart as far as they can get them to go. Then they'd run that bar through there, and it just locks your legs into place. You're already tied and handcuffed. You're handcuffed with your wrists together behind your back, and they're not really handcuffs like we use here, with a chain. They force your wrists together like this (illustrates), and you can't move your wrists apart at all because there is no chain. They could tighten things with something like an Allen wrench. They tightened them down as tight as they could. And then, besides being handcuffed, you're bound with a rope by both upper arms.

With some people, this would separate their shoulders.

So you're already tied up like that, then they take a rope and run it around your neck and back up around your arms so that your arms come way up high. In other words, they force your head down between your legs so that your nose is kind of in your anus. Then they can tie that rope off to the far end of the bar, as tightly as they can. And then they just kind of leave you there like that. It's a pretty painful position to begin with, but then you're contorted in such a way that the circulation is cut off from your feet and your hands and arms. That really starts things tingling. After awhile, it really begins to hurt; it feels like people are putting little needles in you. Then the goons all leave, except one, and he just sits there on a stool and reads the paper— while you're sitting there like that. And they just leave you there as long as it takes. Periodically, the guy in the chair would come over and kick and hit me. Then he'd make sure those ropes were as tight as they could possibly be.

What's going through your mind at this point?

Well, the worst part then is when you give up, because you've done everything you can to stay there and tolerate it as long as possible and not to give up. You know, you think to yourself, I'm going to count to a hundred. Then you count again. Think of anything to keep from thinking about the discomfort. But then the worst part is psychological, because when you do decide "I can't do this any longer," the guy sitting there on that chair over there doesn't speak English, and he doesn't understand what you said. And you're trying to tell him: "I give up. I'll answer the interrogator's questions." Instead, he thinks you're being smart or whatever, so he comes over and starts beating on you some more. And he won't do anything. Eventually, he gets the picture, or maybe he has had it all along, so he leaves and you're lying there thinking, "I've gone to my absolute limit. It's a good thing he finally left." You think he's going to come right back, because you want to answer these questions. Hell, he doesn't come back for a long time. It may be fifteen minutes, but it seemed like fifteen hours—when you're in that situation. But the bad part of that is, psychologically, that you're thinking, "I thought I couldn't do any more, but here I am. I'm actually doing it, because I have no choice." I'm thinking, "I can't get out, and this guy won't come back, so I must have given up too early."

Do you feel guilt about that?

Sure you do. And so when you first give up, when they finally do let you out, then you have this really bad psychological depression.

Did these feelings carry over until your release? Did they haunt you?

No, the real bad part was just the first few days, until you had contact with another American, who could tell you you weren't the first or only one to answer questions. Everyone had done it.

So how long were you in the Hanoi Hilton?

Probably only two weeks. Time went by. I hardly remember any real parts of it, because my arms were troubling me. They were badly infected by that time, and we got no medical attention. These were fairly good-sized cuts on my forearms, that the lady had wrapped in gauze. I'd been in that rice paddy, which was real dirty water, so my arms were really infected. In fact, they were swollen to look like Popeye. The only thing I could do—I was afraid gangrene would set in—was to squeeze my arms every few hours to get all the pus and stuff out. They hadn't sewn the cuts up. Anyway, I would get as much stuff out of them as I could. Then the arms would look more normal but would be real painful. The infection caused a fever. Didn't have enough water to drink. Always thirsty. They had a special section. I didn't know what the prisoners called it at the time but eventually learned that they called it "Heartbreak Hotel." They used stocks, like the Pilgrims used to use. They'd put you on these concrete beds, and then put your feet in these stocks, and clamp you down. The rod that locked you in place could be removed only from outside the cell. So they put me in those. And I was just out of my head most of the time.

Do you remember any hallucinations?

Oh yeah. I kept having these escape hallucinations. I imagined escaping from prison. I had to stay awake because I knew if I went to sleep they would get me again, but I couldn't stay awake. I'd fall asleep, I'd wake up, and I'd be back in the stocks again. That happened over and over. I'm a smoker, and of course I started having nicotine withdrawal too. In every one of these rooms there was a little hole in the bottom of the wall where, during heavy rains, water would run right through—literally for water runoff. You could take a bucket and wash the floor, and it would all run out this hole. One of my recurring hallucinations was that this little wagon, drawn by a couple of little horses, would come through the hole, and these little Gypsies would climb up onto my bed and give me cigarettes. Every time they'd give me a cigarette, I'd just be lighting up and then I'd wake up. That was another one.

The other hallucination that got me in trouble must have coincided with something that was really happening, the cell doors opening. I believed that Matt Dillon, the sheriff on "Gunsmoke," was there, releasing American prisoners and kicking ass on the Vietnamese. And I could hear him opening the doors and letting the prisoners out of their cells. And the sound of this started down at the end, and I could hear this one open, and the guys getting out, and the next one, and the next one, and the next one. Then it came my turn—I was just waiting for him to open the door—and he went by it and went to the next cell and opened that one. So I started yelling at him, "Hey, you forgot me. I'm over here. You've got to come and let me out." And of course, you had to be quiet in the cell, so then when that would happen, the guard would come in. He had this rice broom, and he would ram it in my mouth and beat me around a bit. But I was convinced that Matt Dillon was there. Also, I was not the only one having hallucinations, because I remember one night when I was not having hallucinations, I was perfectly lucid, somebody in the cell across from me was conversing outside his window with Henry Kissinger, who was in the courtyard negotiating the release.

Do you remember any lines from that?

No, I don't, but I remember that he was reporting back to us. I finally got out of there.

What caused that?

I don't know. It seemed to be a kind of classification. Once they had asked you all those questions, they classified you by rank. Things may have been dictated as much by space requirements as anything. I suppose when they captured many more guys, they had to make room for them in the system.

Did you meet anybody at the Hilton?

Never met anybody at the Hilton. Every move was always done at night. During the night they came in and took me out of that little cell and took me to a camp the prisoners called The Zoo. Moved me into a cell with other recently captured pilots. One was Bob Abbott. We had come to Vietnam at the same time, assigned to the same wing. We went to different squadrons. The other guy was Loren Torkelson, who was an F-4 flier, a front-seater, who was shot down.

What did it mean to be with some buddies?

That was much better. Very much better. But we didn't stay at The Zoo very long.

What do you remember that was peculiar about The Zoo?

The weird thing about The Zoo was when the French had it, it had been some kind of film studio. There was a swimming pool in the center of the complex, which was full of film. Except for the Hilton, all the camps had been converted from something else. Every camp had one English-speaking Vietnamese. We had names for all these guys. We called one of the guys at The Zoo "Dumbshit." But I remember one of my first meetings with him. He started asking me questions about what my target was, what my mission was on the day I got shot down. And I told him some railyard and that I had been dropping regular bombs. He was out of his chair and slapped me upside the head. He said, "You're lying. That's not true. Because you were dropping CBUs on this camp." (My target on the day I was shot down.) It was very close to The Zoo. Some stray CBUs did come into the camp that day. I don't know if you know what a CBU is, but it's a pretty lethal weapon—purely anti-personnel. It looks about the size of a softball, and it's metal. It has an explosive device in the center, and all kinds of BBs—ball bearings—embedded in the soft metal around the explosive. It's meant to kill not the guns but the gunners. Anyway, when we flew, we carried four cannisters. Each cannister had twelve hundred CBUs. And he had some of these BBs in his hands. He throws them on the table and says, "You bombed this camp." Of course, I denied it.

So you weren't at The Zoo very long. Where did you go from there?

We went to The Plantation, which was a relatively small camp, more central to downtown. It was very near the Dumer Bridge, the major highway bridge across the Red River. The tracks were right behind the camp, and they were already elevated on their way up to the bridge.

So you could look out the window and see the trains go by?

We didn't have windows, but we made ways to see out.

Ho did you make ways to see out?

By drilling holes. We drilled holes with wire, with things we could find.

You called this other place "The Plantation." That sounds almost luxurious.

Well, the prisoners called it "The Plantation" because in the center of the camp was this two-story French colonial style house, with this big tree in front of it that looked like it should be by a Southern plantation house. It had green shutters on the windows. So we called it "The Plantation." Actually, when the French were there, it must have been some kind of light vehicle repair facility, because around the center house were garage-like buildings. Behind one of those buildings, there were even some jeeps that didn't run anymore.

It sounds like you really felt the presence of the French.

Well, yeah. One of the things that became obvious to me was that a lot of the torture devices at the Hanoi Hilton the French had built in. And some of those things the Vietnamese were doing to us, obviously the French had done to them. One of the devices I mention were the stocks, which were an integral part of the building. Also, in that first room I told you about, in that interrogation room, one of the things the Vietnamese did—though they never did it to me—was run that rope up over a hook and haul you to the ceiling.

How many days were you in The Zoo?

Probably a month. I was at The Plantation until late 1969. About two years.

It seems you were moved all over the place.

Yeah. And then the strangeness really began, because they quit being mean, combative, and confrontive with the three of us. That occurred when we moved to The Plantation. There, we lived in a room on the side of the camp, away from the other POWs, and we could see that we were being treated differently.

Why do you think that was?

Well, it became clear pretty soon. Then they would have one or more of us three to the big house in the evening for—we called it—quizzes. There was a guy, who was not from the camp, obviously higher-ranking and educated, who spoke English better, and he would just talk about things. He would be asking you questions. He would be saying, "What do you think about the war? What do you think about President Johnson? We understand there's a lot of opposition to the war by many Americans." He would offer a cigarette. "Do you smoke? Would you like a cigarette?" He would be almost pleasant as he interviewed us. Asking nothing of us if you didn't want to answer. In one of those meetings, he would ask us, "How would you like to see Hanoi? Well, you're going to see Hanoi because you don't believe your people purposely bomb hospitals and schools. Well, we're going to take you and show you a hospital that's been bombed. We're going to take you and show you a school that's been bombed."

At night they would come, maybe once a week, bring these military-style clothes with no rank or insignia, but green khaki trousers, and tell us to get into them. Then they'd load us into the jeep with an armed guard, and we would go to a school or hospital. And there'd be a doctor at the hospital who'd say, "This is where I used to be a doctor; this is where the bomb dropped." He would say, "Why do you think there are so many people out at night?" We'd say, "I don't know." He'd reply, "Well, it's because we can't go out in the daytime because you're always dropping your damn bombs. But we've adapted. You haven't hurt us at all. Things go on as normal. We just do them in the dark." It was real strange, and we had no idea what they were doing. We had had only sporadic communication with the other prisoners at this point, because we shared no common walls in our cells.

It eventually became clear to us that they were contemplating a release of three POWs to one of the periodic "peace" delegations that visited North

Vietnam. They wanted POWs who hadn't been there long and hadn't been mistreated as badly as most of the others. We finally told them we didn't want to be a part of that.

So they put you back in with the other prisoners when you said you didn't want to go home until everybody went home.

Right. And eventually they got some to do it.

How would you have felt if you'd have said yes and gone home?

I would have felt awful.

You would have been a propaganda tool, right?

Sure. And it was against orders. I was not the senior ranking officer there. That was Dick Stratton at that time in The Zoo. It was his order that no one would accept an early release. I couldn't do it. I felt bad enough even having been offered the opportunity, because I felt the other prisoners were looking a little askance. They might have been wondering why "you guys" were offered the opportunity. They were never offered the opportunity.

So that's another layer of guilt, isn't it?

Yeah, right.

Then you're back in with everyone else.

Now we're back with everyone else. In fact, they split us up then. They put Torkelson somewhere else and put Abbott and myself in this tiny little room in the gun-shed for six months. It was terrible for six months. I didn't know this part, we just called it "the gun-shed." Eventually we moved into a room with two other POWs. We then had a bigger room. Torkelson, plus one other guy, Joe Crecca, and Abbot and myself. And then the four of us were together virtually the rest of the war.

How long were you there?

Till mid-1969. It was the four of us in that room till sometime in '69. After Ho Chi Minh died, late in the year, conditions changed considerably. And we moved from The Plantation to a brand-new prison camp they built. We called it Camp Faith. It was a much better place. And there, they put us in larger rooms with ten guys per room. They had a series of compounds, which included a little building with four prisoner rooms and a center room that the Vietnamese did something in. So in each compound, that meant there were about forty guys. What was totally new here was that they had a window at each end of this room, and it was left open. Furthermore, they would let people out of those rooms, a room at a time, to be outside in the sun.

Because the window was open, you could actually go talk to the other prisoners who were outside. It was a totally new thing.

Do you remember any special conversations you had then?

No real special ones. Just a lot of talk. But that didn't last very long, because that was the year that the U.S. attempted to rescue POWs from Sontay camp. Of course, we didn't know at the time what happened. We knew something had happened. They obviously were worried about security, because Sontay must have been very close to Camp Faith. We knew that because we could hear some of the action. So they moved us back to the Hilton. And because all the prisoners were now at the Hilton, they had to put us in large rooms, the part of the place that had previously been kept for bank robbers and the like. Now we lived in a big room with forty guys in a room, five or six guys together, but we could have communication with virtually all the prisoners.

Did you feel like baggage, being moved all the time?

Your mood varied, of course. We were always confident that we would get out some day. The only question in anybody's mind was when that day would be.

From this point, how long before you got out?

Another three years. We got out in February of 1973.

How many years is that?

That's five years and eight months.

That's incredible.

The last two and one-half years were relatively easy, compared to the first ones, because now the torture was gone. They weren't doing that anymore.

Did you ever wager to pass the time?

Oh, we always wagered. Of course, we couldn't pay our bets in prison. They were always to be paid upon our return. I remember my most outstanding wager. This goes way back to The Plantation. In the room next to me was a guy named Ben Ringsdorf, and he was from Alabama. He and I had a standing wager for all the years we were in prison, for all the football games between our two favorite leagues. I had the Pac-10, and he had the Southeast Conference. It turned out that I had to pay Ben three bottles of Wild Turkey.

Would you have believed the strength of will going in?

I had no idea how strong that will is. Because quite frankly, when I was hit and when I had to bail out, I debated with myself whether to bail out or whether to stay with the airplane. Because I knew that, where I was jumping out, they weren't going to come rescue me. They weren't even going to try. I figured that I would be captured right away, and I never was optimistic about the outcome of the war, as most of the aviators were. I figured, if I'm captured, most likely it's going to be for a long time. And the Vietnamese are not going to be nice. And I thought to myself, because I'd been in car accidents before, and knew they don't hurt initially, that if I just stayed in the plane, it wouldn't hurt. In fact, it would be over real quick. If I got out, it was going to be a lot of pain. So I got closer and closer and closer to the ground, and the will to survive just takes over.

Are there any indelible images?

One of the indelible images or memories I have is of the memorable Christmases I spent there as a POW. And it was because of the fact that you wanted to give something to somebody else for Christmas. And everybody did. We exchanged gifts. And what made it so special was of course that you couldn't run to the store and buy a gift. A gift took real thought, planning, and whatever gift you gave had to be made.

Some examples?

I remember one guy, surreptitiously, with his bread dough—we didn't always get rice, sometimes they gave us bread dough to eat—rolled little balls of it into beads, and made a rosary, which was really authentic. Other times the gifts were humorous. I did usually do a poem or a song about somebody else. Sometimes humorous, sometimes not. I'd pick out a trait somebody had and address it.

What have your learned from the POW years that's helped you in your day-to-day life?

Well, I learned I had some weaknesses I didn't think I had, or know I had, and I learned I had some strengths I didn't know I had. I think what sustained me was the confidence that I would go home some day. The will to survive is pretty strong.

Colonel Bernie Fisher

BERNIE FISHER

Adventures In Ashau

"What's your favorite plane?" I ask Bernie Fisher, feeling a little awestruck at this famous flier.

"The F-15," he answers, explaining that he wasn't checked out in it. "I think I was very partial to the 104. That little rascal would go fast and high."

Fisher is an easy-going, down-to-earth man. No pretentiousness, no braggadocio, here. In that sense, Fisher is not what one might expect from a war hero, albeit of a complex war which divided a nation. There is a sensibility here that is remarkable, as he speaks of the Vietnamese man he met in the waters off the coast of Vietnam. What is clear is his humanity, something lost in the debates and posturing about that conflict.

Fisher participated in ROTC at the University of Utah, then entered primary flying school at Marana, Arizona. After Basic Flying School at Williams AFB, Instrument School at Moody AFB, and Day Fighter School in the F-80 Shooting Star at Tyndall, he had his first operational assignment with the 42nd Fighter Interceptor Squadron in Chicago.

Following stints at Chitose Air Base, Japan, and Malmstrom AFB, Montana, he was assigned to Homestead AFB, Florida, from where he would volunteer for duty in Vietnam to fly the A-1E Skyraider.

Fisher arrived in Vietnam in July, 1965. While assigned to the 1st Air Commando Squadron at Pleiku, South Vietnam, Fisher received nationwide publicity for his actions during the battle in the Ashau Valley on March 10, 1966. For those actions, above and beyond the call of duty, which saved a fellow flier, he was presented the Medal of Honor by President Lyndon B. Johnson at the White House in 1967.

In 1968, Colonel Fisher was transferred to Bitburg Air Base, Germany, and subsequently, assumed command of the 525th Fighter Interceptor Squadron. Then he became Operations Officer of the 87th FIS in Duluth, finally going to the 124th Fighter Interceptor Group in Boise. Fisher is married to Realla J. Johnson; they have six sons and twenty-three grandchildren.

Most pilots have had some precarious landings. Talk about a precarious landing.

I was flying a 104 Starfighter down in the Gulf of Mexico. We were running intercepts. I could smell something very strong in the cockpit. I looked down and noticed my oil pressure was dropping—just going down, down, down—so I started climbing for the base at Homestead. Then I realized the oil was depleted, and the nozzle went wide open. I then realized my thrust had decreased. On the F-104 the nozzles on the engine are controlled by engine oil and, if you lose the engine oil, you lose the nozzles. Eventually what you do is go to about 40 percent thrust. The weather was overcast that night, and so the ground control lined me up with a runway. I could tell with my own DME [Distance Measuring Equipment] just how far out I was. The decision was made that I could make the runway. When I broke out of the clouds, I would land. It was about a three-thousand-foot ceiling. When I got to the runway, I eased her in and made the landing.

How did you feel on that one?

Well, it's kind of scary. It doesn't round out very well. We used to shoot SFOs quite religiously [Simulated Flame Out]. Each time we came back with a little extra fuel, we would come over the field at fifteen thousand feet, shut the engine down to idle, and open the speed boards, which simulated a dead engine. Then we would make one 360-degree turn and come across the runway, starting around at five hundred feet—no lower than three hundred feet. We would just round out and throw our gear down as soon as we had the runway made, when it should lock in.

Your favorite plane?

Oh, I think the F-15 is one of the finest and fastest airplanes. I've just flown in that one—I wasn't checked out in it. It was a good airplane.

Of those you were checked out in, which is the best?

I think we were very partial to the One-oh-four. That was quite an airplane. That little rascal would go fast and go high and was very maneuverable.

Did you get in a lot of situations—dogfights maybe—that demonstrated the ability of the 104?

Not necessarily dogfights but lots of practice intercepts. One thing that was good about it was that you could go very high. But when you went high, you had to wear the pressure suit. That was probably the most uncomfortable suit in the world to wear. For example, water will boil in the atmosphere at fifty thousand feet and above. If you take a jar of water and move it out into the atmosphere, it will boil. Of course, the higher you get, the lower the boiling point, so your blood does the same thing. If you're above fifty thousand feet and you lose the cockpit pressure, you're in trouble.

How did you feel when you got that piece of paper that said "Divert to Ashau Valley" for what turned out to be that famous rescue?

I didn't get a piece of paper. We had just completed one mission, and we were already briefed for another mission. We went out to the airplane, two of us, and they briefed us. We got our parachutes and personal guns and were ready to go.

They said, "Take it to Ashau instead." They told us there was a lot of activity up there. So we stayed low on the deck—right on the trees. We couldn't go high enough in that airplane to get out of the weather. So we stayed below.

Didn't you find the hole in the clouds?

That was the second day. We came into the area. There was a lot of activity. From where we were flying, there were just white clouds. You could see mountain peaks sticking through here and there. We knew Ashau was in there someplace. The air-controllers, who knew the area better than we did, would say, "Hey, I think it's over here in this canyon." So they'd open the flaps on the bird and descend to have a look. Then you'd hear, "No, it's not in this canyon."

Again, the "bird dogs"—similar to the Cessna 172s—would just put the flaps down and descend through the clouds in hopes of spotting the field. The chance of hitting a mountain was very good. When they broke out, they'd say, "It's not this canyon." And another guy would say, "Hey, I think it's over here." Well, I saw a break in the clouds and said, "Hey, I know where we are," so I rolled in and went through the hole into the canyon.

There were nineteen bullet-holes in your plane when you got through. That's a lot of holes, isn't it?

Well, it's a lot of holes, but the airplane seemed to sustain it. In Korea I remember some guys got over a hundred bullet-holes in their airplanes, and they would still be flying. Yes, that's a lot of holes because they hit a lot of vital areas: the fuel tank, the wings.

But your plane still flew for you.

Oh, yes, they didn't hit any vital areas. Anytime they hit anything vital, the plane's going to quit. We have backup systems to the main controls. For example, we had cables going down to the leading edge of the wing and, if they got cut, we always had secondary cables running to the back of the wing—a backup for everything.

Let's talk about the rescue in the Ashau Valley. Didn't you talk Jump Meyers down when his plane was first hit?

We talked to each other. When he first got hit, he was making his first pass, and I was coming in for my second pass. He called me and said he was hit, and I observed he was burning well past the tail of the airplane. He just ignited and was on fire—looked like a torch going through the sky. He was down pretty low on the deck. What a guy should do is jump out of the airplane, but we didn't have ejection seats. And, if you jump out, you have to have five to seven hundred feet of altitude in order to make it, and he didn't have that much. So he bent it around to the left and headed into the strip at Ashau. I reminded him that he still had about six thousand pounds of bombs on the airplane, and he'd better get rid of them. He had a handle in case of emergency, and he dumped it all in the jungle and continued on around the turn. Just before he was ready to touch down, it looked to me like he was a little bit too hot to land on the runway, and I told him he'd better pull the gear up. If you land flat on the belly, the thing's not going to cartwheel quite so badly. So he pulled the gear up and landed on the belly, and I guess he slid five hundred or six hundred feet down the runway, then slid off to the right and hit the bank. I looked out and saw this big ball of fire there. I called the command post and said we had one down. I didn't think he'd made it. I thought he'd been killed in the crash.

When did you realize he'd made it alive?

I made a circle overhead and watched for a moment. He was in the airplane forty-five seconds or so. Then the fire blew away from the right side and he came running out across the wing. When I saw him run, I flew right over him—about twenty-five feet. I waved at him and he waved back and I knew that he was out of the airplane. But when he was running it looked like he was on fire. He was smoking; the smoke was following him, and I figured that he was burned quite badly.

When did you decide to go for him?

When he got out of the airplane, I called the command post, and I told them that he was out of the airplane. I requested a helicopter. Their reply was that they would have a Marine 'copter there in about twenty minutes. The Marines supported from one of their Special Forces camps, so we left it right there and went back to hitting the trenches where the gunfire was coming from. I suppose it took us ten minutes. We dropped all our bombs, shot up about half of our ammunition, and then I called again and asked the command post where the helicopter was. It was time for us to head out of there. They said they didn't know, it might be another twenty minutes before they got there. When I heard that I felt strongly about going in to pick him up. I think, in my own way, we receive a lot of spiritual help that comes from our Heavenly Father. I just prayerfully said, "He's going to need a lot of help, and so am I." I relaxed and things settled down, and I felt like it was the thing to do.

452

People described you in articles I read as "real cool."

Well, no, I don't think so. You know, you do get kind of excited at times like that. I think that after we decided what we were going to do, things settled down and I could think a little better. Half-relaxed, I just called John Lucas—he and these guys on the flight were good shooters. They were real good support. I told John what my intentions were, and he said he would cover me, which means that when you're on the ground, they'll keep people away from you. I told the command post what my intentions were. I asked them the length of the runway, even though I had a map in the cockpit. It's hard to read the map and watch airplanes come around in a box canyon. There was a lot of traffic in there. They told me the runway was thirty-five hundred feet long, and I knew I could land in three thousand feet. But it turned out to be a mistake: the runway was only twenty-five hundred feet long, too short for this airplane.

You needed three thousand feet to land?

I just figured twenty-eight hundred to three thousand feet to land this airplane prior to each mission. You compute your take-off and landing roll, so you know what distance is required, including how much fuel you have left on board.

Weren't there some obstacles on the ground? Did you worry about that?

I didn't realize it. I didn't realize there was all that stuff on the runway. The Vietcong had mortared the PSP [pierced steel planking] on the runways, and there were prongs of metal sticking up three-and-half to four feet. I guess some of the metal was from the camp that had exploded. I think they dumped some rocket parts on the runway, too. Anyway, there was a lot of stuff there—metal, garbage, and debris—plus the fact that they had been hit pretty hard with artillery shells and mortar shells. When I touched down, I tried to avoid that stuff. I realized that I might blow the tires out on the airplane. I really assumed I might wear out the tires during the landing roll.

When I got to the end of the runway after heavy braking, the brakes were hot. I went off the end. It looked like just straight ahead of me was a little brown grass, and I assumed I could go out into there and slow it down. I remember just saying to myself, "Oh, no, not now." I was afraid I'd gotten that far and was losing it. But it was a good-sized grass area. They had dumped fifty-five-gallon barrels out there, and I hit those and did damage to the airplane. I think it was a fuel storage dump. So I went through it and banged the airplane up a little bit, but I did get it turned around.

I got it back up on the runway and taxied about eighteen hundred feet. When I went by him—"Jump" Meyers—he jumped up and waved.

I hit the brakes. I guess in Jump's mind he thought I'd been shot down.

He didn't realize that I had come in to get him, and so he wasn't concerned about the condition of my airplane. And all of a sudden, he realized I'd come in to get him, and he jumped up and I stopped. He made a run for the airplane.

We waited and waited. It seemed like a long while, because they were hitting me while I sat there on the ground. I figured he must have gotten hit, trying to get to the airplane, so I unstrapped to go get him. He was on the right side of the wing, trying to get up on the airplane, but he just couldn't get in. The plane has a fourteen-foot, four-bladed prop on it, which puts out a lot of air. It's characteristic of the airplane that, when you bring it back to idle, it quits. So you don't always bring it clear back. That is why he didn't get up on the wing of the airplane: too much wind. I pulled it back to the stop position and slowed it right down and he was able to make it. One step up on the wing, then on the side, and into the cockpit. He kind of put his head and arms in, and I reached over the top of him and grabbed him by the pants and pulled him into the cockpit.

What's the first thing he said to you?

I don't know. I don't think we could hear what we were saying. He made some comments on something. He gave me some signals. We didn't even strap in. I knew we had to get out of there.

I spun it around, and my initial thought was that I needed more runway. I didn't think we had enough room to take off. I was afraid that I wouldn't get the airspeed we would need to get off. We came off the ground beautifully. They told me to keep the airplane low, so they wouldn't shoot at us so hard. I guess while he was on the ground Jump had a pretty good observation point to listen to the gunfire. He said it was like the Fourth of July celebration. Every time we'd come up over the top of them, the guns would open up on us. We were lucky that they didn't hit us more than they did.

How many Vietnamese were down there?

Special Forces told us after we left that some two to four thousand had come into the canyon. About two to three days or so before the fight, they moved in two companies of Nungs [Hmong] to strengthen the Special Forces camp. These are mercenaries. They have fifty men in each company plus American advisors leading them. It brought the camp to about four hundred and fifty men. Initially there were twelve Americans. I think it came to about seventeen American advisors in the Special Forces camp itself.

When you went down there, it was to save the camp, wasn't it?

Yes. A lot of the information we got was after the fact. Prior to becoming involved in Ashau, the Special Forces people knew that they were probably going to have a fight. They knew that a lot of people had moved into the valley. They observed that and figured that there was going to be a fight and that's why the Special Forces were brought in and the two companies of Nungs—to help.

Early the first morning, 9 March, we hit the camp when the weather was rotten. I don't think it got above three hundred feet ceiling in the canyon that morning. The 123s that we put in the first day—March 9, 1966—those pilots would come in and drop bundles, attached to parachutes. We would observe their drop into the canyon. When the cargo birds turned, we could see one wing just above the trees, the other wing in the clouds. Very, very, poor visibility. On the second day, visibility was up to about eight hundred feet.

When did you feel the most fear?

There was the time when I went off the end of a runway. That was probably the biggest panic I had. I thought I'd lost it right there. When I went into the fuel storage and hit a bunch of stuff, I went, "Oh, no!" in disgust. I realized that I could lose the airplane out there.

You know, things are happening so fast; you're being shot at and you're shooting back: you strike and you direct strike, you get an offer of help and give help—I don't think you really have time to stop and think of fear or anything like that.

Tell me how you felt after the recognitions. How did you find out?

After the mission was over, I took Jump to the hospital. I think he stayed overnight. The next day or the day after that they wanted us to come down to the Seventh air force headquarters at Tan Son Nhat. We went down there. I really don't know how we got there—whether it was the bird, or perhaps the 123. Anyway, we went over to the Seventh air force—stayed in a Chinese home with three storeys. It had a swimming pool up on the third floor—pretty ritzy. They had leased it from the Chinese. It was a pretty swinging place.

Colonel McGinty was the Secretary of Office Information. This colonel was a real neat guy, very friendly and well liked by a lot of people. He called us in and he said, "Bernie, what do you think you deserve?" I said, "I don't know." There was a lot of hoopla about it. And he said, "You've read a citation or two, how would you rate this?" I said,"Well, I think it would probably deserve a Silver Star." He said, "We have just finished visiting with the Chief of Staff at the Pentagon, and they recommended the Medal of Honor, and we agreed with it." That was the first that I knew about it. I had known somebody that had received the Silver Star, but that's as high as I had ever known somebody to go. I didn't know very much about the Medal of Honor—very few of those are given.

Then we headed down to Plei Ku from there. There is a regulation that covers Medal of Honor nominees or recipients. If you are nominated or have received this award, you are supposed to be moved out of the combat zone because of the use it could have if you were captured—or picked up or shot down. So then they had to decide what they wanted to do. I ended up flying about another thirty missions.

One day the group commander called me and he said, "I have two regulations here. One is the Fifth air force regulation, and one is air force regulations. I want you to read these and take them to your squadron commander and have him give me a call."

There was a question there on what had to be done. They had to move me: they couldn't keep me in a combat area. So they decided they would send me to the Philippines or maybe to Hawaii. I had a couple or three weeks left in my tour, so my operations officer said, "Why don't you just send him home?" I just looked at him, saluted him and said, "I'm for that." They put me on an airplane; I didn't even have laundry!

It turned out kind of neat because when I landed at Travis, two guys in orange flight suits came up to me.

"Are you Bernie Fisher?"

"Yes"

"Well, we'll take your bags," and we went out the back door and got into one of those trainers, a T-33, and took off for Boise, Idaho. We were about halfway there when I looked out the window. We were intercepted by a flight of F-102s, and we made about three passes over Boise.

When we landed in Boise, there was a delegation there to meet us. It was quite exciting—and included a parade downtown to the Statehouse and a very warm welcome by state officials and city dignitaries.

Did you salvage any stuff during the war?

No, I didn't salvage anything, but here is a little story. There's a harbor at Qui Nhon but no place for ships to dock. They have to anchor out in the harbor, and the freight and cargo has to be loaded onto amphibian carriers. They called them "Larks." The little Larks were real workhorses.

One of the fellows who was the flight line chief—he was the kind of guy who could get anything from anybody—came in one day to Jump and said, "You know there's a ship out here that has frozen food on it. I could take the little boat and go out and get some frozen steaks."

He had a friend who drove one of the little Larks, and he really had formed a good friendship with him. So they jumped in the Lark and headed out to the ship. Of course, he went on board, saluted the flag and the officer on the deck, just like you would in the navy. To the officer on the deck he said, "Sir, I'm here to get some steaks."

Well, he's visualizing two or three good-sized steaks for the guys to eat. The next thing you know here comes this great big boatswain's net over the side. It must have had a ton of frozen steaks in it. Anyway, the guy didn't even bat an eye. He signed for it. He then went into shore and realized they were in deep trouble because there was no place to keep frozen food. We worked out of tents; even the commander was also in a tent. They got in to shore and took the steaks down to the squadron and they told Jump, "We have to do something."

Jump said, "Just one more minute."

He called one of the First Air Cavalry officers. When they first went over there they had landed at Qui Nhon. It was hot and it was dirty and they were sweating. They didn't have any shower facilities; they had to bathe in the ocean. It was a mess. So Jump took a bunch of our napalm cans and punched holes in them and built some racks and put some canvas around them. He made about half a dozen showers, out of kindness. So he was well liked by the commander.

So he called the commander and said, "I'm in trouble. I need somewhere to put some frozen steaks."

"Don't worry. I'll have something for you in a few minutes."

Soon, down the runway came a forklift, and on it was a walk-in freezer. They took one of the compressors they used to start the airplanes, with an electrical generator on it, and they rigged it to get 220 volts and plugged that into the first food locker and froze those steaks down. And for long as I can remember, on Saturday evening we had a steak fry in Qui Nhon. It would cost you one dollar for all the steak you wanted, all the French bread you could eat, all the rice and booze you could get over there. People would come from all over; more than once the runway would be so full of airplanes, we could hardly get our fighters in. I don't think the army could ever figure out where their steaks were.

Do you remember anything else like that?

One night the aircraft carrier came in and the pilots came ashore, and we hosted them at the officer's club. We had a great party. So the Navy guys invited the pilots out to the ship. They went out to the ship around midnight; I guess many of the guys had been drinking a little bit, and they were pretty drowsy. The next morning three guys woke up when they heard the props turning. They got up and went up to the deck to see what was happening, and found out they were under way. They had fallen asleep on the ship, and the ship had taken off overnight, and they were now somewhere around Da Nang. So finally they sent a helicopter out to the ship to bring these guys back.

We had a fellow who lost an F-104 and went into the gulf and was recovered.

He lived?

Yes. He spent two days and one night in the Gulf of Tonkin, and he almost drowned because he couldn't keep his head up any longer. So I decided if I ever went down I wanted to compensate for that. In my survival kit I had a pair of flippers, a mask, and a snorkel. I thought that if I ever went down in the water, I'd lie face down and I could survive a long time while breathing through the snorkel tube.

I used to do a lot of scuba diving and liked it very much. I used to go out swimming with a snorkel in the harbor in Vietnam. It was beautiful water. People would criticize me a bit, because people would be swimming around and be shot.

One day I noticed some Vietnamese people, local people, were out scavenging the shore for items that had fallen off the ships. They would gather whatever they could find and sell it on the black market and survive on it.

I saw this little guy out in his boat. I swam up to the side of the boat, reached up on the side and jumped in. Scared him to death. I could speak a little Vietnamese by then; we had a conversation, and after awhile he laughed and we joked for while. He let me row for awhile, and I'd scavenge for him. Then I realized it was time to head back, and we gave each other a handshake and hug and I left. I jumped in the water and swam back to shore. I don't suppose we will forget that.

Any other memorable people you met over there?

I was just thinking. They were filming a documentary at Qui Nhon. A young, handsome fellow was in charge of the filming, and we became close. He went on several missions with us. When things would settle down, we would have dinner, and he would talk to us. We would have shows come over— "The Bob Hope Show," "The Eddie Fisher Show"—and there were lots of celebrities.

He said to us one day, "Why don't you guys say 'hi' to these people and welcome them?"

"We don't know them. You hate to go up and say 'hi' to Eddie Fisher. You feel like you're interfering with his life."

"They are the loneliest people in the world. They come over to put on a show for you, you watch the show, you're timid and shy. You know, they would really like to have a friend."

"Okay. We'll take you up on that."

So the next show that came over was the Grand Ole Opry from Tennessee. When the show was over, we agreed we'd go down to the club where everyone went for dinner, and we'd meet them and say "hi." We went around to all the stars there and, you know, they were just as pleased as punch. We realized that some of these people whom you think are untouchable are really moved because very few people come up and really become friendly with them.

Is there anything you can't stand to think about—anything you've had to suppress?

I've seen only a few people in the air force who probably had too much combat. But I think of the guys in the army. It was a dirty, nasty war for those guys on the ground. I don't think it was anything like that in the air force. It wasn't the swamps, the mud, killing people—it was quite clean, quite decisive, for most people. I think there was quite a difference in that respect.

We had a fellow pilot who had a startling experience. When you are flying with support on the ground, there were these things—we called them "skrags"—pieces of trees that stuck above the green timber, dead dry wood. Sometimes they'd stick up fifteen feet above the green trees. They told us about these, but you know you try to forget about it.

One day I was flying a mission on a Vietcong concentration. I was flying two hundred feet over the green trees over the river and dropped down right next to the Vietcong barracks. I dropped the bombs and flew out, and it was a tight place to get in. I was really concentrating on the troops ahead of me, and I didn't even see the skrags sticking up. All of a sudden they were in front of me. I pulled back on the stick and, at the same time, let a bomb go. Boy, it scared me; I almost hit it.

The air-controller said, "Did you drop it?" I said that I pulled back and dropped one. He said, "It didn't go off." About two miles and a few seconds later, it went off—way up in the mountain. I'd tossed this bomb way over after I pulled up. He said, "You'd better get your act together." And by then my heart was beating up in my throat. I'd almost hit that skrag.

We had a few who hit those skrags. A 104 pilot, who preceded me by one month, hit one of those strags and tore the bottom out of his airplane, crashed and was killed. He didn't make it. We had a pilot who hit one of them and tore the plane up. There were pieces of tree in his wing. He got the plane back to Plei Ku, but he was uncomfortable flying after that. It really scared him. He came so close to buying the farm; I thought they should really have sent him home. When he went on a mission and went in to hit a target, he would drop, but he didn't care if he hit the target or not. I think it bothered him. He'd fly the mission and sometimes miss the target. He let it go where he felt like it. He had just had enough.

But you held together all right over there?

I held together fine over there. I guess I thought the most important thing is my flying, and I felt I could handle anything we had to contend with. The only thing that would bother me was if maintenance was doing a sloppy job on the airplanes, and they weren't hanging together. But, in all, the maintenance was great. They brought my airplane back, did you know?

Is it at the Wright-Patterson Museum?

Yes. I was back there about two or three months ago. You know, they filmed a documentary out of Norton, and it brought back a lot of memories. They had a whole filming team to run it; it was great.

When I flew the airplane, it had been damaged of course. We brought it back to Plei Ku and reconfigured it just as we normally would, and it went back into combat. Somebody was flying it around Qui Nhon and got hit. He was trying to make it; it was debatable whether he would have to bail out or whether he could glide along to make the runway. So he kept his gear up, kept his flaps up, and did all the gliding he could, and he made the runway.

Coming in, he bellied it and it caught on fire and it was burned quite badly. They put out the fire, but it sat there for awhile, till the guys that worked with us over at Plei Ku wanted to rebuild it. They had one of the Douglas tech reps come over to look at the airplane, and he said it was a Class Twenty-Six. That meant it wasn't economical to rebuild, but the guys still wanted to rebuild it. The Plei Ku guys offered to rebuild it on their own time, just as a kind of war memorial. So they reskinned it and put a new engine in it and fixed it up in really fine shape. Then before they flew it very much, they put it on an aircraft carrier and took it home.

In the meantime, when I came home, we went to Washington for the presentation and went to New York City and received the gold medal from Mayor Lindsay from the City of New York. We had dinner one night at the New York Athletic Club, a pretty swanky club, and General McConnell was there, the Chief of Staff, and somebody from the Pentagon. Eric Sevareid, the war correspondent, was there, having dinner with us, and I asked General McConnell where the airplane was. He said it was still in combat, and they couldn't bring it home because it was needed very badly. That's the last I heard of it.

Just a couple of weeks later, I heard someone mention to General McConnell that they had decided to bring the airplane home. So that's what they did. They put it on a carrier and sent it to Miramar Naval Air Station, in California. Then, Jump Meyers went out and flew the airplane back to Hurlburt Field, Florida, for just a short time, and then to Wright-Patterson.

What did you think when you saw the old baby again?

That was real nostalgia. There was an open house when they first got the airplane, but I couldn't make it, I had commitments. So they decided to postpone the welcoming ceremony until I could get there. I made arrangements to go there later for an open house, and there were a lot of people there.

460

The fellow who did the work at Wright-Patterson to restore it to extra good shape by polishing it, was a very quiet man and had been there for years and years at the museum. He said, "What do you think of the airplane?"

"It looks quite nice—the best I have ever seen it!"

"Why don't you jump up and try it? Look it over."

So I climbed up on the wing and looked in it.

He said, "You can climb into the cockpit—if you want." I used a mechanical device on the canopy to slide it back, as they never did work electrically.

"What are you doing?"

"I'm going to open the canopy."

"Use the switch."

So I turned the switch and it pulled back. I'd never seen it work in its life! It pulled back, and I climbed in, and the radios worked and the electronics were all intact. They had left the same equipment in it. Just to think, about three months ago, I sat in it and looked around and thought, "Here's the airplane I flew a few years ago."

Any tears in your eyes?

A little bit—a little bit emotional. You sit there and think about the switches and the gauges and the gunsight, the radios and the control panel. The sight of the airplane—you know—it was quite a feeling. You look out the window, and there is the gun you actually shot with . . . It sure did. As you get older, it seems you get emotional a lot easier than when you were younger. I'll be talking sometime and I'll get a frog in my throat. It takes a little while to clear it, thinking of things that happened to people there.

Dale Storr

DALE STORR

Down In The Gulf War

D ale Storr is a member of a flying family. His father was a B-52 pilot; his brother Dave a Marine flier; and his youngest brother Doug is a C-17 pilot. But it was the excitement of a family cross-country flight from California to Iowa that really captured the imagination of young Dale and may have set him on his career flying course.

After graduating from Washington State University in ROTC, Dale began pilot training at Vance Air Force Base, where he graduated in January of 1985. He stayed on as an instructor pilot in T-38s and later went down to Randolph for another five months of training, then back to Vance for a three-year tour as an instructor pilot. He was assigned to the A-10, and after stints at Holloman and Davis-Monthan, he went to England air force base in Louisiana.

During the war in the Gulf, Dale flew eighteen missions before being shot down, captured by the Iraqis, and held as a POW. Storr is tall, probably over 6'4". He sits edgewise by the short round oak table, and in a direct and analytical way, relates his amazing story. His voice, normally flat, peaks remarkably at the point in the interview when he tells the story about the man who straightened his nose, and later on when he tells about the joyous reunion with his colleagues. Dale now flies for the Air National Guard, and when we spoke, he had just returned from Bosnia.

What did you think when the Iraqi conflict arose?

I didn't think much about it. On the second of August I heard about it on the news. "Oh, those guys are always fighting over there," I thought. "Who knows what it's going to turn out to be." In fact, I didn't even know we were deploying until one day when I was waterskiing on a lake down in Louisiana. One of the sheriffs said, "Hey, you guys might want to get back! There's some trouble brewing." When we got back, they started hanging tanks on airplanes. I still didn't know when we were going to go, but they said we were going as a squadron and that we were just waiting on tanker support. On the 26 or 27 of August, we finally deployed. We went from England Air Force Base to Myrtle Beach Air Force Base with twenty-four airplanes, then to Morone, Spain, a 13.7-hour flight. A long flight. We arrived in the afternoon and spent the whole night there, and the next day left in the middle of the night, and got to King Faud base the next day.

How long did it take for you to get into the hot and heavy stuff?

As soon as we landed, they dropped the external tanks and travel pods and gassed the airplanes and put them basically on alert. It was pretty tense when we first arrived. We didn't know what Hussein was planning on doing. He had a whole bunch of forces amassed, north of southern Kuwait. We were a little nervous, what with no army support and no tanks on the ground. It took about a month before we finally settled down and started flying some serious training exercises. Every now and then, tensions would heighten over there and we'd have an exercise. I remember two exercises: Imminent Thunder One and Imminent Thunder Two. These were interesting because they almost duplicated what we did in the war.

Is that just good strategic planning?

I thought the whole war was unusual, in that things went exactly like the training. It was a pretty complex plan that we used, getting airborne, checking in with all the guys on the ground, the deconfliction. Deconfliction involves finding out what everybody else is doing flying through your airspace. We had a lot of people flying out there—F-15s; F-16s; tankers; other A-10s, among others. We used the kind of "big-boy concept" which means that you are supposed to be there, and we would tell people we were there.

On the first day of the Gulf War, it all seemed like such a complex plan, and also we had people getting hit and taking fire. I thought things were going to go to hell in a handbasket, but things worked out exactly like they planned. I flew the day prior to the day the war started, and I flew the next day, and except for about three times due to radio traffic, I flew just as planned.

What was different, or surprised you, from what you had prepared for in the exercises?

There were all kinds of little things that were different, such as when you go up there with training ordnances. For example, if you hang a BDU-33, a small training bomb, it's not going to slow your airplane down significantly, and you're not going to use a lot of extra gas getting home. On the other hand, on my very first sortie, we headed north, just as we had planned in Thunder, where we hit some targets. What was different during the war was that the target was a little farther north than we were used to flying, and so we burned a little extra gas. My wingman went to drop his, but instead he "hung" three bombs. That's a lot of extra weight when you're already low on gas. We're right at bingo fuel, but he's now burning extra gas, he's heavier, and he's got these big cans hanging underneath his airplane, and they're live. The cans didn't release because you've got these little cartridges, like shotgun shells, that fire and spread the hooks to release the bombs. What happened here was the carts fired, but the little hooks got jammed and didn't release right, and the bomb didn't fall off. A lot of times, though, a switch doesn't get thrown, and that bomb hanging there is just as safe as could be. But you don't know that. We got back to King Khalid Military City (KKMC), and my wingman is a bit low on gas. At the time, we find that there are several of us with hung ordnance. As a result, the guys with hung ordnance are flying, letting the others land. If you're going to have a guy down there with a live bomb, and that bomb comes off the wing, he can shut down the runway for a long time. That's one of the little nuances we didn't plan for in Imminent Thunder. Of course, I wasn't one of the planners; I was just one of the little worker bees, but when I went back to KKMC and saw airplanes stacked up on top of each other, I thought, "Oh, we didn't practice this!"

We finally got on the ground, and my wingman's bomb was just as safe as all the others. They finally fixed him up, and we got airborne again. Then, on my second sortie of the day, my radio went out. In fact, my intercom panel, where all the radios went through, failed, so I went ahead and went on to the target. Because of the lack of radio communications, I didn't know I had missiles being fired at me; I didn't hear anybody call them out. I was just fat, dumb, and happy, trying to get a Maverick missile of mine to hit. I finally pulled off, and because the problem was intermittent, I heard all these voices screaming and yelling at me, telling me to look out. It turned out my wingman was a little freaked out when we got back.

Talk about some of the toughest missions. Obviously, the toughest had to be the one where you got shot down.

Some were more frustrating than others. Some were harder to find targets. For some we took a lot more fire than the day I was shot down. There was one sortie where we were trying to get some self-propelled artillery in northern Kuwait and saw some really big stuff shooting at us—a lot bigger than S-60, which was 57 millimeters. In that flight we were close enough so we could see big orange explosions, then a big, black smoke ball. There was some big stuff coming up at us, but we were able to avoid it after we saw it.

It seems to me there were some pretty amazing flying skills over there.

There were. I'm not saying I was part of it. But I did probably spread more bomblets over Kuwait than anyone else. I was pretty good with the gun, and with the Maverick. I liked using those. Also, I could drop those Mark-82 slicks pretty well. They were just gravity, 500-pound bombs. Finally, the CBU-87 was a good weapon. It was an expensive weapon, designed more for the F-16 than for the A-10. It's got little bomblets on it and has a warhead that will go right through armour. If it hit a light vehicle, it would go right through and go off in an incendiary mode. However, if it hits something soft like the ground, it will go off in an anti-personnel mode and destroy troops out in the open. It was a pretty effective weapon. I wish we had had a lot more of them. I could hit targets pretty well with it. It was a pretty accurate weapon.

What about flying conditions? Everything looks pretty much the same over there in the Mideast.

I don't know if I was ever confused, but it was difficult picking out targets. I started using binoculars early in Desert Storm, because as high as we were flying, you couldn't pick out a tank on the ground. I liked going high because it saved gas and it gave you more time to orbit. The higher you are, the harder it is to pick a target. But it is hard to use binoculars in an airplane because of the vibration, which causes you to lose your visual acuity. What I'd do was put my wingman on the tail to cover me, and I'd get the airplane banked up and trimmed up, and I would lean forward in the seat, trying to isolate myself from the airplane as much as I could. Then I could look at the ground for targets. That's the only way I found really viable targets, with my binoculars, because it was fairly easy to hide a tank in the desert with camouflage. I was able to distinguish between tanks and APCs and trucks and decoys. In fact, I found some SCUD decoys one day with my binoculars. They were just big plywood panels put up, and even though they were just two-dimensional, they looked like SCUDs. I almost put a Maverick into them, thinking they were. I called them in as decoys.

What do you think of the A-10? It's an awful-looking plane, isn't it?

It's awful ugly, but it's a good airplane. It's underpowered, but I think any fighter pilot will tell you his airplane is underpowered This one really could use a lot more thrust. It's a good jet, real strong for what it's designed to do. It did a hell of a job in the Gulf War. I remember, though, in training how we were told how tough the A-10 was, and how it was designed to take all these hits. I think I was the first A-10 pilot to take any battle damage, and I remember being in prison thinking, "Oh, God, these guys told me this airplane was so tough, so strong it would get you back. Just one shot took me down."

Tell me about that incident.

It was the second of February, and I was leading a two-ship sortie. Eric Miller and I had already flown one sortie up north. We were working with a forward air controller (FAC) and had hit some targets. But we bingoed out before we hit the last target. I think it was a truck park. So we went back to KKMC, where we were sitting alert, and got scrambled to go work over in the marshes. We got airborne, but we could never find the FAC we were looking for to join up with. He was flying in an F-18D, two-seater, fast FAC. Finally, they figured he had scrubbed the sortie or something. He just never showed up. When I tired of waiting for him, I talked to "bookshelf," and they told me they had a target for me. It was supposed to be a SCUD that was in southern Kuwait. I went down there, though I'd never heard of a SCUD in southern Kuwait. I didn't think they had any there. I left Eric up high, and I went down low.

I had my binoculars out. It was neat seeing all the bunkers where the F-16s and the Stealths had come in and just surgically killed every single airplane that was down there. That was impressive to me, but I certainly couldn't find any SCUDS down there. I looked and looked and looked, but I couldn't find anything. Then a whole bunch of Triple-A started coming up. Even though we had taken out all the airplanes, all the Triple-A was still there. I got out of there just as fast as I could and told Eric to start heading west. I called back and said I couldn't find any SCUD. They said, "Roger," and I said, "We still have a little gas here," that there were still some targets up to the north that we didn't finish. We went up there with our bombs.

You volunteered, basically?

Yes, but I had gas. I wasn't going to haul the stuff back to KKMC for no reason. There were some bunkers we were supposed to hit, and though they were low priority, the bombs we had were good for them. We didn't have any tail fuses for our bombs. All we had were Mark 113 radar fuses, which weren't ideal. The target wasn't really bunkers, but buildings with steel roofs. Using a 113 in that situation isn't going to do much damage. However, I was hoping there were troops inside, or something, and the frag-effect would go through the ceiling. It was all we had for ordnance, so we rippled our bombs on those buildings. After that, because I knew where that truck park was, we headed up there. We had just enough gas and we had full-loaded guns.

I went up on my first pass and shot at about 10,000 feet. I pulled off and Eric called, "Your bullets went long. It's a miss—your bullets went long." I then pulled up and did a penalty lap north of the target area. A penalty lap, as you probably know, is used to get the altitude back before you go back again. I went off to the west and attacked from the east this time. I squeezed off a long round this time—maybe 450 rounds—because I was pretty frustrated missing the first one. As I pulled off, I could hear Eric say, "Good hits, good secondaries." He could see some of the trucks starting to explode. I felt pretty good about that, and I remember looking at my altimeter, passing through at about 9000 or 10,000 feet. I was in a left-handed turn looking for Eric, trying to clear him in. I wanted to get a visual on him before I cleared him in. Suddenly, something hit the airplane. I never saw it—he never saw it—but it hit my plane. It felt like a 50,000-pound sledgehammer just came up and hit the bottom of the aircraft. Strangely, the airplane didn't explode and didn't go out of control. The first thing I did was to look inside, then I looked at the engines—they were both spinning. Then I looked at my hydraulics. I still had good hydraulics, so I thought in my mind I could still fly the airplane. The next thing I did was to call Eric. "Hey, Bolt," I said, "I'm hit bad." I didn't hear anything back from him, not right away at any rate. I was in a climb, a left-hand turn, looking for Eric, when I realized the airplane was in a slow roll to the right. I started trying to correct the airplane, looking over my shoulder trying to find Eric. I started slamming the stick to the left, still looking over my shoulder for Eric. I saw that the aileron out there wasn't moving, and it should have been. It should have been going up and down. That's when I realized I was in a lot of trouble.

The airplane started rolling over on its back. I started getting the negative-G thing, where I was getting pinned up against the straps. That's when I heard Eric say, "Storrman, recover, recover, recover." He thought that I didn't realize that I had been hit, and that I was going after the truck park again, or another target. He hadn't heard my radio call because my antenna had been blown off. The FM antenna is right under the airplane, right under the ejection seat. I was trying to recover, but I was up in the straps, and my airplane was coming back around. That's when I thought of manual reversion, a system on the A-10 that takes all the hydraulics off the flight controls and reverts to a system that flies the airplane with control wires. I finally switched it to the other system, but when you do, you have to wait, to give the tabs in the ailerons time to shift over. Wait. Wait. It still wasn't happening. The airplane by this time is coming back around. Every time it went over on its back, the nose dropped. By now we were getting pretty steep. That was when I heard Eric say, "Storrman, eject, eject, eject!"

Eric was watching the airplane in this big spiral going to the ground. I thought, "No, I'm not ejecting now, not yet, it's too early." I was only five miles from the border, and I wanted to get back with the friendlies. In your mind you're going through all this training you've been given. "Okay, let's try the boldface, which is "Throttles-Idle, Controls-Neutral." "Okay, give the nose a chance to come back around." "Let the plane get some airspeed." So I tried that, still nothing worked. Then I tried isolating the speed brakes and the flaps. "Maybe the flaps have gone out." Now I'm upside down again, trying to get myself back into the seat, trying to get those darn switches activated. I don't know how many times I've been over on my back. The airplane's still not flying. The stick is just limp. So I'm checking the switches with that classic channelized attention. I'm not even looking outside nor am I looking at my altimeter. For some lucky reason, I just happen to look up and I see the ground ahead of me. At that point I figured it was too late. I'd waited too long; I was going to die. Even if I ejected now, I had the feeling that I'd waited too long.

I just got real lucky and got into a good seat position that I'd been practicing since I was a student in the T-38. I grabbed the hand grips on the side of the A-10, and I remember the canopy coming off almost immediately. Then there was a little bit of delay. I remember the white smoke coming up between my legs. Then I felt the seat push against me—a real smooth acceleration—not anything like I thought it was going to be. The next thing I remember hearing was the parachute opening behind me, the ruffling noise. When I finally got my head back enough to look at the chute, I just saw it pop open, and I couldn't believe it. I couldn't believe I had lived through this. It was the most beautiful thing I had ever seen.

Then the next thing that happened was I saw this huge explosion beneath me. I looked down, and it was the airplane. It has just blown up beneath me, and there's a huge fireball coming up. "Jeez, I can't believe this. I just survived the ejection, and now I'm going to die in the fireball." It was either going to burn me up, or it was going to melt my parachute. So I started climbing up on the risers, the way they teach you, trying to get the chute drifting some. I was just climbing that thing as fast as I could. I'm sure it worked some, but not enough. Anyway, the last thing I remember was looking down there and seeing this smoke just about to come up and get me. I thought, "Oh, God," and I closed my eyes. It got really, really hot, but it didn't burn me. I was wearing all my gear, and I had everything covered up. Then in a few seconds, I felt this big rush of cold air come by me, and I opened my eyes. I could see the ground; I'd passed right through the fireball.

I let go of the risers and started doing the things they teach you to go through: canopy, mask, seat-kit, etc. "The little life raft, I'm not going to need that." I punched it right off. You could hear the bullets from the [plane's] guns going off. It sounded like every gun in Kuwait was shooting at me. I thought they were going to get me. So anyway, I come drifting down, and the next thing I see is a truck coming from the truck park. I was pretty bummed because I knew these guys were going to be pretty mad! I started looking for a place to land, but it was all real rocky desert-type terrain. I started thinking, "Oh, God, I'm going to break my legs," but there was nothing I could do because I was drifting backwards in my parachute. In other words, I couldn't see what was behind me. Again, I got real lucky, and I landed in a sand dune, the only sand dune I could see around me. I did the standard feet back, butt up PLF [parachute landing fall] into the sand dune and didn't get a scratch.

I undid my chute, checked to see if I had any broken bones. I got my hit-and-run bag and tried to hide. The first thing you do is go into escape-and-evasion mode, but these guys saw me coming down. Other than behind an A-10 wreck, there weren't a lot of places to hide, so I tried to hide behind the sand dune. I got out my radio in my PRC-90 from my survival vest and tried to get Eric to get some bullets on these guys. When I couldn't make contact with him, I shifted frequencies. "Hey, Bolt, Storrman. I need some bullets on this truck and I need them right now." I couldn't see Eric, but I could see the truck coming to get me. I tried calling him two or three times and then, finally, the truck stopped and six or seven guys jumped out. They sent one guy out there. I was on my knees trying to hide. I said, "Hey, Eric, it's too late." I threw the radio on the ground and put my hands up. I found out after the war that the radio worked, but they told me that it was a yellow radio—a training radio. Training radios are set at different frequencies. I'd just done a practice in Louisiana, and someone had put a yellow radio in my survival vest.

The Iraqis came right to me and slapped me around with the butts of their AK-47s. After that they asked me if I had any food. These were conscripts that were forced into the army—a real ragtag bunch. I had a roll of lifesavers in my pencil pocket, and they took those. They devoured them.

We were sitting about 300 feet from my burning plane, which still had a lot of 30-millimeter ammunition in there. Suddenly, it started cooking off, but these guys didn't seem to care, especially with all the other noises of war surrounding us. I knew I had one Maverick left, and then it cooked off. It just arched up into the air with its launcher still on its back. Luckily for us, it just arched away, but that got the Iraqis' attention. They started screaming and yelling when they saw that, so we jumped in the truck and headed away.

Didn't they put you in a place where fellow Americans were?

First, they did a couple of interrogations on the way to the prison. They were goons and didn't know how to interrogate. They finally got to the spot that I called the bunker. Everybody who got interrogated went through there. This place was pretty bad. During the three days that I was there, they broke my nose and my right ear drum. They dislocated my shoulder, messed up my left knee pretty good. That was just in a couple of days. Still, nothing like what our guys captured in Vietnam went through. I don't know why they were doing it. Sometimes they just beat you after the interrogation was over. Finally, I just got so mad. These guys at this point knew all the resistance techniques I'd been taught, so that was a little frustrating. The techniques are classified, so I can't talk about them, or how I used them and how they recognized them. But they did recognize them pretty quickly. They were good. After that, we went to a prison—an old French prison—that we later called the Biltmore. The place was really strong and sturdy and was like a big dorm. The building was rectangular with a central hallway running outside of it. It had solid steel doors so you could never see outside your room. There was a toilet that didn't work in one corner, and the paint was all chipped and busted up. No running water in the place. The light worked every now and then. We had a tile floor. There was no running water, but there was a little place where we could wash our feet. A rectangular window ran across the very top of the ceiling, but it had frosted glass and wooden slats preventing direct sunlight from ever coming in, so I never got any direct sunlight. I could, however, tell when it was day and when it was night. The guys interrogated me every other day there. These interrogations were a lot easier, though they did hit you with these little whips. These interrogations were pretty much a joke until they found out I was lying to them, that everything I said to them was a lie.

What happened to catch you?

They shot down a couple of other A-10 guys later in the war, and their stories didn't match up with mine.

Do you remember a lie you told them?

Oh, yeah, I told them I was from Dhahran. I told them my commander's name was Col. Elwood P. Hinman. I believe he's a general now. I used everything from Vance Air Force Base in my lies. I just based everything on Vance. I lied about the airport's layout.

Do you remember the exact time they came in the door, knowing you had lied?

I felt something was up because this guy started out by saying, "Oh, mister, I feel so sorry for you." I thought, "Why? Because I'm starving in here—I'm hungrier than hell." I looked over at him, and he starts going on and on. "Well, you know the story you've been telling."

"Yeah, well, so what?"

"Well, we know it's not right. Do you know Colonel Sandy Sharp?"

I didn't go along. "Mister, your Commander, Colonel Sandy Sharp."

I think, "Oh, God, they know. They know I'm lying."

When someone catches you in a flat-out lie, you wonder what can you do. From then on, they beat me up pretty well. They threatened to kill me. They told me I was to be executed on the twenty-third. I found out after the war I was in the regional intelligence headquarters for the Baa'th Party, which is Saddam Hussein's party.

That place was targeted.

Yes, that was a fairly strategic target. The Iraqis decided to use us as shields. That couldn't work, though, because if the US was ever going to let that deter us, they would just start using more and more people for hostages. On the twenty-fourth, the US tried to put their bombs on target there. As far as I can tell, the first bomb went stupid, or the pilot couldn't put it where he wanted, or for some reason had it veer off intentionally. The second bomb hit in the far wing from me; the third hit closer, right next to my room. It went through the cell next to me, and they were all blown up in the basement. The bombs were of the BLU-2000 penetrator variety. Then, a fourth bomb hit farther down on our wing. After this I got more frightened than I had ever gotten— even when I had had pistols to my head.

When the first bomb hit, I had heard the planes fly over. That was no big deal—I'd heard that a lot. Then when the bomb hit, the one that missed, it hit close enough to knock some plaster off the ceiling and the walls. The plaster came down and busted my head open. I just lay down and curled up in a ball, and thought, "God, they've targeted this place. We're goners." Then the second bomb hit. Now when that second one hit, it sucked all the air out of the basement. In addition, it took out this big grate and it landed on me— it landed on my calves and my chest. It was a big, heavy thing and bruised me up pretty good. When the third bomb hit, a big portion of my walls started crumbling down. It was the middle of the night, pitch black. As it happened, the steel grate would take all the punishment from the rocks, chunks of concrete and falling debris. About then, I started smelling smoke and figured we were going to burn to death. I struggled, and it took me about a half hour to crawl out from all that mess. I heard a bunch of screaming voices. It was the first time I knew there were other Americans in there. I couldn't believe it. I was just higher than a kite. I heard Larry Slate, backseat F-14 guy, across the hall. We started exchanging names and airplanes.

There was the front-seater from a F-14, Devin Jones. Larry was Devin's RIO (backseater) and had been rescued, but hadn't heard about Devin. Before long, a guy down the hall starts yelling, "Hey, Storr, is that you?" "Yeah," I answer. "Do you fly A-10s out of King Faud?" "Good to hear you're alive," he says. "Everybody back at King Faud thinks you're dead. In fact, I went to your memorial service." The voice turned out to be Sly Fox, another A-10 guy. It seems Sly had just been shot down and still thought I was dead. I said, "Well, I'm still alive. I'm not dead yet."

Who else did you hear?

We heard this voice yelling, "Are there Americans here?" And we start yelling, "Yeah, yeah." The voice who spoke says, "I'm Bob Simon, CBS News." Larry says, "Hey, this is great. Tell the air force to stop bombing this place. There are American prisoners here." And they say, "Tell the air force Dale Storr is alive—they think he's dead. He's here in Baghdad." Bob Simon is saying, "Okay, Okay, I'll see what I can do."

About an hour later, a guard comes up and starts rattling our cages and clanging keys. The place was just a mess. So we're on the second floor, going down stairs that are half blown apart. It's night; my leg's bleeding and busted up.

I was having a hard time walking. We went through six inches of water in the basement. You could smell kerosene all over the place, because they had had a kerosene-powered generator down there, but the tank had apparently ruptured. They loaded us up in a big Greyhound bus that didn't have any seats in it and made us sit there on the floor with our heads between our knees. I ended up sitting next to Bob Simon, but I didn't know it at first because he had been in there for awhile and had a big old beard, scraggly clothes. I was in my flight suit. So I sit down next to Simon and hear the guards saying, "Don't talk. Don't talk." They're screaming and yelling at us.

The first thing you do is try to find out if this guy next to you is friendly or not. I nudged him, and he nudged back. I nudged him again. "Dale Storr, American," I said. He comes back, "Bob Simon, CBS News." Later, Simon got out a few days before we did, when the war was over, and passed a note saying, "Dale Storr is alive in Baghdad." And that's when the military finally called my mom and said, "You might want to watch CNN when they release the prisoners, because your son might be one of them." They had listed me as nothing but MIA a couple of times.

As I look back on it, the toughest time was in the bunker. I was sick, and then after all the beatings, I couldn't keep any food down. When they dislocated my shoulder, that's when it really started getting bad. I didn't mind having my nose broken, although that bled a lot. One time, though, they let me go to the bathroom and there happened to be a medic there. He did some work on my nose and straightened it out for me. I thought that was pretty nice.

An American medic?

No, an Iraqi medic. It was kind of funny. The medic said, "Oh, mister, who did this to you? Who did this to you?" I said, "You guys did it to me." "No mister, no Iraqis do that." Blood all over my face. "Yeah, right!" But he straightened out my nose.

When you got released, I remember seeing you pictured on TV, and you showed some real emotion.

Yeah, we had just gotten off the airplane. We were all in our yellow pajamas. Everybody was pretty excited. I remember us taxiing in; I figured we were going to land in Riyadh, which was a short drive to Dhahran, which was my base. At the time the Red Cross didn't know what the Iraqis were going to do. In fact, the Red Cross didn't even release our names till we were turned over to US officials.

I had talked to Colonel Eberly and I said, "There's no American flag out there." We had all talked about getting out there and saluting the American flag, and then walking down the stairs and shaking hands. So I'm watching, watching. The Saudis want to make it very political. We had some Saudi prisoners, so they went out of the plane first. (They weren't military—they were firemen.) Next, a Kuwaiti prisoner went off. Then it was followed by rank and order of the rest. We had kind of dropped the plan to salute. Then I saw a C-141 over there. I knew they had a flag over there on the tail, so figured we could salute that. If you look at the footage, you'll see when we step off the airplane, we turn halfway to the right—sort of jerk to the right—salute the flag, then face forward and go down the stairs. That's where we saw "Stormin' Norman." Schwarzkopf shook hands with us. I'm just thinking that we're going to jump on the 141, and I'm going to meet my buddies and go home. I'm just walking along, and I heard someone yelling, "Storrman, Storrman." It's my best friend, Roger Clark. I had known him for four years. We had both flown the A-10 and were roommates before the war. I recognized his voice instantly, and I just went for him. I just lost it emotionally right there. That's when I realized I was really back. So I ran up to him and just started high-fiving. I couldn't believe it. I just went nuts. I just couldn't believe it when I heard his voice. We just didn't stop talking for the next twelve hours.

From there we went to a hospital ship in Bahrain, spent three days there, then back to Andrews and spent the week in the hospital there. We had picked up a lot of bugs over there, and they put some weight back on us. I went home for two weeks. Then I went down to Louisiana to watch my squadron come home. I went home for another three weeks. We had to take thirty days of mandatory convalescent leave. We could have taken as much as we wanted, but I had to get back flying.

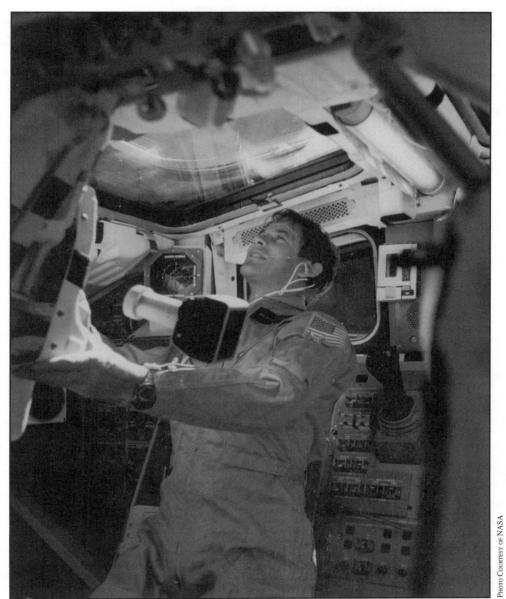

Dr. Joseph Allen

DR. JOSEPH ALLEN

The Scientist In Space

D r. Joseph Allen's older brother helped introduce him to the flying experience. I asked if the two had a rivalry. "No,'" he said, "he is a good physician, a flying doctor. He knows how to fly small airplanes. I know how to fly high-performance ones. He laughs at me when I fly his, because I'm not as good as he is."

Despite a genuine modesty, Dr. Allen has accomplished plenty. For one thing he was selected from eleven thousand applicants for the rarefied atmosphere of astronaut. That led to his becoming a high-performance airplane pilot with about three thousand flying hours. In the interview Dr. Allen talks about the almost coincidental path to NASA, when he finally was selected as a scientist-astronaut.

Dr. Allen went on his space missions as mission specialist, not as a pilot of the space missions. Yet, by all measures, Allen is a pilot, too—for not only has he piloted high-performance jet aircraft, as mentioned, but he has even traveled out in space with the self-propelled backpack (MMU), a kind of piloting that would remind most of a scene out of James Bond. He points out he could have flown as pilot or mission specialist, but opted to use his science background in space. During his eighteen years as an astronaut with NASA, he flew as a mission specialist aboard the space shuttle Discovery, on STS 51-A, from November 8-16, 1984. During that mission the crew deployed two satellites and managed to undertake the first space salvage attempt in history. This led to the retrieval of Palapa B-2 and Westar VI communications satellites. He also flew aboard Columbia on STS-5, the first fully operational flight of the Shuttle Transportation System. That flight marked the first time the program had deployed communications satellites from the orbiter's payload bay. In addition, Allen served as a support crew member for the first orbital flight test of the space shuttle and was the CAPCOM for the earth re-entry phase of the mission. Furthermore, he performed as mission controller (CAPCOM) for Apollo 15 and 17.

Winner of a Fullbright scholarship, Dr. Allen received the M.S. and Ph.D. degrees in Physics from Yale University, and his undergraduate degree from DePauw University. He is author of *Entering Space: An Astronaut's Odyssey* and has published widely in technical and research areas. Currently he serves as president and chief executive officer of Industries International, a technology-based company providing products, technical services, and unique research, test, and evaluation facilities in areas of advanced transportation systems, space, information systems, and simulation and training for industry and government.

When did this Indiana boy decide he wanted to be an astronaut?

I grew up in a small community in central Indiana. I was born right before the war and grew up in the war years. I liked machinery and made model airplanes. We were not the kind of people who had access to airplanes, but when I was thirteen, I took a dollar ride and thought it was pretty extraordinary. In those years there were no astronauts. In my book *Entering Space*, I explained that I wanted to be an explorer, then a race car driver, and then a cowboy. In fact, I was too timid to be an explorer, too timid to be a race car driver, and couldn't sing well enough to be a cowboy, so I guess I was lucky that the profession of astronaut was invented!

I liked science a lot and went off to college in the early fifties to study math and science. I was a college student when Sputnik was launched by the Russians. A great terror went through the hearts of the national leaders when that unique event happened. The communists had stolen our nuclear weapons secrets because they were not nearly so technically advanced to create such devices on their own, and with the launch of Sputnik they demonstrated that they had rocket power enough to put a satellite into earth orbit. Forget the satellite. They clearly had rocket power enough to launch nuclear weapons at us, across the oceans or over the poles. This realization caused a great tremor in our national psyche.

I remember being more intrigued by the satellite than frightened by it. Then I went on and became a Ph.D. in Physics. I was working in the Physics laboratory when the first seven astronauts were selected. By then I was studying cosmic ray physics and nuclear physics. I was intrigued by space physics because some of the problems of cosmic ray physics were explained by very simple experiments that went into the first satellites. For example, in the Explorer (the first U.S. satellite), there were very simple physics experiments that consisted of some Geiger tubes, the old-fashioned radioactivity measuring tubes, invented in the thirties. Lo and behold, these Geiger tubes discovered that there were belts of radiation circling the earth, an important discovery about our solar system. Since I was a scientist working in that field, I was quite excited by that result. In the early space days, however, all astronauts were aviators by profession, not scientists.

Were you flying at that time?

My brother, who is a doctor of medicine, started to fly airplanes, and I was very intrigued by that. I joined a flying club.

That footage of you with orange juice in space has become sort of legendary.

Yes, I took still photographs of orange juice floating. I'm not quite sure why. I also took many feet of video. It turned out these video pictures were used for kids' programs on TV like "321 Contact" to show how astronauts have fun, as well as work in space. Some of the footage is just a howl. It's bizarre to see liquid floating free, and you control it by blowing on it. If you've seen the footage, you know it shimmers and shakes like weak Jell-O. You can cause it to tumble and break apart into globules. Touch a towel to it, and it instantly soaks into the towel. You can touch your tongue to it, and it immediately begins to run all over your face. Funny to watch. You can put a straw up there into the liquid, and then put your mouth around the straw and simply drink the liquid.

You launched the first satellite from the space shuttle.

Yes, I'm an astronaut who cut his teeth during the Apollo years. Thus when the shuttle came along, I was by then a senior astronaut with first choice as to which of the missions I would fly. I chose to be a mission specialist during the first operational flight and was the first mission specialist to go into orbit. Our job then was to carry the first cargo ever aboard the shuttle. (That was the first operational flight, the fifth flight of the space shuttle.) Then I had the good luck to go a second time and on this mission to salvage hardware from orbit and bring it home. That's actually not been done since.

You were in there with Apollo 13. What did you think when you saw the movie?

It was a great exercise in nostalgia for me. It took me right back to the actual experience, now twenty-five years ago. I was in Mission Control during that mission. It was a dangerous mission in the extreme, and there was no certainty that it would be possible to rescue the crew once the explosion in the oxygen tank had occurred. If the crew had run out of a single one of the many consumables aboard the crippled spacecraft before they splashed down in the ocean, they would not have survived.

During the Apollo 13 mission I mainly just stayed out from underfoot, because the "varsity" flight controllers were working the problem, and they made the right decisions.

What did you think about the movie?

I know Hollywood typically takes poetic license, but I saw very little liberty taken insofar as glossing over facts in the *Apollo 13* movie was concerned. They pretty much told the story as it happened. I know of only one thing that was exaggerated. To show trauma out in space, the moviemakers resort to showing a violently shaking spacecraft. When an explosion occurs, I'm sure it shakes, but later in the movie they cause it to shake when the movie depicts the firing of the trajectory correction burns. Such burns are not violent in any sense.

Let's talk about the missions you flew.

The missions I flew were the fifth and fourteenth missions of the space shuttle, and both were largely cargo handling missions.

What did you do during your astronaut years in the late 1960s?

My responsibility as a mission controller was to focus the whole repertoire of science that was to be integrated into the flight plan. I made sure that the flight crew members understood where the science objectives of the mission were and how all the instruments used to make science measurements were to be deployed and set up.

Example?

For example, there was a host of cosmic ray instruments, geo-physics instruments, and geological instruments aboard Apollo 15, and this equipment was needed to carry out the fifteen or twenty investigations that were assigned to the mission. Each investigation has its priorities, requiring time of crew members during the mission. Someone on the ground has to understand all the operational requirements of the mission; to understand how you fly the spacecraft; to understand how you get it from here to there, how you land it, and so on. That person must also understand all the requirements of the scientists; to integrate the operational flying requirements with the scientific requirements and make sure all the mission objectives fit together and are do-able.

That was my job during Apollo, to have an understanding of both fields of spacecraft operations and scientific goals.

How did you get to be a scientist on the space flights?

In the middle sixties, NASA was beginning to train astronauts for elements of the moon landing. Meanwhile, the bureaucracy figured it might be easier to train a scientist in aeronautics than it would be to train the aviators in science. NASA made a decision to try that. At that point they were even looking beyond the moon landing and had envisioned a time of several manned and orbiting space laboratories.

How did you learn about this?

In 1965, NASA sent out information to university laboratories and national laboratories with a request for any Ph.D.s to apply. For a host of reasons, the

Dr. Joe Allen in Space

main one of which was curiosity, I sent in an application. I didn't hear anything for one year. I figured that was just like the government: hurry up and then wait. In January of 1967, the three astronauts lost their lives in the tragic fire on the launch pad. I received a letter from NASA two days later. The letter said NASA had received my application and asked if I was still interested. Read in the context of the fire that had just happened, it was an inappropriate letter. But, of course, the letter had actually been sent out several days before the accident.

Were you spooked?

No, not really, but I thought it was quite bizarre. NASA officials whittled the list down from eleven thousand applicants to twenty-five finalists. Then they took us individually for a T-38 ride for an hour and a half.

What did you think?

That was the first experience I'd ever had with an airplane like that, which could knock your socks off.

During the interview phase, was there anything you said that made you think you really nailed it?

I have no idea (*laughs*). They may have made a typographical error for all I know! Going in, my feeling was that I was a very good research scientist; I was in good health; my age was correct; but I still didn't have my heart set on becoming an astronaut. That probably made it a lot easier for me to get through a tough, aggressive interview. It wasn't that I didn't care, but it's just that I had a good profession already. Since then I have participated in many of the astronaut selection committees, and I will tell you that those who apply today are extraordinarily well prepared. In contrast to me, many of them have always wanted to be astronauts.

Isn't there a schism in the astronaut ranks between those who fly and the research people?

In the early days of space flight, everybody was a pilot. That tradition carried all the way through Apollo with the exception of Jack Schmitt, the last person to step on the moon. Jack was a professional geologist. But when the Skylab flew in the seventies, two out of every three persons aboard it were scientists.

You actually did some flying though, while you were up with Discovery, with that backpack.

Yes, I flew the manual maneuvering unit (MMU). That's the little backpack that goes on the spacewalking astronaut. It's actually been flown only six times.

What did you feel like when you were out there in space?

Well, just about everything you can imagine and more. When you are in a space suit, and out there on a tether, it's spectacular enough. But when one flies the MMU, the minute you untether yourself, you can maneuver yourself from the mother ship, and you are, in every sense, out of the world. Technically, you are a satellite yourself. That is about as extraordinary as you can ever imagine.

Is it hard to fly the MMU?

The MMU is very well controlled and very well behaved, though flying it is not a lead-pipe cinch. It is complicated because you are maneuvering yourself in all three dimensions and in all three degrees of rotation, so you have to control your attitude—the way your eyes point—as well as your velocity in the up-down, aft-forward, and side-to-side directions. And you control the rate at which you change your pointing direction. There are lots of degrees of freedom and, unlike an airplane or a helicopter, your motion is undamped, that is to say, once you start a motion it never stops, unless you give equal and opposite control inputs, in order to effect stopping.

You have to be physically adroit, it seems.

It requires dexterity and concentration. They say you can fly the MMU, but you can't fly it and chew gum at the same time!

What was the most intriguing task aboard your missions?

I was involved in the salvage of the valuable satellite, the Westar. The most difficult aspect of this was that there were many, many steps one had to accomplish, end to end in a series, and if any one of them failed, you were stuck.

Did any fail?

We did get to one that failed and were momentarily stuck. We were able, though, to devise a work-around for a failed clamp designed to grasp the top of the satellite. This was a specially-built tool, designed from the drawing of the satellite on the ground. Unfortunately, we found that the satellite was not the same as the drawing. No one had remembered that it had been modified, and those modifications meant the tool didn't work. We designed on the fly, so to speak, a work-around, which took a lot of physical stamina—an enormous amount.

How much?

We were out for over eight hours.

Eight hours is a long time. Not many astronauts have spent that much time out there at once, have they?

That's about the limit. During the Hubble telescope repair, several times people were out for a similar duration, but none for a longer period of time. After that experience we were pretty spent. To work in a space suit in itself is not unlike being a runner in a marathon. Not a lot of body strength is required, but it demands an amazing amount of patience, and you must meter energy, in a thoughtful way.

483

The Westar weighed half a ton. Talk about any dangerous moments or episodes or potential dangers to life or limb.

You are correct about the weight. Of course, in orbit it weighs nothing at all. Nonetheless, its mass (different than weight) is still over half a ton. Thus you would not want to get an arm or a leg, or your whole body for that matter, between the massive satellite and any part of the orbiter if the two objects were about to bang together.

You had a sign in space that you had some fun with?

Well, just a little bit of humor. We had a flight earlier that had taken the first satellites into orbit using the space shuttle and we called ourselves the "Ace Trucking Company" at that time. On my second flight where we recovered satellites, we renamed ourselves the "Ace Repo Company." The sign also said, "The sky's no limit."

Is there anything you saw in space that absolutely set you back on your heels?

You're looking at the earth, and you're traveling around the earth every ninety minutes at about eighteen thousand miles an hour, one sunrise and sunset every hour and a half. The grandeur of our home planet sets every space flier back on his heels.

What's your metaphor for this?

Well, there are so many metaphors for it, and they all seem very weak. What happens, though, is your appreciation of the planet goes from an intellectual level to an emotional level as well. The space experience hastens this. Before making a space journey, you may intellectually understand and appreciate a number of things about earth, yet not be particularly emotional about them. After making a space journey, I guarantee that you will care enormously about our home planet.

Colonel Stein

HENRY J. STEIN, JR.

Battalion Commander, Army

He is a man of principle—complex and tough in a lot of ways. He is plainspoken and surprising when he sometimes speaks in metaphors. If something has gone wrong, and he has done the right thing, he'll tell you he feels "like a fish in cool, clean, clear water." He is brutal with himself and others. Frank. Introspective. He has his reasons, and as he says, he doesn't back down. But before the interview I didn't know all this. I do know there's a complexity to him. Henry J. Stein, Jr. seems to be the type who must buy into something before he goes full-out in support of it.

He was commissioned second lieutenant, infantry, in 1953. From that experience, he learned to relate to the soldier on the ground, to understand the foibles of other people, and himself. Those lessons paid dividends when Stein decided to pursue flight and received his wings in 1956 (rated for fixed and rotary wing) and went on to an illustrious career in army aviation. He participated in Air Assault Tests, and upon activation of the First Cavalry Division (Airmobile), served as S-3, Fifteenth TC. He then became the deputy Commander, 1st Cav. Division Support Command, and commanding officer, 229th Assault Aviation Battalion. He spent three years in Vietnam with the First Cav. Division. He is surprising on such subjects as his decision to pursue additional tours of duty.

Retired in '79 with close to thirty-five years in the service, Stein logged over 1,200 combat flying hours. He was awarded the Legion of Merit, Meritorious Service Medal, Distinguished Flying Cross, Bronze Star, Air Medal, Commendation Medal, and Good Conduct Medal. A graduate of Gonzaga University, Stein lives in Spokane, Washington, where he raises English setter bird dogs, fishes, and hunts.

He stretches in his chair to relieve his back, which still troubles him some from an aircraft accident. We adjust the mike, and soon he's digging up a past that, until our interview, he hasn't had much interest in recalling.

You seem an unusual mixture of tough and tender.

Funny you should pick up on that. I came in the army as a buck private. I went through the ranks and I served with some bad NCOs and some bad officers. There wasn't anything I could do. As a young private I always thought utopia was at NCO headquarters. So I became a first sergeant and I found out that that wasn't utopia—only a stepping-stone to it. I decided the answer must be in getting a commission.

They sent me up to Chandler AFB (when the army and air force were one). I'd been running a stockade when I came back from Europe. I realized my personality as NCO was contrary to completing OCS because I'm right up front with people. As an NCO, if you step in front of me, we're going to talk about it. I'm not going to back away. At this time they didn't use courts-martial much. They had a boxing ring. I spent quite a bit of time in there. With the old experienced soldier, after you whomp him a few times—he may even beat you—he doesn't want to fight you again. That was prevalent in that time in the non-commissioned officer area.

I had a normal second lieutenancy. Then they started sending people to flight school. I realized that when they started sending officers to West Point, aviation was going some place. I had flown some in the Civilian Air Patrol, so I put in for flight school. I learned something. They used to have maneuvers out near Yakima. As part of going to flight school, I got to be company commander of the aggressor company—those are the people who are put out in the field to fight against the division. Our chief umpire was General Dean, who was captured in Korea. Boy, I wanted things to go right. I was the only first lieutenant commanding a company in the whole damn division. I guess one reason was that old Dean didn't really need a good company commander, he needed a good first sergeant. Maybe I hadn't made the transition from sergeant to officer yet.

I had a gentleman named Harry L. Heads, who had a big gold star on his tooth. Harry was a field man. When we were out in the field, you couldn't ask for a better field man than Harry. Yet, when you got around town, Harry would disappear on you. He'd go into bars. So we had this live ammunition exercise in Yakima. Before we did the exercise, I had to call to insure that all my people were present and accounted for. When we lined the whole company up, we realized that only one man was missing. You guessed it—Harry L. Heads. The first sergeant and I both knew that Harry was in town. I knew in that moment that if I said we couldn't go through with the live fire, because I had a man missing, that the live fire wouldn't have occurred. General Dean would wonder who was responsible. I knew it would be Henry J. Stein, Lieutenant, and that that would be the end of my career.

Sgt. Smith and I sat under the forward slope with field glasses and watched to see if we saw anybody moving out there, because if we did it would be Harry L. Heads. But there was nobody out there moving. We did the exercise without him and when it finished, I couldn't get to Yakima fast enough. The second bar we hit, there was Harry. We took him back to camp.

Part of the failure in command comes from excessive courts-martial. That means the disciplinary record will look bad for the division. You don't want that to happen. So I decided to turn Harry over to Sgt. Smith and I went to bed. The next morning I got up and got in my tent and Harry L. Heads was standing there with a big black eye. He wanted Sgt. Smith courtmartialed. He told me what happened, that Sgt. Smith had hit him. I said, "We can have a court-martial." Then I added, "But you know what I think of your performance and you know what I think of Sgt. Smith's performance. I'll get Sgt. Smith in here and we'll see what happened." When Sgt. Smith came in, he came to ramrod attention, right next to Harry. I said, "Did you hit Corporal Heads?" I expected, "No sir." But he said, "Damn right I did," and he popped him again and knocked him to the floor. I said, "You know, you're lucky I had my head turned. You're lucky I didn't see anything."

Time passed and I went off to flight school. Over the years I lost track of Sgt. Smith and on my second tour in Vietnam, I was Deputy Support Commander. One day I'm in there behind the desk when a Command Sergeant Major walked in and came to attention. He said, "I've been huntin' for you, Col. Stein." I looked at him. He said, "You don't know who I am, do you?" I tried to fake it. I said, "Oh yeah, I knew you in Mannheim, Germany." He smiled. When he smiled I saw that big gold star on this tooth and I said, "Harry L. Heads." We talked, and he wanted to know where Sgt. Smith was. Harry L. Heads had made Command Sergeant Major of the Army. As he explained, his record was squeaky clean. He had never had a court-martial or an Article 15. He told me, "If you had busted me, I wouldn't be a Command Sergeant Major today."

I think you asked about "tough and tender." Nowadays, when that happens, you have a court-martial and that sticks on a person's record for the rest of his life. Even when you change, you don't have a chance. A court-martial and you're out. That big "tough and tender" you asked about comes from an enlisted man's background. I know what it is to scrub a toilet; I know what it is to walk a guard post; I know what it is to try your best and see things go wrong, and you fail. When I was an enlisted man, if my sergeants hadn't done that for me, I wouldn't be here talking to you today.

I really don't think it's tough and tender. I think you see potential in people. My success comes from what you can make them be—what they don't expect to be. You don't destroy somebody. Anybody can destroy. It takes no intelligence to destroy. Most people go through life and never build anything—never create. They just destroy. If you can't replace something you destroy with something better, you've achieved nothing. The biggest achievement is to build something in a man—something that can grow. That's why I'm in scouting now, to do that same thing with kids.

I enlisted at the end of WWII and went to Ft. Lewis and then to Italy. I came back and went to ROTC. I consider myself a good sergeant, a good officer, and a good pilot. There wasn't much I didn't fly in the Army. I know how aircraft work. I understand the aircraft as a person. In terms of maintenance, I understand when an aircraft's sick. I understand when you pick up an aircraft and it talks to you and cries; then you put in down, fix it and take it out to test it and it purrs and it doesn't deceive you. It never lets you down. In some ways an aircraft is more faithful to you than people. My personal belief is that you can take good care of an aircraft; you can listen to it and fix it. People aren't that way.

Idrang: " You'd suddenly hear that wolk-wolk-wolk. . ."

Talk about flying in Vietnam—some procedures, some happenings.

The first call for breakfast was at 5 a.m. I didn't eat breakfast. Then I'd go to the flight line and test hydraulics, test our weapons, radio, and pre-flight kit. I never had a command aircraft. I'd just walk up to the aircraft and say, "I'm flying this today. You step out of the cockpit." The reason for this is that they can't sabotage your aircraft. We all monitored each other's frequencies. We all were aware of the yellow aircraft, your flight leaders. The yellow one is the aircraft who has five or more aircraft behind him. He might be flying troops in. When he gets hit and goes down, the command frequency picks him up.

In Vietnam you'd fly in for the night at about 4:30 or 5 p.m., and everybody found reason to be out on the pad. Maybe you all knew that one aircraft was missing, and then you'd suddenly hear that *wolk-wolk-wolk*, and it'd be your bird. When they'd land, pandemonium; everything came alive with laughter. In fact, you'd go to bed, but in the morning you knew you'd better pump some oxygen to make sure everything was all right inside you. If you weren't all right, you wouldn't fly. Nobody held it against you.

I was coming in one night and I looked out and saw a Huey coming in with a sling loaded. It landed at the Alpha Company's pad. I couldn't figure out what they were sling-loading in at night. A few days later I found out when I got invited down to Alpha Company for an elk dinner.

"An elk dinner?"

"Yes, we got an elk."

"Where in the hell'd you get an elk?"

"Up around Ty Nhin," which was not far from where Teddy Roosevelt used to hunt tigers.

Some guy had gone out and shot an Asian elk. They were planning a big feast. They had even invited Group Commander Col. James Hamlet. I talked to my major. I said, "You know if you were not such a good officer, I'd relieve you." I told him, "You're going to have to get word to Hamlet that the dinner is cancelled. I don't care what you do, but I'm telling you that if you don't straighten this mess out by tomorrow, even though you're a good company commander, you'll be gone." Well, he straightened the mess out. He gave the elk to an orphanage at Bien Hoa, and they enjoyed it very much. Next time I saw this major, he was instructing at Fort Leavenworth.

Later, when I was a comptroller at Ft. Monroe, Virginia, Gen. Hamlet was Inspector General for the Army. Jim was coming down for a visit and so we arranged that he stay with us. When he arrived, we had dove for dinner. He loves dove. That night in the course of conversation, over a glass of bourbon, I told him the story of the Asian elk. He said, "I wondered why that didn't materialize, Hank. It's not very often you get invited for an Asian elk dinner."

Unbeknownst to me, a general officer can prefer court-martial charges against you anytime, anywhere. No statute of limitations. So Jim Hamlet went back to D.C. and wrote up a court-martial: misappropriation of property, endangering lives. He went down to Ft. Lavenworth and confronted the major and told him that he could have him court martialed. Instead, after he'd scared the hell out of him, he decided not to court-martial him. He probably chewed him out the way that I should have.

The best commander I ever had was Col. Hamlet. A fine man. A black man. A good one! In fact, I remember sitting there when he first addressed us. I watched him talk and listened to him. After the meeting I went up to him and said, "You know, Col. Hamlet, I want to tell you something. I didn't know I was prejudiced until now. I just went through an experience where I watched a man talk that didn't have any color." I had had other black officers who were friends, but I always was aware of color. Suddenly, with Jim Hamlet, all I saw was a man I admired.

What's the difference between fixed-wing pilots and helicopter pilots?

It's the difference between a glider pilot learning to fly without an engine and one learning to fly with an engine. When I was in Italy, I thought I was one of the hottest fixed-wing pilots going, and I was. There I met Hans Steiner, who'd been Hans Rudel's wingman. Rudel was Hitler's pilot. He wasn't a war criminal; he was a pilot. I was trained to fly instruments; Steiner wasn't. We

VN rescue, 7th Cavalry, under fire, in the Idrang Valley.

made a trade. I gave him all my instrument manuals, and taught him instruments, and he taught me to fly a glider.

What's the logic to that?

The difference between life and death. A glider pilot never stalls. When one makes a mistake, the only way you can recover is to convert altitude into airspeed. You're never going to gain one without losing the other; you're always going to lose one or the other. You convert airspeed into altitude. You call it flying by the seat of your pants. When you're sitting in a glider and suddenly you feel the cushion move away from your posterior, you know you're in bad trouble. But when you're in a power aircraft, you just add throttle and convert power to airspeed to altitude.

I think the lessons I learned from Hans Steiner are the only reasons I'm here talking to you today, because I got used to flying a fixed-wing much like you'd fly a glider. I always knew the engine was there, but I always knew what I had to do if the engine quit. The tail on an aircraft is offset, as you know, to compensate for torque. As a consequence, when you lose an engine, torque starts to turn you in the direction of the torque. If you try to counter that, you lose fifty feet, so instead you should go with the turn. If I lose an engine, I've got a fifty-foot advantage over the person not glider-trained.

Tell me when this made a difference.

I've had thirteen engine failures. One of the most dramatic was when I took off from Mannheim, Germany. I had a runaway prop on an L-20 and I had to pull the power. We were probably at five hundred feet at the time. I heard the co-pilot come on and call an emergency. All I did then was complete the turn, come back in and made a regular wheeled landing on the runway. If I hadn't turned the direction the plane told me, I think I would have ended up on the Autobahn. We came in with nothing to spare. And you couldn't bail out or eject from that altitude.

Most helicopter pilots who are not fixed-wing trained will think nothing of hovering out of ground effect. They'll come to zero airspeed and sit there and hover. When you lose an engine with a helicopter, you immediately pop to the right and begin to drop. To come out of a stall with a helicopter, much like a fixed-wing, you have to drop your nose and trade altitude for airspeed, and then fly out of it. The helicopter pilot who's fixed-wing trained, you'll find, holds more airspeed than the average helicopter pilot trained only on helicopters.

I put in three tours in Vietnam. I found that in the First Cav. Division, we had about fifteen years' flying as an average in the First Cav., and in VN had about one to three years of flying. When you get out of flight school, you're as hot as can be. Then as you start to fly, you do away with what you've been taught. That's when most are apt to get killed, until you achieve five hundred hours of flying. After that, flying becomes reflex and experience. You change technique. You also select your flying partners very carefully. You realize a pilot's strengths and a pilot's weaknesses. I'd get to where I'd fly on instruments with only three or four men.

When we were flying out of Mannheim into Lebanon in UIA Otters, I'd only fly with certain pilots. We didn't drink; we didn't wear rings; we wore boots and flight clothing in case of fire; we preflighted everything, took nothing for granted. When we made an instrument approach, we called it out by the numbers. None of us are infallible, and I didn't fly with people who thought they were.

Did this selectivity ever create problems?

I don't think so. I think with the aviator, no matter who you are, you are a professional and you recognize a good man, a good pilot. I'll not tolerate anyone under the influence of alcohol or drugs. In fact, the company commander I replaced was rather lax in certain respects. He had an OH1G gunship pilot waterskiing on the Han River in Vietnam. It makes a nice spectacle, but that's grounds for relief right there.

I was flying out of Verona in Italy; we had a Special Forces unit to support. We would drop people off and pick them up, "line-crossers," as we called them. We had a good operation and good pilots. We relied on the Italians for the weather information. One time I had a flight scheduled to bring a surgeon down to Livorno. I took a look at the weather and told Operations, "I don't have de-icing on this aircraft. I'll tell you, Mt. Cimone is five thousand feet, so to even get over her, I'm going to have to be in where I'll need de-icing. I just don't think the flight is mine." So he pulled me off and put me on an "Honest John" rocket shoot. A peer of mine, named Harris, said, "I'll take that flight."

He took that flight and while I'm adjusting artillary fire, I hear Harris over Pisa calling for a GCA, "For real...For real." You can call practice GCA's— practice approaches, but I guess when you call "for real," you want the guy to know it's not a practice; you're in bad trouble. He had taken on ice, and he and the surgeon crashed. Later we went down and found that Harris survived and was sent up to Germany.

When Harris came back to us, he supposedly was cleared for flight. Later, he and I were flying into Vicnza, Italy. Now I don't mind a crab approach to landing, unlike what the army aviation teaches you to fly, which is wing low when you come in. On the other hand, the air force teaches you to fly the crab-in and not to cross-control. Anyway, Harris was flying a crab-in, and since I was trained by the air force in San Marcos, Texas, I wasn't really upset. Then I noticed our aircraft was going in at a huge crab. About two feet off the runway, I said, "Are you all right, Harris?" He said, "Yea," but didn't correct what he was doing. At that point I kicked the rudder out straight and we got in on it. We bounced a little, but landed safely. I knew in that moment there was something wrong. No pilot in his right mind tries to commit suicide. So I turned Harris in. He was sent up for flight evaluation, and they found he had lost feeling in half his body. The last time I saw him he was in a wheelchair in Germany. He couldn't walk; the right side of his body was gone. He still had some movement in the left side.

What was your relationship after that?

I used to fly up there and see him. I'd land in Mannheim and we'd go out and eat. We were friends. He respected me and I respected him. It's the same as when somebody says to me, "Hank, you're grounded now." That happened. I had an accident in VN and damaged my back. As a result, I had a reflex problem and wasn't safe to fly. It hurt, but you don't have any animosity. You respect a man for saying, "Hank, you're going to kill yourself. Let's make a comptroller out of you." So they made a comptroller out of me. I flew a DM-6 [desk, mahogany, six drawers], until I retired.

HENRY J. STEIN, JR.

Tell me about the crash you just referred to.

I lost an engine, but I was maintaining airspeed. Boy, was I maintaining airspeed! Still, I had nothing but rice paddies to go into. So you always take what's in front of you. I was night flying. You turn the light on and see what you've got in front of you. If you don't like it, you turn the light out. Anyway, I hit the dyke on a rice paddy and slid into the paddy. It was a violent strike and it broke the transmission loose. The transmission came down through the cockpit, in between us. As it hit the seats, the transmission sent us sideways. We both had our armour chest plates on and didn't have time to get rid of them. If you don't have time to get rid of the plates, they only add to your injuries. If you're going to crash, you should have the pads off.

Colonel Stein after Idrang Flight, pointing to bullet in the hydraulic system.

The crash banged me up quite a bit. At the time I was commanding a battalion. I didn't want to lose my battalion. If you go to the hospital, the first thing they do is ground you, and you lose your command, so I decided to fly right seat for awhile. I had my warrant officer jump in the left seat. I used a cane to get around, and once I got in the aircraft I had no problems. I never thought much about it until after I got back from Vietnam and went through a flight physical. They said, "Hey, you got some serious damage in your back."

You know, I just heard on TV a mother say that losing her seven-year-old daughter was fast when she and her flight instructor and father crashed from four hundred feet. It only took four seconds at that height. Let me tell you, when I crashed, from the time I felt the skids of my helicopter hit the bank of the rice paddy, time stood still. I could see individual shoots of rice; I could see leaves and floating debris on the surface of the rice paddy and I had time to think of at least fifteen different people I would never see again. That little seven-year-old girl had four seconds of stark raving terror and four years of thoughts in four seconds.

How many helicopters were you in charge of over in Vietnam?

I commanded the 229th Aviation Battalion Consolidated. I had two companies of gunships: OH1G's, Cobras, eighteen ships per company. I had four lift companies: Hueys, eighteen in each company; and I had one company of CH47s, eighteen.

Talk about maintenance.

I've been a maintenance officer most of my life. They call you a test pilot. You know aircraft and you know maintenance. You make sure maintenance is done.

There are two types. You've got program maintenance and demand maintenance. Because you're rated on your efficiency report for the availability of aircraft for the mission, sometimes there's a tendency for the commander or the maintenance officer to have deferred maintenance. "Oh, we'll put this on here, and you can fly with it. We'll take care of this next time it comes down for a periodic maintenance." Some people cannibalize. When they lose a forty-five-degree gearbox, they'll pull her off this aircraft and put it on this other one. As a general rule, you've got to make the system work. At seven hundred hours you'll put an order in for the eight-hundred-hour gearbox. If I have an aircraft that only has twenty-five hours before it goes down for the hundred-hour inspection, I would send it on special missions—short missions, administrative runs. But aircraft with low time will not go on the six- and eight-hour flights.

Any real conflicts on such issues?

You have people trying to make stars. I don't blame them. I'm not a good politician—I wouldn't have made a good general. Sometimes someone in authority would have people do things that they shouldn't do. You just have to say, "Well, I think you need a different battalion commander then, because I won't do it, and I won't permit it," and if you're good, the boss won't relieve you.

You lost men over there. Remember anyone special?

I lost a man named Fanning out of Montana. His aircraft engine quit on him . . . They have a ceremony, flight helmet on top of the casket, boots polished in front . . . I don't go to funerals now. I have nothing to do with them. Not that I don't care for the people. I just can't.

The biggest failures I've ever seen were commanders who don't feel like fish in cool, clear water because they had the ability to do something to prevent a man from being killed or hurt.

Anyway, the Fanning story goes back to 1958 when I was a maintenance officer at Ft. Lewis. During that period I had a close friend named Fanning, a

(OUI) Mohawk pilot. I thought a lot of him. Fanning was great. He was one of the first to go to Nam. I hadn't been over yet. Then he came up missing when his Mohawk went down.

After I became battalion commander, I got a lieutenant in, also named Fanning. He turned out to be my friend's brother. Strangely enough, over the

Henry J. Stein pilots in troops.

years that I knew him, I never did tell Lt. Fanning why I wouldn't put him on a combat mission, but I didn't. And it was nobody's business but mine why I didn't. You tell people things and you get criticized for it. Anyway, I protected Fanning. I wanted to be sure he got home. One day he was on a supply mission to Bong Son and had an engine failure. He crashed and was killed. Maybe I feel that I shouldn't have restricted him, that I should have had him do combat flights like anybody else, but I didn't. I tried to do my best to be sure he got home.

Fanning stands out. They all stand out. By the way, they found his brother while we were there. They found the aircraft; there wasn't much left of anything, just some pieces of the aircraft, and dog-tags.

I remember when I was maintenance officer in Korea, the military wanted CH-37s to be sent to Vietnam. So I sent four of them down. I feel maybe I should have gone. Instead, I stayed there and sent the other guys down. A CH-37 crashed and killed everyone, except a man named Flowers. I got the feeling that maybe I should have been obligated to go.

What was the saddest thing you saw in Vietnam?

This involves the massacre at the Idrang Valley. In it was a Sgt. Patterson, a heavy-mortar platoon leader and a close personal friend of mine. Patterson was forty-seven years old and worked for me when I was on ground duty. His unit, First Battalion Ninth Cav., was in an approach march when they encountered four thousand North Vietnamese regulars. That's three regiments. The North Vietnamese walked right through the First of the Ninth Cav. because there was no flank security. The U.S. troops were decimated.

When this happened, we scrambled everything. I was a maintenance officer at the time, and even I jumped in an aircraft to help people out. We all did. Perhaps I did because I'd served with a bunch of those people before. Let's say I had more at stake emotionally. When I landed, I saw the mortar platoon was eliminated—they were all shot running forward. Nobody was shot in the back.

Probably the saddest thing I ever saw was that massacre in Idrang. In fact, that's the reason I went back two more times to Vietnam. I noticed one thing when we all went back: we all wore 1st Cav. patches on both shoulders. The last tour I had there, everyone of us had a Cav. patch on the left and the right shoulder. We'd been there before. Some people didn't like that because they said it meant they weren't going anywhere in the division. That may be so, but at least we knew what to do and what not to do. We knew how to run our artillary and how to prepare and how not to take chances and how not to lose people. During my last tour in VN, I didn't lose one single pilot to Charlie. I lost them to aircraft failures; I lost them to pilot error; I never lost one man, one aircraft, to Charlie.

I thought the saddest thing in my life was realizing that the same First of the Ninth commander who'd done this thing in training had done it for real at the Idrang Valley. I don't where that person is. I don't want to know. The most important thing we have in the command structure is to relieve those who are unqualified or who are not doing their job. We don't have to tolerate bad performance. If you don't do something about someone, though, you have the Idrang Valley.

You mentioned sabotage?

I had a command aircraft in my command; when they pulled her down for inspection, it had a hand-grenade in the fuel tank with friction tape around it. The pin had been pulled. That's why, after that, I never had a designated command aircraft. I'd walk out and say, "I'm taking your ship today." It eliminates someone knowing which aircraft you will take. Another helicopter had a screwdriver jammed into the main drive of the tail rotor. Maybe it was left there by accident, but you don't take any chances. You do a good pre-flight all the time.

How did you explain the grenade?

I didn't explain it. My jeep driver said, "Colonel, don't go to your tent. Just don't go." Now, I didn't bother asking him why. I didn't have to. If you compromise your informants, then you lose them. Instead, I went to the club, had a drink and called the bomb squad to get an ordnance man out there. It turned out I had a Claymore mine in my refrigerator. When they opened up the door, the light wasn't there and it had wires hooked to a Claymore mine behind the refrigerator door.

Before I got out of Vietnam, one of my companies had already lost a company commander. He was fragged at night: somebody rolled a hand grenade into his hootch. That's when I put Major Tommy Steiner in charge. He took command. We put chain-link wire on the outside of all of our windows. In my quarters I slept with sand bags around my bunk. It was musty and smelly, but it was a good safety precaution.

Now when I was in Korea, they had geese for security. The geese get to know you, but when a stranger comes, they'll honk and raise hell. So I got geese in our compound and they provided security. Also, we put a Vietnamese Ranger in charge of the compound where my officers lived.

Was the Claymore put there by our troops?

I have no idea. My bet was they were done by our own people. We always looked for the guy on drugs for the problem. I don't think drugs were as bad as the papers back in the States suggested, but we had drug problems among a few of the men. At some point, Tommy Steiner found a man involved in heroine in his unit. This guy was a user and he was a distributor, but we couldn't absolutely prove it. He had made statements to others about eliminating a prior commander with a hand-grenade. Anyway, as soon as I got a call from Tommy telling me about the guy, I flew down at night in my helicopter with guards and landed at the pad and picked the man up. Then I flew him back to my battalion. He and I sat down at my office and had a talk. I explained to him there was no way we could prove all the allegations against him. I told him I wasn't going to lose another company commander because of him. Then I said, "Remember one thing—I know where you are at all times, but you don't know where I am." I told him that we had a lot of good people in this battalion and that he might even be one of them. All I did was scare the hell out of him. I knew he had to know I was not a man to fool with. At the time I'm talking to him, I had my .45 on him under the table, but aimed up like this [gestures upward from waist].

During the months to come, he worked in the mess hall. In fact, he practically lived there. He was a model soldier. He didn't want to get out of line; he didn't want to fly on a mission; he didn't want to deal with any of his fellow soldiers who'd not tolerate his outlook on life. His only salvation was to stay where he was protected. But while he had been down at Bearcat, he was one helluva problem. When it comes right down to it, fear can be a terrific motivater.

You mentioned earlier losing a body?

On my ship I always kept a Penetrator, a crane you use to let people down and bring people up. If I'd be on the air and hear one of my pilots was down, I'd get as many gunships as I could and run to where he was. I had the capability—without landing—of picking someone up and taking him home. Sometimes you'd take a few rounds yourself. When you do things like this for your men, you'd be surprised at the loyalty they have for you. They know you'll stick your butt out for them. In a real sense, you get to know people in army aviation, because you spend so much time flying and so much time on ground duty. You really know the commanders on the ground; you really know the sergeants. They work for you. So when they need help, they're part of the family. It's like you still belong to them. Anyway, I had the Penetrator

Colonel Stein places troops on mountain top for security in VN flying a Huey.

in my battalion because I wanted it, and being battalion commander, I got it. There's some prerogative to command. Rank has its privilege; rank has its responsibilities.

One time I got a call from a unit saying that they were in contact with the enemy and that one of their people had been shot up pretty bad and was dead. It took four days for them to locate him, but when they did, they found Charlie was all around him. They needed to get out. They couldn't carry him out because that would have slowed them down. So I said, "I'll take that mission," and I went in.

What you do is bring the aircraft right into the trees and snuggle down so low nobody can see you to shoot you. There you are, on instruments, hovering. You can't let that aircraft move left or right an inch. A guy on the crew cranks the Penetrator down through the trees. It's very important that you don't get off center, even though you have the option to cut the cable. In an emergency the problem is that it takes a split second to do anything, and in that split second, terrible things can happen, especially when you're hovering three or four feet from tree limbs.

Anyway, we picked up the soldier's body with the Penetrator and got it up into the helicopter where we shoved it into the back. Then we started back. Unfortunately, we didn't have our gas masks with us—we should have. I got sick. If you've ever been around a body that's been out in the heat for four days, you'll know what I mean. There's nothing like it. You can be flying an aircraft and lose your stomach, as we did. As a consequence, I said, "Dammit, hang that man out of the ship a little bit, so we can get some air through there." As we did I was crosscontrolled, almost flying sideways. We're flying along and the next thing I hear is, "Colonel, we lost the body."

I turned around and as I did I could see this body bag flying through the air. My whole career flashed in front of me. I couldn't imagine having to go back and answer to anybody on why I didn't have that body with me. After all the people who had gone in and located the body had done their job; I just hadn't done mine. So I turned the bird around and we went back in. We were some distance from where we'd first picked the bag up, so I prayed Charlie wasn't down there. This whole episode took place not far from Bong Son.

When we got back there, my door gunner got on the Penetrator and the other crew member lowered him down. We went into the hover procedure again. Luckily, he found the body again. We somehow had enough stuff with us to tie the bag back together. Then we brought it up and again put it in the back of the aircraft. We're talking about two trips of the Penetrator—first for the body, then for the crew chief.

We were all sick on the flight in, but I was too scared for it to matter, for I realized I'd taken a shortcut and my own career would have gone down the tube. It would have been the end of my command. And if I hadn't been able to correct it, it should have been.

You don't fly any more. Jim Fleming, another helicopter pilot from Vietnam, told me the same thing.

I don't know . . . When I retired I went to a school to learn how to retire. I've been retired nearly 20 years. They taught you not to answer phones; to develop hobbies; and to stay away from stress. Maybe I don't fly because it was such a beautiful life that even when I'm in an aircraft now, up on top, it's very painful. I don't know of anything I love more than flying. I loved it more than life. In fact, life was secondary to taking care of the aircraft and flying. You have a mission: life isn't important. You get the mission done. It's important, but you don't cower, you do the job. Still, when you have to give something up, it's hard.

For another thing, I don't go to military parades anymore. It isn't that I don't like the military. I think it's that when you find a labor of love, rather than being sorrowful when you leave it, you accept the reality and move on. My answer is that I don't like to be reminded of what I used to be, only what I am now.

I didn't tell you this yet. I lost an aircraft during my first tour. I was four days in Cambodia. We all got out. It took me four nights and three days. In the daytime we slept and didn't move and didn't breathe, and at night we crawled and walked. We heard noises—animals and people. I know what Capt. Scott O'Grady, who was shot down over Bosnia, meant when he said he was a scared rabbit; I know what that means. I also know that you develop a very strong sense of battlefield religion and respect for God and your fellow man. In that time I promised myself if I got out, I'd never be unhappy again—I'd never do anything I didn't want to do. I'd live my life to be happy. Life's too precious to waste one second any other way. So that's what you work for. That's what I've lived for, since leaving Vietnam: to forget.

ACKNOWLEDGMENTS

There are many people to thank over the long duration of the project, especially Tom Davis, Donna Zacherle, McKenzie Broughton, Bob Zeller, Norm Pedersen, Sally Graves, the folks at the Museum of Flight in Seattle and those at the Experimental Aircraft Association in Oshkosh, as well as the Collings Foundation (Box 248, Stow, Massachusetts 01775) for the opportunity for me to stand in a restored B-17 and a B-24—for keeping the grand old planes flying. Finally, my apologies in the event anyone was accidentally overlooked. Lines from "Flying the Zuni Mountains" and "Gather My Wings" by Ann Darr. Copyright 1974 by Ann Darr, from *St. Ann's Gut* by permission of author.

Above all, I wish to thank the fliers who gave so fully of their time and who assisted me with photographs. Though it sounds superficial (as thanks so often do), thanks too for the special lives they lead and have shared so fully. Finally, appreciation and remembrance is due to those flyers who risked their lives in the various fields and campaigns chronicled in the book, but never mad it home.

Author's Note: Much effort has been made to cross-check and insure accuracy, but an oral history project this sweeping, it is a formidable task. A strong effort has been made to enable each of the fliers interviewed to go over their remarks; however, I as author take responsibility for any errors of fact that may have come to light.

IB

Author Irv Broughton assumes waist gunner position aboard a B-17.

In both print and film, author Irv Broughton has earned a reputation for his work documenting memorable aspects of the American past. His films, which record a generation of older American writers, have received numerous awards. He is editor of *A Good Man*, an anthology about fathers and sons (Ballantine, 1994), and a three-volume collection of interviews, *The Writer's Mind* (University of Arkansas Press, 1990-1993), as well as a textbook on interviewing for the media. Of one of his writer collections, novelist Fred Chapell said, "This is the best collection of interviews I have ever read." His poems have appeared in many national journals. He teaches writing and humanities at Spokane Falls Community College.